Master and Servant

Leading historian Carolyn Steedman o. _____ and compelling account of love, life and domestic service in eighteenth-century England. The book, situated in the regional and chronological epicentre of E. P. Thompson's *The Making of the English Working Class* and Emily Brontë's *Wuthering Heights*, focuses on the relationship between a Church of England clergyman (the 'Master' of the title) and his pregnant maidservant. This case-study of people behaving in ways quite contrary to the standard historical account sheds new light on the much wider historical questions of Anglicanism as social thought, the economic history of the industrial revolution, domestic service, the Poor Law, literacy, education, and the very making of the English working class. It offers a unique meditation on the relationship between history and literature and will be of interest to scholars and students of industrial England, social and cultural history and English literature.

CAROLYN STEEDMAN is Professor of History at the University of Warwick. Her previous publications include *Strange Dislocations: Childhood and the Idea of Human Interiority, 1780–1980* (1995) and *Dust* (2001).

Cambridge Social and Cultural Histories

Series editors:

Margot C. Finn, *University of Warwick*
Colin Jones, *University of Warwick*
Keith Wrightson, *Yale University*

New cultural histories have recently expanded the parameters (and enriched the methodologies) of social history. Cambridge Social and Cultural Histories recognizes the plurality of current approaches to social and cultural history as distinctive points of entry into a common explanatory project. Open to innovative and interdisciplinary work, regardless of its chronological or geographical location, the series encompasses a broad range of histories of social relationships and of the cultures that inform them and lend them meaning. Historical anthropology, historical sociology, comparative history, gender history and historicist literary studies – among other subjects – all fall within the remit of Cambridge Social and Cultural Histories.

Master and Servant

Love and Labour in the English Industrial Age

Carolyn Steedman
University of Warwick

CAMBRIDGE
UNIVERSITY PRESS

CAMBRIDGE UNIVERSITY PRESS
Cambridge, New York, Melbourne, Madrid, Cape Town, Singapore, São Paulo

Cambridge University Press
The Edinburgh Building, Cambridge CB2 8RU, UK

Published in the United States of America by Cambridge University Press, New York

www.cambridge.org
Information on this title: www.cambridge.org/9780521697736

© Carolyn Steedman 2007

First published 2007

Printed in the United Kingdom at the University Press, Cambridge

A catalogue record for this publication is available from the British Library

ISBN 978-0-521-87446-5 hardback
ISBN 978-0-521-69773-6 paperback

Clio loves those who bred them better horses,
Found answers to their questions, made their things.

W. H. Auden, 'Makers of History' (1960)

'I'll be bound, you're saving – and I'm doing my little all, that road.'

Emily Brontë, *Wuthering Heights* (1847)

Contents

Maps

Acknowledgements

I have had the kindest and most encouraging readers for this book at its various stages of production. Professor Ted Royle was an invaluable source of information about the eighteenth-century West Riding and its religious communities. He alerted me to sources, introduced me to the twentieth-century fiction the worsted field produced, and told me when I had Phoebe Beatson walking along the wrong road to Halifax. Above all I value his judgement that I had pulled it off – that is, convinced him at least, that Nelly Dean from *Wuthering Heights* was (and is) a kind of historian. Professor Jeremy Gregory provided an equally acute reading and alerted me to new ways of thinking about the role of eighteenth-century Anglicanism in self and social formation. I am extremely grateful for his interest. Bertrand Taithe was encouraging, not only in his final reading, but of all the stories of love and labour that I brought home to all of them from Kirklees Record Office. Vicky Taithe provided extraordinary insight into the twenty-first-century West Riding woollen and worsted manufacture and the reproduction of everyday life for its workers. I was pleased that Terry Eagleton read my manuscript and was so taken with the idea of a West Riding Enlightenment (and that his Heathcliff might find a place in it). Without Peter Mack's conversation about teaching the classics in early modern England, I would not have been able to understand what I do of John Murgatroyd's life, teaching and writing. I am extremely grateful for his help (and all his conversation). A version of this book was completed before the award of an Economic and Social Research Council Research Professorship in 2004, to work on 'Service, Society and the State: the Making of the Social in England 1760–1820'; but at the revision stage so much of what I had learned during my first eighteen months of research on the new project has entered the final version, that I must acknowledge the support of the ESRC in completing it (ESRC RES-051-27-0123).

I dedicate this book to Nan Steedman, in acknowledgement of her interest and involvement in these long-dead people and for always promoting the possibility John Murgatroyd might be the father of Phoebe Beatson's child. She was wrong; but counter-narratives are the most useful of things for any kind of writer.

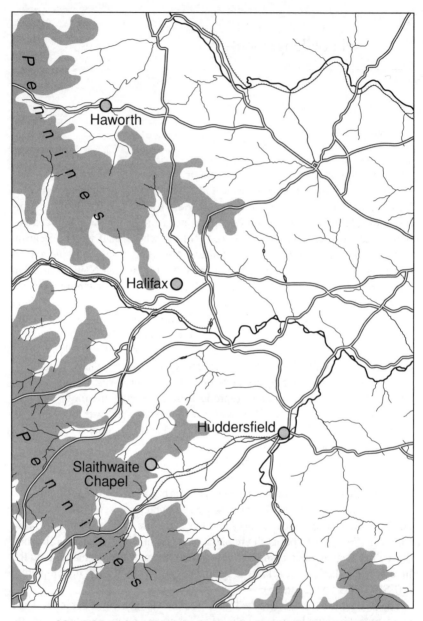

Map 1 Map of the Haworth, Slaithwaite, Huddersfield and Halifax region, 1795

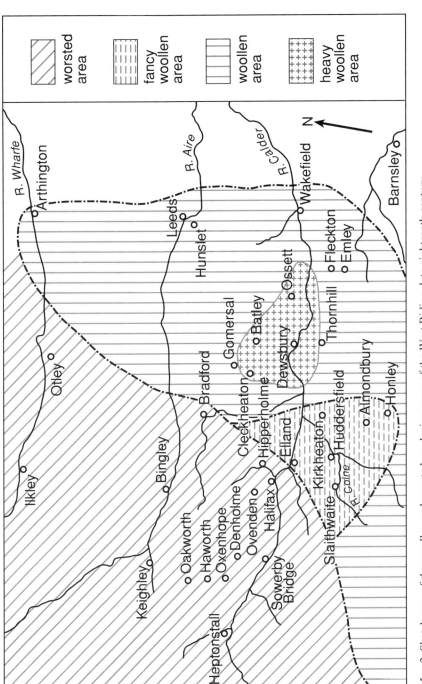

Map 2 Sketch map of the woollen and worsted producing areas of the West Riding, late eighteenth century

Prologue

This is a book about one servant and one master and the changing shape of their relationship, lived out in the time and place of the 'making of the English working class', the industrial West Riding of Yorkshire. It covers the period from about 1785 when Phoebe Beatson first came to the service of the Reverend John Murgatroyd of Slaithwaite, just outside Huddersfield, to the first decade of the new century, after she had borne her illegitimate child, scandalously, in a clergyman's house. The Anglican God whom Murgatroyd served and promoted throughout his very long life changed His shape and form during these years of war, dearth, revolution and counter-revolution; church and state, the law and its practice, redefined the service relationship, and the human and social relationship 'service' inscribed. Here, in what follows, we have one tiny birth pang of modern, industrial society, and some of the minute shifts and stratagems of feeling that countless individuals undertook, in making themselves subjects of modernity.

What I set out to do in this book was explain how its historical actors were able to buck so many of the trends that their historians have seen them – people like them – enacting. Above all I had wanted to understand, and thus be able to explain, why George Thorp refused to marry Phoebe Beatson. She carried Thorp's bastard child through the spring and summer of 1802, and somehow, in some way, he was able to resist the pressures (well known to historians of the English working class) of clergy, poor law officials, employers, ratepayers, landowners and magistrates to make an honest woman of her, and thus relieve the parish of a potential claimant on its funds. These were unusual people, or at least unusual in the twentieth-century social histories we have of others like them, doing things and displaying attitudes that lie at the outer, faint-drawn ends of the bell-curve of 'normally' and 'usually'. What is more, the God they believed in also bucked trends, allowing them all to think, feel and act in ways contrary to His reputation for underpinning strict social morality and obeisance to the laws of church and state.[1]

---

[1] There are disagreements among historians over the influence and effects of eighteenth-century Anglicanism, but William Gibson's argument that 'the level of commitment to the Church was . . .

When I started to write I had in place an almost-intact explanation for the behaviour of Phoebe Beatson's employer. The Reverend John Murgatroyd (1719–1806) had briefly been curate to the Almondbury incumbent during the middle years of the century and schoolmaster for almost fifty years at Slaithwaite (some five miles distant from Almondbury township). Now, for the part of his story that follows, he was in retirement, resident of the hamlet of Lingards (just above Slaithwaite on the other side of the River Colne) and peripatetic preacher in nearly all the churches and chapels within a twenty-mile radius of home. When his servant Phoebe became pregnant around Christmas-time 1801, he did not turn her out; he did not allow her to enter the familiar sentimental plot of seduction and betrayal. By rights (of late eighteenth-century literary convention and some modern social history) he should have dismissed her from his service (the law said he might), made a magdalen of her for the reform imagination, perhaps inadvertently sending her to flit through the greasy alleys of an industrial city (Leeds maybe, or Manchester, where more such descent-into-prostitution stories were actually set), selling herself on the way to salvation by an encounter with her humanitarian superiors.[2] But he did none of these things. He did not, as far as one can tell from the pages of his journal, ever blame her or condemn her. He let her have the baby in his house; he baptised, and loved, and gave house-room to the little bastard girl; he noted her development in his diary. At his death in 1806, he provided a happy ending for mother and child. Indeed, they both seem to have lived happily with him until past Eliza Beatson's fourth birthday.

New forms of feeling came into the world during these crisis years of war and revolution. Ways of perceiving, imagining and understanding self and others that had been prepared for during earlier and other kinds of revolution (proto-industrial, capitalist, commercial, cultural and philosophic) were consolidated. Societal and ideological developments, usually dated from the mid-seventeenth century, involved new versions of the human subject, of God and how He moved, of the kind of entity His creatures were, and of the ways in which it was

---

much greater than historians allow, and the eighteenth century is perhaps the last period in which popular faith can be taken for granted' has been persuasive. William Gibson, *Church, State and Society, 1760–1850* (London: Macmillan, 1994), p. 10.

[2] For 'the sentimental prostitution narratives purveyed by late eighteenth-century humanitarian reformers', see Barbara Taylor, *Mary Wollstonecraft and the Feminist Imagination* (Cambridge: Cambridge University Press, 2003), p. 242, discussing Vivien Jones, 'Scandalous Femininity: Prostitution and Eighteenth-century Narrative', in Dario Castiglione and Lesley Sharpe (eds.), *Shifting the Boundaries. Transformations of the Language of Public and Private in the Eighteenth Century* (Exeter: Exeter University Press, 1995), pp. 41–70. The *apogée* of the Manchester variety is probably Elizabeth Gaskell's *Ruth* (1853). See also Carolyn Steedman, 'Enforced Narratives. Stories of Another Self', in Tess Cosslett, Celia Lury and Penny Summerfield (eds.), *Feminism and Autobiography. Texts, Theories, Methods* (London: Routledge, 2000), pp. 25–39. For what common law said about dismissing pregnant maidservants, see below, chapter 7.

possible to love them. It became a central aim of this book to consider the ways in which these large-scale social and philosophic developments were experienced and thought about in the everyday life of three obscure inhabitants of the late eighteenth-century Yorkshire worsted field.[3] (The significance for such an enterprise of this location and its dominant mode of production will be discussed shortly.) John Murgatroyd's love for a baby (and for her mother, though that was love in a different register) was perhaps part of a relatively modern conception of an Anglican God, still playing a role in constitutional-philosophical thinking as He had done in the century after the English Revolution, but who was now also used as a way of conceiving men and women as social creatures, possessing histories (natural and cultural) that explained them as modern subjects. In all likelihood, the political-constitutional church had always operated in conjunction with the socio-cultural church, proffering social thought and theory to different audiences. Anglicanism as a form of social thought was certainly present in the writing of Eamon Duffy's sixteenth-century Morebath cleric, and the political-constitutional aspects of the Anglican Church were certainly much in evidence in the debates over repeal of the Test and Corporation Acts and Roman Catholic Emancipation in 1828–9.[4] Over the sixty years from which his records survive, John Murgatroyd's immense output of writing shows Anglicanism as a way of individual thinking, feeling and behaviour towards others in a specific local context.

The poor laws, which provided so much of the narrative framework to Phoebe Beatson and George Thorp's relationship (and which also demonstrate the interest of the state in the relationship), expressed social and religious thinking combined; they were perhaps the major institutional expression of the combination during the long eighteenth century. At the same time, an Anglican God was increasingly used to delineate human nature, and to think through social and human relations, past, present and potential. John Murgatroyd, Phoebe Beatson's employer, spent a lifetime in the Church of England and with his God. Literally so. Every day's entry in Murgatroyd's journals started with 'Awak'd with God' – before he went on to describe the weather, and on Sundays to thank Him for having brought his family safely to the end of another week. On New Year's Eve 1802 when he wrote that 'I and my small Family have/ the Lord be thanked/ been preserved to ye End of another month, & ye last Month in 1802 Some Rain and Darkish . . .' his unorthodox little household consisted of

---

[3] The area of worsted yarn and cloth manufacture bounded by Bradford and Halifax has long been called 'the worsted field'. Its outer reaches lay beyond Heptonstall (to the west) and Keighley (to the north). See maps I and II.

[4] Eamon Duffy, *The Voices of Morebath. Reformation and Rebellion in an English Village* (New Haven and London: Yale University Press, 2001). In the 1780s John Murgatroyd mused much on the Test and Corporation Acts in his writing. See below, chapter 5.

himself (a man in his eighties), Phoebe Beatson (an unwed mother in her late thirties) and baby Eliza, who was now four months old.[5]

We must take seriously Murgatroyd's understanding that God was a constant presence. This is a hard task for modern social historians, many of us trained in the visceral revulsion from religion, its fettering of the mind and spirit of so many people in the past, that was inculcated in us by constant reference to the founding texts of modern social history, to Edward Thompson's *The Making of the English Working Class* (1963) in particular. God is indeed a palpable presence in Thompson's work, but appears for the main part in his Methodist aspect. By way of contrast *Master and Servant* deals with the living God of John Murgatroyd's Anglicanism. To take this God seriously – to examine seriously the effects of a theology on everyday life and thought – is not to advocate or promote it (or Him); nor is it to abandon scepticism and atheism (or whatever the personal position of the historian might be). These are obvious-seeming points, but they do have to be made, given that one of the contentions of this book is that our conventional view of the making of the English working class is at least partial, and probably misleading, because it fails to take into account the religious formation and the articulated thoughts and feelings derived from Anglicanism of men and women living through the society's transition to industrial capitalism, in the century after 1750. This point applies particularly to Thompson's *Making*, for it finds most of its evidence of class formation in the Yorkshire worsted field, in the very valleys, towns and hamlets that are the setting for this current book. How John Murgatroyd behaved and how he thought in the case of Phoebe and Elizabeth Beatson is to be understood through his own apprehension of a belief system, at work in the Halifax–Huddersfield district, in the closing years of the eighteenth century. Understanding *his* understanding marks out a project similar to that of Barbara Taylor in her recent account of Mary Wollstonecraft, which is not only to restore religious belief to its full status in an eighteenth-century life, but to make sense of Wollstonecraft's faith, and its emergence as thought, feeling and imagination in a personal, and thus a social context.[6]

Taylor's project is broadly shaped by the sociology of religion.[7] But the historian can fantasise about taking a different path from hers. The fantasy operates like this: historians are perforce interested in events and happenings in the past: what we do is describe and re-describe *what has happened*, whatever its shape or form. Perhaps an Anglican God *happened* in the West Riding between 1780–1810 (and in other places and periods, of course). He

---

[5] Reverend John Murgatroyd, Diaries, KC242/7, West Yorkshire Archive Service, Kirklees District, Huddersfield (31 December 1802). See Naomi Tadmor, *Family and Friends in Eighteenth-century England. Household, Kinship, and Patronage* (Cambridge: Cambridge University Press, 2001), pp. 18–43 for the oddness and typicality of this 'family'.

[6] Taylor, *Mary Wollstonecraft*.   [7] For further discussion of this point, see chapter 7.

was certainly a happening in John Murgatroyd's mind, as well as constituting a form of language for describing all that Murgatroyd thought and believed about himself and the world. Perhaps this God – the idea of Him – had the power to make things happen; and happenings are what we are interested in. This, so far, is to follow Max Weber, whose endeavour in exploring the relationship between Protestantism and early capitalist development in the West was to understand 'the manner in which ideas become effective forces in history'.[8] But what would happen if the historian went beyond this, and behaved as if Murgatroyd's god – an Anglican God, in the West Riding – actually existed? (It would be a behaviour, a methodology, the use of a form of language, not a belief; I cannot *believe* this; but a historian might behave as if she does.) Doing this would be to concentrate on God as some kind of phenomenon, rather than on the presumed human wishes and desires that sociologists and anthropologists say give Him (whatever His particular and local form and aspect) shape and existence. It would be to do something like Mary Lefkowitz, in her *Greek Gods, Human Lives*, where, in the course of describing a pagan theology, its social purpose and the Greek gods' radical otherness (they are not like human beings; they are profoundly disinterested in human kind, and quite unlike the personal God of Christianity), she *thanks them*. She thanks the gods, 'without whose aid no human achievement is possible'. For the course of her book (and perhaps in real life) she believes in the gods: believes that they did and do exist, and are neglected sources for understanding the modern human condition, as well as past circumstances.[9] This, in fact, is a view entirely compatible with the sociology of religion: a shame culture developed out of agrarian subsistence economy and slave-holding social order, thinks through the process and meaning of life with figures, tropes and constructs that go by the names of Demeter and Phoebus. This sociology, however, is nowhere evoked by Lefkowitz; her method is, rather, to believe and believe in the gods, and in their powers.

This may be only an unnecessarily complicated – and quirky – approach to a historical belief system; or a highly effective method for uncovering one. In the early stages of writing this book, I wanted to do the same with an Anglican God, in this place, among these people. Not only might this allow me to see the shape, contours and attributes of this god, and thus understand better what John Murgatroyd believed, but it would allow me to fulfil the intention of the book, to find other, older gods here, among the Pennine Hills and to make a new (historical) mythology to add to all the other ones that have emanated from this place. But I am simply unable to do what Mary Lefkowitz did, for two reasons. First, I live in England under the same union of church and state as did

[8] Max Weber, *The Protestant Ethic and the Spirit of Capitalism*, orig. pub. 1904–5 (London: Allen and Unwin, 1930), p. 90.
[9] Mary Lefkowitz, *Greek Gods, Human Lives. What We Can Learn from Myths* (New Haven and London: Yale University Press, 2003), Acknowledgements.

those who lived in the late eighteenth century; John Murgatroyd's social and ideological context shaped my own. I learned the Creed, and the formularies of the Church of England every Sunday afternoon between 1955 and 1958, and said the Lord's Prayer every day at school assembly, for a much longer time than that. Presumably Mary Lefkowitz did not learn to make sacrifice to Zeus (or any of the Olympian crew) in the back yard of her early years, and has not had to abandon a belief system inculcated in childhood. The gods you have not had to escape are the attractive ones, and much easier to believe in. And in the second place, I simply cannot make this God walk the Pennine Hills, and do things (arbitrary and strange, or familiar and providential), because He was not a god like that.[10] He was what you told the children He was: a Spirit, everywhere present (though *not* in the bread and wine of a Sunday), and deeply personal, and nowhere at all. Nevertheless, I propose this approach to a belief system: to ask questions about this God first, His shape and form, as He actually appears in Murgatroyd's writing and note-taking, as Barbara Taylor has done with the infinitely better organised and original thinker who was Mary Wollstonecraft.

As a reader of John Murgatroyd's writing, I found the cumulative effect of his incantatory and repeated evocations of his God very moving. Being moved by rhetoric (by the shape and sound of the words rather than their referents) was my own route to taking his beliefs seriously. It is, of course, easier to do this with Murgatroyd than with many an eighteenth-century clergyman, who scarcely mentions his Maker (whilst devoting much word-space to dinner).[11] Murgatroyd's simple benevolence moved me as well (that he *was* such a man is attested to in his diary, and in much commentary on him, contemporary and posthumous). In the burial records of Slaithwaite, his is the only one with an addendum: 'Oct 30th [1806] Revd John Murgatroyd, an amiable Man aged 87'.[12] This is an epigraph in a minor key to the most elegant and desirable of them all, penned nearly two centuries later by Sigmund Freud. He wrote of the British psycho-analyst and his former pupil David Eder that he belonged 'to the people one loves without having to trouble about them'. I know I feel for this long-dead Yorkshire clergyman the same response that Freud felt to Eder's 'toleration and great capacity for love' and that I recognise a similar 'simplicity,

---

[10] For the trenchant opinion of Henry Fielding on this very point, and its implications for the writing of 'history' in the eighteenth-century sense and narrative in general, see chapter 10.

[11] But the absence of God from the pages of a journal is no necessary indication that clerics did not have deep religious views. Parsons Woodforde's and Holland's have sometimes been read with an extreme literalness. James Woodforde, *The Diary of a Country Parson: the Reverend James Woodforde 1758–1781*, ed. John Beresford (Oxford: Oxford University Press, 1924). Jack Ayres (ed.), *Paupers and Pig Killers. The Diary of William Holland, a Somerset Parson, 1799–1818*, orig. pub. 1984 (Stroud: Sutton, 1997). Francis Griffin Stokes (ed.), *The Blecheley Diary of the Reverend William Cole, MA, FSA, 1765–67* (London: Constable, 1931).

[12] Slaithwaite Parish Records, Slaithwaite Chapel, Baptism and Burials, 1755–1812, D120/2, West Yorkshire Archives, Wakefield District, Wakefield.

integrity and goodness' in him.[13] At least, I tell myself, I know where I'm coming from in regard to my historical subjects, and some of the ways of my projection, displacement and transference. Transference is an occupational hazard for historians as far as I am concerned, but I do not see how we would ever get going on anything, were it not available as a device for disinterring our historical subjects.[14] What my response to Murgatroyd's writing has taught me, is how very much historical transference (and projection) depends on the knowledge and information the historian possesses. I can make other, overt identifications with Phoebe Beatson of a political kind (a woman, a working-class woman doing the job I would have done had I not had the great good fortune to be born two hundred or so years after she was) and they arise from her story and the account of what happened to her; but I simply do not have enough information about her as a person to be moved by her.

I started to write with the faint outlines of an explanatory structure for John Murgatroyd's behaviour in mind, and also with an over-excited and confident belief that I would be able to explain Phoebe Beatson and George Thorp. Thorp, in my view, is by far the most interesting character in this story, because of the refusals he was able to make, and because, unlike Murgatroyd, it is not possible to give an account of him by measuring what he did against an established and elaborate account of a belief system, that of eighteenth-century Anglicanism. A quick, final trip to Huddersfield (and Halifax and Wakefield, for West Yorkshire Archives are divided between many record offices), I thought; the poor law records, Phoebe Beatson's settlement and bastardy examinations by the magistrates, and with great good fortune, perhaps the examination of George Thorp and the affiliation order that named him the father and obliged him to pay for the child. Just that, I thought, and I would have these people taped, or at least have some inkling, from one tiny deviation in the formulaic lines recorded by the justices' clerk from their statements, of how and why it all fell out as it did. But they are not there; and because I cannot find these documents, I cannot find George Thorp. Even the Slaithwaite Militia Return for 1798 and the Militia List for 1800 seem not to have seen the light of day since a local historian of the Colne Valley had them in his hands in 1896.[15] These returns – what effectively amounted to a census *avant la lettre* – were required of local communities during the invasion scares of these war years. They listed all men over the age of sixteen years and not having more than one child, and thus liable to be called up.

---

[13] J. B. Hobman (ed.), *David Eder. Memoirs of a Modern Pioneer* (London: Victor Gollancz, 1945), p. 21 and Foreword. On the psycho-analytic front, Murgatroyd several times recorded that he counselled those who came to see him 'troubled in their spirit'. See below, chapter 4.

[14] See Carolyn Steedman, 'The Watercress Seller', in Tamsin Spargo (ed.), *Reading the Past* (Basingstoke: Palgrave, 2000), pp. 18–25.

[15] D. F. E. Sykes, *The History of the Colne Valley* (Slaithwaite: F. Walker, 1896), pp. 301–3. Clive Emsley, *British Society and the French Wars, 1793–1815* (Basingstoke: Macmillan, 1979), pp. 99–123.

George Thorp, certainly a Slaithwaite man, is highly likely to have been listed. (He could have had a dozen bastard children and still have been returned, for they did not count as legitimate ones did.) But the returns are not to be found, though great assiduity and a lifetime of diligent searching might produce all the missing documentation, miscatalogued in a West Yorkshire Archive Service repository, or quietly waiting in some private attic, somewhere. I write these lines with some diffidence, for I am a professional, and want to be seen as such by my fellow historians. I ought to have known that it was a long and optimistic shot – the hope of finding George Thorp. Indeed, I am part of the chorus reiterating that poor law records were much less preserved in the north, compared with the south, that I would have been extraordinarily lucky to have found affiliation orders . . . The upshot is, that George Thorp, his obduracy and stubbornness (which I will never know was marvellous, or admirable, or not) are not there to be accounted for.

There was a crisis of documentation with John Murgatroyd too, though of a very different kind. It occurred at exactly the same time as the one to do with George Thorp, when the book had already been started. The Kirklees (Huddersfield) branch of the West Yorkshire Archive Service holds some of Murgatroyd's diaries written between 1781 and 1806 (one for roughly every other year), one of his commonplace books, and a long essay (folded and hand-stitched) on the 'Qualifications of a Minister of Christ'. It is known that he kept a diary in some shape or form, from at least 1739, and that there existed several other notebooks, in which he copied from works of divinity, sacred history, the classics and poetry. One of his nineteenth-century historians who had them available when he wrote also indicated that he intermittently used these volumes as letter-copy books.[16] I was happy to have so little: less is often more in the historical game, and some of us like nothing so much as writing within the strictures of absence. If there's *something* there, we can do something with it, finding a world in a grain of sand, and conjuring a social system from the purchase of a nutmeg grater recorded in a household account book.[17]

Too much documentation poses its own problems. In his postscript to *The General in His Labyrinth* (1991) Gabriel García Márquez's novel about Simón Bolívar's last and terrible journey to the Caribbean coast of Neuva Granada in 1830, he describes the historical overload he experienced in the course of his

---

[16] Henry James Morehouse, *Extracts from the Diary of the Rev. Robert Meeke . . . Also a Continuation of the History of Slaithwaite Free School and an Account of the Educational Establishments in Slaithwaite-cum-Lingards, by the Rev. Charles Augustus Hulbert* (Huddersfield: *Daily Chronicle* Steam Press; London: Bohn, 1874), pp. 105–16. This contains much information taken from Charles Augustus Hulbert, *Annals of the Church in Slaithwaite (near Huddersfield) West Riding of Yorkshire from 1793–1864, in Five Lectures* (London: Longman, 1864). Hulbert was actually Murgatroyd's first historian, and will be used throughout this book in that role.

[17] Carolyn Steedman, *Dust* (Manchester: Manchester University Press, 2001), pp. 18–19.

research for the book.[18] You wade through a swamp of historical facts – mere items of information – that swarm and sting and itch, above and below the water-line. They itch and sting because they have no meaning yet assigned to them; they are blind and deaf in their assault on your person, and they make you numb in panic, too. García Márquez had the advantage of a 'literary audacity' that determined him to 'recount a tyrannically documented life without renouncing the extravagant prerogatives of the novel', and only the last few weeks of that life, to boot; he also had friendly historians at the end of a telephone line to give him 'a first inkling of a method for investigating and ordering facts' (the brilliantly simple stalwart of the file card system); I hope that some of his professional informants also told him how unlucky he was, to have *so very, very much*.

My crisis of too-much occurred when I was told that, far from being lost, some of John Murgatroyd's other note- and commonplace books were in the Special Collections of the University of York Library (a circumstance and deposit quite unknown to the West Yorkshire Archive Service and to the National Register of Archives). They are voluminous.[19] After some days of elation and resentment mixed, I was able to issue myself with the reminder that I was not writing a biography of John Murgatroyd, but rather attempting to understand what happened in his Lingards-cum-Slaithwaite household between 1785 and 1806, and why the people involved in it were able to behave the way they did.[20] I needed to know what was in (but not to transcribe) 'A Book of Records' (900 pages long, consisting of bound loose sheets and separate paper-covered notebooks); 'A Cornucopia; or collection of weighty transcripts transcrib'd out of the scarcest, most necessary, & best chosen books &c' (what its compiler said it was, and near as long as the first); and 'Authors Useful to be Read at School' (smaller and indeed useful, but with only two pages actually devoted to its title). This book is written then, as most histories are, out of absence and silence, out of records missing and lost. And the tiny flotsam of the found has had different kinds of attention paid it: different documents have been read and transcribed in different kinds of ways. The story comes from these records certainly, but also from other places, in particular from my knowing that John

---

[18] Gabriel García Márquez, *The General in His Labyrinth*, orig. pub. 1990 (London: Jonathan Cape, 1991), pp. 271–4.

[19] And alarmingly so to one who, like Nelly Dean from *Wuthering Heights*, knows what Latin and Greek look like, but has not the advantage of knowing them ('It is', as Nelly remarks, 'as much as you can expect of a poor man's daughter'), for a fair proportion of these three thousand or so pages consists of Greek transcribed for teaching purposes. Nelly Dean's role in this current book, as reader, narrator and historian, will be discussed in chapter 10, but readers may care to note that she is already a presence in it.

[20] Beyond elation and resentment a more proper response is gratitude to Professor Ted Royle of the History Department, University of York, for telling me about the Murgatroyd material in York University Library.

Murgatroyd and George Thorp really were unusual men. I could only have that sense of their oddness from a reading of a great deal of modern history of the eighteenth century, and from other accounts of the period and place.

I do not know whether Phoebe Beatson was unusual or not. What *happened to her* was out of the run of the mill, and remarked upon as such by one Slaithwaite inhabitant at the time. But though she appears on a near-daily basis in Murgatroyd's journal from the time she joined his household in 1785 until his death in 1806, and though I have (also from the journals) an excellent account of her work as a worsted-spinning out-worker, the only thing I know about her as a person is that she was afraid of bulls, a fear which necessitated one of Murgatroyd's many journeys to accompany her to her spinning master's place along the old packhorse route from Slaithwaite to Forrest near Halifax. Richard Walker, her spinning master, had just moved there from Hollywell Green, and the last part of the route was new to her. Phoebe Beatson could not write, or at least, she made her mark in the Halifax St John's parish register rather than signing, when she finally married (*not* George Thorp) in 1807, so there is not even that trace of her. She is at once the cipher, the hidden-from-history that twentieth-century socialist-feminist scholarship gave us; and at the same time the most familiar of characters from the melodrama (of a poor woman seduced, then abandoned) that modern social historians learned from the nineteenth century.[21] But she did not actually play this part in real life, for Murgatroyd helped her avoid it. It is not possible, then, to write Phoebe Beatson according to the lines given her by social history, nor within its established conventions and plots. Hence sprang Nelly Dean. Ellen Dean from *Wuthering Heights* (1847) came – in some dream or day-dream I had – before the last journeys to the West Riding archives. Unless they end up before some kind of tribunal and are forced to tell their story to a justice or a judge, and unless the record of their narrative is preserved, eighteenth-century poor women are perforce as silent as the grave, unavailable to the historian except as a name on a list, or an entry in a register of church and state. Exactly the same condition of silence pertains as far as working-class men are concerned of course; but then, with labouring men, there is not the strange – uncanny, even – effect of this almost-perfect silence in conjunction with the clamorous voice of the female domestic servant as story-teller of the Western world. In English literature, at least two major

---

[21] For the relationship between modern social history and melodrama, see Carolyn Steedman, 'A Weekend with Elektra', *Literature and History*, 6:1 (1997), pp. 17–42; also Renato Rosaldo, 'Celebrating Thompson's Heroes. Social Analysis in History and Anthropology', in Harvey J. Kaye and Keith McClelland (eds.), *E. P. Thompson. Critical Perspectives* (Cambridge: Polity, 1990), pp. 103–24, especially p. 116, where one of the claims is that *The Making of the English Working Class* is a form of melodrama. See also Martha Vicinus, 'Helpless and Unbefriended. Nineteenth-century Domestic Melodrama', *New Literary History*, 13:1 (1981), pp. 127–43; Patrick Joyce, *Democratic Subjects. The Self and the Social in the Nineteenth Century* (Cambridge: Polity, 1994), pp. 176–92.

fictional narrators of modernity are servants, and they are women.[22] Between the two of them, Samuel Richardson's Pamela Andrews (from the 1740s) and Emily Brontë's Nelly Dean (from the 1840s) give an account of modern class society coming into being, and the changes in passion and affect – the transformations of intimacy – that accompanied social revolutions in economy, manners and thought. Pamela first occurred to Richardson's imagination out of a 'trewe' story half-remembered and a book of model letters he was writing (and out of fairy stories, 'The Faerie Queen', and God knows what else).[23] Nelly occurred to Emily Brontë's – probably – as a narrative and structuring device sometime between her publisher's rejection of the first version of *Wuthering Heights* and her rewriting of it, in 1846. *Where* she came from has not had anything like the detailed attention paid to the great question addressed to *Wuthering Heights*: 'Who and what is Heathcliff?'; but we may assume that there can be only one place of origin for him and his foster-sister, the servant Ellen Dean, that is, in Brontë's imagination. Here is Edward Chitham on Heathcliff's coming into the world; what he describes applies to Nelly, and to Pamela Andrews, and (if we accept 'history' as a form of writing, as well as all the other things it is) to the Phoebe Beatson who is the subject of this book. 'It would be rash to suppose that [Brontë] had met a prototype of [Heathcliff] in real life', remarks Chitham; 'but contradictory to think that she had not met him in her inner life. Just as Haworth Church becomes "the minster" in two poems, a real poet may become a vision, and a real man contribute to an element of Heathcliff.'[24] Phoebe Beatson lived once, walked the pathways with her worsted bundles, as Nelly Dean (who never actually existed) did not. But here, now, in these pages, Phoebe will emerge from the same place as Nelly: both spring from histories known and histories unavailable to their writers; from all that the past has deposited in the imagination of their creators.

Nelly, here, now and newly invented, is a persistent attempt not so much to give the servant a voice, but to have her tell the story. It is the servant who

[22] I have argued elsewhere that William Godwin's Caleb Williams in *Things As They Are* (1794) should be admitted to their company. Carolyn Steedman, 'Servants and their Relationship to the Unconscious', *Journal of British Studies*, 42 (2003), pp. 316–50. For the 'trewe' and the 'true', the novel, the 'newe' and the 'new' in the early eighteenth century, see Lennard Davis, *Factual Fictions. The Origins of the English Novel* (New York and Guildford: Columbia University Press, 1988).

[23] The process Richardson recorded with the felicitous phrase 'and hence sprung Pamela' has been much discussed. For a relatively recent summary of the search for Pamela's origins, see Carolyn Steedman, *Past Tenses. Essays on Writing, Autobiography and History* (London: Rivers Oram Press, 1992), pp. 1–18, and Notes. The invention of Pamela was described by Richardson in a letter to Johannes Sinistra, 2 June 1753, in Wilhelm C. Slattery (ed.) *The Richardson–Sinistra Correspondence* (London and Amsterdam: Southern Illinois University Press, 1969), p. 28.

[24] Edward Chitham, *The Birth of* Wuthering Heights. *Emily Brontë at Work* (Basingstoke: Palgrave, 2001), p. 42. Chitham has just been discussing the transformations of reality in Brontë's poetry. For a historian imagining the imagination of the past, see Taylor, *Mary Wollstonecraft*, pp. 4–5, 95–142.

must tell. Nelly is also something quite detailed that Emily Brontë knew about a history of service in the West Riding between the 1770s and the very early years of the new century, the topic and the time span of this current book. Fourteen miles or so separate Haworth from Slaithwaite (though you could not go as the crow flies); or maybe there are fewer miles to travel if the fictional village of Gimmerton, and Wuthering Heights and Thrushcross Grange are made out of a topography much closer to Halifax (not Haworth at all) than has hitherto been thought.[25]

Brontë used the voice she gave Nelly Dean to tell what turned out to be a founding myth of modern England, enacted in the same period and the same place as the one where – historians sometimes cruelly say this – Edward Thompson invented the English working class.[26] *Wuthering Heights* has become the myth of modern love, of *amor passion*, of the way we are now and how we got to be that way. In and about the same terrain, Thompson wrote the epic of modern class society, an epic that in its use has also become a myth. *Master and Servant* will draw on and use the perceptions and strategies of two other historians of the West Riding, Emily Brontë and Edward Thompson.

But the historian Emily Brontë dealt with domestic service in West Yorkshire *c.*1770–1800 in a way that, in writing his history, Edward Thompson did not. Nelly's clamorous, insistent voice telling of this time, this place must wait until the end of this book. Phoebe Beatson's silence is where we have to begin, in order to comprehend the profundity of her – the domestic servant's – exclusion from the histories written about the coming into being of her class.

[25] Chitham, *Birth of* Wuthering Heights, pp. 97–107. See below, chapter 10 for the 'new' location of Wuthering Heights.

[26] Thompson was resident in Halifax in the 1950s and 1960s when he worked on and wrote *The Making of the English Working Class*. See Steedman, 'Weekend with Elektra'; Julian Harber, 'Edward Thompson (1924–1993)', *Transaction of the Halifax Antiquarian Society*, 2 (New Series) (1994), pp. 125–8.

1   Introduction: on service and silences

Phoebe Beatson has no voice in Murgatroyd's journal (though she is as much a presence in it as she was in his life). Neither could she write. She was thus in no position to pen the extraordinary (and published) social commentaries and satires that we continue to discover eighteenth-century maidservants producing.[1] She appeared before several magistrates when she was examined as to the state of her settlement and asked to name the father of her unborn child in the early summer of 1802, but any record of her time in a justicing room is quite lost. Neither she nor John Murgatroyd ever turned to a local magistrate to test the limits of the service contract (the hiring agreement) or to complain about its breach by one or the other. So in Phoebe Beatson's case there is no startling, immediate, voice speaking out of a justice's notebook, as does Mary Cant's from Nottinghamshire, in autumn 1785, telling Sir Gervase Clifton, JP that her master has treated her very ill, hit her round the head, and all because when he told her to dress the baby, she had said, 'He might dress it him self for she was busy'.[2]

Many social historians of the eighteenth and early nineteenth century in England have faltered at the silence of the female domestic servant and found a solution by simply leaving her out of account. 'I have not looked at domestic servants,' says Nicola Verdon, considering rural women's work and wages from the 1790s onwards; she and many others.[3] When the later eighteenth-century domestic *is* dealt with as part of a social and economic structure, the preoccupations of historians of later periods are sometimes reproduced: the maidservant is low-paid, has little status; her work can best be described as 'casual'; she is

---

[1] Donna Landry, *The Muses of Resistance. Labouring-Class Women's Poetry in Britain, 1739–1796* (Cambridge: Cambridge University Press, 1990). Carolyn Steedman, 'Poetical Maids and Cooks Who Wrote', *Eighteenth-century Studies*, 39:1 (2005), pp. 1–27. For the literary scholar, eighteenth-century maidservants are not at all silent.

[2] Sir Gervase Clifton JP, 1772–1812, M8050, Notebook, p. 124 (undated; probably November 1785), Nottinghamshire Record Office, Nottingham.

[3] Nicola Verdon, *Rural Women Workers in Nineteenth-Century England. Gender, Work and Wages* (Woodbridge: Boydell Press, 2002), p. 5.

vulnerable to sexual exploitation.[4] Where we have a demography of service, it is often constructed either from metropolitan sources from before about 1750, or from nineteenth-century census material.[5] Deborah Valenze has remarked how very much our assessments of eighteenth-century servants are bound up with our imaginings of nineteenth-century ones. 'The new servant' of the Victorian age (the one with which we perform our reconstructions for sixty years before) 'appears domesticated', she says; she lacks 'any individuality or cunning . . . Incapable of low spirits, [she is] stalwart and decent'; there are no depths to her; she cannot be anything but what she is.[6] This domestication of the domestic servant that Valenze has so strikingly noted was in large part the result of the removal of certain legal rights from household servants, specifically the removal of the right to settlement by service under the Poor Law Amendment Act of 1834. The eighteenth-century women who wrote astonishingly disrespectful verses about their employers' literary and culinary tastes, or who told their master to dress his own baby, were legal bodies with legal personae, in a way that their nineteenth-century counterparts were not. This factor – fact, indeed – of their legal identity explains to some extent their massive, persistent and insistent presence across all the cultural forms that people like their employers produced, across the eighteenth century.[7] But these are not the usual places for social historians to hunt out their historical subjects.

Culturally noisy then, but demographically elusive, the eighteenth-century provincial domestic servant is pursued through contemporary assessments and surveys, with historians reading backwards from a nineteenth-century perspective (as I am now about to briefly do). At the turn of the twentieth century, servants of both sexes represented one person in twenty-two of the general population of Britain; in the 1890s one-third of all women employed were domestic servants.[8] Using contemporary surveys from the later eighteenth century, Jean Hecht and Bridget Hill concluded that one person in eleven was a domestic servant, perhaps one in five or six in the metropolis; or that perhaps 40 per cent of the population of eighteenth-century England been servants at

[4] Katrina Honeyman, *Women, Gender and Industrialisation* (Basingstoke: Macmillan, 2000), pp. 17–34.

[5] Tim Meldrum, *Domestic Service and Gender, 1660–1750. Life and Work in the London Household* (London: Longman, 2000). Edward Higgs, 'Women, Occupations and Work in the Nineteenth-century Censuses', *History Workshop Journal*, 23 (1987), pp. 59–80.

[6] Deborah Valenze, *The First Industrial Woman* (Oxford and New York: Oxford University Press, 1995), pp. 167–8.

[7] Carolyn Steedman, 'Servants and their Relationship to the Unconscious', *Journal of British Studies*, 42 (2003), pp. 316–50. Bruce Robbins, *The Servant's Hand. English Fiction from Below*, orig. pub. 1986 (Durham and London: Duke University Press, 1993).

[8] Lee Davidoff, 'Mastered for Life: Servant and Wife in Victorian and Edwardian England', *Journal of Social History*, 7:4 (1974), pp. 406–28.

some point between early adolescence and marriage.[9] Most of these estimates used Patrick Colquhoun's political arithmetic from 1806, in the *Treatise on Indigence*. He is frequently quoted as reckoning 910,000 servants in England and Wales (in a population of nearly 10 million), 800,000 of whom were women. But Colquhoun did not, in fact, count or estimate servants at all. His intention in the *Treatise* was to calculate national income according to rank and degree of persons, and to compare his own figures, derived from the Census of 1801 and the Pauper Returns of 1806, with the 1688 tabulations and estimates of Gregory King.[10] Colquhoun mentioned domestic servants in order to mark their absence from a category: 'labourers in agriculture, manufactures, commerce, navigation, and fisheries, &c, *exclusive* of menial servants' (emphasis added) are what he actually wrote about. The body of his thesis – which is about the causes of poverty – mentions servants out of place with good characters but unable to procure work, and those out of place for 'fraudulent and pilfering practices and bad behaviour', as examples of remediable and culpable causes of indigence, respectively.[11] The vast figures of 110,000 male servants and 800,000 females are produced during the course of a discussion of friendly societies and savings banks for the labouring poor; he reckoned that these numbers of servants might represent a 'resource for members' for these hedges against indigence. As Leonard Schwarz says, Colquhoun's figures were produced (or invented) to induce moral panic about the habits of 'opulence' in keeping servants.[12] And really, there were simply not enough young, unmarried women in the general population to provide this level of live-in household service.

When we estimate the number of servants in England from about 1770 to 1820, it matters very much what we are counting, whose 'domestic servant' we are reckoning, and their employers' and the law's reasons for calling them what they did. When William Pitt proposed an end to the tax on female servants in 1792, he said that in the previous tax year, 90,000 'different families . . . the poorer class of householders' had paid it, which gives a figure considerably lower than Colquhoun's from a decade later, even if every one of these

---

[9] J. Jean Hecht, *The Domestic Servant Class in Eighteenth Century England* (London: Routledge and Kegan Paul, 1956), pp. 33–4. Bridget Hill, *Servants. English Domestics in the Eighteenth Century* (Oxford: Clarendon Press, 1996), pp. 15–16. Judith Laurence-Anderson, 'Changing Affective Life in Eighteenth Century England and Samuel Richardson's *Pamela*', *Studies in Eighteenth Century Culture*, 10 (1981), p. 445.

[10] Patrick Colquhoun, *A Treatise on Indigence; Exhibiting a General View of the National Resource for Productive Labour . . .* (London: J. Hatchard, 1806), p. 23. E. A. Wrigley and R. S. Schofield, *The Population History of England, 1541–1871. A Reconstruction* (Cambridge: Cambridge University Press, 1989), pp. 2–4, 571–2.

[11] Colquhoun, *Treatise*, p. 11.

[12] Leonard Schwarz, 'English Servants and their Employers during the Eighteenth and Nineteenth Centuries', *Economic History Review*, 52:2 (1999), pp. 236–56.

householders employed a veritable retinue of maidservants.[13] The maidservant tax had been an extremely unpopular tax which only lasted for seven years (unlike the tax on male servants which, inaugurated in 1777, was operative until 1937). It had been criticised from its first proposal in 1785 as a levy on families, a tax on having children, as falling on poorer and middling-sort house-holders (they were the ones who employed a lone woman, to do the work of the house and a smallholding, said Charles James Fox), as spelling out the certain road to prostitution, said several MPs, for who would employ a girl if they had to pay a levy of 10s 6d for her services, and what else was there for her to do if she could not go to service?[14] So insistent and persuasive were these objections that sliding scales of payment and a bewildering range of exemptions were introduced before the bill passed.[15] The exemptions were not at all bewildering to householders, who learned very fast that if they had two or more children (or grandchildren) living with them, they were exempt from payment for their female servants. And even if there were no children in the house, if the servant were a girl under fourteen, or a woman over sixty, then they were exempted as well: 'Appeals before Commissioners, 1770–1785, Hastings Rape. Sussex to wit . . . Wm Gilmore Croft of Battel [appeals] for that he was charged for one Female servant when he was Exempt as having Children under the Age of 14 years appeal allowd & ordered to be discharged . . .'[16] Pitt was thus count-ing households employing women between the ages of fourteen and sixty, and containing no resident (legitimate) children under fourteen.[17] Also, as Leonard Schwarz has pointed out, domestic service was not universally, nor perhaps even generally, provided by live-in domestics. Women, in particular, might go on working in the houses where they had briefly been permanent servants, long after marriage and children, coming in to cook dinner for company, turn out a room, help with the washing; they were paid by the hour or by the day. If the amount of waged domestic work provided by women is reckoned, rather than the strict tax-law definitions with which William Pitt was working, then even Colquhoun's inflated numbers may have been close to the mark. We certainly can speak of ubiquity, of paid domestic service as the most common work experience of women in the society.

[13] *The Parliamentary History of England* (London: T. C. Hansard, 1814), vol. 29, p. 829 (17 February 1792).

[14] *Parliamentary History*, vol. 25, pp. 546–67 (9 May 1785).

[15] *Parliamentary History*, vol. 25, pp. 569–70, 812 (28 June 1785).

[16] 'Appeals before Commissioners, 1770–1785 . . . Hastings, Sussex'; 'Appeals heard determined at Meeting of the Commissioners held at the George Inn Battel the 21st day of January 1785', PRO, IR 83/131, The National Archives, Kew.

[17] The legislation did specify that the children who provided exemption must be legitimate. There is much to say about the late eighteenth-century state's interest in what would now be called family policy to be read out of the servant tax and its operations. See Carolyn Steedman, *The Servant's Dream. Waged Domestic Work and the Making of the Modern World*, forthcoming.

It often made sound sense just to keep quiet about your servants and the domestic labour you bought. A very great deal of the household work performed by extra-family members was not by those footboys, maids, cooks and butlers (all the categories of menial servant that the acts of parliament specified), hired for the purpose, serving a year and being paid their wages at the end; but rather by women (and men) bought in for a couple of hours, half a day, three mornings, to perform housework as piece-work (wash the china in the china closet, do some ironing, clean the brewing equipment, turn out a bedroom).[18] The Somerset widow Frances Hamilton, who ran the substantial farm and quarry that was bequeathed her, employed two properly hired female servants, one man servant (who did a great many things, in garden, quarry and field, besides waiting on table and carrying her library books into Taunton), and a series of parish apprentices – ten-year-old boys – who worked in husbandry and in the house, between 1778 and 1801. But she also frequently recorded in her accounts (these entries are for 1794 and 1799) that:

Sep 28th
 Catherine settled acct with me &
 paid me 10s6d she owed me & I paid her for working
 30 days at washing 6
 4 days brewg at 6
 10 days Ironing at 4 £1 0s 4d

and

January –	Betty Huckleburgh
1	at 12 o clock
2	at 11 o clock
7	Betty sleep here
15	Betty Huckleburgh went Home to breakfast & work for herself: came at night
16	Betty Huckle the same
17	the same
18	the same
19	breakfast and sweep my room
20	Betty here Paid her.[19]

William Blackstone said that domestics were 'the first sort of servants acknowledged by the laws of England; so called from being *intra moenia*'

---

[18] Commissioners of Excise, *Abstract of Cases and Decisions on Appeals Relating to the Tax on Servants* (London: T. Longman and T. Cadell, 1781). Amanda Vickery, *The Gentleman's Daughter. Women's Lives in Georgian England* (New Heaven and London: Yale University Press, 1998), p. 139.

[19] Frances Hamilton, Bishops Lydeard Farming Accounts, DD/FS 5/8–7/3, Somerset Country Record Office, Taunton (28 September 1794, 20 January 1799). Margaret Allen, 'Frances Hamilton of Bishops Lydeard', *Notes and Queries for Somerset and Dorset*, 31: Part 317 (1983), pp. 259–72.

(dwelling within the walls of a house; resident).[20] Tax law and taxing the servant's labour cut right across this legal definition; when later eighteenth-century employers, commissioners and judges talked about 'servants' they had all these definitions in mind, and we can read what they meant by considering the context to their use of the term. Often, as we shall see, there was a good deal at stake in saying that your servant wasn't a 'servant'. We need a definition that reckons both that tiny number of liveried, bewigged, taxed footmen, serving in the big house, *and* the numbers who came and went in all sorts of modest households, like Betty Huckleburgh (Huckleborough) and Catherine Vickery above. New kinds of household work and maintenance had emerged; the proliferation of new household goods (carpets, china, curtains, cooking utensils) demanded new kinds of labour, organised by new rhythms of everyday life.[21]

Late eighteenth-century commentators like Charles Fox knew that the most common experience for what he called 'poorer' householders was to employ a young woman to take charge of the kitchen and to do the outside work on which day-to-day life in the household depended.[22] Quite apart from new tax law, there were good reasons for calling this woman 'a servant in husbandry' (even though she cooked the dinner, dusted and washed the baby's nappies) because then, if she displeased you, you might take your complaint before a magistrate who, authorised by some very old legislation, was bound to take note of you both.[23] Moreover, the servant tax legislation exempted those who employed men and women in the exercise of their trade (this included the trade of farming) and by whose labour the master or mistress earned a living or a profit. Many employers tried this on with their boys and footmen, calling them husbandmen for the purposes of an appeal committee meeting. (They probably *were* farm workers from time to time, digging, shovelling, forking, carting . . .

---

[20] William Blackstone, *Commentaries on the Laws of England. In Four Books*, orig. pub. 1765, 6th edn (Dublin: Company of Booksellers, 1775), Book 1, p. 425.

[21] Bridget Hill, *Women, Work and Sexual Politics in Eighteenth-century England* (Oxford: Blackwell, 1989), pp. 103–47.

[22] Apprenticeship to housewifery of girls (and a tiny number of boys) is illuminating on the permeable boundary between indoor and outdoor household work. See Keith Snell, *Annals of the Labouring Poor. Social Change and Agrarian England, 1660–1900* (Cambridge: Cambridge University Press, 1985), pp. 270–319 for the apprenticeship of women, including apprenticeship to housewifery. Honeyman, *Women, Gender and Industrialisation*, pp. 26–7. It was the work of female servants that blurred the distinction between household work and outside work (though that is the wrong way to put it: for eighteenth-century employers, the work existed on a continuum). See Hill, *Women, Work*, pp. 69–102; Thomas Parkyns, *A Method Proposed, for the Recording of Servants in Husbandry, Arts, Mysteries, &etc. Offer'd by Sir Thomas Parkyns, Bart., One of His Majesty's Justices of the Peace for the Counties of Nottingham and Leicester* (London: privately printed, 1724), p. 40. For the permeable boundary between inside and outdoor work in Buckinghamshire in the 1750s, see G. Eland (ed.), *The Purefoy Letters 1735–1753*, 2 vols. (London: Sidgwick and Jackson, 1931), vol. I, pp. 226–56.

[23] Hill, *Women, Work*, pp. 69–102. Paul Craven and Douglas Hay, *Masters, Servants and Magistrates in Britain and the Empire, 1562–1955* (Chapel Hill and London: University of North Carolina Press, 2004), pp. 59–116.

as well as occasionally waiting at table, fetching water, cleaning out the house, assisting in the kitchen, cleaning knives and forks . . . What they *did* was no more demarcated by the kitchen door than the work of female servants in country places.) You might wish a magistrate to exercise some control over your domestic servant (who milked no house-cow and who never helped with the hay harvest; but who was insubordinate, refused to dress the baby, filched your goods, hid a peck of grain in one of your outhouses for her family to take under cover of darkness . . .) and calling her a 'servant in husbandry' or just 'a servant' (but *not* a 'domestic or menial servant') made this a possibility.[24] Early nineteenth-century lawyers thought that, throughout the previous century, magistrates had responded to both parties in the domestic service relationship, exercised an authority they actually didn't have in law, and assumed that all the women who came before them were actually servants in husbandry. They knew perfectly well that legislation related 'particularly to artificers and servants of husbandry, but it is imagined that it may well be construed to give justices a general jurisdiction over servants of every description, and such jurisdiction is in fact exercised them', said James Barry Bird in 1799.[25] In 1812 Thomas Waller Williams thought that in the previous century (and in a nice example of what is now called legal fiction), magistrates had simply assumed that all servants 'were servants in husbandry, and thus exercised jurisdiction'.[26]

Colquhoun's estimate of 800,000 female domestics in 1806, Pitt's more certain 90,000 households paying the maidservant tax in 1791, measure out at the very least a vast commonalty of experience from both sides of the borderline. Serious attention has been paid to Sara Maza's and Cissie Fairchilds's work on service in France and to their insistence that service was, above all else, experienced as *a relationship*.[27] It is an emotional and affective relationship

---

[24] 'A peck of wheat stolen from me & deposited under Hay in the Stable,' recorded Frances Hamilton of Bishops Lydeard near Taunton on 15 June 1794. It took her two weeks to determine that it was Hannah Burston, who had been with her for at least seven years, who had done it: '29 Jun 1794 Discharged Hannah Burston from my House: She having concealed a peck of Wheat found in ye Stables returning it into the Hutch with an intent not to acquaint me with the transaction.' She did not involve the local magistrate in this affair. Frances Hamilton, Bishops Lydeard Household & Farm Accounts, DD/FS 5/2.

[25] James Barry Bird, *The Laws Respecting Masters and Servants, Articled Clerks, Apprentices, Manufacturers, Labourers and Journeymen*, 3rd edn (London: W. Clarke, 1799), p. 3.

[26] Thomas Waller Williams, *The Whole Law Relative to the Duty and Office of a Justice of the Peace*, 4 vols. (London: John Stockdale, 1812), vol. III, pp. 887–93. See also Richard Burn, *A New Law Dictionary. Intended for General Use, as well as for Gentlemen of the Profession, Continued to the Present Time by his Son, John Burn*, 2 vols. (London: T. Cadell, 1793), vol. II, pp. 325–8; Thomas Ruggles, *The History of the Poor; their Rights, Duties, and the Laws Respecting Them*, 2 vols. (London: J. Deighton, 1793), vol. II, p. 255.

[27] Sarah Maza, *Servants and Masters in Eighteenth-century France. The Uses of Loyalty* (Princeton and Guildford: Princeton University Press, 1983). Cissie Fairchilds, *Domestic Enemies. Servants and their Masters in Old Regime France* (Baltimore and London: The Johns Hopkins University Press, 1984).

that has been investigated rather than a class relationship, an investigation that is always accompanied, as is Amanda Vickery's brief but brilliant account of Elizabeth Shackleton's feelings about her female servants in 1780s Lancashire, by the social historian's familiar and resigned caveat that we are never likely to find out very much about how the servant felt about Elizabeth Shackleton.[28]

It has been unusual to discuss the service question in a provincial setting as Vickery has done; most recent work on domestic service has used metropolitan sources – to uncover the employment of servants by relatively low strata of the artisan population of Augustan London,[29] and above all perhaps, to find women, and women's experience. These women have been seen by their historians to be exercising choice, using domestic service as a way of evading marriage and maintaining independence.[30] From the perspective of the metropolis, English social historians can no longer be accused, as they were in 1976, of ignoring servants because they were women.[31] At the same time, our knowledge of apprenticeship has been much increased, particularly of the many ways in which it was used to provide households with female (and sometimes male) domestic service, particularly in the provinces.[32] In December 1810 at the Leeds assessed tax appeals meeting, the commissioners heard the appeal of Messrs A. and R. Leigh, cloth merchants, against the surcharge on 'a Young Man who is bound an Apprentice to them to learn the Trade . . . not imposed by the Magistrates – the said Apprentice acts as a Livery servant in general by regularly waiting at Table &c, but his masters do not furnish him with a livery as . . . they consider him no more than an occasional servant . . .' The commissioners and the high court judges determined that he was one, and the Leighs liable to the tax.[33] A few years earlier, a Huddersfield clothier and cloth merchant had been asked by the parliamentary commissioners taking evidence on the legal regulation of the woollen trade, whether local 'Footmen . . . might have been in the Clothing Business in the earlier part of their Lives?' He said no: 'they might have been in the Weaving Business, but not in the Cloth Pressing, I am sure', not mentioning the kind of informal arrangement that employers might

---

[28] Vickery, *Gentleman's Daughter*, pp. 134–46. For the service relationship as a class relationship, see Steedman, *The Servant's Dream*, forthcoming.

[29] Peter Earle, *The Making of the English Middle Class. Business, Society and Family Life in London, 1660–1730* (London: Methuen, 1989), pp. 218–30.

[30] D. A. Kent, 'Ubiquitous but Invisible. Female Domestic Servants in Mid-Eighteenth-century London', *History Workshop Journal*, 28 (1989), pp. 111–128. Meldrum, *Domestic Service and Gender*.

[31] Theresa McBride, *The Domestic Revolution. The Modernization of Household Service in England and France, 1820–1920* (London: Croom Helm, 1976), pp. 9–17.

[32] Snell, *Annals of the Labouring Poor*, p. 257. Hill, *Women, Work*, pp. 85–102. Frederic Keeling, *Child Labour in the United Kingdom* (London: P. S. King, 1914). Joan Lane, *Apprenticeship in England, 1600–1914* (London: UCL Press, 1996).

[33] PRO, IR 70/3, 'Assessed Taxes and Inhabited Houses Duties. Judges Opinions, 1805–1830', Vol. III, February 1810–June 1830, 'No. 581 – Leeds – Apprentices', The National Archives.

come to with all their workers and apprentices, in order to get household work done.[34]

John Murgatroyd paid the servant tax on Phoebe Beatson; his was a typical kind of household in tax-law terms. He recorded the local assessor knocking on the door with a schedule in his hand; he sent Phoebe to pay the levy on herself, and the other assessed taxes. There would have been little point to an appeal: no children, one female servant; no exemptions here. It was probably the most typical arrangement under which female domestics lived and worked: a single-servant household. To take an example of one town for which female servant tax records survive: in Shrewsbury in April 1786 householders paid the tax on 176 female servants, 83 (47 per cent) of whom were returned as single servants. (These included women working for lodgers employing their own servants, called 'inmates' of someone else's house in the Shrewsbury returns; they were householders as far as the Tax Office was concerned.) Another twenty-five women (14 per cent) worked with a fellow servant (sometimes male, more commonly female). In this county town thirty (17 per cent) of taxed female servants worked in large establishments of six or more servants (again, male and female).[35] Some of these ostensibly single-servant householders may have been exempt from tax on a second woman because of the children present; some may have employed a young girl or an older woman as well as their assessed maid. This total is certainly an underestimate of the number of servants employed in the town. But these figures do allow us to say with some certainty that a single-servant household was the kind most likely to be lived in by employer and employee in the later eighteenth century. In Doncaster for the assessed tax period ending in April 1789, 167 employers paid the tax on 241 female servants, 129 (60 per cent) of them working as a single maid, 40 (18 per cent) in a two-servant household.[36] The vast army of helpers, part-timers and bought-in domestic workers are not included in anybody's reckoning, not in Shrewsbury, nor in Doncaster; not at the Tax Office, nor up in Slaithwaite.

Domestic servants are no longer absent from histories of women and women's work; but they (men and women) are still not present in larger-scale political and social histories of Britain's transition to capitalist modernity. Domestic service of whatever kind was the largest single occupation for women; a very large number of working-class women worked as servants at some point in their life, many of them living in close proximity to their social superiors. But the

---

[34] PP 1803 III (Part 3), *Minutes of Evidence taken before the Commissioners, to whom the Bill, respecting the Laws relating to the Woollen Trade, is committed*, pp. 871–81; Q. 377.

[35] 'An Assessment of the Township . . . for the Taxes on Male, Female Servants, Coaching Horses, Waggons, Carts, April 1786', 3365/374, Shropshire Records and Research, Shrewsbury.

[36] 'Doncaster Window Duty 1789', AB6/2/17, Doncaster Metropolitan Borough Council Archives, Doncaster. There was one large establishment in town, of seven servants, employing three (taxed) female servants – 1 per cent of the female servant workforce. Seven householders paid up for three maids. There was one in the town who paid for four.

historiography of class relations, from Thompson's *The Making of the English Working Class* (1963) to Anna Clark's *The Struggle for the Breeches* (1995), has not assessed the significance of service for class. Thompson's thesis concerning class and class formation has been scrutinised, adjusted, altered, moved back and forwards in time, and gendered; but servants are no more part of the story than they were when it was first written.[37] In the case of labour and social history, evasion of their massive presence is not a result of difficulties in tracking them down, measuring their presence or even of naming them. Rather they are not there because – as will be discussed in chapter 3 – they are *not already in* the story that social historians are telling (or repeating, or readjusting) and they have not been there since Adam Smith first called their work 'not-work' in the 1770s, Karl Marx used Smith's social theory nearly a century later, and twentieth-century social historians used both their theses to write the history of the working class in England. Phoebe Beatson is silent, not only because she could not write, not only because John Murgatroyd never recorded her speech in his journal, not only because the records of her appearance before magistrates in the summer of 1802 have not survived, but also because the histories that have taken her retrieval and the reconstruction of her experience as a task employ a plot-line that simply does not include women (and men) like her. Adding Phoebe Beatson (and the relationship between her and John Murgatroyd) to the making of the English working class will not demolish the Thompsonian thesis, but it will affect it at the structural level. This book is, in part, the beginning of an attempt to see what happens to a historiography once a majority of the working class are added to their own story.

John Murgatroyd's silence over the events of 1801–2, when Phoebe Beatson conceived and bore her illegitimate child (or in a longer frame, his silence during the years 1786–1806, or 1739–1806) is of a different order. Some of it is probably a function of missing documentation. No diaries survive for 1783–5, or for the years 1787, 1792–3, 1795, 1799 and 1803. Canon Hulbert, Murgatroyd's Victorian historian, noted on the cover of the first surviving diary from 1782, that these were 'not forthcoming'. Missing diaries cannot be read

---

[37] R. J. Morris, *Class and Class Consciousness in the Industrial Revolution, 1789–1850* (London: Macmillan, 1979). R. S. Neale, *Class in English History, 1680–1850* (Oxford: Basil Blackwell, 1981). John Rule, *The Experience of Labour in Eighteenth-century Industry* (London: Croom Helm, 1981). Joan Wallach Scott, 'Women in *The Making of the English Working Class*', in Scott (ed.), *Gender and the Politics of History* (New York and London: Columbia University Press, 1988), pp. 68–90. William H. Sewell, 'How Classes are Made: Critical Reflections on E. P. Thompson's Theory of Working-class Formation', in Harvey J. Kaye and Keith McClelland (eds.), *E. P. Thompson. Critical Perspectives* (Cambridge: Polity Press, 1990), pp. 50–77. Catherine Hall, 'The Tale of Samuel and Jemima. Gender and Working Class Culture in Nineteenth-century England', in Kaye and McClelland, *E. P. Thompson*, pp. 78–102. Patrick Joyce (ed.), *Class* (Oxford: Oxford University Press, 1995). Andy Wood, *The Politics of Social Conflict. The Peak Country, 1520–1770* (Cambridge: Cambridge University Press, 1999).

for his immediate reaction to the outbreak of the French Wars in 1792, nor for accounts of harvest failure and the crisis of dearth in 1795. The Quota Act of 1795 and its demands for Yorkshire to produce 609 men for the armed forces were not mentioned by him in the following year, for which a diary does survive. For 1798 there is a necessary silence over the dismissal of the Lord Lieutenant for the West Riding (the Duke of Norfolk had toasted Charles James Fox as a kind of George Washington, for attempting to make his own country as free as the Americans).[38] There is no later discussion of the Peace of Amiens (1802), or of the embodiment of the militia and mobilisation for the regular army before declaration of war in May 1803, though his diaries cover some of the 'Amiens interlude', which was also the time of Phoebe Beatson's pregnancy and the birth of her child.[39] Murgatroyd probably did write more than has survived about local reverberations of war and its economic and political impact on the West Riding, for in the extant diaries he recorded in some detail effects on the woollen and worsted trade, viewed through the prism of his servant's work as a spinner and the inability of her spinning master to pay for work she had done.[40] He regularly read the Manchester and Leeds press; he borrowed newspapers from visitors and regularly went down into Slaithwaite for the news. He had clear views on some national events and on their godly and local import. On 2 January 1794 he wrote that 'The Parliament must today the Lords for Xt's sake dispose their Hearts to Love, Unity & Peace', knowing the very hour when acknowledgement of the French Republic by the British government was to be debated in the upper chamber.[41] Speaking against continued war and from a perspective recognised in the commercial and trading centres of the woollen and worsted trades, the Earl of Guildford was to say that 'If you dry up the resources in France, you destroy your own markets. If you destroy her, she will have no commodities to exchange with you, or money to purchase what you have to sell.' The Lord Lieutenant of the West Riding (not yet dismissed from office) supported this view. The Earl of Derby 'abhorred the atrocities [the French] had committed', but thought that 'the love of peace should predominate over every other consideration'. But they were in the minority: all the lords spiritual and most of the temporal turned their hearts against peace, commercial or godly. There may well have been more political commentary like this in Murgatroyd's other journals, penned from his perspective as a minister of Christ, and more political observation like that from June 1796 when he noted that 'They are

---

[38] Clive Emsley, *British Society and the French Wars, 1793–1815* (Basingstoke: Macmillan, 1979), p. 67.
[39] Emsley, *British Society*, pp. 38–42, 49, 53, 99–123.   [40] See chapter 3.
[41] Reverend John Murgatroyd, Diaries, KC242/2, West Yorkshire Archive Service, Kirklees District, Huddersfield (2 January 1794). *Parliamentary History of England*, vol. 30 (13 December 1792–10 March 1794), pp. 1045–8 for the King's Speech on Opening the Session; pp. 1062–88 for the Lords' debate on it, which was what Murgatroyd was interested in.

busy canvassing thro' ye Kingdom for Parliament men a New Parliament.'[42] He used his other notebooks in this fashion as well, to observe current events, though here his entries were undated: anxieties about general mobilisation and the defence of the realm were probably recorded in 1802, though they make no appearance in his diaries.[43]

Pitt's war budgets and the tensing sinews of the fiscal military state for combat could have been noted by Murgatroyd in the extant diary for 1794, when taxes on attorneys, spirits, bricks and tiles, and plate glass and paper were introduced.[44] The Murgatroyds' new house in Lingards (built for his retirement from Slaithwaite schoolmastering) had been completed in 1790, but he employed a Huddersfield-based solicitor, drank as much as the next man and purchased a good deal of paper, yet he did not mention the rising cost of living in his diary. In 1795 further levies were introduced – on wines and spirits, tea, some imported wood, life insurance and on hair powder (which used precious corn (wheaten) flour). In 1796 the assessed taxes (on windows, horses, male servants) were raised by 10 per cent; there was a new levy on tobacco; the tax on pleasure horses doubled and a new tax on work horses was introduced. The levy on printed calico was near doubled to sixpence a yard. In 1797 there were increases on tea, spirits, on sugar, and on newly-built houses . . . Patrick O'Brien calculates that during the twenty-two years of war with France (Murgatroyd lived through fourteen of these) from 1793 to 1815, 'something like 63% of the extra taxation required [for] combat . . . emanated from taxes falling . . . upon the incomes and consumptions of the rich', as indeed was the policy of successive governments, where policy can be discerned.[45] But these new and increased taxes fell also and increasingly on the goods and services consumed in modest households; the cost of housekeeping increased steadily during the last ten years of Murgatroyd's life. But he kept no horse, nor a manservant who needed hair powder (though he may have purchased it for his own wig, which he obdurately wore until his dying day); he smoked his tobacco and went on drinking the spirits purchased from Rochdale. He had paid the maidservant tax for Phoebe Beatson during the short life of that extraordinarily unpopular measure, but it had been abolished in 1792. If he contributed anything to the 'Loyalty Loan', which was launched in December 1796 with the intention of raising £18 million for the

---

[42] Murgatroyd Diaries, KC242/3 (6 June 1796).   [43] See below, chapter 2.

[44] Emsley, *British Society*, p. 49. Patrick K. O'Brien, 'Public Finance and the Wars with France, 1793–1815', in H. T. Dickinson (ed.), *Britain and the French Revolution, 1789–1815* (Basingstoke: Macmillan, 1989), pp. 165–87. J. V. Beckett, 'Land Tax or Excise. The Levying of Taxation in Seventeenth- and Eighteenth-century England', *English Historical Review*, 100 (1985), pp. 285–308. J. V. Beckett and Michael Turner, 'Taxation and Economic Growth in Eighteenth-century England', *Economic History Review*, 43:3 (1990), pp. 377–403.

[45] Patrick K. O'Brien, 'The Political Economy of British Taxation, 1660–1815', *Economic History Review* 41 (2nd Series) (1988), pp. 1–32. W. R. Ward, *The English Land Tax in the Eighteenth Century* (Oxford University Press: London, 1953).

war effort, he did not record it in his diaries. All account books are missing from his archive (and so are the West Riding assessed tax records missing). Account books might well obviate most of John Murgatroyd's silences on his commercial and political context; as it is, what we are left with are the writings of a man who considered a diary to be for the purposes of recording the diurnal (the state of play with the builders and the new house, company at dinner and the contents of the kitchen garden, his maidservant's spinning, and a new recipe for cooking tainted meat) and his relationship with God. It is also important to note how very long was the historical perspective from which he intermittently recorded current events and with what kind of public history he aligned the story of his own life: in 1802 he noted that 'King George 3d enters upon his 65th year of age & I entered my 65th year of serving ye Public'. As a clergyman of the Church of England his political times stretched back to the seventeenth century; they existed in a permanent present tense: 'All graciously preserved,' he noted on Martyr's Sunday that year. 'Had pleasant Day. King Charles beheaded very troublesome Times in England.'[46]

Murgatroyd's silences, then, do not need compensation. In this book, I have compensated for Phoebe Beatson's silence by some account of her typicality as a domestic servant; and at the end of it, in a much bolder move, I read Emily Brontë's *Wuthering Heights* (1847) as the historical novel it actually is, its setting the West Yorkshire worsted field between about 1770 and 1800. This tale (or history, as I shall argue) is told by one of the great servant-narrators of literary modernity, Ellen (Nelly) Dean. Here the servant certainly has a voice; large swathes of the text *are* the (invented) voice of one of the Pennine serving class. I am concerned to discover what might be retrieved of the perceptions and understandings of a nineteenth-century novelist who chose to write in the voice of a social inferior and a servant, *and* what Emily Brontë knew, or believed she knew, about domestic service and servants in the recent historical past of the later eighteenth century. Brontë's story (or history) also emerged from a clergyman's household, as does the one that follows here.

But meaning, myth and fiction are preoccupations of this book from the very beginning, long before *Wuthering Heights* is discussed. The major historical account of the West Riding in this period remains Edward Thompson's *The Making of the English Working Class* for which Yorkshire archives, and the annals of its labouring poor that they contain, were important sources. This book is the beginning of an attempt to enter domestic servants into that drama of class formation. And drama it *is* – not *was*: for we are dealing for the main part with dominant and interpretive accounts penned by twentieth-century historians, not by their historical subjects. These historical accounts have in their turn become

---

[46] Murgatroyd Diaries, KC242/7 (4 June, 30 January 1802).

myths of class and nation formation. Histories like Thompson's, and those that modelled themselves on his, remain serious socio-historical accounts; but in their wider social appropriations as arguments and texts, they have become mythological, for they explain a social order coming into being: how things got to be the way they are.[47] This is why it is instructive to read *Wuthering Heights* in conjunction with *The Making of the English Working Class*, for they have both become myths of social origin emanating from and concerning the same geographical terrain and the same historical period. Indeed, *Wuthering Heights* did not need to be made *into* a myth by its readers, as in the case of Thompson's historical myth; according to some literary critics, from the moment Ellen Dean opens her mouth, she tells 'a myth of origins'.[48] A way of reading what follows here is as the replacement of one myth (or set of myths) with another. The new myth is the myth of the West Riding Phoebe; telling of her serves to encapsulate developments and perspectives that deviate from the ones handed down to us. More prosaically, this book describes three intertwined personal histories, and the experiences these people had of life, love and labour, in the classic site of class formation in England. It may serve to adjust and complicate the account we already have of the making of capitalist modernity in England. If the relationship between John Murgatroyd and Phoebe Beatson had been enacted elsewhere – not in the West Riding – it would have less significance for any kind of rewriting of the making of the English working class. As it is, this master and this servant and the life they lived together highlight the material out of which Thompson made his account, so much of it produced in the West Yorkshire worsted field. In this way, it has to ask readers to consider the kind of story that 'history' is, the effects of these stories as they are told, and their constant potential for alteration, as new evidence comes to light.

The West Riding of Yorkshire has been very well studied: the land between the Aire and the Calder (all of West Yorkshire) is – as we shall see – haunted by historians (many of them eighteenth- and nineteenth-century historians) who have written up its demography, accounted for its industrialisation, assessed the relationship between rural manufacturing prosperity and marriage behaviour, and found many of its bastard children, in order to judge the behaviour of its people. At the end of a substantial and illuminating account of two townships north of Slaithwaite, Calverly and Sowerby, Pat Hudson and Steve King question

---

[47] For the movement between formal academic history and its use in popular and political imaginations (including those of historians), see Geoff Eley, *A Crooked Line. From Cultural History to the History of Society* (Ann Arbor: University of Michigan Press, 2005), pp. 152–5.

[48] Susan M. Gilbert and Susan Gubar, *The Madwoman in the Attic. The Woman Writer and the Nineteenth-century Literary Imagination*, 2nd edn (New Haven: Yale University Press, 2000), p. 292.

the techniques of the historical demographers and economic historians (whose techniques they themselves have deployed) who proceed by relating human behaviour to 'general economic climate[s] . . . to real wage movements, degrees of wage dependency . . . [and the] dominant occupation . . .'[49] As they point out, it is notoriously difficult to do this with sub-groups (we must count Phoebe Beatson and George Thorp as part of a sub-group) – to understand behaviour in relationship to these factors at all, partly because records do not exist by which it can be charted (they themselves have performed miracles with the poor law records of Sowerby and Calverly), but mainly because (not a point they make directly) there may have been no such relationship, between the economic forces discernible to the modern scholarly eye and the moment (of passion? abandon? decision? conviction?) in which a child, to be called bastard by law, state and future social historians, is conceived. Their comments make the thought flash – vertiginous and alarming – that the enterprise of economic and social history has served to obscure as much as it has revealed of lives like Phoebe Beatson's. Their proposed solution is dizzying and exciting in equal measure: to stop relying on received histories of economic trends to explain proletarian behaviour in the past; rather to turn to the idea that behaviour and human relationships themselves have power to shape lives. These relationships and behaviours will be 'rooted in local vernaculars' – to do with the hills you walk, the wool you process, the God you believe in. Then your historian may be able to see you, not quietly confirming a demographic trend (like that of the increase in illegitimate births for the assessment of general prosperity in relation to marriage behaviour and as the connection between proto-industrialisation and population increase), nor passively reflecting the movement of real wages for female textile workers, but as an actor in your own life. Your historian will need a very broad definition of material culture in order to do this, one that encompasses all the things made by men and women (that in their turn, make them): love as well as labour, belief as well as the production of bastard children.

This book is constructed as a series of essays, all of them bringing questions to bear on Phoebe Beatson and John Murgatroyd's relationship, and the social, economic and cultural relations of West Yorkshire 1786–1806, more generally. They are relatively self-contained essays: you could read chapters on the worsted manufacture, on West Riding Anglicanism, on Murgatroyd's promotion of the gods of classical antiquity and the Anglican God in Slaithwaite school, without the perspective of other, unread chapters. This organisation has necessitated some occasional repetition – not of argument, but of information – that I do not

---

[49] Pat Hudson and Steve King, 'Two Textile Townships, c.1660–1820. A Comparative Demographic Analysis', *Economic History Review*, 53:4 (2000), pp. 706–41.

believe will irritate those who read (as I hope readers will) chronologically, to discover Nelly Dean from *Wuthering Heights* as historian of English industrial modernity.

We shall proceed now, in the *marxisant* tradition of Slaithwaite's Victorian incumbent, the Reverend Charles Hulbert, who believed that this place produced the habits and manners of its people (though he could scarcely have *approved* the behaviour of Phoebe and George, nor of one of his predecessor's baptising their little girl).

2 Wool, worsted and the working class: myths of origin

This place, this 'narrow bit of hill country' dividing Yorkshire from Lancashire in which the Colne and Calder valleys lie, has been a land of myth for a very long time. It was, according to E. P. Thompson, the *locus classi* of 'the outstanding fact of the period 1790 and 1830 . . . the formation of the "working class"'.[1] Through countless readings and appropriations of *The Making of the English Working Class*, through all the historical work that has confirmed and readjusted the account first published in 1963, what he told in it has acquired the status of myth – a foundational account of modern English society, and of the birth of the social classes that accompanied the early stages of its capitalist development. According to the imaginative strictures of classical mythology, then, we may see a Colossus striding out among the hills. There is, first of all, the ancient and amiable Reverend John Murgatroyd, accompanying his maidservants to the putter-out, the small-time merchant wool comber who supplied the worsted bundles that they would, over the next few weeks, spin into yarn in the spaces of time between the domestic services they were contracted with him to provide. He always went with a new girl, to show her the way; in March 1782, for example, he went 'to Halifax; our Servt. Betty with me to Hollawell=Green & took 5 lbs of yarn, & brought back 9 lbs o' Wool – this her first Time of going – So now She knows ye. Way –'. Often these journeys fitted in with his own family and financial arrangements: on this occasion, having left Betty at Richard Walker's, he 'proceeded fowd. to Halifax – found my sister poorly . . .'[2] In July 1786 he borrowed a neighbour's 'Galloway [mare] . . . to Hollowell Green with

---

[1] J. H. Clapham, *The Woollen and Worsted Industries* (London: Methuen, 1907), pp. 12–13, for 'the narrow bit of hill country'. The Wharfe Valley marks the boundary of modern West Yorkshire; Clapham used it to mark the boundaries of the Leeds/Bradford/Halifax/Huddersfield district. Haworth, situated between the Calder and Aire valleys, faces the River Aire. Its location is important for the later stages of this book. The area in which Thompson's drama enacted itself is that of the Aire and Calder valleys. (The Colne river is a tributary of the Calder, the Colne Valley the site of *this* drama.) Thompson's working class lived – quite precisely – in the Calder Valley. E. P. Thompson, *The Making of the English Working Class*, orig. pub. 1963 (Harmondsworth: Penguin, 1968), pp. 212–13.

[2] Reverend John Murgatroyd, Diaries KC 24/1, West Yorkshire Archive Service, Kirklees District, Huddersfield (1 March 1782).

Worset – 12 lbs – Phoebe went with me – I brought Her back 12 lbs back for spinning as far as ye Outland then turn'd round, & proceeded to Halifax . . .' Richard Walker farmed as well as running an out-working system: he was 'away at the hay' when Murgatroyd called in on his return journey from his sister's.[3] In July 1789 Murgatroyd 'walk'd this morning with our Servant Phoebe . . . over ye Moor to ye Forrest with her Worsted – She brought back Twelve pounds to spin – Richd. Walker being remov'd from Hollowell=Green to Forrest, she did not know the Road well enough'. Phoebe Beatson, whose long service to Murgatroyd and turbulent romantic career are the focus of what follows here, did not like this new route: 'I ventur'd to go with Phoebe, who is afraid of Bulls &c, over ye Moors to Rich. Walkers – she had 12 lbs of yarn, & brought back 12 lbs to spin . . .'[4] Colossus in this first instance simply by way of similitude, for John Murgatroyd was 'a tall and venerable looking man, who wore a powdered wig and a long cloak' long after the fashion for the head gear, at least, had moved on.[5] Most of Murgatroyd's immense walking was done on Sundays, when in his long retirement he took services as far away as Saddleworth, Elland, Ripponden and Raistrick. He never undertook a regular curacy again, after he relinquished the one he had held as assistant to the Almondbury incumbent, between 1755 and 1767.[6]

But Colossus in the second instance by way of metaphor as well, for if we follow John Murgatroyd and Phoebe Beatson along the moorland pathways, the old road, past fields with bulls, winter snowdrifts, lakes of mud in the early spring, then we are bound to be accompanied by two historiographies, of labour and class consciousness, and of political repression and protest. These are weighty and portentous historiographies, straddling the West Riding and indicating it as the birthplace of a modern class society and as 'the raw frontier society of early industrial England.'[7] Labour exploitation and political oppression meet in Edward Thompson's richly detailed making of the West Yorkshire working class (not least because of Thompson's own location in the Huddersfield–Halifax district, when he produced his account in 1963).[8] He shows a swift West Riding

[3] Murgatroyd Diaries, KC 24/1 (14 July 1786).

[4] Murgatroyd Diaries, KC 24/1 (31 July 1789, 8 December 1789).

[5] Henry James Morehouse, *Extracts from the Diary of the Rev. Robert Meeke . . . Also a Continuation of the History of Slaithwaite Free School, and an Account of the Educational Establishment in Slaithwaite-cum-Lingards, by the Rev. Charles Augustus Hulbert* (Huddersfield: *Daily Chronicle* Steam Press; London: H. G. Bohn, 1884), p. 107. See also Charles Augustus Hulbert, *Annals of the Church in Slaithwaite (near Huddersfield) West Riding of Yorkshire from 1593–1864, in Five Lectures* (London: Longman, 1864), pp. 52–60. For wigs, hair powder, the tax on it, and the slow movement of fashion in provincial places, see below, chapter 3.

[6] Morehouse, *Extracts*, pp. 105–16 for a biography of Murgatroyd.

[7] Edward Royle, 'The Church of England and Methodism in Yorkshire, c.1750–1850. From Monopoly to Free Market', *Northern History*, 33 (1997), p. 137.

[8] Andy Croft, 'Walthamstow, Little Gidding and Middlesbrough: Edward Thompson the Literature Tutor', in Richard Taylor (ed.), *Beyond the Walls. Fifty Years of Adult Education at the University*

reaction to national political events, including the sedition trials and Britain's
entering the war against France. The Liberty Tree was planted on these hills,
where it flourished. The London Constitutional Society's proposal for a British
convention to discuss events taking place in France rallied the provincial Corresponding Societies: 'Halifax . . . came forward for the first time, in April 1794',
ascribing their earlier reticence to ' "a number of [local] men, who oppose . . . all
free discussion . . . To see one of the advocates of Liberty in this town, fined or
pilloried or imprisoned, would unspeakably gratify their rage . . ." '[9] Open-air
meetings took place all over the district during April; there were food riots; the
militia were employed; local manufacturers petitioned for peace. William Pitt
saw through the Two Acts (banning seditious meetings and suspending *habeas
corpus)* in November and December, during 'the last, greatest, period of popular agitation'.[10] Six years later, Huddersfield magistrates still feared that ' "an
Insurrection was in contemplation among the lower orders" ', for there were
' "persons going about endeavouring to persuade the People to take an oath, to
support each other in regulating and lowering the Price of the necessaries of
Life" '.[11]

John Murgatroyd noted the effects of general dearth in his diary in 1802,
the day that Phoebe came home from Halifax where she had been to pay the
assessed taxes for him, to collect the rent on the houses he owned in the town –
and to visit her parents, for that was where she had been born and where they
still lived. 'All is distressing poverty I find, at Halifax – as it is here . . .' he
had heard; 'many tenants are sinking under very pinching circumstances – The
Lord be merciful to us.'[12] The connection between trade and war, and between
revolution and local economy, has been long noted by historians of the area.[13]
The 1780s, the interval between the American War and the Revolutionary Wars,
were a boom time for the worsted trade despite competition from cotton; worsted
for hangings, furniture, carpets, stuffs . . . was much in demand. 'From the

of Leeds, 1946–1966 (Leeds: Leeds Studies in Continuing Education, 1995), pp. 144–56. See
also David Goodway, 'E. P. Thompson and *The Making of the English Working Class*', in Taylor,
Beyond the Walls, pp. 133–43. Carolyn Steedman, 'A Weekend with Elektra', *Literature
and History*, 6:1 (1997), pp. 17–42.

[9] Thompson, *Making*, pp. 141–3.

[10] Thompson, *Making*, p. 155; Roger A. E. Wells, *Dearth and Distress in Yorkshire, 1793–1802*,
Borthwick Papers 52 (York: University of York, 1977); Wells, *Wretched Faces. Famine in
Wartime England, 1798–1801* (Gloucester: Alan Sutton, 1988), pp. 133–60; Wells, 'The Devel-
opment of the English Rural Proletariat and Social Protest, 1700–1850', in Mick Reed and Roger
Wells (eds.), *Class, Conflict and Protest in the English Countryside, 1700–1880* (London: Frank
Cass, 1990), pp. 29–53.

[11] Thompson, *Making*, pp. 517–18.

[12] Murgatroyd Diaries, KC 242/6 (28 February 1802). This was part of Phoebe's routine: 'Phoebe
walk'd after Dinner to Halifax to her mothrs & about Rents –'. Murgatroyd Diaries, KC 242/5
(24 June 1800).

[13] John James, *History of the Worsted Manufacture in England*, orig. pub. 1857 (London: Frank
Cass, 1968), p. 357.

years 1782 to 1792, the demand in foreign markets for English worsted goods, far exceeded that of any former period, and in this trade, the West-Riding, especially Halifax, took a large share.' The town 'enjoyed great prosperity until the breaking out of the French War, when its trade, chiefly foreign, declined', wrote John James in 1857.[14] Throughout the summer of 1801 meetings were held all over the West Riding to protest against short wages and short time, for the Two Acts had run their course, and it was technically possible to call public meetings once more.[15] Here, Luddism was to flourish as well, and there was probably a Luddite command centre in Huddersfield by 1812.[16]

Echoing between the lines of Thompson's political account is another, contrapuntal one, which had been in existence for at least a century when he wrote. His story of 'an army of redressers' resisting the effects of mechanisation in the woollen trade as they simultaneously reacted against the curtailment of their legal and political freedoms was a plain tale of worsted in John James's world history of its manufacture, in which having reached the period 1750–1800 and the West Riding, he noted that its wool combers 'were a turbulent, ill-ordered class, and occasioned much trouble to their employers', going on to note extensive and 'exceedingly obnoxious' trade combinations among them, particularly in Halifax.[17] The Yorkshire wool trade and its labour relations had thus had a colossal historiography by the time Thompson came to write of the intersection of labour and politics in the making of working-class experience. Indeed, it was of gigantic proportions by the early twentieth century. In 1907 J. H. Clapham noted that the development of the woollen and worsted industries had 'attracted economists and historians to an uncommon degree, and rightly, for it is connected at all points with the rise of both of the economic and political life and strength of the nation'.[18] He could already draw on a long history of their development. Nineteenth-century accounts like William Hurst's *History of the Woollen Trade of the Last Sixty Years* (1844) or John Burnley's *History of Wool and Wool Combing* (1889) relied in their turn on eighteenth-century technical commentaries on the differences in processing between worsted and woollen and on annals of the trades produced by the men whose technical innovations developed both of them.[19]

---

[14] James, *History of Worsted*, pp. 304, 306.   [15] Thompson, *Making*, pp. 517–18.
[16] Thompson, *Making*, pp. 609, 646.   [17] James, *History of Worsted*, pp. 322–3.
[18] Clapham, *Woollen and Worsted*, p. 1. The connection between worsted and national identity was already well established by 1907. See Collinson, Burton & Co., *The West Riding Worsted Directory containing the History of the Worsted Trade* (Bradford: Collinson, Burton, 1851), p. 93, where it is described as 'the peculiar property of this country', by which was meant England, and not just the West Riding.
[19] Here, as in all these commentaries, 'wool' is the actual fibre; 'woollen' and 'worsted' refer to its processing into two kinds of thread and cloth. As detailed below, woollen manufacture used short staple wool, carded into slubbings and then fulled, frizzed and cropped. Worsted manufacture used long staples, combed into rovings and then spun and woven. If either stuff were to be dyed, it was 'in the wool' (at the wool stage) not as cloth.

Woollen and worsted together not only make a history for this area; they provide a topography as well. This was the first thing that struck Daniel Defoe in the 1720s, when he first visited this 'frightful country', and 'began to perceive the reason and the nature of the thing': why things had to be the way they were. He saw that the land was divided 'into small pieces and scattered dwellings' for 'the convenience of the business which the people were generally employed in . . .'[20] Houses were scattered up and down the moorside, from top to bottom, each finding its own access to the means of production for woollen cloth: fuel and water (Defoe was writing of woollen, not worsted, a yet undeveloped trade). The roads followed the logic of this kind of settlement; 'indeed, no road could do otherwise', he noted, for 'whenever we passed any house, we found a little rill or gutter of water . . . as they could not do their business without water, the little streams were so parted or guided by gutters or pipes . . . that none of those houses were without a river . . . running through their workhouses'. Defoe wrote of a population densely settled throughout the West Riding – 'much thicker than any agricultural population', noted later historians of the Huddersfield district – 'and yet not congregated in towns, nor largely in villages, but dispersed on the hills'. Valley water was used for the preparatory processes of woollen and worsted manufacture, getting the fleeces ready for combing or carding and spinning, and for the last stages of woollen cloth manufacture. Maps of the later eighteenth century show the same pattern of settlement, 'all the hill country from the Calder southwards . . . crowded with the names of separate houses, in strong contrast to the bare spaces between the villages elsewhere'.[21]

Other contemporary observers approved this pattern of settlement and production and the effect it had on the habits and manners of its people. Discussing population growth and the birth–death ratio in 1780s Slaithwaite, John Aikin commented on the healthiness of the township and the surrounding valley and on 'the advantages it offer[ed] for the increase of the human species'. These were the benefits of 'a manufacture carried on in rural situations and at the workman's own house'. There was high employment and high wages ('encouraging early matrimony'; another trend that Phoebe Beatson did not follow); warm clothing, good food and 'abundant fuel' were enjoyed by 'the industrious in this place'.[22] Charles Hulbert thought that Aikin's assessment still held good for 1860s Slaithwaite, and that 'domestic employment, connected with small

---

[20] W. B. Crump and Gertrude Ghorbal, *History of the Huddersfield Woollen Industry* (Huddersfield: Tolson Memorial Museum Publications, 1935), p. 15, citing Daniel Defoe, *A Tour thro' the whole Island of Great Britain*, orig. pub. 1742 (London: Dent, 1928), pp. 193–95. Maxine Berg, *The Age of Manufactures* (London: Fontana, 1985), pp. 199–202.

[21] Crump and Ghorbal, *History of the Huddersfield Woollen Industry*, p. 15.

[22] John Aikin, *A Description of the Country from Thirty to Forty Miles Around Manchester*, orig. pub. 1795 (Newton Abbot: David and Charles, 1968), p. 554.

farms' produced the same 'patriarchal manners and thought' as they had in the late eighteenth century.[23]

The Colne Valley runs for about seven miles south-west of Huddersfield to the Pennine Ridge, 'practically [separating] Yorkshire from Lancashire'.[24] Its centre, Slaithwaite township, was a dynamic place when John Murgatroyd worked his long years there as schoolmaster, and became increasingly so after 1786, when he removed to Lingards, a mile up the hill from the town, on the other side of the River Colne. Slaithwaite-cum-Lingards had coherence as a settlement, and a system of land tenure that made the transfer of property easier than in many other parts of the West Riding, one reason for the proliferation of mills and manufactures there in the later century. The Earls of Dartmouth held it (but not the acres in the adjacent townships of Linthwaite and Golcar, where Phoebe Beatson's lover and husband came from, respectively;[25] George Thorp's family belonged to Linthwaite, owned by Sir Joseph Radcliffe of Milnsbridge, resident magistrate and encountered by Phoebe Beatson in the summer of 1802 when he examined her as to the state of her settlement). Slaithwaite-cum-Lingards had come into Dartmouth possession in the 1720s as part of a marriage settlement, and by the end of the century, the owners were in their entrepreneurial and improving stride, playing an important role in industrial and communications development. Their land agents reported in 1803 that 'the River Colne is now become a Stream of considerable Importance for the number of mills erected on it, for the purpose of Scribbling and Manufacturing Wool, spinning Cotton etc'.[26]

This territory of roads and tracks was improved by turnpiking, from the 1730s onwards. Turnpike roads provided alternative routes from Halifax to Manchester (though the old packhorse route probably still continued to be used by Murgatroyd and his servant when they walked over to Halifax).[27] Canals were cut from 1700, eventually allowing uninterrupted water traffic from east to west coast. In 1803, the Dartmouth agent reported on the last stage of canal

---

[23] Hulbert, *Annals of the Church*, p. x. Forbes was dismissive of these claims for 'domestic comfort, simple manners and social happiness' connected with late eighteenth-century domestic worsted production. Henry Forbes, *Rise, Progress and Present State of the Worsted Manufacture of England. Lectures on the Result of the Exhibition delivered before the Society of Arts, Manufactures and Commerce. Lecture XXI* (London: David Bogue, 1852), pp. 327–8.

[24] Hulbert, *Annals of the Church*, pp. 14–15.

[25] D. F. E. Sykes, *A History of the Colne Valley* (Slaithwaite: F. Walker, 1896), p. 85, for tenant-right. The village of Slaithwaite straddled the River Colne, Bradley Brook and Crimble Brook, and contained parts of the townships of Slaithwaite, Golcar, Linthwaite and Lingards. Only Slaithwaite and Lingards were within the Earls of Dartmouth's Manor of Slaithwaite.

[26] Dartmouth Estate Papers. I Rentals, 1803. Register and Rentals, pp. 79–85. The Manor House, Slaithwaite. Scribbling was a stage in wool carding; it heralded the very early mechanisation of the trade. See Bernard Barnes, 'Early Factories in a Pennine Parish', *Local Historian*, 15:5 (1983), pp. 277–87.

[27] Keith Parry, *Trans-Pennine Heritage Hills. People and Transport* (Newton Abbot: David and Charles, 1981). W. B. Crump, *Huddersfield Highways Down the Ages*, orig. pub. 1949, Kirklees Historical Reprints 3 (Huddersfield: Kirklees Historical Reprints, 1988).

development by the Huddersfield Canal Company, and how it had provided a new watercourse that ran parallel to the Colne. Direct water carriage to Halifax, Wakefield, Leeds and Hull was now available, and there was 'every Probability that the Trade and population on this Estate [would] annually increase as it has lately done'.[28] The new canal meant that the typical small farmer and clothier on the estate could be encouraged to improve his or her land. Lime had been costly to transport by road; it was cheaper now with the new waterway. Its use as a fertiliser, along with clover crops, would be encouraged.

There were a dozen mills along the Colne and the new canal by now, half of them for wool, the other half for cotton manufacture (and one dye works). Constant excavation and building of new mills and their infrastructure made night-time walking difficult: one March Sunday in 1802 when John Murgatroyd had walked to Longwood Chapel along the canal, he 'had to go on ye Hands & Knees over a Wood Bridge for safety' on the journey home.[29] It was an immigrant township. Some came from afar, like the 'spirited Lancashire collier' who assured the Dartmouth agents that the seam of coal found on the estate would pay rich dividends, others from much closer, children whose parents had seen the new opportunities in cotton and wool. Up in Lingards, John Murgatroyd noted that 'Thomas Gleadhill's Boy [had come] to wind Bobbins for ye weaving of Cotton – Quarmby's Girl began to weave for Mr Mellor' (Edmund Mellor had already read the lie of the land, and started weaving cloth for Huddersfield market in the early 1790s).[30] It was a place of families and familiars, and of strangers too, nearly all of them engaged in the woollen and worsted trades in some way or other. Looking at the Slaithwaite militia records for the turn of the century, D. F. E. Sykes found only 5 men out of 202 returned as eligible to serve who did not call themselves 'clothiers'.[31]

The woollen and worsted trades have carried their own historiography with them since the early eighteenth century. More recent accounts have increased our understanding of the organisation of the two branches of the industry in putting-out systems, of product and technical innovation, and the systems of credit financing that supported both of them.[32] It was worsted thread that Phoebe

---

[28] Dartmouth Estate Papers. I Rentals, 1803. Register and Rentals, General Description, pp. 79–85.

[29] Murgatroyd Diaries, KC 242/6 (14 March 1802).

[30] Murgatroyd Diaries, KC 242/7 (8 October 1802).

[31] Sykes, *History of the Colne Valley*, pp. 301–3. Of the other forty-one men who were not liable to serve because they had two or more (legitimate) children, only two were not clothiers.

[32] See John Smail, *Merchants, Markets and Manufacturers. The English Wool Textile Industry in the Eighteenth Century* (Basingstoke: Macmillan, 1999); Pat Hudson, *The Genesis of Industrial Capital. A Study of the West Riding Wool Textile Industry c.1750–1880* (Cambridge: Cambridge University Press, 1996), pp. 25–52. Pat Hudson, 'The Role of Banks in the Finance of the West Yorkshire Wool Textile Industry', *Business History Review*, 55:3 (1981), pp. 379–402. John Smail, 'The Sources of Innovation in the Woollen and Worsted Industry of Eighteenth-century Yorkshire', *Business History*, 41:1 (1999), pp. 1–15. S. D. Chapman, 'The Pioneers of Worsted Spinning by Power', *Business History*, 7:2 (1965), pp. 97–116. Pat Hudson and Steve King, 'Two Textile Townships, c.1660–1820. A Comparative Demographic Analysis',

Beatson spun, and that she (and sometimes her employer and other Lingards friends and neighbours) carried over to Richard Walker's, first to Holywell Green and later to Forrest. Both of them carried not only bundles of thread, but the value of Phoebe's labour: the major nineteenth-century historian of the worsted manufacture pointed out that in the late eighteenth century, whilst woollen cloth making – the processing, spinning, weaving and finishing of it – only doubled the worth of the original fleece, 'that of [worsted] stuffs amounted to five times as much'.[33] When Henry Forbes delivered his lecture on worsted manufacture in 1852, one on which much subsequent accounting for it is based, he was forced to preface his remarks with the caveat that he 'laboured under the disadvantage of having to deal with the subject in reference to which there exist but few historical or statistical documents on which full reliance can be placed'.[34] Part of the problem was, as he noted, that 'up to 1834, the woollen and worsted trades were mixed up together in the Parliamentary returns'.[35]

Despite the weight of information about wool, we know relatively little about the labour process in worsted spinning and even less about the system of domestic production in which Phoebe Beatson took part. Indeed, without John Murgatroyd's recording of his role in this out-working system, we would not know that household servants, properly hired and receiving wages for domestic work done, took part in such an operation.[36] Or rather we knew that something like this happened in late seventeenth-century Furness, for example, where 'gentry women would superintend the spinning of textile fibres into yarn by their female servants and contract with jobbing weavers in their neighbourhood to transform that yarn into cloth', though the practice is presumed to have died out by the later eighteenth century.[37] Even in his editing of the letter books of two eighteenth-century clothiers, Frank Arkinson was forced to comment how very little could be gleaned about the organisation of spinners and spinning in the putting-out system that obviously pertained. Richard Walker probably represented the 'alliance of land and loom' in the emergence of the industrial West Riding and Lancashire (he obviously farmed, or at least grew a hay crop

---

Economic History Review, 53:4 (2000), pp. 706–41. D. T. Jenkins, *The West Riding Wool Textile Industry, 1770–1835. A Study of Fixed Capital Formation* (Edington, Wiltshire: Pasold Research Fund, 1975). Berg, *The Age of Manufactures*, pp. 208–11.

[33] James, *History of Worsted*, p. 285.

[34] Forbes, *Rise, Progress*. James called this lecture 'masterly'. James, *History of Worsted*, p. 323.

[35] Forbes, *Rise, Progress*, p. 318.

[36] Though once you start to look with Murgatroyd in mind, there are suggestions that it may have been a taken-for-granted of the servant's labour, in other, much grander households than his. See, for example, Susanna Whatman, *The Housekeeping Book of Susanna Whatman, 1776–1800*, intro. by Christina Hardyment (London: National Trust, 2000), p. 33.

[37] Amanda Vickery, *The Gentleman's Daughter. Women's Lives in Georgian England* (New Haven and London: Yale University Press, 1998), p. 150, citing Barbara Pidock, 'The Spinners and Weavers of Swarthmore Hall, Ulverston, in the late Seventeenth Century', *Transactions of the Cumberland and Westmorland Antiquarian and Archaeological Society*, 95 (1995), pp. 153–67.

alongside distributing spinning work across the locality), where a new era had opened post-1750, according to worsted's foremost historian, John James.[38] Before the mid-century, the district had mainly been employed in the making of coarse woollen cloth; but now

the clothiers engaged with energy in the comparatively new business of stuff-making... All ranks hastened to learn, in some of its branches, the worsted business – some as sorters, some as combers, more as weavers, whilst the women and children were taught spinning, and for the instruction and employment of the latter, numerous schools teaching spinning were established.[39]

There were probably 4,000 combers at work in the West Riding in the 1770s, each employing fourteen spinners like Phoebe Beatson.[40]

Putters-out (or agents; Murgatroyd called Walker an 'out-putter') were to be found in the most distant parts of the West Riding, and often doubled as shopkeepers (though Richard Walker does not appear to have been one).[41] A rapidly expanding trade in which there was money to be made turned some hand-combers, clothiers (weavers) and agents into merchants and manufacturers. The worsted processes were not always neatly divided from each other – though I do not know whether Richard Walker combed his own wool, or wove the worsted thread after it had been returned to him as yarn. Probably not. Combing in the later eighteenth century was usually done in workshops, not at home, as it involved the use of charcoal fires on which the combs were heated. The move to home was a stratagem by spinning factory owners of the early nineteenth century to break the power of combers working together. Richard Walker combed his own wool only if he owned a share in a workshop. From the evidence of Murgatroyd's diary, he worked alone. He was certainly in the business in a small way, and vulnerable to its fluctuations and reversals of fortune.[42]

An engraving of 1814 (in which it is not clear whether the young woman – clad for the purpose in the 'costume of Yorkshire' – is spinning wool or worsted) has often stood in for want of information about domestic spinning.[43] Eighteenth- and nineteenth-century technical handbooks and histories of the

[38] John Rule, *The Experience of Labour in Eighteenth-century Industry* (London: Croom Helm, 1981), pp. 13–14, 32, 36–7.

[39] James, *History of Worsted*, pp. 267–8.   [40] James, *History of Worsted*, p. 281.

[41] James, *History of Worsted*, pp. 311–13. Colum Giles and Ian H. Goodhall (Royal Commission on the Historical Monuments of England), *Yorkshire Textile Mills* (London: HMSO, 1992), p. 17.

[42] Crump and Ghorbal, *History of the Huddersfield Woollen Industry*, pp. 90–1.

[43] See Hudson, *Genesis*, pp. 34–5, and plate 2, p. 45, and Pat Hudson, 'Proto-industrialisation. The Case of the West Riding Wool Textile Industry in the 18th and early 19th Centuries', *History Workshop*, 12 (1981), pp. 34–61 for the engraving, reproduced from George Walker, *The Costume of Yorkshire, illustrated by a Series of forty Engravings, being Fac-similies of original Drawings, with Descriptions in English and French* (London: Longman, Hurst etc.; Leeds: Robinson etc., 1814). This was evidently produced for the tourism and folklore market. For the marketing of literary 'Yorkshire', see below, p. 58, note 49.

industry are illuminating on the worsted spinning and weaving processes, but they carry no information about the domestic industry in which Phoebe Beatson was employed.[44] Murgatroyd might be surprised to find himself occupying the role of a seventeenth-century gentry housewife, but as the financial arrangements between Phoebe Beatson and Richard Walker were clearly managed by him, not his wife or his sister (who came to live with him after his wife's death in 1797), it is for the moment the only one he has, as far as worsted spinning is concerned.

'Worsted', describing both a thread and the fabric spun from it, is a type of wool product, called thus so as to be distinguished from 'woollen' by the type and length of the filament as it grew on the sheep's back, and by the process of its preparation and finishing. Eighteenth-century definitions made for general audiences were simpler than those produced by the trade itself and those of the nineteenth century, by which time power spinning of worsted yarn was the focus of technical and historical description.[45] 'Worsted is properly, a thread spun of wool that has been combed, and which in the spinning, is twisted harder than ordinary,' stated Chamber's *Encyclopaedia* firmly, in 1788.[46] These were the simplest possible terms in which the differences between woollen and worsted could be discussed, said S. D. Chapman two hundred years on: 'worsted is a thread spun of wool that has been combed, whilst the woollen thread is carded before it is spun'.[47] Combing removed the very short fibres 'leaving a long "sliver" of long fibres for spinning', and in the eighteenth century, the production process involved adding some kind of oil to the fleece (Phoebe Beatson's bundles of wool were heavy because of the oil) so that the fibres adhered to each other and pulling out of the long ones was made easier.[48] The oil-soaked fleeces had to be kept for about a year, hence the particular capital demands of the worsted trade.[49]

---

[44] Frank Arkinson (ed.), *Some Aspects of the Eighteenth-century Woollen Trade in Halifax* (Halifax: Halifax Museums, 1951), p. 1.

[45] James, *History of Worsted*, pp. 253–8. Chapman, 'Pioneers', pp. 97–116. Joel Mokyr, *The Gifts of Athena. Historical Origins of the Knowledge Economy* (Princeton, N.J.: Princeton University Press, 2002), pp. 28–77 for the implications for training and human capital development bound up with textile mechanisation. See also Nicola Verdon, *Rural Women Workers in the Nineteenth Century. Gender, Work and Wages* (Woodbridge: Boydell Press, 2002), pp. 42–3.

[46] E. Chambers, *Cyclopaedia: or, a Universal Dictionary of Arts and Sciences . . . with the Supplement and Modern Improvements Incorporated in One Alphabet, by Abraham Rees* (London: J. F. &C. Rivington, 1778). For a contemporary description of wool combing (as opposed to carding), see R. March, *A Treatise on Wool, Worsted, Cotton, and Thread, describing their Nature, Properties and Qualities* (London: privately printed, 1779), pp. 15–16.

[47] Chapman, 'Pioneers', p. 97.

[48] Chapman, 'Pioneers', cites William Gardiner, *Music and Friends: or, Pleasant Recollections of a Dilettante*, 3 vols. (London: privately printed, 1838), vol. I, pp. 231–3; vol. III, pp. 82–3, 231–3.

[49] Chapman, 'Pioneers'. Jenkins, *West Riding Wool*, pp. 19, 25–37, 175–182. Hudson, *Genesis*, pp. 37–48.

Having shown the 'progress of the worsted manufacture . . . from the reign of George III . . . to the present time' of 1851, the Bradford firm of Collinson & Burton defined worsted as 'all wool which in its process of manufacture is not fulled [the cloth not washed and pounded after weaving in order to thicken it], whether it be confined to the product of the long staple [or 'sliver' of the fleece], or mixed with cotton, silk or other textile material'.[50] Now, in the mid-nineteenth century, with worsted spun and woven by machine, 'worsted' meant wool cloth made with 'a staple of attenuated consistency' *and* cloth used for dress: stuffs like calamanco, scallion, camblet, tammy – fine, light, durable material with a good drape and fine sheen.[51] As Chapman reflects, 'the difference between woollen and worsted yarn is not easy for the layman to define' and the distinction puzzled and fascinated late eighteenth-century observers as well. There was something arcane and glamorous about knowledge of it. The parliamentary committee of inquiry charged with taking evidence on a bill proposing new regulations for the woollen trade in 1803 had the temerity to give Mr Nathaniel Murgatroyd (he had been in the worsted business all his life) a kind of test on types of worsted cloth, evidently highly pleased with their grasp of so complicated a process.[52] When John Murgatroyd's neighbour Edmund Mellor turned his hand to woollen cloth weaving in the early 1790s (Mellor had read the signs of a shift of commerce from Halifax to Bradford, and from worsted to woollen, and this career shift was also a way out of personal financial difficulties), John Murgatroyd listed the twenty-nine 'different Parts of Employment in making one piece of Woolen Cloth wn. made, ordering it for sale' in the notebook he used to make his notes for Sunday sermons (and write bad poetry and remedies for ailments).[53] He was much more familiar with the worsted process and did not need to detail it: spinning took place in his house and he was woven in to the local putting-out system through Phoebe Beatson's labour.

Was it he, not his servant, who was a nodal point of the system? His diaries are not extant for every consecutive year between 1782 and 1804, but in

---

[50] Collinson & Burton, *West Riding Worsted*, p. 80. For fulling, see Jenkins, *West Riding Wool*, pp. 6–9, 127–8.

[51] Collinson & Burton, *West Riding Worsted*, p. 80. Hudson, *Genesis*, p. 26. My own personal definition of 'worsted' as wool and cotton mixed obviously comes from the nineteenth century, and from the Pennine weaving area north-east of Burnley, that is, from *Wuthering Heights* territory. See Carolyn Steedman, *Landscape for a Good Woman* (London: Virago, 1986), pp. 27–47; however, according to John James, this Lancashire definition, learned in my childhood, was the most ancient. *History of Worsted*, pp. 3–4. See also Forbes, *Rise, Progress*, p. 304 for worsted defined as silk and wool, or cotton and wool, mixed.

[52] Parliamentary Papers 1803 III, Part 3, p. 238. Mr Nathaniel Murgatroyd, evidence, pp. 228–41.

[53] Reverend John Murgatroyd, Notebook, 'Ask, Read, Retain, Teach', KC 242/9, p. 84, West Yorkshire Archive Service, Kirklees District, Huddersfield. List dated 12 December 1791. Murgatroyd Diary, KC 242/2, 'Edmund Mellor sold one piece in ye Hall – it is the first piece he sold from begin'g to be a piecemaker' (5 January 1794).

individual calendar years and in the notebooks where it is possible to track Phoebe Beatson's visits to the wool comber's across two, she delivered yarn and collected wool every twelve weeks on average, though the most usual gap between coming and going was seventeen weeks. It had been the same for Murgatroyd's previous servants, Molly Wood and Betty Sykes. The domestic servant's year did not follow the same timetable as the one mentioned in all the contemporary literature on spinning, and Murgatroyd's at least produced just as much yarn in the summer months as they did in the winter.[54] Spinning was usually performed in cottages by women and children, and it was mainly done in the winter months. Phoebe spun all year. Her production fell off when she herself was ill, at the time around and after Mrs Murgatroyd's death in 1797 (in this year, John Murgatroyd did most of the fetching and carrying of wool and yarn); during the turbulent months of her pregnancy, she spun very little out of the 13 lb of wool she had brought home in March (the baby was born at the end of August 1802). Murgatroyd's nephew Joseph 'rode to Halifax about my Rents he took Phebe's worsted with him' in July, and in August Richard Walker paid her for just 1 lb of yarn.[55]

In a long historical perspective and a national context, hand spinning as a source of income for proletarian women was declining; but not here in the 1790s for Phoebe Beatson.[56] She usually collected 12 or 14 lbs from Richard Walker, thus in ordinary times producing about 1 lb of yarn per week. Remembering full-time domestic spinners of the 1790s, Thomas Crosley reckoned that – in the Bradford area at least – they could spin 'nine or ten hanks a day', for which they were paid a ha'penny a hank: 'I gave a half-penny per hank, and sometimes one shilling and two-pence for every twenty four hanks over.'[57] For Phoebe Beatson, spinning really was a part-time occupation. She may have used 'the old one-thread wheel' (the one in the much-used illustration) for there was 'no innovation of the [small domestic] jenny in worsted spinning parallel to its development in the cotton and woollen trades', though the traditional distaff would have allowed her to spin whilst performing some of her domestic tasks.[58] In the irritating way of one's historical subjects, Phoebe Beatson and Richard Walker (and the whole of the Halifax–Huddersfield district) reckoned their products by the pound, not by the hank, so working out Phoebe's wages

---

[54] James, *History of Worsted*, p. 312 ('Reminiscences of the Worsted Manufacture, by an Octogenarian', pp. 311–13).

[55] Murgatroyd Diary, KC 242/6: 'Phoebe went to Rich.d Walker's with 13 lbs of worstot & brought 13 lbs to spin' (4 March, 8 July, 3 August 1802).

[56] Verdon, *Rural Women Workers*, pp. 42–3. Bridget Hill, *Women, Work, and Sexual Politics in Eighteenth-Century England* (Oxford: Blackwell, 1989), pp. 63–4.

[57] James, *History of Worsted*, p. 325.

[58] James, *History of Worsted*, p. 324. Hudson, *Genesis*, p. 42. For other later eighteenth-century technical innovation in domestic spinning machines, see March, *A Treatise on Silk*, pp. 17–19. For the distaff, Berg, *Age of Manufactures*, pp. 139–43.

for spinning must depend on two entries in her employer's diary. In January 1791 'Phoebe went to Richd Walker's with 12 lbs of yarn . . . Ricd paid Her all due Hers at his reckoning came to £1.10.4d', that is, 2s 6¼d per pound, in which case – and there is nowhere else to reckon it from – a Bradford hank weighed less than half an ounce, and anyway, the fineness of the yarn was measured by the 'count', that is, the number of hanks to the pound. So the weight of a hank – which was of a standard length – depended on the fineness of the thread: the higher the 'count', the lighter the hank.[59] A fragment from the 1770s suggests that hanks of yarn produced for warp and weft weaving were of different weights. Warp thread was spun double, twisted as well as spun, and a hank of it weighed 5 oz. Single weft thread made up a 2 oz hank.[60] Phoebe Beatson probably spun single thread yarn, and a distaff would have made for a finer thread than the spinning wheel. Anyway, the further you were from Halifax, the less you were paid for spinning, one possible reason for making the six-mile round trip from Slaithwaite to Holywell Green (near enough in Halifax) worthwhile.[61]

Metamorphosed into a full-time Bradford spinner, Phoebe Beatson could have spun her 12 lb of wool in six weeks, rather than the twelve or so it usually took her. If rates of payment in the 1780s and 1790s were roughly the same across the worsted-producing districts of the West Riding, then it is reasonable to reckon that Phoebe the part-timer took twice as long to spin her yarn as did full-timers. Or perhaps this reckoning of Richard Walker's in January 1791 included payment for the period before, when Phoebe went over with 4 lb of yarn (and 'Rich'd did not pay Her'). His debt was reckoned by Murgatroyd at 4s. 9d., making the wage for 1 lb of spun yarn 1s 1¼d, a price very close indeed to the Bradford 1s 2d for twenty-four hanks. Whatever the weight of a hank actually was, Phoebe Beatson could, by spinning perhaps 50 lb of wool a year, add between £2 10s and £3 to her annual wage as domestic servant. We do not know what those wages were, as no record of her service contract with Murgatroyd exists (nor do account books); but wage rates for a maid in a

---

[59] For the multiplicity of terms for describing, measuring, weighing and reckoning worsted thread, see Society for the Promotion of Industry, *An Account of the Origin, Proceedings, and Intentions of the Society . . . in the Southern Districts of the Parts of Lindsey in the Country of Lincoln*, 3rd edn (London: R. Sheardown, 1791), pp. 51–99; J. Huntingford, *An Account of the Proceedings, Intentions, Rules, and Orders of the Society for the Encouragement of Agriculture and Industry, instituted as Odiham in Hampshire . . .* (London: Frys and Couchman, 1785). Both of these provide detailed descriptions of attempts to introduce worsted spinning to cottage families as a source of income. It was recommended and prizes given to outstanding boy spinners as well as girls.

[60] This is a calculation to do with the cost of actually producing worsted (not wages paid). James, *History of Worsted*, p. 280.

[61] Worsted spinning took place in the environs of Huddersfield and in Slaithwaite, obviously; but Slaithwaite was at the edge of the worsted field, properly defined (see Map II). Huddersfield was the centre of the fancy-woollen trade in the 1790s.

single-servant household across the country in the years 1786–95 ranged from 4 to 5 guineas a year (the equivalent of about 1s 5d–1s 9d a week).[62]

Most discussion of eighteenth-century wage systems has followed the blue-print of contemporary economists like Adam Smith, which was refashioned by Karl Marx into a history according to which workers increasingly lost control over the means of production. In the nineteenth century this was understood to be the result of mechanisation, but earlier on, when such theories of labour were first evolved, it was seen as a consequence of a 'divorce from the materials on which they work[ed]'.[63] A historian really must complain about the validity of this model, when one of the largest occupational categories in the society, domestic servants, is entirely missing from it. The work of menial servants is simply not there, in the reckonings of labour, labour value and labour theory that we currently possess – an absence that must concern us much in consid-ering Phoebe Beatson in her major role as household servant. But Phoebe in her second role as domestic worsted spinner must complicate the picture we have as well. She did not own the worsted on which she worked; it was never hers, neither in bundle form nor after she had exercised her energies on the bun-dles, mingled her labour with greasy mass, and turned it into a commodity – yarn – for sale. It was lent her, loaned her, given to her on trust, for payment that came only after the labour was completed. And of course, to exercise our full theoretical objection to the system of political economy that has dictated most of the ways in which historians have been able to see her as a worker, we must add to the list of lacunae surrounding her as a historical figure the observation that we do not even know whether she owned her own tools (let alone what kind of mechanism her spinning wheel (or distaff) was). (Though she probably did own it, or it was her family's.)

Quite often Richard Walker was unable to pay Phoebe, though he always took the yarn and gave her more wool, even during the decade's two great crises of dearth (1794–6 and 1799–1801), which Murgatroyd's extant diaries do cover, for the main part.[64] Sometimes Wilson's problem was what Pat Hudson has called the shortage of small coin, which persisted in the region well into the nineteenth century.[65] In an entry of Murgatroyd's already noted, Walker gave her a payment of £1 11s 6d in January 1791 for 12 lb of spun yarn, though by his reckoning, he only actually owed her £1 10s 4d. A week later, Murgatroyd

---

[62] Just over the Pennines at Ponden near Haworth, Robert Heaton, merchant manufacturer in the worsted way (his family a possible point of origin for *Wuthering Heights*), contracted with a new maid for 1s 2d a week in 1791. Robert Heaton, Account Book of Robert Heaton, Heaton B149, West Yorkshire Archives, Bradford District, Bradford. Note of Agreement dated 26 September 1791 (though this was not a single-servant household). Here in the north, they had started to reckon maidservants' wages by the week, not by the year as was still common in the south (though it is unlikely that cash was handed over weekly).

[63] Rule, *Experience of Labour*, p. 31.   [64] Wells, *Dearth and Distress*, pp. 1–7.

[65] Hudson, *Genesis*, pp. 142, 143, 150.

'walk'd this morning to Richard Walker's to have a Guinea, not weight, chang'd
Phebe received it for her worstet – He changed it & I gave Him ye . . . 1s 2d
which She owd Him . . .'[66] In 1796 the problem was 'light gold' (lightweight
gold coin) with which he was reluctant to pay her. He 'put it to another Time'.[67]
But in September 1794 when Phoebe had been over with 4 lbs of yarn, non-
payment was a result of economic circumstances wider than unsteady cashflow
and dodgy coinage: 'Rich'd did not pay Her – He owes her 4 shillings 9 . . .'
Still in her debt three months later, and unable to pay when she took over an
accumulated 14 lb of yarn, Murgatroyd noted in his diary: 'Hard Times'.[68]

All through the spring of 1797, Richard Walker was unable to pay. In this
year at least, it was Murgatroyd for the main part who carried the yarn and
wool. It was the year of his wife's death and discussions with his sister about
her leaving Halifax to move in with him. Forrest was on his way to the town, and
Phoebe presumably busy with sick nursing, and then after March, with greater
household responsibilities than she had had before. She also undertook many
of his public duties in this year of crisis and change. He sent her to funerals in
his place, when he was unable to move for want of sleep. She paid the assessed
taxes on his behalf, and attempted to collect the rents on his Halifax properties
in January 1800: 'Phoebe gone to Huddersfield to J. Bentley [Murgatroyd's
solicitor] about Halifax Houses – She return'd safe, & in good Time, but brought
neither Money nor Encouragement'; 'Phoebe walk'd after Dinner to Halifax to
her mother's & about Rents'; 'Phoebe returned from Halifax & brought some
Rent Money.'[69] In July 1800 'Phoebe walk'd to Hudd. paid Mr Mellor for Gin,
was at Whitworth Doctor abt her Ancle – was with Joseph Bentley who gave
her Money on Houses Acct – bought papers, Tobacco, &c – then returned by ye
canal safe Jonathan went with Her to Hudd.: & helped to carry ye Gin Runlet,
returned to Gin man –.'[70]

A household adjusted itself to changed circumstances – the death of a mistress, and sister Ann Murgatroyd's arrival (Phoebe's father and one of her
brothers brought her things over from Halifax in August 1797).[71] For five
months between the death of one Ann and the arrival of the other, Phoebe
was, if not mistress of the house, or in charge of it, a household presence in
a way she had not been before. The first recording of 'Molly May . . . at our
House, mak.g Servt. Phoebe a Gown' is dated August 1797, and brewing day,

---

[66] Murgatroyd Diary, KC 242/1 (21 and 28 January 1791).
[67] Murgatroyd Diary, KC 242/3 (2 February 1796).
[68] Murgatroyd Diary, KC 242/2 (24 September, 22 December 1794).
[69] Murgatroyd Diary, KC 242/5 (28 February, 18 March, 24 June 1797). Also entry for 26 June
1800.
[70] Murgatroyd Diary, KC 242/5 (22 July 1800). See Margot Finn, *The Character of Credit. Personal
Debt in English Culture, 1740–1914* (Cambridge: Cambridge University Press, 2003), pp. 64–
105 for similar perambulatory debt payment and collection.
[71] Murgatroyd Diary, KC 242/4 (6 August 1797).

which Murgatroyd had always intermittently noted, became 'Our Brewing Day'.[72] Murgatroyd was certainly, and increasingly after his sister's death in January 1801, in a new relationship to Phoebe. Now he notes (for the first time in March 1800) 'Our Baking Day';[73] he records her sowing peas and beans in the kitchen garden. He had done this before, but now they are 'her small seeds'.[74] They are treated by the community as a social unit, as on New Year's Day in 1802 when 'I & Phoebe drank tea & supped at neighbour Mellors'.[75] (She was pregnant, but he did not yet know this.) Her role as his representative increased.[76]

Through all of this, Phoebe went on spinning, until her pregnancy decreased her output to just 1 lb of yarn in August 1802 (for which Richard Walker did pay, cash on the table – for he came over to Lingards to collect it from her).[77] It was her system, and her arrangement, though Murgatroyd's involvement in it at the practical level was considerable. There can only be speculation about how much her earnings at spinning went into the calculation of her wages as domestic servant. Murgatroyd clearly held money for her, and knew exactly what she was earning. Phoebe had come to his service in May 1785, though their reckoning day seemed to be in August.[78] Most domestic servants were paid annually, and on the one occasion in the extant diaries when this is mentioned, Murgatroyd wrote, 'I reckoned with Phebe; she paid me all due to Me so we begin again', probably referring to Phoebe's borrowing from him against her wages during the preceding months.[79]

The material culture of the Colne Valley made manners (as Canon Hulbert, in his role as cultural-materialist historian of the 1860s noted); perhaps it also made forms of love and feeling. Worsted, or at least worsted spinning, is needed to tell the story that is about to be told, of Phoebe Beatson and George Thorp, their little bastard daughter, and George Thorp's resolute refusal to marry her mother. Worsted can help us begin to consider the structures of romance, passion and affection that pertained in West Yorkshire, round about the turn of the century (at least allow that they might have existed). We could, for instance,

---

[72] Murgatroyd Diary, KC 242/4 (11 August, 8 December 1797).
[73] Murgatroyd Diary, K6 242/5 (6 March 1800).
[74] Murgatroyd Diary, KC 242/2 (28 March 1794); KC 242/3 (12 April 1796).
[75] Murgatroyd Diary, KC 242/6 (2 January 1802).
[76] See Naomi Tadmor, *Family and Friends in Eighteenth-century England. Household, Kinship, and Patronage* (Cambridge: Cambridge University Press, 2001), p. 23 for the 'set role for a female housekeeper' in the eighteenth-century family-household system.
[77] Murgatroyd Diary, KC 242/6 (3 August 1802).
[78] Murgatroyd Diary, KC 242/7 (29 May 1804).
[79] Murgatroyd Diary, KC 242/2 (8 August 1794). For gifts to servants, bought on their employer's account, and borrowing against an annual wage, see John Styles, 'Involuntary Consumers'? Servants and their Clothes in Eighteenth-century England', *Textile History*, 33:1 (2002), pp. 9–21.

look at spinning, and at the human hand. Love and worsted spinning was a trope, an image of erotic potential, at least by the end of the eighteenth century. William Gardiner remembered 'a pretty sight in the villages' of this time, in Leicestershire: 'a cluster of girls spinning under the shade of a walnut tree, combining with their love songs the whizzing of their wheels . . .' 'Mechanised contrivances for spinning' – the single thread wheel of the famous illustration included – were, as he pointed out, all 'imitations of the finger and thumb, in drawing out the thread from the wool', involving (he did not exactly say this) a particularly graceful series of gestures to observe (though tiring to perform) that displayed a well-toned arm, and moved a bosom, perhaps alluringly so. It may have been the case that southern landowners and magistrates, gathered in their societies for improving the lot of the poor by teaching the art of spinning to their children, also dimly apprehended the cultural meanings attached to the process. For among the certificates, prizes, monetary awards and celebrations they promised to teenagers with the highest output of yarn, was the ceremony that would crown two of them Spinning Queen and Spinning King.[80] And the hands. Gardiner quoted a poem in point:

> As I sat at my spinning wheel
> A bonny lad came passing by:
> I ken'd him round and liked him weel,
> Good faith! He had a bonny eye.
> My heart now a panting gan to feel,
> But still I turned my spinning wheel.
>
> My milk-white hand he did extol
> And praised my fingers long and small;
> And said there was no lady fair,
> That ever could with me compare.
> To kiss my hand he down did kneel
> But still I turned my spinning wheel.[81]

The hand mattered in ways that have now disappeared from our own erotic registers.[82] The oil in which the worsted bundles were soaked and the natural lanolin of the fleece kept a working woman's hands whiter and softer than they would have been if they spent all their time (as Phoebe must have spent

---

[80] Society for the Promotion of Industry, *Account of . . . Lindsey in the Country of Lincoln*, pp. 1–51; Huntingford, *Account of . . . Odiham in Hampshire*, pp. 69. Thomas Ruggles, *The History of the Poor; their Rights, Duties, and the Laws respecting Them*, 2 vols. (London: J. Deighton, 1793), vol. I, pp. 94–100.

[81] Gardiner, *Music and Friends*, vol. I, pp. 231–3, 112–13.

[82] George Eliot seemed to know something of the erotics of all of this, when she described a first sighting of Hetty Sorrell in the dairy. George Eliot, *Adam Bede* (Edinburgh and London: Blackwell, 1859), chapter 7, 'The Dairy'. *Adam Bede* is set in the 1790s. I am indebted to Jeremy Gregory for pointing all of this out to me.

much of hers) raking out grates, scouring iron vessels and cleaning carbon-steel knives. None of this is to say what Phoebe Beatson's hands were like, nor that George Thorp ever saw her spinning; it is rather to point to the cultural and social specificity with which men and women do their fancying, and find each other and themselves delightful and desirable; it is a way of reconstructing the moment when Phoebe and George decided to do what it was they were going to do and produced the history that follows.

3   Lives and writing

Phoebe Beatson had been just nineteen years old when she came to live with the Murgatroyds, in the new house built at Lingards for their retirement: 'Phoebe Beatson came to my Srvc. ye 29th of May 1785 19 years since,' noted Murgatroyd in May 1804; 'as I began my 67th year she began her 20th yr'.[1] A father, a mother, two brothers (one of them called Tommy) and a sister appear in the pages of the Murgatroyd diaries, and so does much communication between the Lingards house and Phoebe's Halifax home.[2] Brothers visited Phoebe, the sister came to stay for days at a time, and the whole family knew and did service for Murgatroyd's Halifax sister Ann. The measure of the relationship between the two households is exemplified in two diary entries. In April 1786 'Phoebe's Father was this Morning at our House for 2 Hours. My sister is hearty, but wonders yt I do not go over.'[3] In December 1791 Murgatroyd walked over to Halifax (as he often did, after leaving Phoebe and her yarn at Holywell and later at Forrest) and visited Phoebe's father, giving him a divine poem he had composed and bringing back with him cotton yarn so that his daughter might knit Billy Beatson a pair of stockings. He also brought home some leather for mending Phoebe's stays.[4] She had bought this pair on a trip to Huddersfield in May 1790 ('Mrs Mellor and her two promising Daughters walk to Hudd: today – Our Servant Phoebe goes with 'em to buy stays &c'), a sign that she was in a

---

[1] Reverend John Murgatroyd, Diaries, KC 242/7 (29 May 1804), West Yorkshire Archive Service, Kirklees District, Huddersfield.

[2] There was another brother of whom I have found no trace in Halifax baptism registers. In September 1802, a month after baby Elizabeth was born, Murgatroyd was in Halifax and visited Phoebe's mother, 'whose son Jno was buried Friday before'.

[3] Murgatroyd Diaries, KC 242/1 (23 April 1786).

[4] Murgatroyd Diaries, KC 242/1 (17 December 1791). For Murgatroyd's published poetry see *A Choice Collection of Family Prayers for every Day of the Week. To which are added a few Divine Poems by the Collector, Jos. Miller, Schoolmaster, Halifax* (Halifax: P. Darby for the author, 1760). This is mentioned by Charles Hulbert; see Henry James Morehouse, *Extracts from the Diary of the Rev. Robert Meeke . . . Also a Continuation of the History of Slaithwaite Free School and an Account of the Educational Establishments in Slaithwaite-cum-Lingards, by the Rev. Charles Augustus Hulbert* (Huddersfield: *Daily Chronicle* Steam Press; London: Bohn, 1874), p. 109. Murgatroyd's contribution is almost certainly 'An Hymn, by J. M.' There is also 'Part of the 145 Psalm imitated, by J. M.' and 'Part of the 15 Psalm imitated' with the same initials, p. 68.

good place, for a good new pair could cost twice a domestic servant's average annual wage.[5]

The Halifax St John's parish register shows a William Beatson (he was a joiner) giving information about four children at their baptism. Phoebe was the eldest of these, being christened in June 1770 (four or five years old, if it is – as is pretty likely – the right girl). William was baptised in December 1771, Thomas in April 1780 and Elizabeth in 1784. Another William was recorded in May 1792. This child may possibly have been named in replacement for the boy who died in 1788. 'Our Servt. Phoebe's Brothr died last Saturday – two men came to acquaint Her the Day after. She [went] wth. 'em.'[6]

Murgatroyd's own origins had been as humble as those of the young woman who lived in his household for twenty years: 'he was a native of Weathercock Fold, in the parish of Halifax. His father was William Murgatroyd, a blacksmith by trade . . .' The family had some freehold property in the town, which provided an income for a very long time indeed.[7] Murgatroyd, and Phoebe in her role as his proxy, frequently tramped the road to Halifax to collect the rents on it, though this was increasingly difficult to do as the 1790s passed; tenants simply could not pay.[8]

John Murgatroyd thought his own rise and progress through the world a sign of God's good grace. He often contemplated his life's story, not in vanity or pride, but in just and humble appreciation of it. Every year in May he remembered 'This afternoon', or 'This day' in 1738, when he came 'to Slaithwaite to teach School'; and then always recorded the passage of years between Then, and whatever Now he was writing in.[9] He may have seen his career resonate with that of his maidservant, wondering, in the passage already noted, at the strange conjunction of their courses, in each coming to Slaithwaite to start their life's labour at exactly the same age, of not quite nineteen. In his early teens, he

[5] See Carolyn Steedman, 'Englishness, Clothes and Little Things. Towards a Political Economy of the Corset', in Christopher Breward, Becky Conekin and Cardine Cox (eds.), *The Englishness of English Dress* (Oxford: Berg, 2002), pp. 29–44 for this calculation.

[6] If the second William Beatson replaced a dead one, then the first died at age 16. Halifax Parish Records, Parish Register, St John's, D 531/11, West Yorkshire Archives, Calderdale District, Halifax. Murgatroyd Diaries, KC 242/1 (20 April 1788).

[7] Morehouse, *Extracts*, p. 107. Halifax Valuations 1735–1852. 155, Valuation 1797, 'General Regulation or Rate of Assessment of All the Lands and Houses within the Township of Halifax; Rev. John Murgatroyd, Weathercock Fold'; also Folio 6, West Yorkshire Archive Service, Calderdale District, Halifax. Thirteen properties were rated, two of them standing empty. Murgatroyd listed the same number 'of ye Present Tenants in ye Houses at Halifax' in April 1797. Reverend John Murgatroyd, 'Authors Useful to be Read at School', 1745–1802, Special Collections, Slaithwaite Parish Collection, University of York, York. He sold the properties in 1803, when six of them were demolished. Phoebe Beatson was witness to this sale, but did not sign. Murgatroyd Diaries, KC 2426 (September 1802). On the question of her writing abilities, see below, chapters 6 and 10.

[8] Murgatroyd Diaries, KC 242/5 (15 March, 24 June 1800).

[9] Murgatroyd Diaries, KC 242/2 (29 May 1794). KC 242/7 (29 May 1804).

had left Halifax for the township of Rishton, placed under the care of the school-master there, Mr Wadsworth. He had been schooled in the classics, making a particular study of 'the Greek Testament, Homer, Juvenal and Persius', said his first referee in trying to get him a position with the Kirkleatham incumbent, and explaining that 'his father is unable to send him to the University, therefore humbly begs you to be so good as to take him into your care, as being your usher, or any other preferments you shall think proper'. He was 'a sedate, thinking and promising boy . . . with tolerable judgement . . .'[10] This was a way into the church, without benefit of powerful patrons and conventional education; and whilst the attempt at Kirkleatham failed, the next year Murgatroyd was appointed master of the Free School (parochial school) at Slaithwaite, a dif-ferent kind of first rung on the Anglican career ladder. This was a momentous event in his life, to be remembered every year he lived it. In 1786 he noted that 'This afternoon I resign'd Slaithwaite School into the Hands of the New chosen Trustees I have been Master from May 29th 1738 – near 48 years'; 'This afternoon / 56 years ago / I came from Rishworth to Slaithwaite to teach School – a noble Undertaking for a person, not quite 19 . . .'[11] The first day of a new life remained quite clear across the years, often described as a kind of vignette of an ever-present moment of potential. In May 1802, eighty-three years old, after a heavy day of tramping to Longwood and taking both services there, right in the middle of pregnant Phoebe Beatson's worrying and preoccu-pying encounters with the poor law, he reminded himself, 'Nota bene – May ye 30th 1738 is ye 1st Day of teaching at Slaithwaite ∼ Daniel Eagland [chapel warden] took down for ye School a Large Elbow Chair & chair'd me by ye window . . . I waited there for Scholars, who came in plenty I look'd on 'em very lovingly & began very chearfully to teach 'em – my willingness was great willingness . . .' Moreover, 'it was beg.ing to get money, instead of Paying – it was helping my Parents – repaying 'em for Education – '.[12] He was, long before twentieth-century educational and social history provided the category, a scholarship boy.[13] He had hopes of a living of his own, seeking nomination for two local ones in 1750, but was passed over.[14]

---

[10] Information from Charles Augustus Hulbert, *Annals of the Church in Slaithwaite (near Hudders-field) West Riding of Yorkshire from 1593 to 1864, in Five Lectures* (London: Longman, 1864), pp. 52–3, which gives as source 'the first Volume of his M. S. Collection'. This was his 'Book of Records', which he used as a letter-copy book in its final pages.

[11] Murgatroyd Diaries, KC 242/1 (23 January 1786); KC 242/2 (29 May 1794).

[12] Murgatroyd Diaries, KC 242/6 (30 May 1802).

[13] Carolyn Steedman, 'Writing the Self. The End of the Scholarship Girl', in Jim McGuigan (ed.), *Cultural Methodologies* (London: Sage, 1997), pp. 106–25. Richard Hoggart, *The Uses of Literacy*, orig. pub. 1957 (Harmondsworth: Penguin, 1958), pp. 241–63.

[14] John Murgatroyd, 'Book of Records', unpaginated, nd, Copy of a letter to Dr Legh (Vicar of Halifax) 11 September 1750, 082.2 MUR, Slaithwaite Parish Collection, Special Collection, University of York, York.

He remained a schoolmaster after he formally entered the church, and long after he quitted the curacy at Almondbury in 1767. Schoolmasters had to be licensed by a bishop, which Murgatroyd was by 1740. Licensing involved reading aloud the Thirty-Nine Articles, declaring conformity and swearing the oaths of allegiance and supremacy – not much less than he would have to do to be ordained deacon in 1754 and priest in 1755.[15] This was as curate of Almondbury parish church, on the nomination of its vicar, the Reverend Edward Rishton – very old, very conservative ('intense in his dislike of enthusiasm', notes Judith Jago) in this centre of Evangelical revivalism – and increasingly reliant on the eyesight of his assistant John Murgatroyd for reading and writing. Rishton was thus assisted by a man who lived 'five miles and two valleys distant', and who held down a full-time job in Slaithwaite school.[16] John Murgatroyd probably only attended to Almondbury parish on Sundays, but Rishton's increasing use of him as amanuensis, and filler-in of forms and returns to the archbishop, suggests that the years as Almondbury curate pressed on him very hard indeed.

He was passed over for a living of his own at Marsden, but came to cultivate good relations with the successful man.[17] He resigned the Almondbury curacy in 1767 when he married into the Lingards' Mellor family ('Ann Mellor, daughter of Edmund [d.1755] and Martha Mellor . . . one of the most respectable families in the place,' noted Hulbert[18]). The house they had built in Lingards after his quitting the Slaithwaite school mastership in 1786 was probably erected on his brother-in-law's land (no Murgatroyd paid ground rent to the Dartmouths here, though the entire parish was in their possession, but Ann Mellor's brother had two houses on his acres).[19] The Murgatroyds' house reverted to the Mellor family on Murgatroyd's death, when he left it to his eldest niece by marriage. The peripatetic preaching he undertook after 1786 (nearly every Sunday, every church and chapel in the vicinity) probably brought in an equivalent, if not greater sum, than had the regular curacy at Almondbury.[20] This was not a career that followed the sociological norms of the eighteenth-century Church

[15] Judith Jago, *Aspects of the Georgian Church. Visitation of the Diocese of York, 1761–1776* (London: Associated University Press, 1997), pp. 64–5. Hulbert, *Annals*, p. 53.

[16] Jago, *Aspects of the Georgian Church*, pp. 166–70. For Rishton in the context of Huddersfield Evangelicalism, see Edward Royle, 'The Church of England and Methodism in Yorkshire, c. 1750–1850. From Monopoly to Free Market', *Northern History*, 33 (1997), pp. 137–61; and chapter 5, below.

[17] Hulbert, *Annals*, p. 58. See below, chapter 5. He may have held hopes of the Honley living as well. Murgatroyd Diaries, KC 242/1 (15 January 1788); he is remembering back to 1761.

[18] Morehouse, *Extracts*, p. 106.

[19] Dartmouth Estate Papers. I Rentals, 1803. Register and Rentals, Lingarths, p. 66: 'Name of Tenement . . . Top . . . Tenant . . . Edmund Mellor . . . The Buildings consist of a good House, Barn, Stable and another good Dwelling House', The Manor House, Slaithwaite.

[20] Morehouse, *Extracts*, p. 105. Marriage into the modestly propertied Mellor family also brought Murgatroyd a degree of security. See below, chapter 5, for Murgatroyd's interest in their financial circumstances.

of England: most clergymen born in the early century were university educated and, whilst curacy (temporary and perpetual) was one of the ways in which the established church adjusted itself to the situation of a growing population, want of personnel and absence of buildings (only 44 per cent of Yorkshire parishes had resident incumbents at this time), it was unusual for a clergyman never to hold a living.[21]

Yet it was a life well ordered, well financed and well lived. It had involved several severe professional disappointments, but at his death John Murgatroyd had near £1,000 to leave behind him, so he could be seen as representative of the growing wealth of the clergy in the long eighteenth century.[22] And Phoebe Beatson did very well too, out of a life she had shared for such a long time. To do nicely in the end, to reap the rewards of having lived well, was a fitting end to many of the plots, divine and secular, by which this young woman and this old man might interpret their own and each other's lives, and implies no calculation on anybody's part. But in a will made two weeks before his death, John Murgatroyd bequeathed to his 'faithful Servant Phebe Beatson, Three Hundred pounds . . . One Hundred & Fifty Pounds of the said Sum for her own use, the other Hundred & Fifty for her child Elizabeths use, in Trust with her Mother as long as she remains unmarried'. There were other bequests (ranging from £5 to £40) totalling £670 in all, so Phoebe Beatson received the greater part of his fortune (he left the house, his library and his literary papers to one of his nieces). Phoebe also was left 'Bed and Bedding at her choice', three oak chairs, a dresser and a dressing box, 'a clothe case', the warming pan, the

---

[21] Noreen Vickers, *Parson's Pence. The Finances of Eighteenth-century North Yorkshire Clergymen* (Hull: University of Hull, 1994) for the eighteenth-century curate. See Richard Hall and Sarah Richardson, *The Anglican Clergy and Yorkshire Politics in the Eighteenth Century*, Borthwick Paper 94 (York: University of York, 1998), p. 8 on how 'it was virtually impossible to become a clergyman in the Church of England without having attended either Oxford or Cambridge'. Judith Jago and Edward Royle, *The Eighteenth-century Church in Yorkshire. Archbishop Drummond's Primary Visitation of 1764*, Borthwick Papers 95 (York: University of York, 1999), p. 9. Edward Royle, 'The Church of England and Methodism in Yorkshire, *c.*1750–1850. Fron Monopoly to Free Market', *Northern History*, 33 (1997), p. 145, explains how difficult it was to create new parishes until the District Churches Act of 1843. It was not, on the other hand, difficult to build new churches. All that was needed was a patron to provide the money. Sir Joseph Radcliffe provided a private chapel in Milnsbridge in 1749, for example, to serve his part of the parish of Huddersfield. But such chapels could not have a formal district (that is, an embryonic parish) assigned to them until 1843. I am grateful to Professor Ted Royle for pointing this out to me.

[22] John Walsh and Stephen Taylor, 'The Church and Anglicanism in the "Long" Eighteenth Century', in John Walsh, Colin Haydon and Stephen Taylor (eds.), *The Church of England, c.1689–1883. From Toleration to Tractarianism* (Cambridge: Cambridge University Press, 1993), pp. 1–64, p. 7. For the general poverty of northern curates, see E. J. Evans, 'The Anglican Clergy of Northern England', in Clyve Jones (ed.), *Britain in the First Age of Party, 1680–1750. Essays presented to Geoffrey Holmes* (London and Rounceverte: Hambledon, 1987), pp. 221–40. For want of cultural as well as monetary capital among Lancashire clergy in this period, see Michael Snape, 'The Church in a Lancashire Parish. Whalley, 1689–1800', in Geoffrey S. Chamberlain and Jeremy Gregory (eds.), *The National Church in Local Perspective. The Church of England and the Regions, 1660–1800* (Woodbridge: Boydell Press, 2003), pp. 243–63.

dining table and 'the little table in common use', the best corner cupboard, silver tea-spoons, sugar-tongs and other silver, a bookcase, smoothing irons and the 'Iron things about the fire with the Oven', and Murgatroyd's watch. The globe was for the little girl, by this time nearly four years old.[23] All of this was done because Murgatroyd had fallen in love with a baby, but was also the proper fulfilment of the servant's story, told over and over again in a thousand books of household advice management for two centuries past (or longer, if we take the Bible's blueprint for such tales as their origin) about rewards on earth for good and faithful servants.

Murgatroyd was much concerned that his niece look after the books, papers and sermons mentioned in his will. She was to take very great care of them, especially any marked with the name of 'my mother's relations who lived at Sowerby Bridge, Near Halifax on account of the Fairbanks name'. However humble and artisanal his birth, John Murgatroyd always knew he came from somewhere, as Phoebe Beatson probably did not. In one of the many occasional volumes and notebooks bequeathed to Hannah Mellor, he had contemplated death in a society ordered by rank and station, wishing, in the most hackneyed and thus the most comforting of heptameters, that 'Beneath this venerable shade contented I can lay me down/Unmindful of what ye Great Ones do or if ye. might smile or frown'.[24] Thus might death be like a life ordered by 'kind Heaven': 'a Country Life The purling Rill, ye Shady Grove/Some choice Books, whch suit my Taste, but above all ye. friend I love'. He had made notes on the topic of 'Rising in Life' in 1789, emphasising that 'a private independt Station, even when call'd Obscurity, is far more eligible yn. ye most conspicuous Condition of Honour, Emolumnt. & Office, recd as Wages, Vice or Prostitution'.[25] It is unlikely that Phoebe Beatson was ever paid the wages of servility in the Lingards-cum-Slaithwaite household (though she was indeed, a household servant) and Murgatroyd's bequest assured to her and her little bastard daughter a private, independent station in life, and certainly helped her avoid the dark movement in the former servant's tale, demonstrating her descent to prostitution. So well known was this story, of the failed service career as direct route to street-walking (told everywhere, from religious tract to social realist novel), that it was used as the first and obvious objection to William Pitt's proposal for a tax on the employment of maidservants in 1785: anything that made young women's employment in households more expensive for employers would naturally encourage prostitution.[26]

---

[23] Will of the Reverend John Murgatroyd of Lingards, p.Almondbury, 1806, Borthwick Institute of Historical Research, University of York.

[24] Murgatroyd, 'Ask, Read, Retain, Teach', KC 242/9, p. 87, 'Observe'.

[25] Murgatroyd, 'Ask, Read, Retain, Teach', KC 242/9, p. 89, 'Rising in Life/1789'.

[26] *Parliamentary History of England* (London: T. C. Hansard, 1814), vol. 25 (1785–1786), p. 574. Modern historians continue to tell this story. See Bridget Hill, *Women, Work, and Sexual Politics*

The purling rill and the little house in the shady grove are an emblem of the household relationship discussed here (and moving too, because it so much prefigures the great kindness and sympathy to come, on both its sides). Nevertheless to the modern eye, these reflections on rising in life seem to miss the point of Phoebe's social journey and Murgatroyd's own, in the way that Murgatroyd's nineteenth-century historians also appear to wilfully miscast it. James Horsfall, FRS, eminent scientist and former pupil of Slaithwaite Free School (d.1785), was made much of by both Canon Hulbert and James Morehouse in discussing Murgatroyd's excellence as a teacher and his devotion to his pupils. Horsfall had been son of the Slaithwaite blacksmith, and this was one of the points of telling the story of his spectacular social and intellectual rise, but neither of them drew the connection between the smithy fathers of teacher and pupil.[27] I am much more interested in class origins and class transition than Hulbert and Morehouse (and indeed, John Murgatroyd) were; their lack of attention to it is not really very odd. In fact, Murgatroyd's 'Rising in Life' is not a reflection on the social at all, but rather a moral contemplation of early lives spent in 'Dissipation and Extravagance' – the time when desire is strong and reason underdeveloped – with redemption as an end-stop, for

this delirium is seldom of long Duration – [people] discern its Folly regard.g Fortune, Reputation Happiness – They perceive sensual Pleasures only of momentary Continuance, & their season Transient by no Means a Foundation for build.g reputation & Happiness such Reflctns wn judged with Enjoyment will bring 'em to consider their dangerous Situations – leading to Ruin.

By contemplating their own life and making comparisons with others, Murgatroyd argued, all manner of people might forsake the foolishness of youth and wrest their course on to a more satisfying path. The model offered by others was important in this process. They must watch, and notice that 'Persons of Foresight have disdain'd such low Gratifications & aspir'd to Happiness in Virtue, rais.g ymSelves by deserving ye esteem of ye good and pious'. Much, much later, when Phoebe was pregnant by a man who would not marry her, the lesson to be learned from contemplation of one's own follies was a more practical one. On the afternoon when she returned from a delayed and difficult interaction with the administrative state ('Phebe went [to] Garside this morning

in *Eighteenth-Century England* (Oxford: Blackwell, 1989), p. 238. For a contemporary novel in which prostitution is the unspoken though palpable threat of Pitt's proposals regarding a tax on maidservants, see Anon., *The Widow of Kent; or, the History of Mrs Rowley. A Novel in Two Volumes*, 2 vols. (London: F. Noble, 1788).

27 Morehouse, *Extracts*, pp. 111–15. Henry James Morehouse, *Village Gleanings, or Notes and Jottings from the Manuscripts of the Rev. John Murgatroyd, Master of the Free School of Slaithwaite . . . Including some Account of his distinguished Scholar, James Horsfall, Born at Slaithwaite, the Son of the Village Blacksmith* (Huddersfield: Parkin, 1886). See Trevor Harvey Levere and G. L'E. Turner (eds.), *Discussing Chemistry and Steam. The Minutes of a Coffee House Philosophical Society, 1780–1787* (Oxford: Oxford University Press, 2002), pp. 23–4, 32.

to be examined at Milnsbridge – Lingarths must be her Place of Settlement – a warrant got for George Thorp & served by ye Constable'), he wrote that 'this will, I hope warn her effectually – will keep her from Mans deceit, as long as she lives'.[28] But now, in 1789 with Phoebe just four years into his service, he reflects not on the social climb that he and she had made in their different ways, but on the elevation that is honour and good reputation, enacted in the eye of God and in the dignity and modesty of an independent life. He was convinced, anyway, that happiness in everyday life was part of God's plan for his creatures, and that it followed on showing 'Others a good Example', and in the

satisfaction of seeing ye wise in heart follw.g our Hope & living with Us is a kind of Heaven upon Earth – We all of Us spend the Time whch Almighty God grants Us here, for a happy Eternity hereafter – Such is ye Way of Living design'd Us on our Coming into this World – We are as happy as we can expect, while we are here, and shall be happy in death . . .[29]

Such happiness resided in God's subjects – in their hearts and minds – not in the things of the earth that made them happy: 'Happiness does not live in the Object enjoy'd but in ye Temper and Disposition of mind tow. ye Object . . .'[30]

There was an account of domesticity and familial relationships – which the law still just about upheld – of Phoebe as a member of his household, not the analogy of a child, but someone occupying the customary and legally under-pinned role of domestic servant.[31] Indeed, William Blackstone's assertion that what pertained between master and servant measured out the first 'great relation of private life', superseding in its importance that between husband and wife, and parent and child, was still being repeated in the 1780s and 1790s.[32] We have seen – in summary form so far – what seems like the plot of popular romance

---

[28] Murgatroyd Diaries, KC 242/6 (17 June 1802). For other pregnant servants' troubles with the laws of settlement and the poor law, see chapter 4.

[29] Murgatroyd Diaries, KC 242/1 (31 December 1788).

[30] For the echoing of Thomas Nettleton's *Treatise on Virtue and Happiness* (1729) through all of Murgatroyd's pondering on the relationship between human beings and the natural world (or between creatures and their Creator), see below, chapters 8 and 9.

[31] For a recent account of the servant's place in legal and political thinking of the first half of the century, see Tim Meldrum, *Domestic Service and Gender, 1660–1750. Life and Work in the London Household* (London: Longman, 2000), pp. 37–46. See also Pavla Miller, *Transformations of Patriarchy in the West, 1500–1900* (Bloomington: Indiana University Press, 1998), pp. 1–40.

[32] William Blackstone, *Commentaries on the Laws of England. In Four Books*, orig. pub. 1765, 6th edn (Dublin: Company of Booksellers, 1775), Book 1, p. 425. Changes in the formulation that the servant was analogous to the child, or made a relation of the master or mistress by a legal agreement, can be tracked through Anon., *The Servant's Calling, With Some Advice to the Apprentice* (London: G. Strahan, 1725), p. 52; John Taylor, *Elements of the Civil Law* (Cambridge: privately printed, 1767), pp. 247–63; James Barry Bird, *The Laws Respecting Masters and Servants*, 3rd edn (London: W. Clarke, 1799), p. 1 and *passim*; Anon., *A Familiar Summary of the Laws respecting Masters and Servants* (London: Henry Washbourne, 1831), Foreword.

in the seduction and betrayal of the servant, at work in Murgatroyd's assessment of Phoebe's relationship with George Thorp. Here, the heavily pregnant maidservant, still 'on her Legs' and going about her household duties at eight months gone, was a picture of virtue in distress that the contemporary romantic novel prepared for, but did not really discuss.[33] Murgatroyd was able to rescue Virtue in this case, give her a home (or allow her to stay in the one she already had), allow the baby to be born there, and neatly and benevolently rewrite the plot of the descent-into-prostitution variant of the romance.

Here then, in Lingards-cum-Slaithwaite, the domestic epic, the marriage plot (which is how George Eliot characterised the Edenic household of Milton's *Paradise Lost*) was played out in a somewhat unorthodox register. Milton's epic (and the contemporaneous efforts of political philosophers) had also played a part in establishing the archetype of marriage – married love and its vicissitudes – as an essential unit of the English state.[34] Murgatroyd was a watchful and concerned witness to the secular management of the divine story all through the spring and summer of 1802, as the administrative state swung into action in the case of Phoebe Beatson. It acted with a maddening combination of swiftness and inefficiency. The Lingards overseer gave notice at the house that Phoebe was to be examined as to her settlement on 21 April; a summons was delivered on 7 May; then two constables arrived on 2 June to 'tell Phebe to go to Kirkstile tomorrow for Exam'n abt her settlement'.[35] Lines of communication were crossed, thought Murgatroyd, as he had already talked to the local resident magistrate on her behalf ('went down to Justice Radcliffe about my Servants Phebes affair got some Lines to ye overseer of Lingarths'[36]). But Radcliffe's note (which Murgatroyd handed over) did not satisfy, so on 17 June Phoebe was off to Milnsbridge to be examined. Murgatroyd was certain that her settlement was at Lingards: she had been there for seventeen years, in service. He was worried that she was late home from her day of shame in having to tell her story to strange men and magistrates.

The pressure then eased off for a couple of months; but on 14 October, the baby six weeks old, 'Phoebe went to Milnsbridge to filiate, but Mr Radcliffe was not at home – would be home tomorrow morning.'[37] She was off the next day, accompanied by the same neighbour, only to be told that the filiation order must

---

[33] R. F. Brissenden, *Virtue in Distress. Studies in the Novel of Sentiment from Richardson to Sade* (London and Basingstoke: Macmillan, 1974). See comments on Brissenden's thesis in G. J. Barker-Benfield, *The Culture of Sensibility. Sex and Society in Eighteenth-century Britain* (Chicago and London: University of Chicago Press, 1992), *passim*. Murgatroyd Diaries, KC 242/6, 'Our brewg Day – Sally Baxter helped Phebe to brew' (13 August 1802); 'Phebe still on her Legs' (22 August 1802). The baby was born on 29 August.

[34] For Murgatroyd's discussion of sex and the marriage plot, see chapter 9.

[35] Murgatroyd Diaries, KC 242/6 (21 April, 7 May, 2 June 1802).

[36] Murgatroyd Diaries, KC 242/6 (30 May 1802).

[37] Murgatroyd Diaries, 242/6 (14 October 1802).

be signed by two magistrates, and that 'she must be at Kirkstile tomorrow'.[38] This time she borrowed a horse, with the overseer walking beside her. The order was finally signed; 'She was rather late Home, wch, fearing misfortune, caus'd uneasiness – '. Thorp did pay up. The last recorded visit of Phoebe to the Holstead overseer for her money was for the second payment, on 19 July 1804, some two weeks before Murgatroyd died and left her enough to do without state benefits.[39]

George Thorp's life is not entirely contained by Murgatroyd's writing as Phoebe's is (except for her one, pathetic mark in the Halifax marriage register, five years later), though his absences had been worrying and provoking and his presence sometimes violent, all through the summer of 1802. All of Slaithwaite was owned by the Dartmouth family, except for some few acres in the possession of Joseph Radcliffe of Milnsbridge House (later to be scourge of the Luddites, now the officiating magistrate in the case of Phoebe Beatson and George Thorp).[40] Slaithwaite town had many Thorps (half a dozen of them called George) paying rent to the Dartmouths; but this George Thorp, or rather, his mother, is highly likely to have been one of Radcliffe's tenants: at Stock Carr Head (the modern spelling is Stocker Head) there was a Widow Thorp who paid rent on some eight acres.[41] Her sons were possibly the Thorp brothers who were paid to carry building materials from Huddersfield when the Murgatroyds were building their house at Lingards in 1786.[42] In June 1802 when Phoebe was six months pregnant, and two days before her settlement examination, Murgatroyd found 'G. Thorp in ye Kitchen' late at night. Talk did nothing: 'He will not marry her,' though Murgatroyd tried his mother again the next day.[43] Thorp's appearances at the kitchen door and in Phoebe's life seem to have something to do with the due process of the poor law, for he visited just before and just after her examinations (the examination as to settlement, and the one at which she named him as father of the child). West Riding quarter sessions was ultimately responsible for the delays and confusions that Murgatroyd and Phoebe Beatson experienced during these months. The country magistrates paid for legal advice in 1805, on how to proceed in bastardy cases, and to find out whether or not they were going about things in the right way. London barrister G. S. Holroyd confirmed that an application for a bastardy order should be made by the parish overseers to the justices; they should issue a warrant, and the man named by the

---

[38] Murgatroyd Diaries, 242/6 (15 October 1804).

[39] For the wide variety of parish practice in enforcing men's payments for their illegitimate children, see John R. Gillis, *For Better, For Worse. British Marriages 1600 to the Present* (Oxford: Oxford University Press, 1985), pp. 128–9.

[40] Dartmouth Estate Papers, 'Slaithwaite and Lingards, General Information', I Rentals, 1803. Register, Survey and Rentals, pp. 78–85, The Manor House, Slaithwaite.

[41] 'Survey of Sir John Radcliffe's Estate and Linthwaite and Golcar, made by Joshua Biran, 1786', Radcliffe MSS 50, West Yorkshire Archive Service, Leeds Office, Leeds.

[42] Murgatroyd Diaries, 242/1 (21 April 1786).   [43] Murgatroyd Diaries, 242/6 (30 June 1802).

woman should be brought before them. He should then give security to indemnify the parish, or enter into recognisances to appear at the next general quarter sessions to appeal. West Riding magistrates asked particularly what should happen if six weeks had passed after the birth of the child and no filiation order had been made (the mother might be too ill to attend the magistrates, or the father in jail – if he had failed to gives recognisances); the opinion here was that the man had a right to discharge under these circumstances.[44] West Riding magistrates were certainly following the structure of this procedure, no matter how many frustrating and inexplicable delays Phoebe Beatson experienced, from misinformation and poor communications (about whom she should see, how many of them, and where).

Her baby was born on 29 August 1802, and George Thorp, who had not been around since June, turned up on 24 October, just over seven weeks after the birth and eight days after filiation. He had not been in jail, had presumably given securities, and had lodged no appeal.[45] He may have wanted to talk to her about the filiation order; or he may have just wanted to see the baby. In any case, John Murgatroyd 'got hold of G Thorp at our Door about 10 – but he forced Himself from me . . .'[46] This was Thorp's last appearance (though the diary for 1803 is missing, and he may have turned up in that). Phoebe filiated, and he paid up (there is no way of telling what maintenance was fixed at).

There really is no more to be said about Phoebe Beatson, between 1786 and 1806: she is entirely contained within the pages of Murgatroyd's diary. There are no settlement or bastardy examinations extant to give the tiniest inkling of what it was that happened between her and George Thorp in 1801 and 1802. She emerges somewhere else, in February 1807, three months after Murgatroyd's death and before the granting of probate on his will, to make her mark in the Halifax parish register and marry John Sykes, a clothier of Golcar, Huddersfield. She may have been a catch now, never mind the illegitimate child, with an inheritance due and a cartload of household goods to her name. She

---

[44] 'The Opinion of G. B. Holroyd, Grays Inn, on Bastardy Cases', Quarter Sessions Records, QD 552, 1805, West Yorkshire Archive Service, Wakefield District, Wakefield. This is legally and historically informative – the West Riding got its money's worth. Holroyd discussed the Elizabethan origins of contemporary law, and then focussed on 6 Geo. 2 c. 31, 'An Act for the relief of parishes, and other places, from such charges as may arise from bastard children born within the same' (1733).

[45] Thorp's name does not appear in the Quarter Sessions Order book with other men who contested the charge of fathering a bastard child. At Skipton sessions that July, a farmer of Esington 'judged to be the Putative Father of a Male Bastard Child lately born in the township of Sawley' was ordered to pay the mother £12 9s 6d for a month's lying in 'and also the sum of four shillings weekly and every week so long as the said Bastard Child shall be chargeable to the said Township of Sawley'. This considerable maintenance may well have been a reflection of the social status of the couple.

[46] Murgatroyd Diaries, KC 242/6 (24 October 1802). It was a Sunday; he had been preaching at Deanhead in the morning.

had probably gone home to Halifax with Eliza, no longer having anywhere to live in Lingards. And John Sykes might have been the man who was bought-in by Murgatroyd to do some gardening in 1790.[47] He was a wool sorter 'at Mr Charles Hudson's near Halifax', wrote Murgatroyd. He had his dinner with Murgatroyd and Phoebe, and visited throughout the 1790s.[48] Perhaps Golcar township was the birthplace of the man she married; he may have moved to Halifax. Phoebe and John Sykes appear not to have had children – at least none baptised in Huddersfield or Halifax over the next ten years, by which time conception would surely have been unlikely because of Phoebe's age. And the story cannot be brought to a conclusion, for there is an absolute failure to trace Elizabeth Beatson (or Sykes, as she may have been known). We may assume (though we really do not know) that Phoebe Sykes saw what happened to her as a secular version of the rising in life story, or as a fairy story, or as a wild variant of the sentimental romance. Virtue in distress was rescued in religious tract material, and increasingly so, as the new century passed – but not by the device of having an illegitimate child in a clergyman's house and living there with the baby until she was four years old. There really were no conventional literary narratives by which Phoebe Beatson could have interpreted her own life – except for the one hinted at by the servant Zillah in *Wuthering Heights* (her hint is one of the epigraphs to this book) when, in a tiny aperture in the text and in what, in this obsessively dated historical novel, is the spring of 1801, she points out that, however bad it may have been for any servant in that crazy Pennine household, at least Ellen Dean has been able to stash away some savings. But that fleeting glimpse is afforded forty years on, in a type of literature (the deckered novel, designed for the circulating library market) that did not really exist, and was certainly not available to the likes of domestic servants, in the 1790s.

Murgatroyd thought George Thorp a bad and irresponsible man, a seducer – 'deceitful', in his words. He thought about these things, not only to have something to say to George Thorp and his mother, but because he was interested in the habits and courtship manners of the people he found himself among. There is a strange 'Love Letter' (headed so) copied out right at the end of his 'Book of Records', not I think because he wrote it himself, but because it is a fine fragment from a brisk and pragmatic Yorkshire courtship, an amusing anthropological example from a land of rough hill farmers and clothiers, a far thing from the gentle decencies of his own love-relationship with Ann Mellor.[49] Murgatroyd

[47] Murgatroyd Diaries, KC 242/1 (18 March 1790).
[48] Murgatroyd Diaries, KC 242/2 (10 August 1794).
[49] Murgatroyd, 'Book of Records'. 'Yorkshire' (its dialect, the characteristics of its people, their dress, habits and manners) had in any case long been a literary trope. It frames William Hogarth's 'Harlot's Progress' series and all the later literary production that used his Moll Hackabout to say something about love and language, service, prostitution and the arrival of West Yorkshire in the

is interested in them, their habits and manners. He came from them, but is not of them now. With his God, he watches them.

By the late eighteenth century, a life – the idea of a life – was infinitely and inextricably bound up with the capacity to write a life story. To tell, to write, to live a life, was an act made by the written word; or to put it another way, the life narrative, verbal or written, was the dominant (by now possibly the only) way of imagining, or figuring one. This major ideational component of modernity – the way in which the modern self is understood to be made in narrative, in the plot structures of the emergent novel, in the particular genre of autobiography – has been much discussed in recent scholarship, across many fields of inquiry. A life was not now, as it may possibly once have been, a given thing, a moment in the Deity's mind, the fragment of an eternal stasis, but rather, a plot, a sequence: a thing with a beginning, a story and an end. The literature charting this profound and convoluted move into modernity, and into our still-current way of understanding narrative and life itself, is enormous; the move is understood to have taken a very long time indeed.[50] Given that we have this knowledge of how John Murgatroyd (and Phoebe Beatson, and all their neighbours) may have imagined and understood their own lives, and represented them to others, what we are most in need of are the interpretive devices for unlocking the particular ideational and self-reflexive practices of West Yorkshire, 1780–1810. There is a problem here for readers of this book, for I, as intermediary reader of John Murgatroyd's writing, have found all of it moving in its ordinariness. The contemplations, the effusions, the regular recording that he had 'Awaked with God' (always immediately followed by a weather report, like 'hrd Frost still & fine cold Day'),[51] the immense historical detail of a day's doing lost in the effacatory 'my ordinary concerns', the way in which each Sunday he noted that his household had been 'all graciously preserved' – the very conventionality of his observations are part of what moves. A further problem with his contemplations and the account he gives of his

---

metropolis. See the Yorkshire girl Margery listing her domestic skills in a London employment office in John Reed, *The Register-Office; A Farce in Two Acts. Acted at the Theatre Royal in Drury Lane* (Dublin: H. Saunders, 1761). They include spinning. Also see Jonathan Myerson, 'A Harlot's Progress', BBC Radio 4 (broadcast January 2006).

[50] The making of the self in narrative has been charted for example, by Franco Moretti, *The Way of the World. The* Bildungsroman *in European Culture* (London: Verso, 1987); Robert Elbaz, *The Changing Nature of the Self* (London: Croom Helm, 1988); Anthony Giddens, *Modernity and Self-Identity. Self and Society in the Late Modern Age* (Cambridge: Polity Press, 1991); Michael Mascuch, *Origins of the Individual Self. Autobiography and Self-Identity in England, 1591–1791* (Cambridge: Cambridge University Press, 1997). All of these accounts implicate writing in the making of the modern self. Mascuch's moves the argument forward by relating it directly to the practice of autobiography and biography, as they emerged in the early modern period. For the Italian philosopher Adriana Caverero, self is impossible without its narration by another. See *Relating Narratives. Storytelling and Selfhood*, orig. pub. 1997 (London: Routledge, 2000).

[51] Murgatroyd Diaries, KC242/1 (1 March 1782).

God, and of the everyday pleasures of human relationship and decency that Murgatroyd saw Him allowing, is that there is no way of transcribing it without reiterating everything we think we know, historically speaking, about the later eighteenth-century Church of England. Here, surely, are 'the fat slumbers of the church' that Gibbon wrote about, and that everyone quotes when they discuss what it meant to think, feel and be an Anglican in a period of theological quietism and self-satisfaction in anti-intellectualism.[52] Murgatroyd looks like a majority of his fellows, for whom 'the Bible and John Locke had explained the essentials', and whose 'ingrained rationalist assumptions about human nature and social harmony' contributed to the generosity and sympathy with which he viewed what was, for him, an essentially benevolent world.[53] Beliefs like these, in God's rule of order and harmony in a social world that mirrored the divine, have been very well explained and shown to be at work in the writings of many clergymen contemporaries of Murgatroyd.[54]

But unlike Parson Woodforde, or the Reverend Coles, John Murgatroyd wrote – copiously and regularly – about his God and about Anglican theology. Moreover, he found Anglican Protestantism a continual source of intellectual and philosophical interest, a body of ideas and propositions that provided him with food for thought, until the very end of his days. He enjoyed thinking through this body of ideas. As well as this, there also always remained about him something of the eager and willing pupil, as if he were forever the young man of humble origins and impressive education, seeking an increasingly unusual entry to a career in the church. He was never a beneficed priest; he was refused at least two livings that he might have expected to obtain. He wasn't quite a gent, in an increasingly gentlemanly church. His ardour, in understanding and appropriating the theology and social thought of an institution that had denied him a full place within it, was – perhaps – an expression of feeling on the outside of a system, and a demonstration of his fitness to occupy a position actually denied him. Had he gained a living, and actually embodied the tenets and principles he debated with himself and his friends and neighbours for over

---

[52] This traditional (nineteenth-century) assessment of the established church has been much complicated over the past twenty years. There are very few accounts now written according to Gibbon's pattern. See Jago, *Aspects of the Georgian Church*, pp. 14–17 for an excellent summary of the recent historiography of the Church of England and Anglicanism.

[53] Alan Smith, *The Established Church and Popular Religion, 1750–1850* (London: Longman, 1971), p. 9 for Gibbon's 'fat slumbers', and pp. 8–13 for a preliminary survey of the Anglican belief system. R. A. Soloway, *Prelates and People. Ecclesiastical Social Thought in England, 1783–1852* (London: Routledge and Kegan Paul, 1969), pp. 19, 5, 22–3 for the quotes above, and *passim* for a more extended survey of Church of England theology and social thought.

[54] James Woodforde, *The Diary of a Country Parson. The Reverend James Woodforde 1758–1781*, ed. John Beresford (Oxford: Oxford University Press, 1924). Jack Ayres (ed.), *Paupers and Pig Killers. The Diary of William Holland, a Somerset Parson, 1799–1818*, orig. pub. 1984 (Stroud: Sutton, 1997). Francis Griffin Stokes (ed.), *The Blecheley Diary of the Reverend William Cole, MA, FSA, 1765–67* (London: Constable, 1931).

sixty years, he may well have devoted more space to his dinner as did more famous clergymen writers; he may then have written less.

His practice of writing was learned from very old models. One was educational, had probably been learned in his own youth and was used by him in Slaithwaite school. 'Commonplacing' had been devised for schoolboys' study of pagan texts. You ruled lines and columns on the pages of a blank notebook, and under different headings, noted the grammatical structures of the Latin tongue, collected your *sententia*, proverbs, maxims and striking passages from the histories, poetry and orations that were more advanced teaching material.[55] It was a method of reading and note-taking designed to enhance memory, to allow comparisons to be made between different forms of language, and to serve as a storehouse of sentences and formularies for those advanced pupils who went on to compose their own Latin texts. Murgatroyd's 'Ask, Read, Retain, Teach' notebook indicates its pedagogic origins and the use he may have made of it in his teacherly role, as schoolmaster and preacher. However, commonplacing was extravagant in its use of the blank page: its columns and headers (means to cross referencing) used up a lot of expensive paper. By way of contrast, Murgatroyd's notebooks are the muddle of a writer trying to save paper and money.

Devised for the purposes of secular education, the note-taking method of reading (and listening, to sermons and other forms of public discourse) was appropriated for religious purposes during the long sixteenth century. 'For Protestant Christians, the school notebook proved a useful aid to worship,' notes Michael Mascuch, and he gives many examples of individuals who used it for the purposes of remembering sermons, contemplating the scriptures, and pondering the providential or merely strange experiences they had recorded.[56] It is clear that the practice of reading over these entries, at the end of a day or a week, was also deeply imbued in writers, so much so that some surviving notebooks were thumbed and turned over to the point of disintegration. More written reflection might follow on these perusals, a further stage in the devotional technology that commonplacing had provided. Often, it was these collections of notes and observations that were smoothed into coherent texts by editors, either family members shortly after the writer's death, or much later by academic compilers and commentators. They gave us – either in the seventeenth or the twentieth century – the form and shape of something that we are much more familiar with: the published diary. These 'diaries' have often been read on the assumption that they are autobiographical in the modern sense; that there is an individual life expressed in the text, self-reflexive and authoring itself.[57] Once you go back to the original texts, says Mascuch, you will find something

[55] Mascuch, *Individualist Self*, p. 82. Peter Mack, *Elizabethan Rhetoric. Theory and Practice* (Cambridge: Cambridge University Press, 2002), pp. 31–2, 44–5. M. L. Clarke, *Classical Education in Britain, 1500–1900* (Cambridge: Cambridge University Press, 1959), pp. 38–45.
[56] Mascuch, *Individualist Self*, pp. 82–6.   [57] Mascuch, *Individualist Self*, pp. 84–6.

very much like Murgatroyd's 'Ask' notebook: a heterogeneous, and to the modern eye, disorganised collection of notes, observations, prayers, poetry – and recipes for carrot throat gargle.

But there are means within the corpus for distinguishing one kind of writing (and reading) from another. When Murgatroyd made notes on what he had read, especially in his early years, he used forms of abbreviation and contraction that he did not employ when he was actually composing in writing. (Much more obviously, he often recorded the title of the work he was noting.) This way of proceeding was typical of the 'Cornucopia', put together in the 1740s. Here, when he writes out of his own resources – or creatively – he uses the extended, or full form of most key words (he nearly always contracted prepositions, articles and conjunctions, as his diary writing shows). The much later 'Ask, Read, Retain, Teach' does contain some unreferenced transcription from published texts; but even when he goes back to the 'Cornucopia', or his 'Book of Records' (compiled fifty years before, and catalogued as part of the library that sat on his parlour shelves), he used extended writing, and incorporated the much earlier notes on John Locke, Thomas Nettleton, *Gil Blas* and *Tom Jones* into his own thinking-in-writing. Extended word form is, then, a pretty reliable marker of originality of composition in his case. There is here the extreme good fortune of possessing so very much of a lifetime's writing, to give a material shape to postmodernist assertions about the realm of intertextuality: that there is nothing ever thought anew; that every written word is the echo and remaking of some other word.[58] This kind of intertextuality operated between the notebooks as well, for Murgatroyd often copied out from earlier volumes into new, a necessary labour that saves on memory and searching, for anyone who uses the commonplace method.

Murgatroyd's commonplace books were also a device for Christian devotion, kept a century or so after the practice was developed among the Protestant 'saints' of seventeenth-century England. His diary (and this was a diary in the strictest meaning of the term, for there were daily entries) was also a devotional device, though it seems a much more conventionally autobiographical production to the modern eye. It notes the writer's daily doings with God, as well as keeping a detailed account of the state of play between Phoebe Beatson and the putter-out, Richard Walker. It describes tea drunk and dinner taken and conversation with fascinating ladies from Manchester, as well as Murgatroyd's weekly service of God, in tramping the twenty miles round Slaithwaite to take divine service. It chronicled the building of the new house at Lingards in very great detail of stone cutting and timber sawing, until, in despair at the slowness of the builders ('Wt Josh Pogson & his Men are doing, I do not know'), he

---

[58] Mary Orr, *Intertextuality. Debates and Contexts* (Cambridge: Polity Press, 2003).

banished them from the diurnal, into another notebook, all of their own.[59] The diary is no seamless narrative account of spiritual growth, as we once used to think earlier, Puritan self-writing might have been; there can be no end-stop to the fully fashioned autonomous self because, after all, this is a diary, but more profoundly because Murgatroyd understood that self-effacement rather than self-reflection before his God was what was required.[60]

Even so, to suggest a kind of self-effacement in the diary and the early notebooks is probably to go about things in the wrong way. Murgatroyd did not have, was not conscious of, the kind of self that literary historians and philosophers might ascribe to him, two hundred years on. He did not write, or read, to find a self affirmed. For example, he read and made extensive notes on Le Sage's *Gil Blas* in the early 1750s.[61] It is truly surprising to the modern historical eye, to see what it is he does with this very long narrative, in which the amiable young hero – from a humble background – moves through social space and varieties of community in a fictionalised Spain (that is really France) never knowing himself yet being made plain to the reader through the ways in which he is tricked, duped, liked and made friends with, by a remarkably wide range of people. Perhaps it is Gil's position as a servant that obviates Murgatroyd's identification. Gil is in service in the vaguely feudal form of apprenticeship to many masters on his way to the university, rather than on the modern English manner of contractual arrangement, yet domestic servant is what he is, for vast swathes of text. But the modern reader expects the identification of a young man from humble circumstances with a literary similar; two centuries of novel reading have taught us that that is what novels are *for*. But there is not one moment of textual identification in Murgatroyd's note taking. Rather, he commonplaces *Gil Blas*, pleased when he can record a maxim from Cicero via its pages ('"Cicero says, Ne'er be so much defeated as to forget you are a Man"'); he lists useful observations, such as '"In these Days all Virtue appears Hypocrisy to young people"', and '"Virtue its:'s too diffict. To be acquir'd, so we're satifd. wth possessing ye appearance of virtue."' It is certainly the case, as with his reading of *Tom Jones*, that the passages he commonplaced are preponderantly to do with love, passion and the ways of women (loose women,

[59] Murgatroyd Diaries, KC242/1 (5 and 29 May 1786), 'Abt ye Masons &c respecting our intended House, in another Book'. For a full account of his relationship with Joseph Pogson and his men, and the house they built, extracted from the journals, see Edward Law, 'The House that Jack Built', Huddersfield & District History, http://homepage.eircom.net/~lawedd/HOUSEJACKBUILT.htm. For the Manchester ladies, see below, chapter 9.

[60] Mascuch, *Individualist Self*, p. 84.

[61] Alain René Le Sage, *The History and Adventures of Gil Blas of Santillane* has a complex publishing history. Books I–VI were published in 1715, VII–IX in 1724, and X–XII in 1735. I have used the facsimile reprint of the English translation of 1716 (London: Jacob Tonson, 1716; New York: Garland, 1972). Murgatroyd's notes show him reading beyond the sixth book; maybe he read the lot.

in the notes from Le Sage). In the 1740s and 1750s he was truly interested in these questions. But as novels, *Gil Blas* and *Tom Jones* are to be treated as any other text, as a source of insight and information about God's creation, not a point of reference or identification for an individuated self.

And yet the life he contemplated did have a shape and plot, which might be reflected on at the year's turn, or the day the anniversary came round of his arrival at Slaithwaite school, and he could measure the similarity between the earnest, loving lad, willing to serve his God as teacher, and what he still was, now. There is plot, sequence, and the reflection of one life in another in the diary; as a text, it has made the move into modernity; it is autobiographical. It is, at the same time, an autobiography in which the individuated self is muted; it concerns God, much more than it concerns John Murgatroyd; it sits on the parlour shelf next to 'Ask, Read, Retain, Teach', which declares the origin of both volumes to be the practice of piety established in the late seventeenth century.

Phoebe Beatson could not write. We deduce that from the mark she made in the Halifax parish register when she got married. She could – almost certainly she could – read, if the extensive history of seventeenth- and eighteenth-century literacy we have to refer to is anything to go by. But neither Murgatroyd nor anybody else ever taught her to write. If an eighteenth-century girl of the poorer sort received any kind of schooling, it usually stopped short of writing, for the teaching of writing was intimately tied to the teaching of Latin, the province of boys.[62] Instruction in writing usually started when the child was about eight years old, and could read well enough to cope with the Bible and other simple literature of the faith. The deeds of trust of Slaithwaite school specified that girls were to be catechised and taught to read, but not to write. It was typical of parochial schools in this way.[63] Murgatroyd did a great deal that he was not meant to do during his forty-eight-year regime, including the teaching of Latin to the 'poorest children' that the deeds specified were to be recipients of its schooling, and it is likely that he did instruct some of the girls in writing. He certainly taught other little girls of the better sort to write: there are times when 'Ask, Read, Retain, Teach' turns into Hannah Mellor's copy book, as she practises her name in copperplate, and copies out book inscriptions in a

---

[62] David Cressy, *Literacy and the Social Order. Reading and Writing in Tudor and Stuart England* (Cambridge: Cambridge University Press, 1980). Margaret Spufford, 'First Steps in Literacy. The Reading and Writing Experiences of the Humblest Seventeenth-century Spiritual Autobiographers', *Social History*, 4:3 (1979), pp. 125–50. See also Carolyn Steedman, 'A Woman Writing a Letter', in Rebecca Earle (ed.), *Epistolary Selves. Letters and Letter-Writers, 1600–1945* (Aldershot: Ashgate, 1999), pp. 111–33, and notes 65–67. See David Levine, 'Illiteracy and Family Life during the Industrial Revolution', *Journal of Social History*, 14:1 (1980), pp. 3–24 for a suggestive and important placing of literacy within the context of the social and affective life of eighteenth-century England.

[63] Chapter 6, 'Teaching', discusses these points in more detail.

tidy hand. He left all his literary remains to his eldest niece, not to his nephew, and he clearly admired the patient intellectuality of his wife in her highly literate approach to God. But Phoebe Beatson, resident in his household from her nineteenth year, did not learn to use a pen. This is unsurprising, given contemporary practices of literacy teaching and theories of education, but for me the fact that Murgatroyd did not teach her to write will always be the one historical silence about this story that I cannot even begin to fill by speculation. Anyway, here Phoebe Beatson both represents and denies the historical norms which are practically our only means for interpreting her. She could not write, and was typical in this way; but not really so for several studies of literacy in the West Riding show that in Halifax parish between 1799 and 1804 nearly half of brides were able to sign, and can be presumed to have been able to write. Moreover, these same studies of industrial parishes across the region suggest that it was more likely than not, that literate grooms would marry literate brides.[64] John Sykes married his (relatively atypical) bride with a fine flourish of the pen; she had other attributes now, fire irons, furniture and a fortune, quite apart from the personal qualities we will never discover.

[64] W. B. Stephens, *Education, Literacy and Society, 1830–1870. The Geography of Diversity in Provincial England* (Manchester: Manchester University Press, 1987), pp. 1–14. W. B. Stephens, 'Literacy Studies. A Survey', in Stephens, *Studies in the History of Literacy. England and North America. Educational Administration and History*, Museum of the History of Education Monograph 13 (Leeds: University of Leeds, 1983), pp. 1–19.

4   Labour

The agreement to serve in a domestic capacity and the contract between man
or maid and master or mistress (the moment of hiring) constituted the most
common labour agreement of the later eighteenth century. It was governed by
legislation that originated in the seventeenth century, when the law of service
(reformulations of the ancient Statute of Artificers) became inextricably bound
up with the newly inaugurated poor laws.[1] The point of connection between
these two bodies of law was 'settlement': the right of a poor or indigent person
to maintenance from the parish to which he or she 'belonged', and the obligation
of the parish to provide it, if that person could demonstrate a settlement within
its boundaries. (Their relief was funded out of a local property tax – a poor rate
levied on local householders.)

Settlement was frequently discussed by contemporaries as the patrimony
and privilege of the poor, and historians of the old poor law have emphasised
this perspective.[2] Pamela Sharpe has claimed that 'settlement can be seen as
a property right for the poor'.[3] Both she and Keith Snell (who refers to some

---

[1] Paul Craven and Douglas Hay, *Masters, Servants and Magistrates in Britain and the Empire,
1562–1955* (Chapel Hill and London: University of North Carolina Press, 2004), pp. 59–116.

[2] Keith Snell, *Annals of the Labouring Poor. Social Change and Agrarian England, 1660–1900*
(Cambridge: Cambridge University Press, 1985), pp. 71–4. Pamela Sharpe, '"The Bowels of
Compation". A Labouring Family and the Law, *c.*1790–1834', in Tim Hitchcock, Peter King
and Pamela Sharpe (eds.), *Chronicling Poverty. The Voices and Strategies of the English Poor,
1640–1840* (London: Macmillan, 1997), pp. 87–108. James Stephen Taylor, *Poverty, Migration
and Settlement in the Industrial Revolution. Sojourners' Narratives* (Palo Alto, Calif.: Society for
the Promotion of Science and Scholarship, 1989), p. 42 calls settlement 'an important patrimony
of any poor child, for good or ill'. Also Lynn Hollen Lees, *The Solidarities of Strangers. The
English Poor Laws and the People, 1700–1948* (Cambridge: Cambridge University Press, 1998),
pp. 29–33.

[3] Pamela Sharpe, *Adapting to Capitalism. Working Women in the English Economy, 1700–1850*
(London: Macmillan, 1996), p. 34. Earlier historians writing in the aftermath of the 1834 legislation that abolished settlement by service were entirely disapproving of this attitude. Robert
Pashley shook his head at the days when 'an imagined, but mistaken analogy between a settlement and a right of property' had preoccupied both claimants and high court judges, in that
once-upon-a-time when 'as it appears in the [eighteenth-century] Law Reports . . . judges used
to speak of a settlement as a thing to be favoured in the law, and when, they seemed to consider
it . . . as a peculiar privilege of the poor'. Robert Pashley, *Pauperism and Poor Laws* (London:
Longman, Brown, Green and Longman, 1852), pp. 268–9.

thousand settlement examinations in *Annals of the Labouring Poor*) outline the many bids and stratagems made by the poor to gain a settlement of their own. By these efforts they chart the course of typical eighteenth-century working lives. For the early part of the century, Snell emphasises the importance of being hired for a year as 'virtually the only method to gain one's own settlement', from which followed the typical pattern of leaving home at about fourteen years of age, and then moving from one annual hiring to the next. Many settlements might be gained by working and receiving wages in a parish for a full 365 days, with each new settlement supplanting the last. On getting married, a man might move from being a yearly servant, to being a labourer, hired (and paid) by the week or by the day.[4]

Women could gain their own settlement in exactly the same way as men, by a series of annual hirings. For women, just as for men, the contract of service was practically the only way of doing this. Indeed, it is likely that more women than men sought settlement in this way in the period 1750–90 – certainly more disputed women's cases reached the higher courts, for 'the decline of service' that began in mid-century and accelerated from 1780 onwards was actually a decline in the involvement of *men* in a particular kind of labour contract. The decline had involved a concomitant shift of service, to women undertaking more resident domestic work. The difference between men and women was that, on marriage, a woman took her husband's settlement. Modern historians draw our attention to the difficulties of proving settlement for groups like 'women or children needing to show a "derivative" settlement from husband and parents', and for married women claiming relief for whatever reason, on their 'maiden settlement'.[5]

Cases went on appeal to London because a settlement claimed by a man or a woman had become a matter of dispute between two local authorities. Cases were batted backwards and forwards over parish and often county boundaries and eventually (or actually, rather rapidly) shot off to King's Bench, in a final attempt to rid a parish of a claimant for relief. Women whose settlement by service was in dispute raise more interesting questions than do the smaller number of men in a similar situation, because women, viewed from the perspective of legal process, raised the more complex and perplexing questions about settlement itself, and the rights it conferred on its recipient.[6]

---

[4] Snell, *Annals*, pp. 73, 105–8; see pp. 17–18 for legislation creating and affecting settlement. Sharpe, *Adapting*, pp. 109–21. Paul Slack, *The English Poor Law, 1531–1782* (Cambridge: Cambridge University Press, 1996), pp. 51–6.

[5] For the case of Rachel Clark of Colchester, married to a Scot who, having no settlement in England, appealed for relief through his wife, see Sharpe, *Adapting*, pp. 118–20, and notes. For Richard Burn's analysis of the difficulties arising from there being 'not the same measure of justice between the two kingdoms of England and Scotland', see Richard Burn, *The History of the Poor Laws: With Observations* (London: H. Woodfall and N. Strahan, 1764), pp. 283–4. He would have thought it odd that James Clark had gained no English settlement.

[6] See Carolyn Steedman, 'Lord Mansfield's Women', *Past and Present*, 176 (2002), pp. 105–43.

We can estimate how many disputed settlement cases, forwarded by litigation-happy courts of quarter sessions, passed before the Lord Chief Justice and his colleagues. Joseph Burchell's *Arrangement and Digest of the Law in Cases Adjudged in the King's Bench and Common Pleas*, which covered the years 1756 to 1794, reported on more than a hundred disputed settlements.[7] Over a third of these involved questions of hiring and service, or entitlement to settlement by service. Other means of gaining settlement (by birth, apprenticeship, marriage, officeholding, purchase or paying rates) did not give rise to anything like as much litigation. Francis Const's 1793 revision of Bott's standard *Decisions of the King's Bench Upon the Laws Relating to the Poor* devoted the most space to the question of 'Settlement by Hiring and Service', in that 'late and most active period' in the making of 'law positive' (statute law) and legal judgment, in the 1770s and 1780s.[8] James Taylor used 985 settlement examinations to produce his 1989 account of poverty and migration during the early industrial revolution, of which 679 had hiring and service as the basis of settlement.[9] These were cases settled locally, some of them not even forwarded from parishes to quarter sessions for adjudication; had they gone on appeal to King's Bench, he would not have found them in the local records. But the number of settlements by service he did find underlines the implications of Burchell's and Const's collections: that it was through settlement legislation, and the judges' adjustment of it into case law in the higher courts, that the poor laws had the greatest effect on the largest number of lives in the last quarter of the century. Taylor further remarks on both the 'special problems domestic servants encountered with the Law of Settlement', and on how little attention those problems have received.[10] Part of Phoebe Beatson's story involves paying attention to those difficulties. Her case suggests, as do many others, that the abolition of settlement by service under the 1834 Poor Law Amendment Act constituted a profound change in the legal structures supporting many working lives. Settlement by service had certainly produced more litigation than any other aspect of the poor laws since their sixteenth-century inauguration.[11]

It was female domestic servants who forced questions about settlement as a form of possession, or property. Their cases still raise questions about labour, value and the ownership of labour. If domestic service is understood as one of the largest of late eighteenth-century occupational categories; if the overwhelming

---

[7] Joseph Burchill, *Arrangement and Digest of the Law in Cases Adjudged in the King's Bench and Common Pleas from the Year 1756 to 1794, inclusive* (London: J. Jones, 1796).

[8] Francis Const, *Decisions of the Court of the King's Bench, Upon the Laws Relating to the Poor, Originally Published by Edmund Bott Esq. of the Inner Temple, Barrister at Law. Revised . . . by Francis Const Esq. of the Middle Temple*, 3rd edn, 2 vols. (London: Whieldon and Butterworth, 1793), vol. II, pp. 315–541.

[9] Taylor, *Poverty*, p. 188, note 2.   [10] Taylor, *Poverty*, p. 190, note 13.

[11] Taylor, *Poverty*, p. 24. Pashley, *Pauperism and Poor Laws*, pp. 268–9. See also James Willis, *On the Poor Laws of England* (London: John Lambert, 1808), pp. 67–9.

contemporary evidence that by this time this workforce was largely female is taken into account; and if domestic service is understood both as a form of labour and as the major route to achieving independent settlement rights, then new questions have to be asked about the permeable boundaries between two bodies of legislation: the law of settlement and the law of service. There was a brisk trade in the informal codification of all the law (statute law and common law judgment) relating to the management of domestic servants in the second half of the century. Its form was various, ranging from the handbook for magistrates, advice books for employers, legal instruction for servants (wrongly named 'friendly advice'), and tracts and stories for a fantasised audience of servants and children. Several writers chose to codify by telling the history of 'our ancient constitution' as the transition from vassalage to domestic servitude. In one of these guides from 1774, Jonas Hanway's *Virtue in Humble Life*, Mary, being instructed by her father on all the whys and wherefores of going into service, is forced to break the bounds of meekness that her author has given her, and to exclaim, 'Do people reason so much about servants?' – to which the only possible response was, Yes, they do.[12]

Confronted by a woman whose settlement was in dispute, local justices and high court judges had to move between two systems of law – poor law and master and servant – using one as if it were the other, so that law might give some kind of answer to the problems they presented. In these encounters, poor law becomes labour law and labour law settlement law. Phoebe Beatson's case never went to King's Bench (it did not even go to quarter sessions, as there was nothing to dispute; her settlement was at Lingards); but it raises similar questions about property in one's person and in one's labour. Cases like hers offer insight into contemporary debates in legal and political theory, about service, self-possession and self-ownership.

---

[12] See for example Anon., *The Laws Relating to Masters and Servants. With Brief Notes and Explanations to render them easy and intelligible to the meanest Capacity. Necessary to be had in all Families* (London: Henry Lintot, 1755); Anon., *A Present for Servants, from their Ministers, Masters, or other Friends*, 10th edn (London: J. F. and C. Rivington for the SPCK, 1787); J. Huntingford, *The Laws of Masters and Servants Considered* (London: privately printed, 1792); Charles Jones, *The Story of Charles Jones, the Footman. Written by Himself* (London: J. Marshall, 1796); T. E. Tomlins, *The Law-Dictionary, Explaining the Rise, Progress and Present State of the English Law . . . originally compiled by Giles Jacob*, 2 vols. (London: Strahan, 1797); James Barry Bird, *The Laws Respecting Masters and Servants, Articled Clerks, Apprentices, Manufacturers, Labourers, and Journeymen*, 3rd edn (London: W. Clarke, 1799); Anon., *Domestic Management, or the Art of Conducting a Family with Instructions to . . . Servants in general, addressed to young Housekeepers* (London: H. D. Symonds at the Literary Press, 1800); Anon., *Reflections on the Relative Situations of Master and Servant, Historically Considered* (London: W. Miller, 1800); Anon., *A Familiar Summary of the Laws Respecting Masters and Servants* (London: Henry Washbourne, 1831). Jonas Hanway, *Virtue in Humble Life: containing Reflections on the Reciprocal Duties of the Wealthy and the Indigent, the Master and the Servant . . .*, 2 vols. (London: Dodley Brotherton and Sewell, 1774), vol. I, pp. 361–2.

The work of domestic servants also occupied a central position in eighteenth-century political philosophy, and thus in the labour law and the fiscal policy that it underpinned. The philosophy of labour, originating in the seventeenth century, concerned itself with work as an abstract quality, as a thing that might be contracted for and transferred from person to person, in an agreement made to perform it for another, for some kind of compensation. The general meaning of 'servant', as a he or she who worked for some kind of recompense in this way, was what John Locke had in mind when he contemplated these questions in the *Two Treatises of Government* (1689). In the second *Treatise*, Locke describes how 'every man has a property in his own person; this nobody has any right to but himself'.[13] The labour of his body, the work of his hands, are properly his, and he has property in them. In the great abundant world that God made, people may mingle their labour with the fruits of the earth, behave like the Maker who made them, and the natural things with which they mix their labour become theirs: their property.[14] A free person, of his or her own will and volition, might 'make himself a servant to another by selling him, for a certain time, the service he undertakes to do in exchange for wages he is to receive'. In that moment of hiring (in such an act of contract) the labour becomes the master's, not the labourer's. The moment in which the transfer of labour occurs is famously described: 'the grass my horse has bit; *the turfs my servant has cut* . . . become my property . . . The labour that was mine removing them out of that common state they were in, hath fixed my property in them.'[15]

Locke was interested in the *employer's* capacities, not the servant's. His turf-cutting servant is a mere cipher (or automaton), as the master uses the man and the horse to take grass and turf into his personal possession. The servant exercises the master's capacity to labour rather than his own. Eighteenth-century legal commentators expounded on the unfortunate social necessity that brought about the situation Locke described. The most famous of them all, William Blackstone, explained that the relationship between master and servant was 'founded in *convenience*, whereby a man is directed to call in the assistance of others where his own skill and labour will not be sufficient to answer the cares incumbent upon him'.[16] Really, 'in strictness every body ought to transact his own affairs', noted James Barry Bird in 1799; only 'by the favour and indulgences of the law . . . can [he] delegate the power of acting for him to another'.

---

[13] John Locke, *Two Treatises of Government*, orig. pub. 1689 (London: Dent, 1993), pp. 127–9 (Second Treatise, chapter 5, sections 26–8).

[14] James Tully, *A Discourse on Property. John Locke and his Adversaries* (Cambridge: Cambridge University Press, 1980), pp. 116–24. Robert J. Steinfeld, *The Invention of Free Labour. The Employment Relation in English and American Law and Culture, 1350–1870* (Chapel Hill and London: University of North Carolina Press, 1991), pp. 78–81.

[15] Locke, *Two Treatises*, p. 129.

[16] William Blackstone, *Commentaries on the Laws of England. In Four Books*, orig. pub. 1765, 6th edn (Dublin: Company of Booksellers, 1775), Book 1, p. 422.

That was why 'the acts of servants are in many instances deemed the acts of the masters'.[17] Throughout the eighteenth century the servant cutting turf, the boy cleaning the knives, the kitchen maid milking the house cow, were conceived of as aspects of their master's capacities and abilities. Post-1777 tax law reinforced this visceral relationship between employer and servant. It was the master or mistress who was taxed for the servant's labour – labour that had been acquired in an act of hiring, or of contract, and that was understood to be in their possession from that moment onwards, whether or not the servant was actually *at work* (cutting turf, handing round a dish of beans at table, playing with the children) or not. Tax law cut through and around many legal assumptions about the master–servant relationship; but where the contractual relationship existed, which allowed for the legal absorption of one (inferior) body in another, this central assumption remained undisturbed.

The propositions of Locke's turf-cutting passage are to do with the conditions of early capitalism and a very wide variety of occupational categories. Robert Steinfeld has reminded us that for more than a century or so after Locke wrote, the idea of free labour remained 'uninvented' (although such invention was in process in the former American colonies, from the 1780s onwards), and that 'all those who worked for others for compensation on whatever terms were in some sense "serving" their masters'. It was not simply a linguistic hangover from Tudor legislation to call workers 'servants', says Steinfeld, for 'the broader usage of the term "servant" [captured the] common qualities of all versions of labor relationship'.[18] Though domestic servants comprised a very large occupational category in mid-eighteenth-century England, at the end of the seventeenth century Locke had been discussing a condition of labour that pertained much more widely. Within the legal and economic category of 'servant', domestics were indeed a minority, but it was the weight of their presence as a type of worker, and the domestic service relationship as one of the most widely experienced in the society, that underlay the assertion of Sir William Blackstone that the contract between employer and servant embodied the first of the 'three great relations of private life' in which the law must be interested.[19] Domestic servants were 'the first sort of servant . . . acknowledged by the laws of England . . . menial servants; so called from being *intra moenia*, or domestics'.[20]

In the social theory derived from Locke, Blackstone's 'first relation' of private life was seen as by far the most complex. In all of Locke's writing, and

---

[17] Bird, *Laws*, p. 6.
[18] Steinfeld, *Invention of Free Labour*, pp. 18–21, 85–6, 102, 105. See also Peter Karsten, *Between Law and Custom. High and Low Legal Cultures in the Lands of the British Diaspora, the United States, Canada, Australia, and New Zealand, 1600–1900* (Cambridge and New York: Cambridge University Press, 2002).
[19] Blackstone, *Commentaries*, Book 1, p. 425.   [20] Blackstone, *Commentaries*, Book 1, p. 422.

particularly in the *Two Treatises*, man is a maker, and his making makes him a person. People fashion things out of the material of the earth, which is provided by God. Labour transforms the earthly provision into objects of use; those who labour have a property in the product. And yet, quite conventionally, and in those everyday acts of hiring and contract that Blackstone described and that the legal system increasingly emphasised, men and women acquired the labour of social inferiors. The rent or lease of the servant's time and energies, the turfs stacked, the corn threshed (the dinner cooked? the sheets ironed? the room turned out and dusted?) became that of the master or mistress. One of the capacities that made people possessive individuals in law and polity was exercised on a daily basis by people who were not, in some commentators' view, persons at all, in the way that 'person' was coming to be defined during the seventeenth and eighteenth centuries.[21]

Readers of *The Wealth of Nations* (1776) will remember that the 'labour of the menial servant . . . does not fix or realize itself in any particular subject or vendible commodity. His services generally perish in the very instant of their performance, and seldom leave any trace or value behind them for which an equal quantity of service could afterwards be procured.'[22] This kind of social and economic theory, worked over and reformulated by Marx, was the twentieth-century historian's legacy for understanding of service in both the nineteenth and the eighteenth centuries; or rather, for its absence in our conventional histories of labour and class.

Was 'labour' really the problem here? Between 1847 and 1867 Marx moved from an understanding of labour as a kind of commodity – something that could be sold and bought – to an account in which labour does not 'really' exist, or rather is only existent in its moment of realisation, when an abstract capacity or ability is congealed, or crystallised into a thing, or object: something made for sale and for use.[23] Indeed 'in order to be sold as a commodity in the market' labour would have to exist in its own right before it was sold – something

---

[21] MacPherson's is the classic statement that, in the seventeenth century, the employed labour force (including servants in husbandry, domestic servants and day labourers) were not really persons, in legal and political understanding. C. B. MacPherson, 'Servants and Labourers in Seventeenth-century England', in MacPherson (ed.), *Democratic Theory. Essays in Retrieval* (Oxford: Clarendon Press, 1973), pp. 207–33. 'Person' also had a quite separate and lay meaning, as 'body'. This is important for John Murgatroyd's musings on the second great relation of private life, that is, the sexual relationship within marriage. This point is discussed below, in chapter 9.

[22] Adam Smith, *The Wealth of Nations. Books I–III*, orig. pub. 1776 (London: Penguin, 1986), p. 430; see also pp. 133–40. Gender does, of course, have much to do with all the omissions being discussed. But had Smith noticed maidservants, he would still have claimed that *her* services perished in the very moment she performed them.

[23] Karl Marx, 'Wage Labour and Capital', *Neue Rheinische Zeitung*, 5–8 (Apr. 1849). Karl Marx and Frederick Engels, *Selected Works. In Two Volumes* (Moscow: Foreign Languages Publishing House, 1958), vol. I, pp. 70–5. Karl Marx, *Capital I*, orig. pub. 1867 (Harmondsworth: Penguin, 1976), pp. 128–31.

patently impossible, for 'if the worker were able to endow it with an independent existence, he would be selling a commodity, and not labour'.[24] Marx formulated the idea of labour power, or the potentiality to labour – to start work on the iron, or the yarn, or the length of linen, whatever – as a conceptual bridge over the absence of labour as a real thing with shape and form in the world.[25] Labour was not a commodity; it was produced in a moment of action, and deposited and straticulated in things which *were* commodities. What determined the value of these different commodities was 'the labour-time necessary for [their] production'.[26] In a structure of argument which proposed that the worker sells his or her labour power (not his or her labour); that the moment labour actually begins, it ceases to belong to the worker, and can no longer be sold by him or her; that labour may be the substance and immanent measure of value, but has no value itself – it would be difficult to incorporate the work of domestic service (or service in general). Marx deprecated the demography of nineteenth-century England which showed domestic servants to be (still!) one of the largest groups of employed persons; then irony covered over their existence and their history (and their former place in an elaborate economic and fiscal theory of the later eighteenth century[27]). For they were, he said, as he contemplated statistics from 1861, 'domestic slaves . . . an elevating consequence of the capitalist exploitation of machinery'.[28] Or they were the mere (though massive) legacy of a much older feudal form of society. Overall 'types of work that are consumed as services and not in products separable from the worker, and not capable of existing as commodities independently of him . . . are of microscopic significance when compared with the mass of capitalist production. They may be entirely neglected, therefore . . .'[29]

The distinction between productive and non-productive labour was encountered again and again by twentieth-century scholars, notably by Nicos Poulantzas and David Harvey.[30] What their reading made plain at least, is that *Capital* is a story about – capital, not labour; that the productive work that produces surplus value does so for the capitalist (or more strictly, for capital); that 'the only productive labour is that which is directly consumed in the course of production for the valorization of capital'.[31] In the beginning, this was not a

[24] Marx, *Capital I*, p. 675.
[25] E. K. Hunt, 'Marx's Theory of Property and Alienation', in A. Parel and T. Flanagan (eds.), *Theories of Property. Aristotle to the Present* (Waterloo, Ontario: Wilfred Laurier for the Calgary Institute for the Humanities, 1979), pp. 283–315, p. 298.
[26] Marx, *Capital I*, p. 130.
[27] For the servant as 'good to think with' in eighteenth-century England, see Carolyn Steedman, 'Servants and their Relationship to the Unconscious', *Journal of British Studies*, 42 (2003), pp. 316–50.
[28] Marx, *Capital I*, p. 574.   [29] Marx, *Capital I*, p. 1044.
[30] Nicos Poulantzas, *Classes in Contemporary Capitalism* (London: Verso, 1975); David Harvey, *The Limits to Capital* (London: Verso, 1999).
[31] Poulantzas, *Classes*, pp. 209–23. Marx, *Capital I*, p. 1038.

story about labour, labouring people, nor their consciousness of being so. *Capital* is about what it says on the title page: about the great dramas, ebbs and flows in fortune, about the tragedy of the colossus Capital. Somewhere then, between Adam Smith and Karl Marx, servants got lost, at least lost for the twentieth-century social historian working within the broad framework of their economic and social theory. This is how a majority of the eighteenth-century labouring population came to be missing from *The Making of the English Working Class*.

Harry Braverman called the distinguishing characteristic of capitalism the worker selling and the capitalist buying, not an agreed amount of labour, 'but the power to labour over an agreed period of time'.[32] In 1765 William Blackstone had explained time and the labour contract to his readers, pointing out that all questions of the servant's time devolved on the contract or hiring agreement: 'if the hiring be general, without any particular time limited, the law construes it as a hiring for a year . . . upon a principle of moral equity, that the servant shall serve and the master maintain him, throughout all the revolutions of the respective seasons; as well as when there is work to be done as when there is not'.[33] Authority over the servant's time was perpetual: the employer had obtained the day-in, day-out attentions of a servant in a relationship of some reciprocity.[34] From the very early eighteenth century onwards, magistrates adjudicating disputes between employers and their servants consistently noted that what a servant was compensated for was his or her *time*, as in 'Widow Greenland parted with her Servt. Mary Kerwin by Consent & paid her 40/- for her Time'.[35] By the middle of the century, 'time' was used to describe what the servant contracted to provide in the Law Reports; following Blackstone, law manuals reinforced this point.[36]

---

[32] Smith, *Wealth of Nations*, p. 430. See also pp. 133–40. Harry Braverman, *Labour and Monopoly Capitalism. The Degradation of Work in the Twentieth Century* (New York and London: Monthly Review Press, 1974), pp. 54, 59–83. For a detailed and suggestive discussion of this point, comparing nineteenth-century England and Germany, see Richard Biernacki, *The Fabrication of Labour. Germany and Britain, 1640–1914* (Berkeley, Los Angeles and London: University of California Press, 1995).

[33] Blackstone, *Commentaries*, p. 425.

[34] Bird, *Laws*, p. 5. The law of mutual obligation in the service relationship was explained to servants in terms of time. See, for example, Anon., *A Present for Servants*, pp. 14–15: 'they are such [i.e. servants] *by Reason of Poverty*, or a meaner Condition in the World, [and] have voluntarily submitted themselves, by Contract, for a certain Time to the Disposal of others, according to the Word of God, and the Laws of the Realm'.

[35] The Brockman family of Beachborough, Kent, a positive race of magistrates, preserved their informal notebooks throughout the long eighteenth century. Brockman Papers, vols. XIII–XV, Add. Mss. 4260, 42598, 42599, 42599du, British Library, London. Three Justices' Diaries, kept by the Brockman Family of Beachborough, Newington, Kent. Filled in by several hands, the use of 'Time' to describe what the servant received wages for, became common in the 1730s. The entry concerning Greenland and Kerwin is from 1734. Add. Mss. 42599 (1725–81).

[36] Bird, *Laws*, pp. 4–6. By 1800 when the anonymous *Domestic Management* gave advice on 'the art of managing a family', it told its imagined audience of 'young housekeepers' and their

And yet time was not what was taxed when levies were raised on the employment of domestic servants, from 1777 onwards. Rather, the servant's labour that had been reckoned in an abstract fashion by John Locke, as an analogy of the constant making and transfer of property in modern society, was used by fiscal authority to calculate the value of cleaning knives and planting rows of beans in a kitchen garden. In England, in the later eighteenth century, the domestic servant's labour was made concrete, moved beyond philosophical example, into a concrete, taxable thing. Tax law had a discernible effect on definitions and understandings of what a servant was, and what a servant did. Interpreted by the common law courts, it named a worker's skills and capacities, what he or she *actually did* in the labour of service, as defining characteristics. Above all, it located labour in the cook, the groom, the maid, the man (even in the turf-cutter), not in the turf-cutter's master, nor in the philosopher watching from the window.

The tax on servants was a tax on their masters and mistresses for having in their households such visible unit measurements of luxury and ostentation; in other words, it was a tax compatible with the Smithian view that domestics did not *really* perform labour. The liveried and bewigged manservant was an index of conspicuous consumption, just as was the hair powder increasingly purchased for valets rather than for their masters, and rather in the way of certain kinds of carriage and coats of arms, and indeed playing cards, dice and newspapers, all of which were taxed to fuel a war economy.[37]

Contemporaries knew, of course, that a liveried man was a luxury item; but they understood also the arbitrariness of choosing servants as a fiscal target in times of war, and the pressing need for revenue, collected from anywhere and anything that would pay. Government reasoning behind the proposals of 1776 was that luxuries ought to be taxed 'because the first weight ought to fall upon the rich and opulent'; land and windows could yield nothing more; 'the governmental view was . . . that the rich must suffer as the elasticity of the tax structure was enlarged by duties on luxuries . . .'[38] In even more pressing times, in 1785 when a tax on the employment of maidservants was proposed, it was

servants, that whatever the contract, it was for *time*: the servant had contracted to give the master time, and to waste it was to rob him.

[37] J. V. Beckett, 'Land Tax or Excise. The Levying of Taxation in Seventeenth- and Eighteenth-century England', *English Historical Review*, 100 (1985), pp. 285–308. E. Baigent, 'Assessed Taxes as Sources for a Study of Urban Wealth', *Urban History Year Book*, 7 (1988), pp. 31–48; 39. W. R. Ward, *The English Land Tax in the Eighteenth Century* (London: Oxford University Press, 1953), pp. 156–7.

[38] This account is from Ward, *English Land Tax*, pp. 123–4. For the impossibility of an income tax in the 1770s, see Beckett, 'Land Tax', p. 301. See also Martin Daunton, *Trusting Leviathan. The Politics of Taxation in Britain, 1799–1914* (Cambridge: Cambridge University Press, 2001), pp. 43–7.

a taken-for-granted that the servant tax had never been a levy on luxury alone, but also upon the use of a particular kind of contracted labour.[39]

William Pitt promoted the tax on female servants on the grounds of its 'qualities': it had virtues that 'he should always look for in moments of pressing exigency, namely, the sum being paid being open and perceptible to those who were to pay it, and that of falling principally upon the opulent'.[40] But it was already apparent that by taxing female domestic labour a burden was to be placed on the middling sort – farmers who kept 'a number of women servants for the double purpose of doing the work of their house and of their farm' were made a particular point of objection – and that luxury and opulence in an employer had dropped out of the argument.[41] A month later, the proposal had incorporated the suggestions of Charles James Fox to make exemptions, and to attend to the plight of families with children – a sliding scale of tax payment was thus first forced by the prospect of assessed female labour. In families 'one servant should be allowed [tax free] to every two children of a certain age', and to make up the shortfall in revenue – 'how much, impossible to say' – every bachelor keeping one male servant was to pay an additional sum of 25s, over and above the regular rate for a manservant. The same legislation established that 'Every person who shall have living in their houses two or more lawful children, under the age of fourteen, shall, in respect . . . of [these] children or grandchildren, be exempted from the payment of duties . . .' Moreover, female employees aged less than fourteen and more than sixty were not liable.[42]

This tax system has been used as a basis for calculating the relative numbers of male and female servants in the population in the eighteenth and nineteenth centuries, and the decline of both categories between 1781 and 1851.[43] Male

---

[39] The proposals concerning a tax on maidservants produced much ribaldry, especially among the denser members of the House, who purported to believe that it was domestics themselves – or perhaps womankind – who were to be taxed. There were facetiously dark reminders issued, of the last time a Chancellor of the Exchequer had tried taxing 'female commodities', and 'a man famous in his day, and whose story is well-known yet, called Wat Tyler . . . raised a violent commotion'. *Parliamentary History*, vol. 25, pp. 558–9, pp. 571–4.

[40] Moreover – important, as the economy was wrenched into funding war – 'its produce [was] nearly ascertainable'. *Parliamentary History*, vol. 25, pp. 552–3.

[41] For the extreme difficulties of separating the work of female 'servants in husbandry' and domestic servants, see Bridget Hill, *Women, Work, and Sexual Politics in Eighteenth-century England* (Oxford: Blackwell, 1989), pp. 69–84, 103–24.

[42] 25 Geo. III c.43 s.13, 14 (1785); 26 Geo.III c.77 (1786); 32 Geo.III c.3 (1792); 4 Geo.IV c.9. The servant taxes never brought in very much. They were finally repealed in 1937 under the Finance Act – though in 1823 in Ireland, under 4 Geo.IV c.9. In Ireland, the tax was more apparently 'a partial tax upon labour . . would anyone say that the master would not employ more servants, if there were no tax at all? . . . The tax cramped labour . . .' *Hansard's Parliamentary History* (New Series) (London, 1823), vol. 8, pp. 603–9.

[43] Leonard Schwarz, 'English Servants and their Employers during the Eighteenth and Nineteenth Centuries', *Economic History Review*, 52 (1999), pp. 236–25. Schwarz uses the resources of

livery servants were a very small occupational group, greatly exaggerated by contemporary critics of 'luxury', only some 50,000 of them in the whole of England and Wales, perhaps 0.7 per cent of the population.[44] The demography of the female servant must be approached from a different direction, as she was uncounted and unlisted (except between 1786 and 1792). In proposing repeal of the maidservant tax legislation, Pitt told the Commons that a charge upon 90,000 families had brought in only the trifling sum of £31,000 in the previous tax year; and he conceded that it had been a tax largely paid 'by the poorer class of housekeeper' (and of course, those without children living in the household, or employing young girls or older women as servants).[45]

Leonard Schwarz's argument allows us to go in an entirely different direction: that of labour, its hiring and its use, and what it was that servants actually *did*. He raises the neglected topic of 'Charring, that is the work undertaken by paid living-out servants'.[46] One of the problems, though, in adding the eight-year-old boy, son of the regular charwoman, bought in for a few pennies to help his mother during the four days she was paid for brewing in September 1794,[47] is that both of them were domestic servants in the social sense, but nothing at all in the legal and fiscal meaning of the term. The servant tax statistics net a tiny proportion of those who performed paid domestic work, but do allow us to discern men and women in households, carrying on the business of life for their employers, with men doing work that seems to bear strict comparison with what 'charwomen' or 'work women' performed: a vast, unplumbed sea of labour that is nowhere enumerated; an army of servants who were defined as such by what they *did*, but who fell outside all contemporary definitions of what a servant *was*.

In William Blackstone's *Commentaries*, in famous justices' manuals like Dr Burn's, and in a host of lesser known guides to parish law and the law of

PRO, T47/8, a compilation list of male servants employed across the country during 1780 when the system was under Excise Office control. This listed male servants, of course. Maidservants were not yet taxed.

[44] Schwarz, 'English Servants', pp. 239–40.

[45] *Parliamentary History*, vol. 29, pp. 816–849. As far as calculating the number of female domestic servants in the population is concerned, and beyond saying that in 1791, 90,000 households did pay a tax on their maids, as much has been done as is possible with the servant tax figures: they can only (fairly) reliably count the number of male servants (see chapter 1). But perhaps there were lists that would allow us to be more reliable about women. There was certainly one, now apparently (and it is to be hoped, temporarily) lost, made in 1787, a year after the tax on female servants was inaugurated. 'Land Tax, Property Tax, Assessed Taxes', PRO T22/8, Letter Book, 1777–1805, pp. 322–3, National Archives, Kew: 'To: paid for making an alphabetical list of Persons keeping Servants, Horses and Carriages throughout England, persuant to a Treasury Order of 17th October 1787 – £483.11.6'. These accounts were for the year ending 5 January 1788.

[46] Schwarz, 'English Servants', p. 236.

[47] Frances Hamilton, Bishops Lydeard Farming Accounts, DD/FS 5/8, Somerset County Record Office, Taunton (28 September 1794).

service, what made a servant a servant was that he or she was resident in a household.[48] Over fifty years, this basic principle did not alter – at least, not in the law books. 'Servants', wrote Thomas Waller Williams in 1804, 'are either menial or not menial . . . Menial servants are the domestics living within the walls of a house.'[49] When Blackstone called menial servants the 'first sort of servants . . . acknowledged by the laws of England', his point of contrast was not casual, bought-in domestic staff (which he nowhere mentioned) but rather, labourers and other workers who undertook non-domestic service under contract (a hiring agreement, verbal or written) and who were subject, like menials, to the substantial and extensive law of service.[50] Magistrates, going about their regular business, were frequently faced with hiring and service agreements that involved domestic servants living out, or whose local lodgings were paid for by employers (the system of board wages); but they dealt with cases like these as if to preserve a legal fiction, that a servant was a domestic *because* he or she dwelt 'within the walls', and was *thus* a domestic servant. The new tax laws of the 1770s and 1780s cut right across this ancient legal assumption. Now, a man did not have to be living under your roof and eating at your (kitchen) table to be a taxable item. His (or her, between 1786 and 1792) being liable to tax depended, in these new definitions, upon what kind of work was performed, and whether or not it contributed to the employer's income or profit. (All servant tax law exempted servants kept for the purposes of husbandry, manufacture or trade, 'whereby the master earns a livelihood or profit'.) Between 1777 and 1792, a servant became a different kind of legal category, became one whose skills, capacities and actual work were detailed in order to declare him or her one; it remains to be seen whether or not he or she became a different kind of worker as well, in a new kind of relationship with the employer. And it becomes impossible to use menservants as an index of luxury, ostentation or, in the modern historian's preoccupation, urban wealth. Many of them were used as the male equivalent of the charwoman, brought in from field or kitchen garden, to do domestic work around the house, on a casual basis. Frances Hamilton's Somersetshire kitchen door is a good place to look (she farmed her own 100 acres just outside Taunton) in order to see Jonathan (properly hired manservant) going out (without his wig) to drive the cart to the quarry, and her charwoman's teenage boy going in from the kitchen garden (maybe he borrowed the wig) to wait on the company at table, all of them keeping the enterprise of a particular household going.[51]

---

[48] Blackstone, *Commentaries*, p. 425.

[49] Thomas Waller Williams, *The Practice of the Commissioners, Surveyors, Collectors and Other Officers, under the Authority of the several Acts relating to the Assessed Taxes* (London: W. Clarke, 1804), p. 879.

[50] Steinfeld, *Invention*, p. 18.

[51] The boy was allowed by law to use the hair powder! 36 Geo.III c.6 allowed the certificates obtained for servants' powder to cover their successors. John Smee, *A Complete Collection of*

There *is* an eighteenth-century guide to charring, though it is a little early for assessing the small army of helpers who worked with Phoebe Beatson between 1785 and 1806. Mary Collier's 'The Woman's Labour' (1739) was published as a response to Stephen Duck's 'Thresher's Labour' (1730), a 'so-what?' and more, to his account of the work and life of the field hands making up the pool of village labour that could be called on at particularly intense times of the agricultural year.[52] Both Edward Thompson and Donna Landry draw our attention to the poem's substantial sections of 'effective critique of the hard-nosed middle class mistress for whom poor women "char"'.[53] This account, of 'washing, cleaning, brewing . . . at the houses of the wealthy, is unfamiliar, and for its time, probably unique'. We may certainly learn from it about the nature of charring, albeit for the 1730s; Collier's detailed itinerary of house-work performed as piece-work suggests its more permanent structures, held in place by whatever resident domestics there were, and supplemented regularly by an army of casual labour that, being nowhere mentioned in the servant tax legislation, escaped all assessors', collectors' and excise men's eyes, fifty years on.

The household objects on which Collier's skill was exercised and the timetabling of the domestic day changed in that half century after 1739 (plates to be washed rather than pewter to be scoured, for example); but Collier's inventory of domestic labour still suggests what it was that servants actually *did*, on a regular basis. She presents charring as antiphonal to the servant's work. Early on a winter's morning, the village women rise by prior arrangement ('our Work appointed') and go to the big house for the wash. They can't get in, for the maidservant is tired out 'with work the day before', and it takes a while to rouse her. The laundry ('Cambricks and Muslins . . . Laces and Edgings . . . Holland Shirts, Ruffles and Fringes') takes all day, for the consumer revolution has already changed the nature of the servant's work.[54] The mistress of the house appears at noon, with *perhaps* a mug of ale for the women, but mainly to nag and scold about being gentle with the ruffles and lace, sparing with fire and soap, and to complain about items lost in former washes. The women work until dusk, sometimes having to 'piece the Summer's day with Candle-light';

Abstracts of Acts of Parliament and Cases with Opinions sought of the Judges upon the following Taxes, viz, upon Houses, Windows, Servants . . . , 2 vols. (London: J. Butterworth, 1797), vol. I, pp. 282–3.

[52] Stephen Duck and Mary Collier, *Stephen Duck, 'The Thresher's Labour', Mary Collier, 'The Woman's Labour', Two Eighteenth Century Poems*, ed. E. P. Thompson and Marian Sugden (London: Merlin Press, 1989), p. viii.

[53] Donna Landry, *The Muses of Resistance. Labouring-Class Women's Poetry in Britain, 1739–1796* (Cambridge: Cambridge University Press, 1990), p. 59.

[54] The increased use of cotton as the century passed also spelled changes in washing techniques. For the impact on servants who undertook laundry work, especially the washing of children's clouts, see Carolyn Steedman, 'A Boiling Copper and Some Arsenic. Servants, Childcare and Class Consciousness in late Eighteenth-century England', *Critical Inquiry*, forthcoming.

by now the 'Blood runs trickling down/Our wrists and fingers'. This seasonal wash (perhaps organised thrice yearly, for in winter, frozen pumps and wells meant storing up dirty linen against the spring) earned the women 'Sixpence or Eightpence' each.[55]

Mary Collier was emphatic about the characteristic of charring, which was that 'we oft change work for work'. Scouring the pewter was next on her list, another task that took from early morning until late at night. Then, a little while later, the message would be sent by the mistress to the cottages that 'She wants our Help, because the Beer runs low'. Hard work, lack of sleep, constant nagging by the mistress, are all part of Collier's complaint about the charwoman's lot; but so is what the job does to 'all the Perfections Woman once could boast', now 'quite obscur'd, and altogether lost'. She emphasises the state of her hands, ruined and bloodied by cleaning 'brass and iron' and, of course, by the eighteen-hour laundry session. (The servant tax appeal system shows just how much metal-cleaning char-men undertook in the post-1777 era, particularly the filthy job – and the sure ruination of hands that it involved – of cleaning carbon-steel knives.[56])

Householders and employers recorded these comings and goings by casual domestic staff – male and female – fitfully and ambiguously. It was unusual to do what Frances Hamilton did in 1798 and 1799 and devote two whole pages of one of her numerous ledgers and daybooks to Betty Huckleborough, who came in for mornings or afternoons to sweep the bedrooms out, and on one occasion to get breakfast ready,[57] though without this meticulous kind of recording one wonders how anyone ever arrived at an agreed final payment. Washing, ironing and brewing were household activities that called upon this kind of labour seasonally, though in Phoebe Beatson's case, pregnancy and child care had more to do with her need for help. The Lingards household brewed every three months or so, with Phoebe collecting the ingredients ('Phoebe went for 2 Sticks & 1 Peck o' Malt & Hops'), Murgatroyd usually noting the event in his diary.[58] The first record of Phoebe having help with it is during the last stages of her pregnancy, in August 1802. In May 1804 when the baby was nearly two years old and 'poorly', help was also noted.[59] The same Sally Pogson came in later

[55] Landrey, *Muses*, pp. 20–2.
[56] Many thanks to the CookShop of Regent Street, Leamington Spa and the Metal Conservation Department of the Victoria and Albert Museum, for helping me to understand what you did with non-stainless steel knives before you could take a Brillo pad to them. Sand and tallow, or emery (aluminium oxide) and oil were probably used. Lisa Pickard, *Dr Johnson's London. Life in London, 1740–1770* (London: Weidenfeld and Nicholson, 2000), pp. 118–19. Phillipa Glanville and Hilary Young (eds.), *The Art of Elegant Eating. Four Hundred Years of Dining in Style* (London: V&A Publications, 2002), pp. 54–9.
[57] Hamilton, DD/FS 5/3, Farm Diary (December 1798 and January 1799).
[58] Murgatroyd, Diaries, KC 242/1 (12 September 1789).
[59] Murgatroyd Diaries, KC 242/(13 August 1802): 'Sally Baxter helped Phoebe brew'. KC242/7 (2 and 4 May 1804): 'Sally Pogson brewing for us this day . . . Sally Pogson got tea with us gron'd for Phebe, Child poorly, helped her to turn . . .'

in the month to help Phoebe with the cleaning.[60] There is no record of what Sally Pogson and the rest of the Slaithwaite crew who helped out were paid. Earlier, before the baby, Murgatroyd's niece Hannah had 'helped' during one of Phoebe's absences in Halifax, and her labour surely came free.[61]

The time between washes (and thus ironing seasons) probably contracted over this period, and there is some evidence that washing work might devolve on to resident domestics, especially in substantial households. Did Thomas Cooper of New Place Farm, Guestling, in Sussex specify in the hiring agreement of 1793 that his new maidservant Lucy Lambert was 'to do the young Child's washing' in exchange for a month's holiday, because Dame Hilder, usually bought in to do a two-day wash, refused to handle dirty nappies?[62] He had agreed an extra guinea a year with Ruth Eversfield, his cook maid in 1792, for doing the baby's washing,[63] and in 1803 gave Addy Griffin, another in his stream of cooks, 'a present of a gown for Washing the child's clouts'.[64] Households obviously came to a variety of arrangements for doing small washes. For rural Norfolk Mary Hardy's daybook shows little change in the thirty-six years her household diary covers. Her two maidservants and one outside washerwoman (often a former maid, now married, who knew the ways of the household) did the heavy wash every four, five or six weeks; they also did more frequent, lighter washes: 'Maids and Goody Thompson washed a fortnight's linen'; 'Day maid and Goody Ram washed'. In April 1791 in a moment of experiment, they 'borrowed Mr Davy's Washing Mill & washed 3 weeks linnen without a work woman'. The use of the washing-mill was a one-off for the Hardy household, but washing machines were available, and promoted widely at least in the West Country. Henry Murrell, who advertised their use to the Bath and West of England Society, thought their great advantage was that you could get 'a stout lad' to stand there turning it, and conserve the maids' skill for the later stages of the laundry process.[65]

In a recent account of eighteenth-century servants, Bridget Hill warned against our post-nineteenth-century assumptions, in taking too much notice of what label a servant was given (groom, cook, footman, man, maid) as any

---

[60] Murgatroyd Diaries, KC232/7 (18 May 1804).

[61] Murgatroyd Diaries, KC 242/5 (25 June 1800).

[62] Thomas Cooper of New Place Farm in Guestling, Household Account Book 1788–1824, AMS 6191, East Sussex County Record Office, Lewes (14 March 1795, 21 January 1790).

[63] Thomas Cooper, Account Book (29 December 1792).

[64] Thomas Cooper, Account Book (30 December 1803). From a much later hygienic perspective, the kitchen was, unfortunately, the best place to do a baby's washing: the only source of painfully acquired – and possibly hot – water in the winter months. Mountains of filthy nappies could not be kept for the regular wash.

[65] Mary Hardy, *Mary Hardy's Diary. With an Introduction by B. Cozent Hardy*, Norfolk Record Society, vol. XXXVII (1968), pp. 5, 31, 45, 73, 78. I am grateful to Mrs Margaret Bird for new information about Hardy's household arrangements. Henry Murrell, 'On a New Washing Machine', *Letters and Papers on Agriculture*, vol. V (Bath: Bath and West of England Society, 1793), p. 469.

kind of guide to what it was they actually did by way of work, and also against interpreting 'housework' in its modern, narrow meaning of cleaning, dusting and polishing – in a house. Hers, along with Peter Laslett's and Peter Earle's, is a claim for the relatively ungendered nature of mid- to late-eighteenth-century domestic labour, and for a fuller meaning of 'housework', as that which kept everyday life going within a household.[66] Like maids, menservants engaged actively in 'housework' regardless of their formal titles (though in 1773, whilst Mary Hardy's maids washed and the men 'cleansed', they were actually skimming the yeast off the beer to arrest fermentation, not washing down the yard or doing any kind of housework); but in a much grander Doncaster household than this Norfolk one, in 1801 'Charles Browning came into . . . service as under butler . . . he engages to assist in cleaning through the dining room and hall . . .'[67] Hill points to what can be read out of newspaper advertisements, about the plethora of tasks that might be assigned to male and female servants, and indeed, most arguments for this kind of domestic multi-tasking have been read from similar sources, or from advice manuals. Mary Cooke of Doncaster, devoting the years of her widowhood to safeguarding her little boy's inheritance, recorded in her day- and letter-book the notices she had placed in the York newspaper. In 1763, she was after 'A Sober Orderly Man who understands a Kitchin Gardin & knows how to Wait at Table &c'; and in 1766 'a Grave Clean handy Woman that can Wash & get up Linnin well and do plain Work knows how to clean Rooms to Pickel & make Pastry & have some knowledge in the Cooking so as to inspect ye Dinners being sent up neatly'. What was wanted was a woman 'used to family Business'. In the much grander household that Hester Piozzi (formerly Thrale) presided over at Streatham Park during the 1780s, even the lovely Mary Johnson, the 'femme de chambre' who possessed all the qualities of beauty and amiability that her mistress required in such a servant, often turned her hand to house cleaning along with the other, inferior maids.[68] Here, in Doncaster in the 1760s and Streatham in the 1780s, 'family business' did not include activity in the kitchen garden, though we must assume that it did for many domestics in one- or two-servant households. Up near Huddersfield, in March 1794, Phoebe Beatson was employed in putting down 'ye peas and Beans in ye Garden'; and in April 1796, Murgatroyd recorded that for

---

[66] Bridget Hill, *Servants. English Domestics in the Eighteenth Century* (Oxford: Clarendon Press, 1996), pp. 22–3, 26, 32–3. Peter Earle, *A City Full of People. Men and Women of London, 1650–1750* (London: Methuen, 1994), p. 83. Peter Laslett and Richard Wall (eds.), *Household and Family in Past Time. Comparative Studies in the Significance and Structure of the Domestic Group over the Last Three Centuries* (Cambridge: Cambridge University Press, 1972), p. 151.

[67] Mrs Mary Cooke, Copy Letter Book, 1763–1767, Davies-Cooke of Ouston, DD.DC/H7/1/1, Doncaster Metropolitan Borough Council Archives, Doncaster.

[68] Edward A. Bloom and Lilian D. Bloom (eds.), *The Piozzi Letters. Correspondence of Hester Lynch Piozzi, 1784–1821. Volume 1, 1784–1791* (London and Toronto: Delaware University Press, 1989), p. 65.

one whole day she had 'garden'd, sow'd her small seeds – She has put down ye Beans and peas'.[69] The multiplicity of tasks undertaken by Frances Hamilton's 'footman' in the 1780s have already been noted, here and elsewhere; the ubiquitous Huckleborough family, who provided her with so much casual labour, produced Richard in November 1796, who was paid 2s 6d for waiting at table, 2s for one day's labour on the farm, and 17s 6d for '15 days in ye Garden'.[70] His work was dictated by the way in which a particular household organised itself, his labour bearing strict comparison with that of the woman hired to cook, clean, attend the kitchen garden and clean out the necessary house. This kind of labour blurred the distinction between outdoor or husbandry work, and domestic work, for high court judges, and in everyday understanding. Boys apprenticed by the parish to a householder were perhaps most likely to perform heterogeneous services indoors and out – and in one case at least it was most likely for it to be recognised that that is what they *did* and what they *were*: the indentures of Delavel Forster Kerr were produced at the assessed tax appeals meeting in Berwick upon Tweed in February 1805 to show that the boy had actually been bound 'as a husbandry servant' and 'in every other Domestic capacity' (his employer was attempting to avoid the tax by showing that domestic service was *included* in the exempted category 'servant in husbandry').[71]

On these first questions of the servant's labour, we may conclude, then, that domestic work was not confined to the four walls of a house; that a household was managed and organised in its kitchen garden as well as its kitchen, in the yard and stable and byre as well as in its houseplace and bedrooms. Casual labour was bought in regularly and irregularly to 'help'. This was the word used by Mary Collier in the 1730s to describe the charring work she did along with the other village women. She possessed a full, sophisticated and resentful understanding of this kind of labour relationship, and a nice and sardonic interpretation of the mistress's motives (in chivvying, complaining, bringing on appropriately timed refreshments). The vocabulary of 'help' aligns itself with what Robert Steinfeld and others have noted about the United States, where hatred of the term 'servant' forced into being the noun 'help', in legal and domestic usage.[72] In England, 'help' remained the word of those who embodied it, and those who employed it; there was no place in English law where it might gain currency. Except, perhaps, under post-1777 taxation law. In her history of housework over a three-century span, Catherine Davidson claims that from the

---

[69] Murgatroyd Diaries, KC 242/2 (28 March 1794); KC 242/6 (12 April 1796).

[70] Frances Hamilton, Household and Farm Account Book, 1791–1799, DD/FS 5/8 (21 November 1796).

[71] 'Assessed Taxes and Inhabited Houses Duties. Judges Opinions, 1805–1830', Vol. 1, July 1805–May 1807, Opinion 17 'Male Servants Parish Apprentices', PRO, IR 70/1, The National Archives, Kew.

[72] Steinfeld, *Invention*, p. 26. Hill, *Servants*, p. 35.

1780s onwards, 'almost everybody was discouraged from employing boys and men in a domestic capacity', and that the servant tax 'meant that apprentices and farm labourers could not do any housework on a part-time or casual basis, without their employers taking the risk of financial penalty'.[73]

Even Sarah Trimmer may help us with this shift in perspective, on service, labour and gender in the later eighteenth century. In disguise as the 'Servant's Friend' in 1787, she has a rector's wife pause to wonder whether her new boy was going to find it all too much for him; feel 'afraid he was too young to undertake all their work, as they kept a horse, two cows, four pigs, made butter, and had a little garden to weed and water, besides waiting at table, cleaning shoes and going on errands'. In this musing, she omits the child care that was also clearly a duty.[74] In non-fictional Soham, Cambridgeshire in 1779, John Peach, surgeon and apothecary, was charged by the tax commissioners for twelve-year-old James Bye who, Peach claimed, was 'chiefly employed about the shop [and] plays with and takes care of the two children'. Satirising the domestic arrangements of 1780s' central Warwickshire from the perspective of the 1830s and its hierarchised job descriptions, the novelist Kate Thomson described a 'man-servant . . . [who] had for many years held the multifarious offices of groom, valet, master of the robes, inspector of wigs, coachman, gardener, butler, brewer, footman and keeper to [his employer]'.[75] Dimly, out of the mist of our conventional understandings of the gendered division of labour, and all our post-nineteenth-century categorisations of 'servant', there emerges the figure of the char-man. Looking northwards, to Haworth, or Hipperholme (or to the end of this book), we could call him Joseph, for the curmudgeonly old man hired as a servant in husbandry to the Wuthering Heights masters for some sixty years also cooks (porridge for the main part), carries trays up and down stairs, helps the gentlemen dress, and looks after the children.[76]

Phoebe Beatson, along with the fictional servants labouring with passions and porridge up on the Pennine Ridge, served her time in a period of great structural change in the service relationship. Under the old poor law, high court judges increasingly emphasised the importance of contract in measuring and regulating it. And tax law was perhaps more deeply implicated in creating new ways of understanding and living the domestic contract. The law itself and its

---

[73] Caroline Davidson, *A Woman's Work is Never Done. A History of Housework in the British Isles, 1650–1950* (London: Chatto and Windus, 1982), pp. 180–1. Hill, *Servants*, pp. 22–43.

[74] Sarah Trimmer, *The Servant's Friend, an Exemplary Tale; Designed to Enforce the Religious Instructions given at Sunday and other Charity Schools, by Pointing Out the Practical Application of Them in a State of Servitude*, 2nd edn (London: T. Longman, 1787), pp. 42, 48–9.

[75] Commissioners of Excise, *Abstract of Cases and Decisions on Appeal Relating to the Tax on Servants* (London: Mount and Page for T. Longman and T. Cadell, 1781), Cambridgeshire. Katherine Thomson, *Constance. A Novel. In Three Volumes* (London: Richard Bentley, 1833), vol. I, pp. 283–4.

[76] See below, chapter 10.

administration in provincial places, asserted the servant's personhood, and his or her capacities. Tax law named him or her a luxury item, but at the same time, minutely considered what he or she *did*, and what kind of labour was involved in cleaning the knives and watching the children. In the Lockean servant, the skills and capacities are the master's: they do not exist in the man or the woman doing the work. All the deliberations that accompanied the servant tax, on the other hand, located them *in* the man or the woman performing certain acts and tasks. The servant will become what he or she does, capacities and skills named and recognised obliquely by the law that must, in that recognition, make them legal persons.

The surprise of John Murgatroyd at being served a notice of assessment on Phoebe Beatson was the surprise of thousands of employers across the country; they saw for the first time how very great was the interest of the fiscal-military state in the everyday arrangements by which they conducted their various household enterprises and the ordinary business of life. They may have heard with some astonishment the interest of the local commissioners in details of payment, the wearing of a wig by the boy you had just called in from the field to serve unexpected company, the dish of beans served in the elegant manner from behind by him in his temporary guise (a servant!), or merely carried to the dining room door by the wigless, grubby lad hurried in from the yard (not a servant!); their interest in the times when your serving maid was called to the house from your furniture showroom to play her other role, do bits and pieces in the kitchen and milk the household cow. But the taxes on horses produced more overt restructuring of time and work in some households. Gentlemen might alter the pattern of their pursuits to avoid the tax: 'when he rides . . . any one of the Horses', the commissioners reported of John Atkinson of Kirkland in Cumberland, 'he saddles it himself and when he returns home he takes care of it and on the day of such riding he has been particularly careful that neither his Servants or his son should take care of . . . [it] so he rode or saddled or bridled the same . . .'[77] All of this was to prevent the man being declared a groom, and thus liable to the tax. Crown surveyors were extremely interested in the saddling of horses, the leading of them out of the stable, the holding of bridles, the assistance with mounting. Mr John Kirby, schoolmaster of Catherick (Catterick) in the North Riding, told the appeal meeting that his school *was* his business. The surveyor may have seen his man 'act in the capacity of a groom, by leading . . . the horse out of stable' and waiting for him to mount, but his real work was to clean the schoolhouse and the boys' shoes, heat up the oven every morning for their food, do the brewing for this extended household and to work

---

[77] 'Assessed Taxes and Inhabited Houses Duties. Judges Opinions, 1805–1830', vol. 3, Feb. 1810–June 1813, PRO, IR 70/3, No. 609, 'Labourers or Husbandmen as Grooms or Cleaning Boots', The National Archives.

the land Kirby owned, in the capacity of a husbandman.[78] But none of these employers should have felt surprise at interest in these domestic arrangements, for the fiscal-military state had been interested in them for a very long time indeed, in the minute questioning of household arrangements under the law of settlement.

---

[78] Not a servant, thought the commissioners in this case, and the judges upheld their opinion. Commissioners of Excise, *Cases*, pp. 43–4, Catherick, North Riding of Yorkshire, 19 Dec. 1779. Richard Burn, *The Justice of the Peace and Parish Officer*, 15th edn, 4 vols. (London: T. Cadell, 1785), vol. II, pp. 126–31. Richard Burn, *The Justice of the Peace and Parish Officer. Continued to the Present Time by John Burn, Esq. his Son*, 17th edn, 4 vols. (London: A. Strahan and W. Woodfall, 1793), vol. IV, p. 156.

5   Working for a living

In some abstract realm of legal theory and political philosophising, Phoebe Beatson exercised John Murgatroyd's capacity to labour: she was an aspect of his legal personality, not he of hers. When she planted, and tended, and harvested the peas and beans in the kitchen garden, she turned his labour capacity into an object of use and consumption. He used no proxy in exercising his own energies and capacities in the service of the Church of England over an extraordinarily long period of time, in holy orders and as parochial schoolmaster. This was work as much as hers was, undertaken in the context of several West Riding parishes, and it needs to be seen as such, in order to understand the differences between him and his maidservant, and what bound them together in a relationship to each other.

Actually, he may have turned a hand on 'our Brewing Day', for all across the country (in grander households than the Lingards one, and with a faint air of the Marie Antoinette about them) gentlemen descended to back kitchens and brew houses, to try out the very latest in tubes and pipes and wort-boilers.[1] He seemed not to think himself above physical labour; he turned his hand to house-building as opposed to housework on one occasion, in June 1786: 'A hot day – look.g & helping ye 4 masons a little in carry'g on our intended Build'g.'[2] He was very interested in his maidservant's making of what appears to be a rag rug, recording over a week in 1790 her 'sewing ye sacking & (making) ye holes'.[3] Thirty years before in Blecheley, Buckinghamshire, the Reverend

---

[1] See, for example, the diaries of Bertie Greatheed of Guy's Cliffe, Warwick, owner of 600 War-wickshire acres (more elsewhere) and married to a niece of the Duke of Ancaster. 'Brewing' and 'brewed' were regular references in his diaries, 1805–19. Warwickshire County Record Office, CR 1707, Heber-Percy of Guy's Cliffe, 1759–1826. CR 1707/120 (18 March 1812, June 1814). As the pronounless 'brewing' (23 March 1812) was fitted in between a reading of Herodotus and helping his granddaughter practise her handwriting, perhaps his involvement was not great.

[2] Reverend John Murgatroyd, Diaries, KC 242/1, West Yorkshire Archive Service, Kirklees District, Huddersfield (2 June 1786).

[3] Murgatroyd Diaries, KC 242/1 (16 and 17 June 1790). It may not have been a rag rug at all, of course, but this is the way of making one. The presence of one in 1790s Slaithwaite disturbs a carefully constructed historiography of their domestic production. See Carolyn Steedman, 'What a Rag Rug Means', *Journal of Material Culture*, 3:3 (1998), pp. 259–81.

William Cole (a cookmaid and a boy made up his household) always noted 'Brewing', 'Washing' and 'Ironing' days in his diary, inscribing the elision of self and servant in the completion of tasks that is a feature of many eighteenth-century employers' writing. It is true that clerical diaries of this period belong to a distinct literary genre, in that they are not works of spiritual introspection so much as records of 'practical attempts to live a Christian life, and to minister to a congregation amid the practical difficulties of the real world'.[4] But it is true only where their point of comparison is the challenging odyssey of the seventeenth-century confessional sort, and when the practical domestic difficulties that so many of them enumerate are ignored. All diary-keeping householders used the same truncated diary-ese. With pronouns missing, it is quite impossible to work out who did what by way of household task. It was a convention of writing that inadvertently supported the legal fiction that master and man and mistress and maid were one person, engaged in the same work. Sometimes the presence of a pronoun effaced the servant. 'I carried 7 more loads of Hay from the Clay Pit Close,' the Reverend Cole recorded in July 1766, though there was clearly 'help' present, driving the cart and forking the hay, just as there was in the more descriptively accurate 'Had my Raspberry Jam & Currant Jelly made'.[5] In fact, Cole's involvement in the preservation of soft fruit was considerable – 'sent Jem to Wroughton to fetch me a Basket of Damsons from Mr Troutbeck's, with which my Maid made Damson Marmelade'; and he was surely present, or hovering, when two of the regular army of helpers who had come to cut out his new shirts and run him up some nightcaps and pillowcases, took over the kitchen to re-boil some runny elderberry jelly ('from 12 Cups full reduced it to 6 & a half').[6]

Who 'wip'd, dry'd, numbered' John Murgatroyd's 'Greek Books' in January 1794, and again in 1799 when he inventoried his entire library?[7] He may have shared the task with Phoebe Beatson, though with the first person singular absent, master merges with maid. Up near Colne, Elizabeth Shackleton merges with hers, in the washing of all the china in the china-closet. As Amanda Vickery remarks, we are never to know exactly how this task was carried out, who did what, and whether Mrs Shackleton got her hands wet or not.[8] If they did cart and boil, and wipe and dry, then William Cole, Elizabeth Shackleton and John

---

[4] J. C. D. Clark, 'England's Ancien Regime as a Confessional State', *Albion*, 21:3 (1989), pp. 450–75; p. 469.

[5] Francis Griffin Stokes (ed.), *The Blecheley Diary of the Reverend William Cole, MA, FSA, 1765–67* (London: Constable, 1931), pp. 71, 243.

[6] Stokes, *Blecheley Diary*, pp. 278, 275.

[7] Reverend John Murgatroyd, 'Authors Useful to be Read at School', Notebook, 1745–1802, unpaginated, 082.2 MUR, Slaithwaite Parish Collection, Special Collections, University of York, York.

[8] Amanda Vickery, *The Gentleman's Daughter. Women's Lives in Georgian England* (New Haven and London: Yale University Press, 1998), pp. 146–7.

Murgatroyd were briefly exercising capacities of their own that contract had bestowed on their servants. When the servant did these things, household tasks were brief enactments of a legal formulary. In that moment, by the mingling of their labour with the elderberries, Mrs Holt and Mrs Goodwin enabled William Cole to mingle *his* with the fruits of the earth, and take them into his possession, in the form of a well-set jelly. Things are harder to determine with the Greek books in the Lingards' parlour, for here, no commodity was produced. (Adam Smith faltered at the distinction between producing a jar of jelly and dusting something, as we have seen, though these were not his examples.[9]) The legal formulary depicted a one-way deal: the service contract did not alter by one jot the master's or the mistress's legal identity, whilst in dusting and washing and wiping, the servant *was*, in some sense, the employer.

John Murgatroyd gained a living inside and outside the structures of the labour contract. Contract regulated his schoolmastering, where the agreement to serve the trustees of Slaithwaite Free School could technically have been enforced in law. Ordination as a priest – the reading aloud of the Thirty-Nine Articles, the oaths of allegiance – constituted an agreement, or bond, to perform certain duties, in certain ways; but these things were not done under the kind of labour contract that regulated the relationship between him and Phoebe Beatson. Murgatroyd was interested in the legal framework of his profession. He copied out passages on the law as it affected parish clerks, and wrote an essay on the judgment of Lord Chief Justice Kenyon in 1799 (or it could have been a later one of Kenyon's, from 1800) on the question of clerical residence. In 1799 the Reverend Mr Blake's barrister produced elaborate reasons for his client's residing on his Devonshire estate rather than in the clergy house attached to St Leonard's Shoreditch in London. The action was brought by Blake to recover the eleven penalties for non-residence his bishop had extracted from him. He was in a poor state of health, it seemed; London made it worse. Lord Kenyon observed that a gentleman might suffer from the gout in Devon as well as London. ('Is it inconsistent with his very existence to reside in his parish?' The Lord Chief Justice thought not: 'I do not see that the case has been made out.') But the principle was more important than Blake's feeble plea, was, in fact, of matter to 'the general happiness of the community', for in every 'well constituted Government, there must be an attention to the service of God'. Indeed, 'religion must always be in strict alliance with the State, otherwise it is impossible, humanely considering things, anything can go on profoundly . . .' In former times, 'before the Reformation, it was among the crying offences of the Kingdom, that those to whom the celebration of religious service was committed, received the emoluments without any attention to the duties of their office'. Kenyon believed, though he was not certain, that it was 'among the

---

[9] See above, chapter 4.

preliminaries of every Vicar . . . to take an oath of residence'.[10] If he was not resident, he ought not to be paid. And in Kenyon's opinion – he had often been asked this – 'residence must be in the Parsonage-house'. A vicar must preach a weekly sermon, and should be there 'to look over the morals of his people, to set a good example, to conciliate their temper, and, if possible to bring about Christian charity and good will . . .' No matter if a bishop had intimated that an individual might dispense with residence: that 'would have had no legal effect on the consequences of this action': it was of 'infinite importance to the Public that the law . . . should be actively promulgated – that the Clergy must reside in their livings'. Murgatroyd took from this what he already knew, noting that 'Any Clergyman's tak.g on Himself in any Xn. Assembly, ye Cure of Souls, took on Himself at ye same Time to reside am.g 'em – the Bond only requir'd Him to do wt in Duty, Justice, & Morality, he was bound to do without it – so it was perfectly legal.'[11] He never held a living himself – was indeed, disappointed in his hopes of one, on more than one occasion – yet the living is the swiftest route to understanding the situation in which he exercised his capacities and labour, over a very long life. The living focused contemporary criticism of the Church of England, and its response – or lack of response – to changing social circumstances. Particularly after 1786, Murgatroyd was in person one of the many solutions the church devised for the problem of very large and sprawling West Riding parishes, increased population in new forms of settlement, want of buildings for worship and want of personnel.

Parishes were the vital administrative units of the state and local government as well as of the Church of England, and Murgatroyd knew three of them well. Halifax, where both he and Phoebe Beatson had been born and grew up, was one of the largest in England.[12] The church's hold was notoriously weak in its upland districts of independent weavers and farmers; the Baptist revival spread from the upper reaches of the Calder Valley, and it was an early centre of Methodism.[13] Now, in the later part of the century, both Murgatroyd and Beatson lived a

[10] 'Law Report', *The Times*, 10 May 1799, p. 3. Kenyon was right in his supposition. See John Henry Blunt, *The Book of Church Law*, 11th edn (London: Longman Green, 1921), pp. 227–53. Richard Burn, *Ecclesiastical Law. Corrected by Robert Philip Tyrwhitt*, 8th edn, 4 vols. (London: A. Strahan, etc., 1824), vol. III, pp. 294–317. Richard Burn, *Ecclesiastical Law*, 6th edn, 4 vols. (London: T. Cadell and W. Davies, 1799), vol. III, pp. 295–318. William Watson, *The Clergyman's Law; or, the Complete Incumbent*, 4th edn (London: privately printed, 1747). For the later case involving residence that Murgatroyd may have been discussing, see 'Law Report', *The Times*, 11 November 1800, p. 3.

[11] Reverend John Murgatroyd, 'Ask, Read, Retain, Teach', KC249/9, West Yorkshire Archive Service, Kirklees District, Huddersfield, pp. 2, 107, 'Law'.

[12] Hitherto thought to be the largest, it now seems that Whalley in Lancashire had that distinction. See Michael Snape, *The Church in an Industrial Society. The Lancashire Parish of Whalley in the Eighteenth Century* (Woodbridge: Boydell Press, 2003), p. 6.

[13] Edward Royle, 'The Church of England and Methodism in Yorkshire. From Monopoly to Free Market', *Northern History*, 33 (1997), pp. 137–61.

confessional life divided between two other parishes, those of Almondbury and Huddersfield. Almondbury (sprawling too, but not as large as Halifax), where Murgatroyd had been non-resident curate to Edward Rishton between 1755 and 1767, contained the township of Lingards. Slaithwaite, just the other side of the Colne, was in the parish of Huddersfield, and its living on the nomination of its Evangelical vicars. In terms of land tenure, Slaithwaite and Lingards were one – 'the two townships . . . form one manor' – held by the Dartmouth family, and the chapel in Slaithwaite (there was none in Lingards) was kept in repair by a church rate levied on both townships.[14] (This did not prevent the vicar of Almondbury's objections to the Slaithwaite incumbent between 1761 and 1767, Samuel Farley, preaching in Lingards and in Linthwaite.) Lingards was separate in secular terms, however, at least as far as the poor law was concerned. It was the Lingards overseer who came 'for Phoebe to go to Justice abt. Belonging to ye Town', in April 1802.

Not only were Lingards and Slaithwaite two settlements, but the two parish structures to which they belonged inscribed two different theologies and confessional convictions within the Church of England. Murgatroyd experienced both Rishton's highly conventional Anglicanism, and Huddersfield's Evangelicalism. From 1761 onwards, Slaithwaite's perpetual curates were appointed by the vicar of Huddersfield, all of them men in the mould of Henry Venn (vicar between 1759 and 1771) who had played a key role in the Evangelical revival within the Church of England.[15] (Thomas Wilson, Slaithwaite incumbent from 1771 to 1809, had the greatest personal effect on Murgatroyd.)

When William Cobbett saw the Church '*everywhere*' in this period, he looked at a landscape given its depth and perspective by church and chapel spires, noted the sheer number of functionaries the Church employed, and the way in which there was simply no place outside the parish and its church, as both a secular and

---

[14] Charles Augustus Hulbert, *Annals of the Church in Slaithwaite (near Huddersfield) West Riding of Yorkshire from 1593–1864, in Five Lectures* (London: Longman, 1864), pp. 14–15. Judith Jago and Edward Royle, *The Eighteenth-century Church in Yorkshire. Archbishop Drummond's Primary Visitation of 1764*, Borthwick Papers 95 (York: University of York, 1999), p. 30.

[15] Judith Jago, *Aspects of the Georgian Church. Visitation of the Diocese of York, 1761–1776* (London: Associated University Press, 1997), pp. 170–1. Henry Venn (ed.), *The Life and a Selection from the Letters of the late Henry Venn, MA*, 4th edn (London: John Hatchard, 1836), pp. vii–viii. C. J. Stranks, *Anglican Devotion. Studies in the Spiritual Life of the Church of England between the Reformation and the Oxford Movement* (London: SCM Press, 1961), pp. 149, 205. Royle, 'Church of England', p. 137. Hulbert, *Annals*, pp. 56, 68–9. William Gibson, *Church, State and Society, 1760–1850* (London: Macmillan, 1994), pp. 58–87. Chapelries (places of public worship, but dependent on established churches), like curates (essentially, assistants to beneficed clergymen in their regular churches), were both part of a solution to the want of church buildings in districts like the West Riding. See F. C. Mather, 'Georgian Churchmanship Reconsidered. Some Variations in Anglican Public Worship, 1714–1830', *Journal of Ecclesiastical History*, 36:2 (1985), pp. 255–83. Noreen Vickers, *Parson's Pence. The Finances of Eighteenth-century North Yorkshire Clergymen* (Hull: University of Hull, 1994).

confessional unit of the society he surveyed.[16] This 'everywhere' is also the foundation of modern historical theses about the eighteenth-century Church of England. Being all-pervasive and inextricable from the parishes in which it had material existence, it was impossible to avoid. Its spiritual, legal and topographical dominance measured out a commitment that was 'much greater than historians allow . . . [this] is perhaps the last period in which popular faith can be taken for granted'.[17] The Church of England was thus 'a form of identification linking rich and poor in a common world view', and 'the spiritual face of the English state'.[18] Or, in other discussions of these religious and secular structures, there emerges the idea of the 'confessional state', of a society and a social order bound together by the precepts and management of a particular faith.[19] The parish was the place where church and state were literally *seen* as a union, and experienced as such.[20] This confessional state was not particularly well staffed. In the later eighteenth century, only about half the parishes in the West Riding had resident incumbents.[21] Pluralities (the holding of two, or even three livings by one man) were common, though they were rarely more than two or three miles apart. In his retirement, Murgatroyd was a one-man solution to the problems of multiple livings, a godsend to the clergymen of the Halifax–Huddersfield region, making their elaborate arrangements to keep the system going. Above all, he helped the West Riding church fulfil what was understood as its most important duty, which was to provide public worship on Sundays. The expectation was that there would be two services, with the sermon being delivered in the morning rather than the afternoon.[22] Murgatroyd's walking and riding of a Sunday maps an area twenty miles or so around Lingards. Arrangements were often as elaborate as they were in January 1802, when 'Rev Bellas sent his Son to ask me to take his Duty tomorrow – He takes ye Duty at Mirfield for Revd Cookson – I promised if Health & weather permit to go to Marsden.'[23] He did go the next day, borrowing a horse from the village and taking his nephew Joseph with him to ride behind. He did all the duty

---

[16] Jeremy Gregory and Jeffrey S. Chamberlain (eds.), *The National Church in Local Perspective. The Church of England and the Regions, 1660–1800* (Woodbridge: Boydell Press, 2003), p. 2.

[17] Gibson, *Church, State and Society*, p. 10.

[18] John Walsh and Stephen Taylor, 'The Church and Anglicanism in the "Long" Eighteenth Century', in John Walsh, John Haydon and Stephen Taylor (eds.), *The Church of England, c.1689–1883. From Toleration to Tractarianism* (Cambridge: Cambridge University Press, 1993), p. 27. Jago and Royle, *Church in Yorkshire*, p. 6.

[19] Clark, 'England's Ancien Regime as a Confessional State'.

[20] William Gibson, *The Achievement of the Anglican Church, 1689–1800. The Confessional State in Eighteenth-century England* (Lewiston, N.Y.: E. Mellen, 1995), pp. 191–2, 195.

[21] Jago and Royle, *Church in Yorkshire*, p. 19.

[22] 'Morning service could be said at any time before about half-past one in the afternoon, depending on the weather and how far the clergyman (and the people) had to travel.' Jago and Royle, *Church in Yorkshire*, p. 4.

[23] Murgatroyd Diaries, KC 242/7 (16 January 1802). When he had been severely ill in 1789, Phoebe Beatson had had to tramp all round the neighbourhood with letters cancelling similar

at Marsden, packing in '2 Xtenings & 1 Church'g' ('ye Woman gave me 1 shillg.') between morning and afternoon service, and having his dinner with Mrs Bellas.[24] If he stayed the whole day to do both services, dinner was usual, though bachelor incumbents might take him to the pub rather than ask a maid to cook on a Sunday.[25] This kind of 'neighbourly help' in leading public worship – 'the duty' – was reciprocated by fee and hospitality.[26] Murgatroyd appears to have earned the fee that was common across the country, for curates taking other men's services (they were known as 'the gallopers') – 10s 6d; only when he was very old, or the weather very bad, did Murgatroyd borrow a horse to do his Sunday work.[27]

Preaching was central to worship, 'a good sermon was expected by the congregation as well as the archbishop', and Murgatroyd had many up his sleeve and bound in volumes in his house.[28] Sermonising inscribed John Murgatroyd's identity as a minister of Christ, certainly for himself, and probably for his many congregations. He devoted more written words to copying and composing sermons than to anything else in the massive quantity of writing he produced during his lifetime, and possessed more than fifty volumes of them, published between the 1660s and 1790s. He never used the mail-order services that were available to lazier or less scrupulous clerics.[29] Over a forty-year period he kept careful records of the biblical texts he preached on, and the churches and chapels where sermons had been delivered (these records became even more important after 1786, when he became peripatetic).[30] Looking over Murgatroyd's immense

---

arrangements. Lancelot Bellas was the Evangelical who had obtained the Marsden living by popular demand instead of Murgatroyd, in 1777. See above, chapter 3.

[24] See Anthony Russell, *The Clerical Profession* (London: SPCK, 1980), p. 54 for the two-hour interval between services, in which churching, baptism, marriage and burial were performed. Murgatroyd Diaries, KC 242/7 (17 January 1802).

[25] Murgatroyd Diaries KC242/6 (4 April 1802). On 3 April at Meltham, he had dined with Revd Armistead at the public house after service.

[26] Jago, *Aspects of the Georgian Church*, pp. 165–6 for 'neighbourly help'. Russell, *Clerical Profession*, p. 53 for leading public worship as the 'foundation charter' of the cleric's role, known simply as 'the duty'.

[27] Russell, *Clerical Profession*, p. 55.   [28] Jago and Royle, *Church in Yorkshire*, p. 6.

[29] The Reverend John Trusler had set his mail-order scheme going in 1769, an off-shoot of his academy for teaching pulpit oratory 'mechanically'. James Downey, *The Eighteenth Century Pulpit. A Study in the Sermons of Butler, Berkeley, Secker, Sterne, Whitefield and Wesley* (Oxford: Clarendon Press, 1969), pp. 7–8. Twelve of his sermons (set in cursive print, so you could pretend they were your very own) are appended to John Trusler, *Memoirs of the Life of the Rev. John Trusler. With his Opinions on a Variety of Interesting Subjects and his Remarks through a long Life, on Men and Manners. Written by Himself. Replete with Humorous, Useful and Entertaining Anecdote. Part I* (Bath: John Brown, 1806). It is not clear whether they were still available in 1806. They had been ten years before. The London supplier's name was given in the appendix.

[30] Murgatroyd, 'Authors Useful'. See Françoise Deconinck-Brossard, '"We Live so far North". The Church in the North East of England', in Gregory and Chamberlain, *National Church in a Local Perspective*, pp. 223–42, and Françoise Deconinck-Brossard, *Dr John Sharp. An Eighteenth-Century Northumbrian Preacher* (Durham: St Mary's College, 1995), for a similar kind of record-keeping.

labours in planning and recording them, the Reverend Hulbert (who occupied the Slaithwaite parsonage a century after Murgatroyd might reasonably have hoped to do) did not think very highly of him as a preacher. 'I do not think he was very eminent,' he concluded, 'but labourious and conscientious, and took great pains in the preparation of his sermons.' He discerned in them 'the moral style' of one of Slaithwaite's previous parsons, Joseph Thorns (fl.1727–60), and was convinced that after Thorns's death, Murgatroyd used 'the actual sermons of that gentleman', with 'doctrine . . . not very distinct; the subjects being chiefly practical or rational'.[31] But if you spend – for example – thirty pages, as Murgatroyd did in 1747, in extracting from the second volume of Beveridge's sermons, subjecting them to critical analysis, noting the rhetorical moves that have been made, and turning back to the biblical texts on which each is based, then you can scarcely help using your data-bank over the coming years.[32]

Sermon piracy was rampant, clergymen eager to learn shorthand so that they could filch each other's rhetoric, and bequeathing clerical neighbours one's sermons was common.[33] Hulbert conceded that Murgatroyd may have rewritten and reformulated Thorns's sermons. The last commonplace book he kept shows him in the process of composing what may have been his own orations. Here his thoughts are too brief (what he wrote would take perhaps ten minutes to read aloud, at the slow pace demanded by eighteenth-century church architecture) to be the reworking of somebody else's full forty-minute sermon.[34] They were probably notes, or summaries, to be developed from the planning stage once in the pulpit. His subjects were, indeed, often rational and practical (though I think that Hulbert was right, in detecting a certain Evangelical enthusiasm in some of his 1790s sermons, when he came more under the influence of Slaithwaite's Reverend Mr Wilson). Yet a preacher who served so frequently in other men's churches must have developed a fine sense of what local people and

---

[31] Hulbert, *Annals*, pp. 25–44, 56. Murgatroyd's own sermons have not survived, so it is impossible to judge whether he really did use Thorns's sermons as his own. Hulbert's judgement may have been based on a note in the 'Book of Records', of 'The great Mischief of Detracting & evil Speaking: wth an Enquiry into ye Motives & Inducemts to ym. A Sermon preach'd in ye Parish Church of Batley, in Yorkshire, on Sunday October 26, 1729, by Joseph Thorns, A. B. Curate of Slaighwaite in Yorkshire. London: printed in 1732 price 6d'.

[32] Murgatroyd, 'Book of Records', 'January 14 1747: Extracts from Beveridge's Sermons, Vol. 2'. William Beveridge, *The Works of the Right Reverend Father in God, Dr William Beveridge . . . Containining* [sic] *all his sermons, as well those published by himself, as those since his death*, 2nd edn, 2 vols. (London: William Innys, 1729). Some time later he devoted eighteen pages of densely written foolscap pages to Robert Warren, *Practical Discourses on Various Subjects. Proper for all Families. In two volumes* (London: Edmund Parker, 1723).

[33] Downey, *Eighteenth-century Pulpit*, p. 5. W. Fraser Mitchell, *English Pulpit Oratory from Andrewes to Tillotson. A Study of its Literary Aspects* (London: SPCK, 1932), pp. 30–8. Sermon piracy may have been the reason for Murgatroyd's very great interest in shorthand (see below, chapter 6); but he scarce had time to listen to anyone else preach, being always at the job himself.

[34] Trusler's mail-order sermons take forty minutes to say aloud, at a slow pace. I base this judgement of Murgatroyd's sermon writing on the notebook he kept in the 1790s, 'Ask, Read, Retain, Teach'.

incumbent wanted, and tailored what he wrote to their expectations.[35] He was taking services at Slaithwaite regularly by the mid-1790s. He rarely repeated himself. He laid out the pages of the notebook in which he recorded sermon topics and texts so that he could compare what he had preached, across the years. He sometimes noted that he had laboured hard on a particular sermon: 'Revel in my Sanctuary: I am the Lord – this written 2nd Time,' he wrote in 1788.[36]

Clergymen had long been counselled to say what had to be said '*plainly, – seriously, – tenderly, – patiently*', and so Murgatroyd seems always to have done, dispensing good advice, to good neighbours, so that they might 'learn with Continuance what is to be done by 'em – what thoughts they must have – what words they must speak – what things they must do, while pushing thro' this world, to a world where they must be forever'.[37] Everyone, clergy and laity alike, should attempt to live as comfortably 'as is to be expected in the Passage thro' a cumbersome & troublesome world'. The way to do this was to contemplate one's life and its uncertainty, and the sureness of death.[38] He saw himself perhaps as the mainstream of the Anglican clergy did, 'not as priestly mediators between God and man, dispensing sacraments, but as partial educators and spiritual and moral leaders and guides'.[39]

But he did dispense the sacraments. One of the few occasions on which he complained about the congregation waiting for him after a Sunday tramp was at Deanhead on Christmas Day 1794, when he 'did all ye Duty . . . [but there were] only 3 yt received Sacrament . . . it is a Pity yt People are so inconsiderate'.[40] Of the two sacraments administered by the eighteenth-century Church of England, baptism was by far the most popular with the laity; for the main part, they displayed as little enthusiasm as did the Deanhead congregation for holy communion. It was difficult to find a communion service anyway, as they were mostly limited to festival Sundays (though some towns had one once a month).[41] Offering bread and wine as part of the service decreased as the century passed – it was offered perhaps four times a year – and an ante-communion (the normal service of morning prayer) became usual. This was what John Murgatroyd officiated over on most of his Sunday mornings across

---

[35] For sermonising and what the laity wanted, see Michael Snape, *The Church in an Industrial Society*, pp. 15–16.

[36] Murgatroyd, 'Authors Useful'.

[37] Peter Doddridge, *Sermons on the Education of Children. Preached at Northampton. With a Recommendatory Preface by the Reverend Mr David Stone*, 3rd edn (London: M. Fenner, 1743). This compilation of excellent advice for 'pushing through this world' was not actually in Murgatroyd's library. Murgatroyd Diaries, KC 242/6 (31 December 1802).

[38] Murgatroyd Diaries, KC242/2 (31 December 1794).

[39] Walsh and Taylor, 'Church and Anglicanism', p. 14.

[40] Murgatroyd Diaries, KC 242/2 (25 December 1794).

[41] Mark Smith, *Religion in an Industrial Society. Oldham and Saddleworth, 1740–1865* (Oxford: Clarendon Press, 1994), p. 51. Jago and Royle, *Church in Yorkshire*, p. 6.

the Colne Valley: it involved following the service as laid out in the Book of Common Prayer, but stopping short of administering the host and the wine.[42] There were powerful popular beliefs about communion which explain the small number receiving the sacrament at Deanhead. It was thought that you had to be exceptionally well prepared to receive the host, and that preparation demanded a high level of commitment. Contemporary guides to worship wavered between urging attendance on everyone ('Such among you as *are* in Business or service, and have not much Time at Command, [should] never make that an excuse for not coming to the Holy Sacrament'), whilst simultaneously presenting detailed procedures for readying yourself for such a duty. There was reassuring advice about a well-managed daily life being the best form of preparation, advice that Murgatroyd copied out in one of his notebooks, but in general, getting ready for communion seemed a harder thing than that.[43] One guide from the early nineteenth century recommended days of prayer in order to achieve the proper humility of mind, and the setting of a mind and heart to 'penitence and resolution to amendment'. Only then were you fit to attend the Lord's table.[44] Working people were offered this kind of advice as well. Sir James Stonhouse instructed those in 'the lower Stations of Life' in 1794 that they were to believe in God, to pray daily and praise Him. 'You are to be baptized', he continued; but above all 'you are to receive the Lord's Supper at which Bread and *wine* are to be eaten and drank . . . This is to be done in remembrance of Him who died as a Sacrifice to obtain pardon of Sin.'[45] There were particular concerns about domestic servants, left at home when a household went off to church. When Murgatroyd noted Phoebe's attendance at Slaithwaite chapel, it was nearly always at the afternoon service, by which time he might conceivably be home from morning duties the other side of the valley. But it is quite clear that many of the poorer sort – servants included – believed that holy communion was not for them, demanding a sophistication of spirituality that they did not possess and a form of preparation that could not easily be fitted into working lives.[46] Anyone who had spent a childhood in a parochial school, or all the Sundays of their thirteenth year having explained in kind but tortuous distinction what the difference between the 'Real Presence' and 'the Gift' was, might feel unfit to attend and that this was a game for gentlefolk, not for them. Instruction concerning holy communion was meant

---

[42] Russell, *Clerical Profession*, p. 101.

[43] 'The best Preparatn for ye Sacrament is the general Care and Endeavour of a good Life – is to live as become Xtians to live.' Murgatroyd, 'Ask, Read, Retain, Teach', KC249/9, p. 19.

[44] Peter Waldo, *An Essay on the Holy Sacrament* (London: J. F. & C. Rivington, 1821), pp. 14–21. Gibson, *Church, State and Society*, p. 25. Russell, *Clerical Profession*, p. 102.

[45] James Stonhouse, *The Most Important Truths and Duties of Christianity. Designed for those in the lower Stations of Life. Particularly for the Instruction of those who cannot read* (London: J. F. & C. Rivington, 1796).

[46] Snape, *Church in an Industrial Society*, pp. 16–19.

to be kind and tempered to a child's understanding; but it was just all rather difficult stuff, especially as the ideological enemy of Roman Catholicism was rarely named – except by the extraordinarily bold Dorothy Kilner who in her *Clear and Concise Account of the Origin and Design of Christianity* has one of her child characters exclaim, on hearing of the doctrine of the Real Presence, '"But Ma'am, how can they think that *bread* and *wine* is changed into *flesh* and *blood*, cannot they see?"'.[47]

Baptism was a sign of entry into the church, and was almost universally administered in childhood.[48] It did not involve the will or volition of the baptised; perhaps the enormous popularity of the rite of confirmation was an attempt to exercise that faith and will as an adult. Confirmation involved the now adolescent and catechised child repeating the vows that had been made on its behalf by god parents. This was to be done in the presence of a bishop. Mass confirmations attracted large crowds of onlookers, well-wishers – and of adults going through the rite for the second or third time. With only twenty-six bishops to 10,000 or so parishes in England, the candidates had to be packed in and processed: there was necessarily something of a production line about the occasion.[49] 'The Arch = BP confirms at Hudd: this day,' noted Murgatroyd in June 1786. 'Our Phoebe wth ye Girl in ye next House is gone to be confirmed there.'[50] At nineteen or twenty she was older than a confirmation candidate was meant to be, but not older than many actually were. In August 1800, Murgatroyd 'walked to Hudd: with neighbour Mellor's children to be confirmed – Hannah, Ann, Betty and Joseph, their servant Hannah Wood & servt. Matthew were all of 'em confirmed [by the Bishop of Chester]'.[51]

So popular was confirmation that stern warnings had to be issued about doing it more than once. 'How often ought any Christian come to be confirmed?' asked the nameless interlocutor of John Lewis's *The Church Catechism Explained*. 'But once,' was the answer. And were they not very ignorant people 'who go to the Bishop to be confirmed every time he confirms'? Yes, indeed, was the

---

[47] Dorothy Kilner, *A Clear and Concise Account of the Origin and Design of Christianity Intended as a second Part to the Work entitled 'The First Principles of Religion and the Existence of a Deity, explained in a Series of Dialogues adapted to the Capacity of the Infant Mind'*, 2 vols. (London: John Marshall, 1783), vol. II, pp. 133–41. This genre of literature is discussed in chapter 6 below. See W. K. Lowther Clarke, *Eighteenth-century Piety* (London: SPCK, 1944), p. 13. Christopher J. Cocksworth, 'The Presence of Christ in the Eucharist and the Formularies of the Church of England', *Journal of Ecumenical Studies*, 35:2 (1998), pp. 197–209.

[48] Jago and Royle, *Church in Yorkshire*, p. 19. Smith, *Religion in an Industrial Society*, p. 51.

[49] Robert Cornwall, 'The Right of Confirmation in Anglican Thought during the Eighteenth Century', *Church History*, 68 (1999), pp. 359–72.

[50] Murgatroyd Diaries, KC 242/1 (29 June 1786).

[51] Jago and Royle, *Church in Yorkshire*, p. 19 for age at confirmation. Murgatroyd Diaries, KC 242/5 (29 August 1800). The Mellor children were, in this order, 23, 20, 15 and 17 years of age. Murgatroyd, 'Ask, Read, Retain, Teach', KC249/9, pp. 88–9. Perhaps the older ones were doing it for the second time, with Murgatroyd's approval.

answer to that; but they did it because they did not really know what confirmation was – not a sacrament but the receiving of a bishop's blessing. That was why ignorant people called it 'being Bishop'd'.[52] For some, wary of communion, being bishop'd was perhaps an individual confession of faith, or at least of allegiance to the church, public in that it took place among crowds of teenagers and their audience of friends and family, and private at the same time, in that the motives and faith of those seeking it were not very likely to be discovered.

A child was prepared for confirmation by catechising. He or she had to be able to say the Creed, the Lord's Prayer, the Ten Commandments, and make the right responses to the Catechism, as laid out in the Book of Common Prayer. Making sure that this was done was one of a clergyman's most important duties, not only for the cure of individual souls, but because catechising produced the right kind of congregation for a preacher's later endeavours. 'The preaching of Sermons without catechising is like Building without first laying the Foundations,' was one contemporary opinion, and failure to undertake it was severely criticised.[53] It was thought that pluralities prevented catechising, for in them there was simply no clergyman to teach the children. In Huddersfield the enthusiastic Henry Venn had held an hour-long class once a fortnight in the 1760s; under the Reverend Rishton's regime in Almondbury there had been no classes at all in his later years of blindness and infirmity. His curate John Murgatroyd was schoolmastering and catechising the children of another parish, in Slaithwaite, five miles away.[54] Nevertheless, there was 'widespread catechising activity across the diocese of [York], in parishes large and small, urban and rural . . . evidence of a genuine and continuing effort by the local representatives of the established Church to bind their parishioners of the next generation in the fabric of the faith and worship of the nation'.[55] Murgatroyd helped produce this success story (though not in Almondbury when he was curate there between 1755 and 1767). In July 1781, for example, he 'catechiz'd above 40 young Persons at Sowerby,' giving them certificates ('Tickets') to show that they had been successful. He did this between morning and afternoon services, along with baptising three children, churching 'Some Women', and burying a corpse.[56]

---

[52] John Lewis, *The Church Catechism Explained, By Way of Question and Answer; and Confirmed by Scriptural Proofs*, 13th edn (London: John Rivington, 1766), pp. 94–5.

[53] Lewis, *Church Catechism*, p. vii. See Revd James Stonhouse, *The Religious Instruction of Children Recommended* (London: J. F. C. Rivington, 1791), pp. vii. Criticism like this repeated the strictures of Archbishop Tillotson, that public catechism was the foundation of a child's education. John Tillotson, *Six Sermons. I Stedfastness in religion. II. Family-religion. III. IV. V. Education of children. VI. The advantages of an early piety* (London: B. Aylmer, 1694), pp. 158–64. See Robert Hole, *Pulpits, Politics and Public Order in England, 1760–1832* (Cambridge: Cambridge University Press, 1989), pp. 138–40.

[54] Russell, *Clerical Profession*, pp. 130–41.

[55] Jago and Royle, *Church in Yorkshire*, pp. 11–14.

[56] Murgatroyd Diaries, KC 242/1 (1 July 1781). The churching of women was another popular rite of the Church of England. 'Phoebe Beatson was 'churched & her child baptized this afternoon by

He undertook all the sacramental, ritual and pastoral activities of a regular incumbent, over a very long period of time, in many parishes, and across many versions of Protestant Christianity. He may have been influenced to some extent by Huddersfield Evangelicalism; but in this year-in, year-out activity, he promoted the formularies and ideology of conventional Anglicanism. As preacher, friend, neighbour and employer, responding to the different congregations he found himself among, he is an example of the way in which Anglicanism was made by its laity, in its attitude and response to what it was provided with.[57] Murgatroyd believed that a good minister should be 'wise to enquire into the State of his Flock to discern their particular Tempers and Constitutions: and even (as it were) to search into their hearts and secret Inclinations'.[58] He did this nearly every Sunday of his working life, in a wide variety of circumstances.

There were other services and provisions made by the Anglican clergy that Murgatroyd also undertook, even though he had no parsonage from which to operate, and no regular clerical income (after 1767) to support the work – of counselling, for example. He visited neighbours all across the Colne Valley (though it is not clear whether this was at their request), and on several occasions he received a 'Woman troubled in her Spirit' at his Lingards house.[59] (It may have been the same woman on these occasions.) He thought this an important part of a clergyman's work, that 'he must be wise to administer private Counsels and reproofs, duly observing of ye Circumstances of Time, of Place, of Person, of Disposition; for a Word fitly spoken, says the wise Man, is like Apples of Gold in Pictures of Silver. . . .' A good minister would be plain in conveying his advice: 'He must be wise in his common converse with his People, that he be neither too easy, nor of too morose & difficult Access.'[60] It is unlikely that he was faced with 'the pathological aspects of private life' during these visits: seeking a clergyman's advice for psycho-sexual and domestic problems was a development of the late nineteenth century.[61] There was, however, a good deal of advice around for clergymen receiving confidences from men and women labouring 'under Melancholy, Dejection of Mind, or Despair', though Murgatroyd seemed not to have possessed Stonhouse's *Most Important Truths*

Rev. Mr Wilson . . .' And this by an Evangelical at a time when in some places clergymen were refusing to perform it for unmarried mothers. Russell, *Clerical Profession*, pp. 81–4. Murgatroyd Diaries, KC242/6 (26 September 1802).

[57] 'A creation of the laity, not through theology, but through piety,' say Walsh and Taylor of eighteenth-century Anglicanism. 'Church and Anglicanism', p. 26.

[58] John Murgatroyd, 'The Qualifications of a Minister of Christ', KC242/8, West Yorkshire Archive Service, Kirklees District, Huddersfield.

[59] House-to-house visiting was not very popular according to some historians of the Church of England. See Russell, *Clerical Profession*, pp. 113–14. For other pastoral duties of this sort, see Smith, *Religion in an Industrial Society*, p. 57, and Walsh and Taylor, 'Church and Anglicanism', pp. 13–14.

[60] Murgatroyd, KC242/8, 'The Qualifications of a Minister of Christ'.

[61] According to Russell, *Clerical Profession*, pp. 123–9.

and Duties of Christianity (1796) which, with psychological sophistication, told the melancholic and depressed that they needed more confidence in themselves and their God: 'You may be blameable in thinking *too ill* of yourself . . . You may not *at present* be a proper Judge in your own Case.' Disorders of the body and of the mind were what produced their psychological states of despair and depression; but God's regard for them did 'not Change with the Frame of [their] Mind'.[62] If Murgatroyd's sermons are anything to go by (and if 'Grief' of 1788 *is* a sermon, in note form), then he noted a similar understanding of the animal system, and the physiological relationship of body and mind. He advised that 'Grief is, of all ye Passns, most destructive . . . sink.g deeply into ye Mind . . . it changes into a fixed Melancholy, wch presses on ye Spirits, & wastes ye Constitution . . . destroys Appetite etc.' A solution was to keep occupied, 'engag'd in some useful Pursuit', advice that he may have handed over in parlour as well as pulpit.[63]

Murgatroyd had been trained for the exercise of his capacities in the office of clergyman, but not in the by-now conventional way of reading divinity at the university. His time at Almondbury under the care of Edward Rishton was clearly viewed as a kind of apprenticeship by his father and the patrons who had written references in support of his earlier applications for positions like this. His 'Qualifications of a Minister of Christ' has the form and structure of an extended essay; it may have been required of him by Rishton during the 1740s. There was also a considerable amount of self-help literature around for a young man in Murgatroyd's position, directed at those who 'who have no University education, but are left to themselves', like Henry Owen's *Directions to Young Students in Divinity*.[64] He had two of these in his library: a very old copy of Bishop Sprat's 1695 charge to the newly ordained priests and deacons of Rochester, which belied its first advice that a thorough reading of the forms for the ordering of priests was really all they needed, with sixty pages of instruction on reading aloud, the cultivation of a rhetorical persona, and advice about daily, personal devotion.[65] Murgatroyd's other home-educator, William Wotton's *Thoughts concerning a Proper Method of Studying Divinity* (1734), laid out a course of study more rigorous than Sprat's, advising a starting-point in the Old Testament, accompanied by explorations in Jewish history and politics. Then, proceeding to the New Testament, the comments of Grotius, the Christian Apologists, Greek ecclesiastical history and histories of primitive

---

[62] Stonhouse, *Most Important Truths*, pp. 20–3.

[63] Murgatroyd, KC242/9, 'Ask, Read, Retain, Teach', p. 111, 'Grief'.

[64] Henry Owen, *Directions to Young Students in Divinity, with regard to Those Attainments which are necessary to Qualify them for Holy Orders*, 2nd edn (London: privately printed, 1773). See Clarke, *Eighteenth-century Piety*, p. 23; Russell, *Clerical Profession*, pp. 23–4.

[65] Thomas Sprat, *A Discourse made by the Lord Bishop of Rochester to the Clergy of his Diocese on the Occasion of his Visitation in the year 1695; published at their request* (London: Edward Jones, 1696).

Christianity would be found useful accompaniments. Young men should remember that they would be preaching to post-Reformation English people, and there was nothing like the sermons of the great Tillotson for reminding them of that. You could be sure that Hebrew was not necessary for all of this, but each of them needed a body of divinity in his head, as the best guard against the enemies of the Church of England. You could guard against these adversaries by discovering in advance what the arguments of local Quakers and Presbyterians might be; you could prepare yourself for dispute with atheists (Deists). Young men should make notes about religious controversies in their commonplace book (it was taken for granted that they would have one), for 'the Knowledge of what our Adversaries say, is of almost absolute necessity for an *English* Divine'.[66] Like Sprat forty years before, Wotton considered the first among enemies to be Roman Catholics, an arming for controversy which in Murgatroyd's case and on the evidence of his journals seems to have been completely unnecessary. Murgatroyd's two home-teachers also urged him to become a particular kind of man, of 'Innocency and Sincerity': by the 'Comeliness and the Amiableness of every Word, and Action of [their] Lives' young men like him would be judged.[67] The best they could do, the highest achievement of their work, would be to distinguish the sinner from the sin. Sprat was also particularly practical on sermon writing and sermonising, considered it to be the most important part of a minister's work, and that which made the role of preacher indistinguishable from that of teacher.[68]

In one perspective, Murgatroyd behaved and acted just as the composite figure of the late eighteenth-century Anglican clergyman devised by his nineteenth-century historians would lead us to expect. But the temper and outline of the type has changed a good deal in recent years. He is no longer amiable, scandalous and fond of his drink, as he makes his way through eighteenth-century novel and the historical imagination of the nineteenth century.[69] He is not non-resident and mad to boot, but rather an earnest and cheerful worker for an institution and a faith, with an astonishing grasp of administrative details and the arrangements needed to keep going one of the largest enterprises in the kingdom, in the number of personnel employed and the plant it owned.[70] Murgatroyd is a clergyman of this modern historical type. But from another view, he does not fit. He had no living, nor even a permanent curacy. He did not derive an income from

---

[66] William Wotton, *Some Thoughts concerning a Proper Method of Studying Divinity* (London: William Bowyer, 1734), p. 11.

[67] Sprat, *Discourse*, p. 55.   [68] Sprat, *Discourse*, p. 7.

[69] Mark Smith, 'The Reception of Richard Podmore. Anglicanism in Saddleworth, 1708–1830', in Walsh et al., *Church of England, c.1689–1883*, p. 110–23; 113.

[70] The law rivalled the Church of England in its number of personnel; the army and the navy provide examples of similar enterprises, in the scale and detail of their operations. See John Brewer, *The Sinews of Power. War, Money and the English State, 1688–1793* (Cambridge, Mass.: Harvard University Press, 1990).

benefice, and was thus an outsider to resentment and dissent that the tithe system produced. The tithe was the clerical income derived either from a levy on local agricultural production, or from land granted in lieu of the 10 per cent due.[71] Tithes were particularly resented by Nonconformists, who were obliged to pay for the preservation and continuance of the established church.[72] But Murgatroyd had no part to play in West Riding versions of a much more general drama of established church and society. He does not seem ever to have written about the tithe question. His income was derived from fees (for taking divine service, and from private tuition given at Slaithwaite school), from letting out the Halifax properties inherited from his parents, and from some investments made with the inheritance that Ann Murgatroyd brought him on marriage. These were private economical circumstances, whilst for the regular clergy their income was not only public knowledge, but connected with pressing political questions to do with established church and the social order, and dissent from both.[73]

He encountered West Riding dissent in vivid form in Marsden in 1779, the year that its living was vacant, and as Hulbert was to note, he expected to be appointed to it, 'and it seems with reason'. The Marsden congregation had very clear ideas about their next pastor and what they wanted from him. Murgatroyd arrived to take services one Sunday in March (from Slaithwaite; he and Ann Murgatroyd still occupied the schoolhouse in the town at this time), and found the church door locked against him 'by the Chapelwarden, encouraged by the Methodistical party . . . so we had no service'. Two weeks later, the door was shut again, both morning and afternoon; 'they got foolish Taylor, of Saddleworth Church, to interfere and do the duty, Vesp [the afternoon service]. They at noon kept the chapel doors fast, and turned the people in at the other door. Shameful work,' he noted. This rejection of Murgatroyd's preaching and confessional persona continued well into June. One Sunday at the end of April, he felt threatened when, walking up to Marsden, he encountered 'three or four men placed in . . . [the] wood to abuse me, who did so in a shameful manner'. Going home at night, he found them there again, but he was accompanied now, and 'they walked off without giving any abuse . . . Oh pity.' Messages were contradictory: the new vicar of Almondbury sent messages for him to go to

---

[71] Slaithwaite's Reverend Wilson farmed some seven acres on the Dartmouth lands in Lingards. Dartmouth Estate Papers, Rentals, 1803. Register, Survey and Rentals, The Manor House, Slaithwaite, I.

[72] Gibson, *Church, State and Society*, pp. 28–32. Hole, *Pulpits*, p. 124. Peter Virgin, *The Church in an Age of Negligence. Ecclesiastical Structure and Problems of Church Reform, 1700–1840* (Cambridge: James Clark, 1989), pp. 33–41.

[73] So private were his financial arrangements that, in the absence of an account book, I have to assume that, through Sir Joseph Radcliffe, he invested in the Huddersfield Canal Company. 'Phoebe at Home poorly – Mr Radcliffe's clark came this afternoon just after Even'g Service with ye year's Interest,' he recorded in July 1802. Murgatroyd Diaries, KC 242/7 (Sunday 4 July 1802). For old Edmund Mellor's legacy to Ann, see Murgatroyd, 'Authors Useful to be Read at School'. His interest in the Mellor will is dated 20 May 1768 and 13 March 1769.

Marsden all through the early summer, and he did. He returned to his rejection in his diary, to Marsden's preference for Launcelot Bellas, who did indeed take the living, and for whom Murgatroyd amiably preached on Sundays for the next twenty years. When he contemplated his disappointment of the Honley living in the early 1760s, he wrote of 'Unfair Things' done to him, the choice of the Reverend Haselham over him, but asked God 'for Xt's Sake [to] forgive my enemies' – and just got on with it, for forty years.[74]

Edward Royle has likened West Riding Methodists and Baptists in this period to 'guerillas in the rough terrain' occupied by the regular troops of the Church of England.[75] It was the Baptists who made the initial forays into parts remoter than Marsden. In 1790 at Pole Moor (a settlement high above Slaithwaite) the Particular Baptists established a chapel, another expression of dissatisfaction by a congregation with how the established church went about its business. The Pole Moor chapel was a gesture at Slaithwaite's Evangelical Mr Wilson in particular, a comment on his failure to stress the doctrine of special election (the Calvinist doctrine of Grace) in his sermons; but it was directed at Murgatroyd as well, if only by default, for by now he was regularly taking Sunday services at Slaithwaite chapel.[76] And congregations had to go somewhere. One part of these confessional conflicts and dissensions was the severe difficulties the Church of England experienced in planting these territories: as Royle points out, there were no new churches built in Almondbury and Huddersfield parishes between 1764 and 1819.[77] Moreover, the enthusiasm of a young curate, intent on pursuing exciting and elaborate doctrinal questions in his sermons, could inadvertently lead a congregation to Methodistical thought, or even to Pole Moor and Particular Baptism. Something like this happened in many of Huddersfield's and Almondbury's numerous churches and chapelries. The printing presses of Huddersfield and Halifax kept congregations and their priests abreast of controversies and the dramatic developments they might produce. Between 1730 (the earliest date at which Murgatroyd could have become a book buyer) and 1806 (the year of his death) they produced 122 volumes (or at least, 122 of these local publications survive). The vast majority of them were religious in the broadest sense, 50 of 71 Halifax productions being published sermons, hymn collections, divine poems and autobiographical accounts of schism. In the 1790s and early 1800s reprints and new editions of seventeenth-century

[74] This account is taken from Hulbert, *Annals*, pp. 57–8. Diaries from before 1781 are not extant. Hulbert was a patient and exact transcriber of Murgatroyd's writing, though he did expand his abbreviations and conventionalise his punctuation by mid-Victorian norms. Murgatroyd wrote about the Honley disappointment in Murgatroyd Diaries, KC 242/1 (15 January 1788). There is a brief account of the Marsden affair to be found in 'Why Bellastown?' at http://www.bellastown.demon.co.uk/btown.htm.

[75] Royle, 'Church of England', p. 144.

[76] Royle,' Church of England', pp. 144–5. Over the next thirty years, upland communities 'were won over by the Baptists'.

[77] Royle,' Church of England', p. 145.

theology found a market.[78] It was easy to keep up with local controversy, especially from the viewpoint of the Colne Valley Particular Baptists.[79] This was modern, intellectually compelling 'religious' argument. Three editions of Alexander Disney's *Reasons for Methodism briefly stated, in three Letters to a Friend*, for example, were published in Halifax between 1793 and 1796. It is an engaging, enthralling (and local) spiritual autobiography, in the West Riding Enlightenment manner, for Disney had abandoned conventional Anglicanism via a reading of Voltaire and the *Analytical Review*.[80]

The way in which Murgatroyd operated as a writer often makes it difficult to work out what his own opinion actually was. This is probably why Hulbert thought him unoriginal and undistinguished as a preacher. He did what most users of a notebook method do: he transliterated, or copied verbatim, passages from works that had particularly struck him. Sometimes he worked up what he had read, and his own view of it, into something that had the emphatic form of an essay, with a relatively sustained argument, that reached a conclusion. His working out of extended discourses (that may be sermons) in his 'Ask, Read, Retain, Teach' notebook often had this form.[81] As many notebook keepers find themselves doing, he often used books that were entitled for one purpose, for a quite different one, writing remedies for tainted meat between reflections on chastity and good neighbourliness. Within the notebooks, his titles are often no guide to what followed. A heading suggested a topic that he did indeed start to discourse upon, but that then (in the space of a few minutes or some days) became a listed compilation from his reading. The passage headed 'Ministers' is typical (possibly written in 1790, if page order is anything to go by; or perhaps in 1788, if the reference to Slaithwaite church is current):

[78] Fifteen of fifty-one Huddersfield publications were 'religious' in this way. The next largest category was 'literature': poetry, play-scripts, literary miscellanies, though much of the religious material was in verse form as well.

[79] Particular Baptist Church, Yorkshire and Lancashire Association, *The Nature and Importance of Repentance. The Ministers of the Denomination of Particular Baptists, assembled in Association at Hebden-Bridge, near Halifax, the eleventh and twelfth of June, 1794, send Christian Salutation to the several Churches they represent* (Halifax: privately printed, 1794). Particular Baptist Church, Yorkshire and Lancashire Association, *Christian Communion. The Ministers of the Denomination of Particular Baptists, assembled in Association at Halifax, on the 30th and 31st of May, 1798, send Christian salutation . . .* (Halifax: privately printed, 1798).

[80] Royle,' Church of England', pp. 151–2. Alexander Disney, *Reasons for Methodism briefly stated, in three Letters to a Friend* (Halifax: J. Nicholson, 1793). See below, chapter 8, for further discussion of this kind of text in the context of West Riding Enlightenment. Sixty years on, Canon Hulbert was to write in detail about doctrinal dispute in late eighteenth-century Slaithwaite. Hulbert, *Annals of the Church*, pp. 73–4.

[81] They did not follow the rhetorical structure inherited from the seventeenth century, of proem, and case to be argued, laid out in a legal fashion. Downey, *Eighteenth Century Pulpit*, pp. 15–16. Murgatroyd's were not sermons with an ultimate destination in publication. They were directed at the ungrand audiences of the industrial West Riding, and not designed to be read by anyone but their author. Hole, *Pulpits*, p. 85.

It's good to keep up Friendship with Families, in whch Relig. Prevails. Let Us nevr. look disdainfully on those below Us, as we know not, how soon we may need 'em. – By ye wise disposal of Providence, one Country has need of anothr, & is benefited by anothr for mutual Correspondence & dependence, to ye Glory of God, our common Parent – strengthen Friendship wth ye honest & fair, lest new Friends prove not so firm & kind as old ones – Great persons sho'd consider their Servants must rest as well as they . . . Wn a village becomes more numerous ye place of meet.g needs Enlargement . . .[82]

It really is not possible to be certain about someone's opinion or belief in writing circumstances like these, though probably safe to assume that a proposition that the writer violently disapproved would be disputed in some way. I think that encroachments of Evangelical opinion and rhetoric into his writing (and perhaps sermonising) happened in something of this way. Hulbert saw him coming under the influence of the Reverend Wilson in the 1790s, and I agree that this did happen, though I have not been able to read the sermons on which Hulbert made his judgement. By the 1790s, Murgatroyd was regularly taking all Slaithwaite Sunday services and Slaithwaite was, anyway, his and Phoebe Beatson's local church, which she attended and at which he took communion. Wilson paid him for these services, not just in fee, but in intellectual and theological attention. In April 1802, on a Sunday when Murgatroyd had done both services at Slaithwaite (though Wilson actually delivered the sermon), the younger man made him a present of 'some Tracts He'd bought in London to read'.[83] Several things happened to these pamphlets: he gave them to neighbour Mellor 'to read – and practice according to ye Teaching yre'; they may have ended up in his notebook, in his consideration of death and judgment, or in his startling reflection on the story of Jezebel and the feast for worms of the vile body.[84] This is, in fact, a transcription of passages from *The Beauties of Henry*, a nice example of the ways in which in the 1790s, a conservative, counter-Enlightenment movement within the Church of England revisited and reworked the anti-scepticism of seventeenth-century divines. Though this new edition of Henry was published between 1797 and 1803, and though Wilson could easily have brought it back from London with him, a work in three substantial volumes could scarcely be called 'tracts'.[85] Murgatroyd copied the passage late in life,

---

[82] Murgatroyd, 'Ask, Read, Retain, Teach', KC 242/9, p. 79. Slaithwaite church was rebuilt and enlarged in 1788, on a new site just up from the river.

[83] Murgatroyd Diaries, KC 242/6 (25 April 1802).

[84] Murgatroyd Notebook, 'Ask, Read', KC242/9, p. 46, 'See in Jezebel the end of pride and cruelty & say the Lord is righteous . . . Jezebel's name no where remains, but stygmatiz'd in sacred writ – They could not so much as say, This is Jezebel's Dust; this is Jezebel's Grave, or this is Jezebel's Seed. Thus ye Name of Wickedness shall . . . rot above ground.'

[85] Matthew Henry, *The Beauties of Henry. A Selection of the most striking Passages in the Exposition of that celebrated Commentator. To which is prefixed a brief Account of the Life . . . of the Author, by John Geard*, 3 vols. (London: privately printed, 1793–1803), vol. I, p. 374. Nigel Aston, 'Horne and Heterodoxy. The Defence of Anglican Beliefs in the Late Enlightenment', *English Historical Review*, 108 (1993), pp. 895–919.

but in a notebook used back to front and every which way, with blank pages used ten years after the preceding one was written, we cannot know whether Wilson's tracts prompted it. What we can know is that he gave them away, for someone else to read, mark and learn. There may indeed have been levels of irony in this second-hand present to his friend, brother and neighbour; this may have been a comment on what Mellor was *not* like, and did not read. It may have been a joke. It is pretty difficult in any case to see the course of Evangelicalism running here, up the hill to Lingards. Historians of the Church of England have, anyway, sometimes discerned a spread of Evangelicalism in what was ordinary, mainstream Anglicanism.

Murgatroyd turned his mind to the great issues of the political and Anglican order and dissent from both of them, on many occasions. He thought – or at least copied out approvingly from somewhere – the opinion that 'the Magistracy is an Ordnance of God for ye good of ye Church, as truly as ye Ministry is – it is happy for a Kingdom, wn its civil and sacred Interests are jointly minded – '.[86] But most of his thinking – or at least his note-taking – on these questions was in relation to the Test and Corporation Acts, and the questions this legislation raised about the relationship of the established church to the legal framework of contemporary society.

His long essay on the acts was probably written in 1787 or 1788, when the longest-standing and most potent marker of the conflict between established church and religious dissent came to the political forefront and was much in the news. Test and corporation legislation had been a way of containing and managing dissent from the established church, from the end of the English Revolution and the Restoration. An Act of 1673 required all civil and military officeholders to take oaths of allegiance and supremacy. A declaration against transubstantiation was also required. (Was there a Real Presence in the taking of bread and wine during Holy Communion? The answer was a resounding No! – to be dinned into small children being catechised by men like Murgatroyd a century later.) Anyone applying for a government or ecclesiastical post must receive the sacrament after the forms of the established church. An Act of 1678 further required members of Parliament to take the oaths of supremacy and allegiance before they took their seats. As enacted, these laws were intended to exclude Roman Catholics from office, though their major effect during the course of the eighteenth century was against Protestant dissenters. There were many attempts at repeal (though only one between 1770 and 1827), and various forms of indemnity enacted; but the Test and Corporations Acts remained on the statute book until 1828.

[86] Murgatroyd, 'Ask, Read', KC249/9, p. 18. I think these remarks must have been made in 1798: he thinks much about the militia in these pages, evidently preoccupied with all the means available for defending the realm.

For dissenters across the country the issue was encapsulated in the requirement to take Holy Communion according to the Anglican form.[87] In the particular controversies of the 1780s and 1790s there was a relatively new secular argument at work: that politics and faith were separate things, that the state could have no real jurisdiction over people's conscience; and indeed, that there already existed societies in which civil and ecclesiastical institutions were entirely separate, to look to as models.[88]

This may have been a new political and philosophical world, but it was one in which very old arguments indeed were reiterated, in line with the retrieval of seventeenth-century theology just noted. Pamphlets and polemics of the 1780s brought to the forefront Bishop Sherlock's standard apologia for things-as-they-were, of 1718.[89] Murgatroyd made extensive notes on the anonymous *Bishop Sherlock's Arguments* – though he does not seem to have bought the work of 1787 in which the long-dead bishop's arguments were rehearsed to refute 'a paper now circulating styled The Case of the Protestant Dissenters'.[90] He noted the title carefully and made two pages of notes (an indication that the book was borrowed), being mainly interested in the rather glamorous question of whether or not a monarch should be obliged to show his allegiance to the Church of England by taking communion according to the Anglican rite. He noted Sherlock's historical account of the way that allegiance of church and state had formed national identity, so that 'Nothing but a perswasn of Error & Corruption . . . [could] excuse Separation . . .', but was far more taken with the conundrum of a king 'come [into] ye Possession of ye Crown [and] obliged to join in Communication with ye Church of England as by Law established', but who did not actually have to have himself *seen* in the act, as did naval officers, parochial schoolmasters and crown surveyors appointed by the Tax Office. He noted Sherlock's justification with care:

Receiv.g ye Sacrament as a Test is not requir'd of a King because, respect.g private Persons, ye Public cannot judge wt. Communion they belong to yn opens a Proof, a test of their Communion wth ye Church established, is required of ym but a King's public person, lives in ye Eyes of all of his Subjcts its as easily known, to wt Communion a King belongs to & wt Kingdm. he governs so no particular Test or proof of joining in Communion need be requir'd.[91]

---

[87] This was not a particular difficulty for Methodists, who had no problem with taking communion in their parish church. And Methodists did not see themselves as 'dissenters' anyway.

[88] Hole, *Pulpits*, pp. 53–4. G. M. Ditchfield, 'The Parliamentary Struggle over the Repeal of the Test and Corporation Acts, 1787–1790', *English Historical Review*, 89 (1974), pp. 551–77.

[89] Edward Carpenter, *Thomas Sherlock, 1678–1761. Bishop of Bangor 1728; of Salisbury 1734; of London 1748* (London: SPCK, 1936), p. 103.

[90] Anon., *Bishop Sherlock's Arguments against a Repeal of the Test and Corporations Acts; wherein most of the Pleas advanced in a Paper now circulating styled The Case of the Protestant Dissenters etc are discussed* (London: privately printed, 1787).

[91] Murgatroyd, 'Ask, Read, Retain, Teach', KC249/9, pp. 101–2.

He recorded Sherlock's Latitudinarian generosity over the privileges that dissenters already possessed, and in a time of some nervousness about national security, chose to observe that

if peace & Security of Conscience will not satisfy, without power & Authority in ye State, it shou'd be no Offence to 'em to tell em yt wth a Regard for our own Consciences, as well as theirs – tho' we rejoice in their Liberty we see no reason to part wth our own Security ~ The Test Act is but a reasonable Provision for securing ye establishmt agt. suspected Enemies yrfore a good in evr'y Respect, where yr's probable Ground for such Suspicion.

As for the shocking view that the upshot of all of this was communion with our Lord being treated as a mere civil oath, Sherlock's difficult argument was made more so, in Murgatroyd's transliteration of it:

An Oath is required – to Speak it again – of a Witness as a test or Proof of his veracity – it's ye Act of a man, considered as a relig.s Creature for, if ye take away ye sense of relign yrs then no pretence for requiring an Oath since An Oath has all its Force from ye Relign of ye Man, it's this alone yt makes it a Test in Virtue of ye strong Obligation undr whch it puts Him to speak Truth ~ Whoever takes an oath, pawns / as twere / ye Love & Fear of God wch are in Him, & all his Trust & Hope in God for the Truth of his Evidence.

What is opinion and belief, in documentary circumstances like these – the amalgam of all that a man has read, heard, thought and half-thought through a long life: an active consciousness, working on new ideas to the very end? These ideas were brought to him not only by eager Evangelicals back from London with handfuls of tracts to distribute, and from weekly discussion with his more traditional brethren, but from working within a multiplicity of confessional and social circumstances that were themselves dynamic and earnest of inquiry.[92] The upshot is, of course, that reading all of Murgatroyd's massive output of words, we would not know much more than we already know about the conflicts of faith, and of church and state, in the West Riding between 1740 and 1800: we would find confirmed the judgement of Judith Jago that many religious practices and beliefs – Evangelicalism and orthodoxy – 'were both separately and together the inheritance of many parochial clergy'.[93]

Clerical magistrates focused questions of church and state in their very persons, and all magistrates administered a law that found its origins and justification in the moral precepts of the church.[94] If this is hegemony, then it could not be more perfectly expressed than in the person of the justicing parson,

---

[92] See below, chapter 8, for Murgatroyd's communication with his neighbours and clerical friends over new theological and philosophical ideas.

[93] Jago, *Aspects of the Georgian Church*, p. 18.

[94] James E. Bradley, 'The Anglican Pulpit, the Social Order and the Resurgence of Toryism during the American Revolution', *Albion*, 21:3 (1989), p. 375.

exercising his authority in a parish during years of war (American, French, Revolutionary wars) when the clergy became the 'most pro-governmental body in the nation'.[95] But Murgatroyd is not in this picture. He was always puzzled when the administrative state came knocking at his door, to deliver a tax return for the enumeration of Phoebe Beatson as domestic servant, or to tell her where to go for her settlement examination by a magistrate. When she returned from this, and later from the filiation meeting where she named George Thorp as father of Elizabeth, Murgatroyd had nothing to say about the system she had encountered (probably two clerical magistrates were involved in the last), only shook his head wonderingly, at the pity of it all.[96]

---

[95] Bradley, 'Anglican Pulpit', p. 36.
[96] In 1802 sixteen of the sixty-three acting magistrates for the West Riding bench were clergymen. 'Names of the Acting Magistrates and Principal Officers within the West Riding of County of Yorkshire', Radcliffe Mss 309 ©/12, West Yorkshire Archive Service, Leeds District, Leeds.

6   Teaching

It was held that the first duty of a Protestant church was to instruct the laity.
Education – of children in parochial schools rehearsing the catechism, or gathered elsewhere to learn their responses, or of adults in a Sunday congregation
attending to a sermon – this was what, in its own estimation, marked the Church
of England off from the Roman Catholic Church's expectation of unquestion-
ing, superstitious faith in the laity.[1] John Murgatroyd understood himself, first
and foremost, to be a teacher. He wrote extensive and considered accounts of
the ministry, and the qualifications of a minister of the church; but when he
thought about himself and what he had done through a very long life, he called
himself a teacher, in pulpit, schoolroom, and 'in my Life and conversation'.
His duty – always, he wrote, done with very great willingness – was to enable
the laity to hear from him consistently ('with Continuance') what the Christian
story was: 'ye End of coming into ye world . . . answered – ye way of Salvation
taught'.[2] He thought he had done well enough over the sixty years he had taught
in school and pulpit; that his method had reached many sorts of people: 'my
Teaching has been plain & . . . fit for any capacity – it has come from my Heart
& by ye close attention & silence of the Heavens it has appear'd plainly to have
powerfully come to their Hearts'.[3] The image of his younger self, earnest and
willing, come to Slaithwaite fresh from one school to teach in another, was
often before him, especially on New Year's Eve. Forever, in the realm of his
imagination, he sat by the window in the schoolhouse, waiting for pupils and
looking on them with love when they did arrive.

In sermonising, the teaching was often practical, telling best how to push
through a troublesome world. His last commonplace book contains notes on
slander and defamation ('ye only method for never increasing ye Charge of

---

[1] John Walsh and Stephen Taylor, 'The Church and Anglicanism in the "Long" Eighteenth Century', in John Walsh, Colin Haydon, and Stephan Taylor, *The Church of England, c.1689–1883.
From Toleration to Tractarianism* (Cambridge: Cambridge University Press, 1993), p. 14. Jeremy
Gregory, *Restoration, Reformation and Reform, 1660–1828. Archbishops of Canterbury and their
Diocese* (Oxford: Clarendon Press, 2000), pp. 235–54.
[2] Reverend John Murgatroyd, Diaries, KC 242/6, West Yorkshire Archive Service, Kirklees District, Huddersfield (31 December 1802).
[3] Murgatroyd Diaries, KC 242/7 (31 December 1804).

Calumny, is never to speak to any one's disadvantage'), on how to forget affronts, how to behave fairly in any kind of group endeavour ('ye more they are, ye better is ye Body evry Member hath Use for ye good of ye whole ∼ mak.g it by Lot prevents quarrel.g in yr Disposal ∼ None can be charg'd with partiality – none can say They had a wrong done'), how friends should behave towards each other, how to avoid the 'fix'd Melancholy' that could develop from grief, and on sexual relations.[4] He told about death and judgment, and the irreducible plot line of the Christian narrative; he copied out practical advice about preparation for confirmation and holy communion from the printed guides he possessed, and we can assume that he probably delivered it, often on a Sunday under the heading of a biblical text.

There is little in the 'Ask, Read, Retain, Teach' notebook that cannot be traced back to the books in his personal library; the title of the notebook proclaims its function. What he called the earlier volumes like this, the ones he had had bound and put on the parlour shelves, was 'Remarks'. That anyone might be interested in the distinction between his own and someone else's thoughts (as Canon Hulbert obviously was) might have struck him as odd. He was a conduit for an accumulated wisdom and body of advice, collected by the reformed church, over the past two centuries. Hulbert was probably right in judging that he exercised great patience and assiduity in copying out from the many works of theology, history and moral guidance for young men that he owned and borrowed, rather than using writing to express original thought.[5] This was his teaching: the basis of a common conversation between him and his neighbours, and the West Riding clergymen he dined with on Sundays. They may have considered his discourse a straightforward expression of his opinion, at a time when 'opinion' did not have the connotations of individuality and originality that it now has. At a distance of two hundred years, however, it is only possible to say that he was struck by many arguments and ideas, and that in writing them down, he did not disapprove of them. Here for once, John Murgatroyd does not buck a trend; he *is* a trend, or rather, the amalgam of Anglican theology, working with new-ish accounts of the historical past and models of the human body (the modern body–mind relationship of late eighteenth-century physiology, to be discussed in chapter 8), to adjust a divinity to ever-changing social circumstances. He *is*, in this instance, a norm.

It is the clear advice about how to live as part of a community and a family in the industrialising Colne Valley that is the most compelling. It appears a secular world, full of other people, their irritating habits and bad behaviour. But it is not;

---

[4] John Murgatroyd, 'Ask, Read, Retain, Teach', KC 242/9, West Yorkshire Archive Service, Kirklees District, Huddersfield, p. 17, '1788. Calumny'; p. 90, 'Order and Dealing Justice'; p. 93, 'Duties that shou'd subsist between Friend & Friend'; p. 111, '1788 Grief'.

[5] Charles Augustus Hulbert, *Annals of the Church in Slaithwaite (near Huddersfield) West Riding of Yorkshire from 1793–1864, in Five Lectures* (London: Longman, 1864), p. 56.

or rather, the division between the religious and the secular, an invention of this period according to Callum Brown, is not one that occurs to Murgatroyd, taking his notes and dispensing his advice.[6] E. P. Thompson's account of the West Riding textile villages, of all the movements their inhabitants made away from the established church and from a theocentric world view, makes it difficult not to see Murgatroyd's notes and observations as designed for a later de-Christianised society. But they are not. All of the people he figures in these pages of extracts and contemplations, the annoyance they occasion, their obstinacy, are held in the eye of God. How to react to them? How to behave?

'We stand in Need of true Courage ev'ry Momt. of our Lives', he noted, 'for enabling us to bear up undr. ye Misfortunes happening [to] us without express.g our Weakness in Complaints & to accommodate Ourselves to ye Extravagance of troublesome people, with wm we're oblig'd to live.'[7] (He looked forward to dining with a neighbouring cleric who wanted his advice about setting up a Sunday school in 1786, because, like him, the Reverend Hadwen was 'situated amg troublesome People'.[8]) His notes on troublesome people in general were headed 'Heroick Virtue'. They prescribed a manner of public behaviour and self-management that was learned both from the Roman satirists and from the prescriptions of Christian forbearance. Everyday sermonising and teaching like this, never intended for transmutation into the most popular literary genre of its day, the published sermon collection, is sometimes thought to have involved only simple things: the teaching of contentment, resignation and the formularies of the church, to simple unlettered people.[9] But palpable in these notes is a kind of shrewd respect for the varieties of wool combing and weaving (and professional and entrepreneurial) congregations he encountered, and an earnest desire to tell them things that they needed to know, to get through the next week and the rest of their life, on a journey heavenward.

His teaching on how to manage sexual relations may offer some insight into his reactions to Phoebe Beatson's pregnancy and her relationship with George Thorp. He made notes on 'Chastity' in 1788, naming it a virtue that helped people tame the wild excesses of love, and that might also secure its real blessings, which were faithfulness, honour and the friendship of a husband or wife. In considering the 'hurtful & prog.sly fatal effects' of passion given way to, his notes emphasised the woman's story. He wrote of the 'Wretchedness,

[6] Callum G. Brown, *The Death of Christian Britain. Understanding Secularisation, 1800–2000* (London and New York: Routledge, 2000), pp. 16–34.

[7] Murgatroyd, 'Ask, Read, Retain, Teach', KC 242/9, pp. 95–6, 'Heroic Virtue 1788'.

[8] Murgatroyd Diaries, KC 242/1 (26 August 1786).

[9] Robert Hole, *Pulpits, Politics and Public Order in England, 1760–1832* (Cambridge: Cambridge University Press, 1989), p. 85. James Downey, *The Eighteenth Century Pulpit. A Study of the Sermons of Butler, Berkeley, Secker, Sterne, Whitefield and Wesley* (Oxford: Clarendon Press, 1969), pp. 1–29. William Gibson, *The Church of England, 1688–1832* (London and New York: Routledge, 2001), pp. 158–61.

Infamy and Ruin of ye Person once beloved . . . who repos'd too great Trust
in ye slippery faith of Man'. He had the interesting and instructive example of
Lucretia's story – one of the best known of them all in plebeian circles (at least
according to Samuel Richardson) – up his sleeve.[10] His advice on adultery was
more severe than even her story delivered: 'next to Homicide [it] deserves to
be most sever.ly punish'd of all othr Crimes, for it is one of ye most evil of
Robberies yt can be committed by one Man agt Anothr'. He emphasised the
psychological effect on women – the baby born after a failed attempt at abortion,
the child unloved, 'for no Act of maternal Tendr.ness is to be expected . . . from
a vicious Mother who sees in [it an] Object . . . of stinging Reproval for her
conjugal Unfaithfulness . . .' Another historical example was noted to emphasise
the point: 'Our Saxon Ancestors condemn'd to ye flames a Woman caught in
Adultery – &, in ye midst of her Ashes, a Gibbet was erected, on which ye
Accomplice of her Crime was executed.'[11]

His preoccupation was the children of such unions – 'helpless victim[s] . . .
daring to behold ye Light' – and his favourite text, 'Train up a child in the way he
should go' (Prov. 22.6). He made more notes on education, and delivered more
sermons to this text, than to any other topic. He owned over fifty volumes of
published and manuscript sermons, many of which emphasised an educational
perspective. One of them was Archbishop Tillotson's long-running best-seller
from the 1690s. This emphasised the duties of parents to make a child a social
being through the processes of religious education.[12] It was both good and
useful to educate children, Tillotson told the long eighteenth century, not only
because 'we bring up Children for the Publick', but also because 'Our Children

---

[10] Mr B. thinks that the serving maid Pamela is much better educated than she is (or sneers at
her so-called learning) when she quotes Lucretia at him. Samuel Richardson, *Pamela, or, Virtue
Rewarded*, orig. pub. 1740 (Harmondsworth: Penguin, 1986), p. 63. Murgatroyd may have taken
his reference from John Clarke, *A Compendious History of Rome by L. Florus with an English
Translation*, 6th edn (London: Hawes, Clarke and Collins, 1763), one of his 'School Books',
and may indeed have had his boys read it. But there's no need for such minute tracing: Samuel
Richardson (and Ian Donaldson) tells us that the story was everywhere, particularly in chapbook
form, in the earlier eighteenth century. Ian Donaldson, *The Rapes of Lucretia. A Myth and its
Transformations* (Oxford: Clarendon Press, 1982).

[11] Murgatroyd 'Ask, Read, Retain, Teach', KC 242/9, p. 28, 'Chastity'.

[12] John Tillotson, *Six Sermons. I. Stedfastness in religion. II. Family-religion III. IV. V. Education
of children. VI. The advantages of an early piety* (London: B. Aylmer, 1694). This is certainly
the edition that Murgatroyd possessed. As a young man arrived in Slaithwaite, he made notes on
the twelve volumes of the collected sermons, concentrating on the first, second, sixth, eighth and
twelfth, leaving gaps in his contents page for when he had completed the task. John Murgatroyd,
'A Cornucopia: or Collection of weighty Extracts transcribed out of the scarcest, most necessary & best chosen Books &c according to this proper Maxim, that every Man shou'd take down
in Writing what He learns for fear of forgetting any useful Circumstance. By John Murgatroyd,
Master of Slaithwaite School. Anno Domini 1742', quarto Notebook, nd, unpaginated; Special
Collections, Raymond Burton Library, Slaithwaite Parish Collection, University of York, York,
'A Catalogue of the Books and Names of ye Authors, whose Writing I've quoted and abstracted
in this Cornucopia'.

are part of our Selves'.[13] It took a pleasurable sagacity to 'discern their particular disposition and temper'.[14] Here is the Lockean model of the child mind and a prescribed responsiveness of an adult towards another embryonic individual, a further confirmation of Carmen Luke's proposition that it was the printing press and piety that together transmitted to the largest number of people from the seventeenth century onwards new psychologies and new propositions about the teaching relationship between adults and children.[15]

Murgatroyd was also familiar with a range of advice literature that mourned the long-lost days of home education, when 'ye Mother's chief Care was to instill into her Daughters ye Principles of Virtue', as well as 'Cookery, Spinning, weaving, sewing, knitting, and in such Knowledge, as a Domestic Life – required', and the reading, spelling 'truly', writing and the 'Figures & cypher.g' needed for 'ye common Course of Life'.[16] This was a yesterday regretted everywhere, by Mary Wollstonecraft as well as a remote West Riding clergyman; such lamentations had been a clerical constant since the early days of Christianity. Murgatroyd was also interested in his actual historical examples of domestic teaching by men, noting that 'Cato instructed his Son, Augustine ye Sovereign of the World did teach his Grandchildren to write – Timothy was taught ye Holy Scriptures from a child wch was ye reason he was so expert in 'em wh. a Man.'[17] He undertook the education of his little nieces and nephew in his house, and his last notebook was used by Hannah Mellor to practise her French in great big copperplate, and her handwriting with 'Hannah Mellor is my Name ∼ with my Pen I write the Same/ If my pen had been better – I would have mended every Letter.'[18] This arrangement for teaching the children (Ann, Hannah and Joseph) seems to have continued even after they started going down the hill into Slaithwaite, to new school arrangements at the church. Hannah and Ann

---

[13] Tillotson, *Six Sermons*, pp. 71, 232.   [14] Tillotson, *Six Sermons*, pp. 93.

[15] Carmen Luke, *Pedagogy, Printing and Protestantism. The Discourse on Childhood* (Albany, N.Y.: State University of New York Press, 1989).

[16] The reflection that begins 'They was happy Times, when ye Mother's chief Care was to instil into her Daughter's ye Principles of Virtue . . .' is repeated across two of his notebooks, 'Ask, Read, Retain, Teach', KC 242/9, p. 82, and John Murgatroyd, 'Authors Useful to be Read at School', Notebook, 1745–1802, 082.2 MUR, Special Collections, Slaithwaite Parish Collection, University of York, York. I have been unable to trace its source. He had in his library Albrecht von Haller's *Letters from Baron Haller to his Daughter on the Truths of the Christian Religion. Translated from the German* (London: J. Murray, 1780) – this was purchased after he stopped teaching school – and Wetenhall Wilkes's *A Letter of Genteel and Moral Advice to a Young Lady*, 8th edn (London: L. Hawes, 1766) for the education of daughters (many more books about the right education of sons). He did not transliterate his pastoral of regret from either of these. Indeed, Wilkes had no objection at all to a young lady amusing herself with Latin, and prescribed a considerable reading list of classical authors to her.

[17] Murgatroyd, 'Ask, Read, Retain, Teach', KC 242/9, p. 82, 'Education'.

[18] Whose Book I am, if you wou'd know In Letters two I will show/The one is H. full great of Might the other M in all men's Sight/Now set these Letters orderly, And they will tell you whose am I?/And, if in spelling you – it miss, Look underneath & there it is.

had in fact started with Murgatroyd's successor at Slaithwaite Free School two years before, when they had been taught by young Mr Bolton ('He appears to be well-behaved') and his sisters.[19]

Murgatroyd agreed – was bound to agree – with the enormous consensus of eighteenth-century educational opinion, that the basis of all teaching and learning was the catechism: 'Children should begin as soon as they are able to learn [it] . . . and go on by degrees 'till They can say it perfectly by Heart, & They are to continue to be instructed in it, 'till They do understand it so well as to be fit to receive ye Sacrament of ye Lds Supper at 16 or 17 years of Age,' he wrote.[20] On the question of catechising, Thomas Sprat had advised that it was best just to confine yourself to the Book (of Common Prayer) in country places; in towns 'where youth is better educated' you could go further, and 'annex some text of scripture to each article and clause; do it drop by drop', so that the children stored up in their mind 'a little Body, as it were, of Orthodox Divinity'.[21]

Tillotson had particularly approved the question-and-answer form of the catechism as laid out in the Book of Common Prayer, for the way it developed the faculty of memory in children.[22] All sorts of teaching primer and teachers' manual not only approved it, but used the same interrogative form. The most up-to-the-minute presented themselves to the book-buying public as part of the new genre of children's literature.[23] Editors and clerical authors laid out the

---

[19] 'My little Scholars. Han:nah, Nancy & Joseph Mellor began School this Morning with Mr Basildon's daughter in Rev. Wilson's Hall.' Murgatroyd Diaries, KC242/1 (2 May 1788). KC242/1 (6 March and 4 September 1786) for earlier arrangements at the Free School.

[20] Murgatroyd, 'Ask, Read, Retain, Teach', p. 82. He possessed several commentaries on the catechism, including Thomas Adam, *Practical Lectures on the Church Catechism* (London: C. Hitch and L. Hawes, 1755) and Peter Newcome, *A Catechetical Course of Sermons for the Whole Year. Being an Explanation of the Church Catechism. In Fifty Two distinct Discourses. In two Volumes* (London: J. R., 1702).

[21] Thomas Sprat, *A Discourse made by the Lord Bishop of Rochester to the Clergy of his Diocese on the Occasion of his Visitation in the year 1695; published at their request* (London: Edward Jones, 1696), pp. 32–6.

[22] Tillotson, *Six Sermons*, pp. 158–64.

[23] John Lewis's *The Church Catechism Explained, By Way of Question and Answer; and Confirmed by Scripture Proofs*, 13th edn (London: John Rivington, 1766) was the century's best-seller. Gregory, *Restoration, Reformation*, pp. 235–54. Murgatroyd did not have this in his library. But he did possess, not a catechism, but an abridged Bible for small children, that used the *non plus ultra* sales pitch of informing its purchasers that it was published by John Newbery's successor: *The Holy Bible Abridged, or the History of the Old and New System. Illustrated with Notes, and adorned with Cuts. For the Use of Children* (London: T. Carnan, Successor to Mr J. Newbery, 1782). For John Newbery's publishing house, see John Rowe Townsend (ed.), *Trade and Plumb-cake for Ever, Huzza! The Life and Work of John Newbery, 1713–1767. Author, Bookseller, Entrepreneur and Pioneer of Publishing for Children* (Cambridge: Colt Books, 1994). See Dorothy Kilner, *A Clear and Concise Account of the Origin and Design of Christianity Intended as a second Part to the Work entitled 'The First Principles of Religion and the Existence of a Deity, explained in a Series of Dialogues adapted to the Capacity of the Infant Mind'*, 2 vols. (London: John Marshall, 1783), for the most modern of aids to catechising.

principles of a faith that was based on a 'Gospel covenant that lets us into the Knowledge of the whole Religion'.[24] The imagery of Locke's *Some Thoughts Concerning Education* (1693) is everywhere; Murgatroyd had read and made notes on it in the 1740s.[25] Adults are reminded that the mind of the child they are teaching through the medium of this book in their hands is 'like Wax', ready for impressions to be made by the adult wielding the stylo, or like the stream that might be turned this way or that by the attentive agriculturalist, watering his 'Domestick Plantations'.[26] Echoing Tillotson, the teacher was reminded that what he or she was doing in that moment was their 'present Pleasure': 'your natural Love for your Children, makes it pleasant to you to do any Thing, which may promote their *real* Interest'.[27] Parents of the polite classes of society (and those they employed as teachers) had long been advised to adopt an informal and friendly approach towards children. Indeed, this had been Locke's advice, as far back as 1693, in his disapproval of the distant, magisterial voice of the Filmerian patriarch-turned-teacher. Now, in the middle years of the eighteenth century there were anxieties not just about teacherly stance but also about the potential terrors of the Christian message for little children. Throughout numerous editions of his *Sermons on the Education of Children* Peter Doddridge had acknowledged the very great importance of children's early imbibing of 'an *Awe* of God . . .'; but at the same time, 'great Care should be taken not to confine our Discourses to these awful Views, lest the *dread* of God should *fall upon them*, as that *his Excellencies* should *make them afraid* to approach him . . . the Father is not to be represented as severe, and almost inexorable'.[28] Anxieties about educators who gave instruction 'with a *magisterial* Air, or in the Way of a Solemn Lecture' were around for a very long time. Doddridge thought that the child kept 'at a Distance, and not allowed to propose, or answer Questions' was in effect prevented from learning and remembering. Lessons should be short and frequent, and delivered with 'great Seriousness, so as to show that your own Hearts are affected with what you teach your Children . . . They will be likely to feel, when they see that you feel.' He thought there was no harm in crying whilst you instructed them: 'a *weeping* Parent is both an *awful* and a *melting Sight*'.[29]

The message was indeed awe-full – and awful: that the child was both an immortal creature, but also sinful; that the child must learn the ways of

[24] Lewis, *Church Catechism*, Introduction, p. vii.   [25] Murgatroyd, 'Cornucopia', pp. 233–59.

[26] James Stonhouse, *The Religious Instruction of Children Recommended* (London: J. F. & C. Rivington, 1791), p. 23. P. Doddridge, *Sermons on the Education of Children. Preached at Northampton. With a Recommendatory Preface by the Reverend Mr David Stone*, 3rd edn (London: M. Fenner, 1743), p. 37.

[27] Stonhouse, *Religious Instruction*, pp. 26–7.

[28] Doddridge, *Sermons*, pp. 20–1.   [29] Doddridge, *Sermons*, p. 57.

repentance.[30] This knowledge could be conveyed by stages, according to modern clerical educators like Sir James Stonhouse. The first task was to tell children what God was, that is, a Spirit, everywhere present, who 'knows all things you do . . . hates sin and naughty children . . . is full of mercy and loves good children'.[31] Having established that, then the parent or educator could lead them to an understanding of themselves as spiritual and physiological entities. 'Tell them what their wants are', counselled Stonhouse, drawing on some very old publications indeed; tell them about bodies, and 'how sad [it is] to endure cold and hunger'.[32] The basic needs of the human body were 'health, food, raiment', which only God could provide: 'You cannot keep yourself alive. It is God alone can do this.' The next step was to insist on the importance of prayer. Children needed reassurance about praying in the dark: when talking to their God, they should not be afraid. Their own experience would tell them *how* to pray, whether to pray aloud or in their head: 'whatever will best keep up your attention', said Stonhouse, addressing the child directly. Then, this stage reached, you might teach the child the essential points of Christian doctrine – when they had this ontologically secure picture of the world in place (*not* a phrase used by Stonhouse), their position in the universe secured by an all-encompassing God.[33] He laid out these principles as teaching goals to be achieved: it was the child's task to understand that Christ was the son of God, at one with the Father ('in a union that none can explain', Stonhouse added, to sighs of relief from the adult helping the child through these lessons). Christ was also a teacher sent by God. He suffered to make an atonement for the sins of humankind. He now dwelt in Heaven, pleading mercy for all penitent sinners. It was good to ask him to mediate between you and God in your prayers.[34] As for the Holy Spirit – more than likely to provoke the child's eternal question, 'Why?' – the teacher had to be more reticent, saying somewhat vaguely that 'You must believe in Him', not grieve him by any sin; you might be made holy and fit for Heaven by his influence in your heart. Most teaching material was discreet and diffident about this most difficult of concepts. The pupil in Richard Challoner's *Young Gentleman Instructed* (Murgatroyd had this in his library) was led through a

---

[30] James Stonhouse, *The Most Important Truths and Duties of Christianity. Designed for those in the lower Stations of Life. Particularly for the Instruction of such as cannot read* (London: J. F. & C. Rivington, 1796), pp. 3–6.

[31] Reverend Mr Richards, *Hints for Religious Conversation with the Afflicted in Mind, Body or Estate, and with such as stand in need of spiritual Assistance* (London: Williams and Smith, 1807). Appendix III reproduces this advice of Stonhouse, 'Selected from Bishop Wilson'. Bishop Wilson had first published in the 1690s.

[32] Richards, *Hints*, Appendix III, pp. 30–1.

[33] Doddridge made it quite clear that his educational prescription derived from his own sense of security, at having been very well taught and cared for in his childhood. Doddridge, *Sermons*, pp. 71–2, Footnote.

[34] Stonhouse, *Most Important Truths*, p. 22.

hundred pages of dialogue and intellectual exchange with his tutor to the final declaration that 'the Holy Ghost is the true God, as well as the Father and the Son; and consequently the same God with them; since the whole Scripture and Christian Church, from the very beginning, acknowledges no more than one God . . .' A brief prayer, and absolutely no more questions from the young gentleman, who has disappeared from the text a page before, in silent conviction of Unity in Trinity.[35] Even the engaging *Holy Bible Abridged* that Murgatroyd possessed forgot its voice of charming indulgence to its child readers on this point, retreating to a mysticism that may have silenced questions for a moment: 'God is in himself from eternity to eternity, without beginning and without end, the most perfect and blessed Being; in his substance, spiritual and eternal; in his person, three united in one; in his name. Father, Son, and Holy Ghost . . .'[36] The narrative voice had promised to deal only with those 'portions of the Scriptures as are both *instructive* and *entertaining*; such as will not only feed the fancy, but mend the heart'; but the Fifth Article of the Thirty-Nine was too important to be conveyed by modern pedagogical principles.

In all of these texts the framing Christian narrative of the first Sin, the Fall, Atonement, Death and Resurrection was put in place, by first making the child understand his or her place in the universe, and in the sustaining and reliable hand of God. These were relatively simple lessons, compared with what the new Georgian lady educator might attempt.[37] Dorothy Kilner's *Clear and Concise Account of the Origin and Design of Christianity* (a much less amusing production than her *Perambulations of a Mouse*, which came out a year later) proclaimed its liberal credentials by assuring children that 'you can run and laugh on the Sabbath . . . [God] delights to behold his creatures happy'; but also undertook the stern task of explaining the relationship between Judaism and Christianity.[38] It dwelt in particular on the mystery of circumcision, and the ways in which Christian baptism had replaced it. The point most emphatically to be made was that there were only two sacraments within the Church of England, and that this was one of them.[39] Kilner instructed that all of this theology was to be imparted by the child reading a designated portion of the Gospels, and then playing his or her part in her printed dialogues concerning it. The adult voice could become very emphatic indeed, almost shrill, on the question

---

[35] Richard Challoner, *The Young Gentleman Instructed in the Grounds of the Christian Religion. In Three Dialogues between a Young Gentleman and his Tutor* (London: T. Meighan, 1755). Challoner was a Roman Catholic of an Enlightenment frame of mind. See Eamon Duffy (ed.), *Challoner and his Church. A Catholic Bishop in Georgian England* (London: Darton, Longman and Todd, 1981), p. 21 for his writings; and Richard Lucker, 'Bishop Challoner. The Devotionary Writer', in Duffy, *Challenor and his Church*, pp. 71–89.

[36] Anon., *Holy Bible Abridged*, chapter 1, 'Treating of God'.

[37] Mitzi Myers, ' "Servants as They are Now Educated". Women Writers and Georgian Pedagogy', *Essays in Literature*, 16:1 (1989), pp. 51–69.

[38] Kilner, *Clear and Concise Account*, p. 182.   [39] Kilner, *Clear and Concise Account*, p. 158.

of confirmation: 'But as I have before explained to you, that a *Sacrament* means some *outward sign*, or *ceremony*, appointed by Christ himself, to be used as a *means* of obtaining some *inward* grace; and as he was so pleased to appoint only two, *baptism* and the *Lord's Supper*, men can have no right to constitute any more; or impose any more *ceremonies* as *necessary* to be performed in order to our being true Christians.'[40]

The children in these texts, and in parlours and schoolrooms across the country, were provided with a story that provided the possibility of ontological, and thus psychological, security: they existed because someone wanted them to exist; they were watched, and they were loved; they would be forgiven. The influences of John Locke's *Some Thoughts Concerning Education*, the model of the child mind and the education for nurturing it that it provided right through to the twentieth century, have long been acknowledged.[41] The role of the Church of England, as an artery for transmitting its central propositions about the needs of children, has not really been recognised. These works not only decorated their pages with colophons and epigrams from Locke, but inserted spiritual content into his areligious formulations regarding child psychology. The content was God – a highly specific Anglican God – and his all-seeing concern for his creatures. Their gentle formulations are, perhaps, one point of origin for much later psycho-analytic accounts of the child mind, particularly those developed in mid-twentieth-century object-relations theory. This eighteenth-century Anglican God is a presence that, in Donald Winnicott's much later propositions, promoted the capacity to be alone, a capacity that is paradoxically only possible where there is someone or something *there*, containing the child's absorption and self-reliance in play.[42] And this literature, directed at children and their teachers, provided a rich and suggestive account of the world as it was, and how it had got to be that way: fuel for an imagination, and in their account of the Anglican God, a necessary component of what is now called self-esteem: a child's sense that it matters, and is important to someone else. We have much evidence (most of it drawn from the nineteenth century) of children taught by the disapproving tenets of Evangelicalism – tenets that were, indeed, *à la mode* in Huddersfield parish in the second half of the eighteenth century. The Evangelical vicar of Huddersfield Henry Venn's sermons make a

---

[40] Kilner, *Clear and Concise Account*, pp. 148–51.

[41] James L. Axtell, *The Educational Writings of John Locke. A Critical Edition with Introduction and Notes* (Cambridge: Cambridge University Press, 1968), pp. 3–68.

[42] D. W. Winnicott, 'Playing. A Theoretical Statement', 'The Location of Cultural Experience' and 'The Place Where We Live', in Winnicott, *Playing and Reality* (Harmondsworth: Penguin, 1971), pp. 44–61, 112–21, 122–9. For the capacity of concentration, or attention, emerging in the Enlightenment study of natural history, see the compelling account in Lorraine Daston, 'Attention and the Values of Nature in the Enlightenment', in Lorraine Daston and Fernando Vidal (eds.), *The Moral Authority of Nature* (Chicago and London: University of Chicago Press, 2004), pp. 100–26.

marked contrast with the teaching of a Stonhouse, or Murgatroyd's notes for his. These last are about some*thing*. In their narratives people (and God) do things. A world of intention and action is displayed. The child in the ultimately satisfying and comforting narrative is approved.

John Murgatroyd noted several times that the great end and point of instruction was 'form.g ye Minds to ye principles of relign.', and this was done not just by catechising and instilling the principles of Protestantism, but by the ways and means of a liberal education. Teaching the correct doctrine to schoolchildren was strongly safeguarded throughout the eighteenth century, as it was in the books for children discussed above. The master of a parochial school was qualified and licensed by obeisance to the Thirty-Nine Articles of the Church of England, and by his sworn allegiance to the union of church and state. The Archbishop of York made specific inquiry into the background and work of schoolmasters in his visitation questionnaires.[43] Education was a form of religious instruction, in a county that was relatively rich in schools – about half of Yorkshire parishes had a school, either a free grammar, or one endowed by charity, or a private or petty school, and these grew apace as the century passed.

Slaithwaite Free School was a parochial charity school, first endowed in 1721 by the then curate, Robert Meeke – though to designate it in this way is to use the categories of a much later history of education. Schools established by charitable bequest were probably the most common type of school during Murgatroyd's half-century as a teacher. A minority of these were grammar schools, which were intended for instruction in the classical languages, and a main route to a university education. Most endowed schools were elementary, common parish schools, established for instruction in reading and writing. Slaithwaite school was endowed as one of these, but in practice, under Murgatroyd's regime, the curriculum was much more like that of the grammar school that he himself had attended at Rishworth.[44] It was endowed to take ten children, boys and girls, 'the poorest objects and chosen out of the townships of Sleigthwaite and Lingards'. The master was to teach them the catechism, 'catechise them once a week in school', and make sure that the children attended divine service. He

---

[43] Judith Jago, *Aspects of the Georgian Church. Visitation of the Diocese of York, 1761–1776* (London: Associated University Press, 1997), pp. 64–5, 120–30; 128.

[44] Richard Tompson estimated some 4,000 endowed schools in later eighteenth-century England, about 700 of them grammar schools (schools 'instituted for instruction which includes classics, which school sends students to universities and/or is staffed by graduates, but which may have gone under any of the common descriptive terms for such a school, i.e "free school", free grammar school, grammar school, public school'). During the course of the century, these types of school were added to by 'charity schools' (endowed elementary schools supported by public subscription). Richard S. Tompson, *Classics or Charity? The Dilemma of the 18th-century Grammar School* (Manchester: Manchester University Press, 1971), pp. 1–3, 16, note 2.

was to 'take care of ye manners and behaviour of the scholars', in particular correcting lying and swearing. Parents were expected to ensure school attendance: genuine illness was to be the only excuse for absence. There were provisions for expulsion should a course of 'due admonition' and 'moderate correction' not change bad behaviour. Boys, when they 'could read competently well', were to be taught to write a fair, legible hand, and be grounded in an arithmetic 'sufficient to qualify them for common apprentices'. Girls were only to be taught to read well and to be catechised, 'except the master has a wife, who can teach them to knit and sew'. The master himself had to be a member of the Church of England, 'of a sober life and conversation, and one who frequents the Holy Communion'. He was required to have 'a good genius for teaching youth to read', possess a fair writing hand, and to understand basic arithmetic.[45]

John Murgatroyd was greatly over-qualified for the position, and does not appear to have followed the outlines of this elementary curriculum during his mastership of the school. 'Some educated clergymen found it difficult to identify wholeheartedly with the practices and curriculum of a school which taught reading and writing accounts, when their own learning had comprised Latin and Greek,' says Judith Jago.[46] This was not a constraint felt by John Murgatroyd, nor does he appear to have resented teaching his socially undistinguished scholars. The advertisement for his replacement placed in the *Leeds Mercury* in 1786 mentioned the ability to teach Latin, Greek, other languages, writing, arithmetic and book-keeping as qualifications.[47] He taught the classics to generations of scholars during his term of office at Slaithwaite.[48] He kept a notebook of 'Authors Useful to be Read at School' (it came to contain a great deal else besides), in which the opening entry listed fourteen books, three of them providing exercises in English grammar, three being works of theology, one *Aesop's Fables*, and seven works by classical authors. This was a wish-list, or recommendation to someone else (perhaps drawn up for the new, well-behaved Mr Bolton), rather than an inventory. 'School Books', dated October 1792, counted an actual library of fifty-seven books, of which thirty were works of Latin or Greek, in the original and translation, and including grammars, dictionaries

---

[45] I have been unable to trace any of the records of Slaithwaite Free School. This account is from D. F. E. Sykes, who transcribed the original deeds of trust and Meeke's will in 1896. D. F. E. Sykes, *The History of the Colne Valley* (Slaithwaite: F. Walker, 1896), pp. 138–42, 391–3. See also his *Huddersfield and its Vicinity* (Huddersfield: *Advertiser* Press, 1898), pp. 415–16.

[46] Jago, *Aspects of the Georgian Church*, p. 127.

[47] Murgatroyd, 'Authors Useful to be Read at School'. The 'Book of Records' contains the draft advertisement.

[48] 'There is one free school in which 20 children, boys and girls, are taught reading, writing and arithmetic and Latin,' noted Samuel Furley (curate from 1761 to 1767) filling in the Slaithwaite Visitation return in 1764. Cressida Annesley and Philippa Hoskin (eds.), *Archbishop Drummond's Visitation Returns 1764 III: Yorkshire S–Y*, Borthwick Texts and Calendars 23 (York: University of York, 1998), 'Slaithwaite'.

and commentaries.[49] Some of these were very old works indeed, that would have been familiar to a seventeenth-century – or indeed, a sixteenth-century – schoolmaster (some of them were in editions so old that he must have inherited them from friends and relatives in order to undertake his own instruction in the 1720s). He had a 1695 edition of Lily's *Grammar*, originally designated for use in schools during Elizabeth's reign, and an even older *Methodi Practae*, from 1660.[50] He possessed Hoole's *Accidence* (one of the books he called 'useful') from 1697, a work which, like the others, suggests a very old teaching method as well, in which the grammatic principles of Latin were learned 'without book', in the question and answer form of the catechism:

Qust: How many Parts of Speech be there?
Answ: Eight . . .
Q: What is the Indicative Mood Present tense of Edo?
A: Sing. Edo. I eat.[51]

After learning these rules, the student was meant to proceed to simple texts – epigrams, fables, dialogues – studying them by reading aloud, describing their syntactic structure, and possibly, by translating them. Again, Murgatroyd owned schoolbooks that would have suggested this traditional teaching method, though by the mid-eighteenth century he had the choice of up-to-date editions of the *Colloquies* of Erasmus and Cordery, and Lucian's *History*, and these were volumes he also possessed.[52] The glossaries of rhetorical terms and grammars in his schoolbook library were probably his own teaching aids, as were his

---

49 Murgatroyd, 'Book of Records'.
50 For Lily's *Grammar*, see Tompson, *Classics or Charity?*, p. 19. William Lily, *The Royal Grammar Reformed . . . for the better Understanding of the English and the more speedy Attainment of the Latin Tongue* (London: A. and J. Churchill, 1695). Christopher Wase, *Methodi Practae Specimen. An Essay of Practical Grammar, or an Inquiry after a more easie help to the construing . . . of Authors and the making and speaking of Latin* (London: privately printed, 1660).
51 Charles Hoole, *The Common Accidence Explained by Short Questions and Answers. According to the very Words of the Book* (London: A. Armstrong, 1697), pp. 3, 57.
52 John Clarke, *Erasmi Colloquia Selecta: or, the Select Colloquies of Erasmus*, 22nd edn (London: J. F. C. Rivington, 1789). John Clarke, *Corderii Colloquior mu Centuria Selecta, or, a Century of Cordery's Colloquies*, 15th edn (London: W. Smith, 1773). John Clarke, *A Compendius History of Rome by L. Florus with an English Translation*, 6th edn (London: Hawes, Clarke and Collins, 1763). He had given up teaching by the time an edition of Corderius was published in Huddersfield: John Clarke, *Corderii Colloquiorum. Centura Selecta. A Select Century of Corderius's Colloquies; with an English Translation, as Literal as Possible; designed for the Use of Beginners in the Latin Tongue. A New Edition. Corrected* (Huddersfield: Brook and Lancashire, 1798). For the traditional method of Latin teaching, see the preface to any of Clarke's textbooks, including this Huddersfield edition; and particularly, Peter Mack, *Elizabethan Rhetoric. Theory and Practice* (Cambridge: Cambridge University Press, 2002), pp. 11–47. See Ian Michael, *The Teaching of English from the Sixteenth Century to 1870* (Cambridge: Cambridge University Press, 1987), pp. 317–20 for the relationship between teaching Latin and teaching English.

several dictionaries. He had half a dozen of these, including Farnaby's *Index Rhetoricus* and Smith's *Rhetorick*.[53]

When John Murgatroyd first came to teach in the 1730s, there was also available a new genre of Latin schoolbooks, and he made careful note of some of their editors in making his inventory. Gentlemen and clerical scholars like John Clarke fulminated much about the arid and impenetrable method of older works. In all of his prefaces, Clarke referred his schoolmaster readers to his thoughts on translation available in his *Essay upon the Education of Youth in Grammar-Schools* (1734, 1740).[54] He was particularly scathing about the teaching method implied by someone like Hoole: boys sitting around to hear two or three lines of Cordery construed by the master, maybe twice, if they were lucky. This was meant to keep them occupied for a couple of hours, copying out the lines and parsing them; but needing more help, 'they must sit doing of nothing, or be continually pacing it up and down the School to the Master'.[55] He thought this 'tedious, lingering Way of Proceeding' particularly hard on boys not destined for university. 'The five or six years spent [in school] . . . is Time absolutely thrown away, for almost double the Time is necessary for the Attainment of but a moderate Skill in [Latin].'[56] Translation was the answer, the absolutely modern method, using text set in parallel if possible.[57] He promoted literal translation for beginners. In his parallel text *Colloquies of Erasmus*, he altered the word order of the English translation rather than of the Latin, for it was after all Latin that they were learning: 'All concerned with the Instruction of young Boys in the Latin Tongue cannot but be sensible of how much their Progress is retarded by the Difficulty arising from the perplexed intricate Order of the Words in that Language. This is a continual Rub in their Way . . .'[58] Others, exercised by the word-order question, went about things in a different way. John Stirling, in his edition of Phaedrus's *Fables*, dealt with the problem by not offering a translation at all. Rather, 'for the greater ease and assistance of Boys, below every Fable, the Words are taken out of their respective Places as

---

[53] Thomas Farnaby, *Index Rhetoricus et Oratorius. Scholis, & institutioni Aeatis accomodatus* (London: G. Conyers and J. Clarke, 1728). John Smith, *The Mystery of Rhetorick Unveiled* (London: George Eversden, 1693). Murgatroyd's schoolbook inventory reads much like Henry Fielding's list in *Tom Jones*; by having '*Erasmi Colloquia, Ovid de Tristebus; Gradus ad Parnassum* . . . Echard's *Roman History* . . .' end up with Jones the barber 'a little torn', he comments on the extraordinary longevity and usage of educators like these. *The History of Tom Jones A Foundling*, orig. pub. 1749 (Harmondsworth: Penguin, 1985), p. 341.

[54] John Clarke, *An Essay upon the Education of Youth in Grammar-Schools*, 3rd edn (London: Charles Hitch, 1740). See also his *Dissertation upon the Usefulness of Translations of Classick Authors, both literal and free, for the easy and expeditious Attainment of the Latin Tongue, being an Extract from the Essay upon Education* (London: privately printed, 1734).

[55] Clarke, *Coredrii Colloquior*, Preface.   [56] Clarke, *Lucius Florus*, Preface.

[57] It was not new at all, as a method. From the early seventeenth century, textbook writers had been concerned with innovation in the layout and general presentation of Latin texts. See Mack, *Elizabethan Rhetoric*, pp. 11–47.

[58] Clarke, *Erasmi Colloquia*, Preface.

they stand in the Text, and ranged in a proper Order, as they are to be construed into our Language'.[59] For the little sons of wool combers, sitting out their five years of Latin, this text could not have produced the startling and arresting effect of the play with English word order in Clarke's *Erasmus*.

Some thought that the translation method had been taken too far. Murgatroyd approved of Nathan Bailey's *English and Latin Lessons for School-Boys* (or at least, listed it twice in his inventories). Bailey thought that the 'great *Heap of Words* with which our common Word Books do so frightfully swell' ought to be discarded, as he had so industriously laboured to do. He meant by this the efforts of other translators to make Latin more acceptable to little English boys by inventing words to describe the things of the modern world they inhabited. But 'why should a Person that is to be prepared for the Reading of Corderius, Phaedrus &c be led through a series of *modern Barbarisms*, and loaded with a Multitude of Words which the Romans never heard of?'[60]

Most of the modern, eighteenth-century readers that Murgatroyd had in his possession promised to be as diverting as possible in their instruction in Latin, or as James Greenwood put it, to be as 'Natural and Entertaining [as] the Subject is capable of', in his preparation of children for a reading of Corderius, the Latin Testament, Phaedrus, Aesop, Cato and Ovid.[61] Incidental entertainment that came with this teaching territory had been available for a very long time, as long as you had not restricted your pedagogy to the all-Latin, all-grammar strictness of a Hoole, or a Smith. Colloquies, in particular, proceeded by an amiable mixture of the zany and the utterly familiar, in which in some timeless realm mothers were too busy in the morning to prepare your lunch box, fathers handed out pocket money when the fair came round, where the fish did swim and the birds did fly. Long, shaggy-dog stories, proceeding by question and answer (to the eternal question of narrative: what happened then?), dealt with a social world, only ever-so-slightly odd, full of people living lives in particular ways. Long, entirely familiar exchanges between teachers and pupils fill their pages – a kind of joke that proceeds by dissolving the boundary between the now of the Slaithwaite schoolroom and the then of the text.[62] Some decades after this, the radical George Holyoake remembered this kind of book from his

---

[59] John Stirling, *Phaedri Fabulae: or, Phaedrus's Fables with . . . Improvements . . . in a Method entirely new*, 9th edn (London: J. Rivington, 1771), Preface. Murgatroyd had this, though not necessarily this edition.

[60] Nathan Bailey, *English and Latin Exercises for School-Boys: Comprising the Rules of Syntaxis, with Explanations, and other necessary Observations on each Rule*, 11th edn (London: R. Ware, 1744), Preface.

[61] James Greenwood, *The London Vocabulary. English and Latin put into a new Method, proper to acquaint the Learner with Things, as well as Pure Latin Words. Adorned with Twenty-six Pictures*, 11th edn (London: C. Hitch, 1749), Preface.

[62] Clarke, *Erasmi Colloquia*; *Cordery's Colloquies*.

childhood; he compared the great ordering of the natural world to the ordering of grammar rules he had acquired in the 1820s.[63] Bailey's grammar of 1744 was weirdly arresting because of that great eternal, timeless universe, in which the sun always rises and sets, and dogs and cats behave as they do, but also because of the odd conjunction of visual images in many of his examples of cases, tenses and moods. Moreover, were you in a school that allowed you to have *English and Latin Exercises* in your hands (rather than the master reserving it as his method book), then you would not have to be very accomplished in the Latin tongue to discover what going with a whorish woman might do for – and to – you.[64] For two hundred years at least, a broadly humanist conception of education had encouraged the reading of Ovid's *Metamorphoses*, for example, because of the moral lessons that could be extracted from it, for its retelling of the Greek myths, and for the general knowledge about the natural world that it contained. Murgatroyd had two editions in his schoolbook collection. Like generations of schoolmasters had done, Murgatroyd would have had to find a way of incorporating the pragmatic approach of the pagans to social and sexual behaviour into the framework of a Christian education.[65]

The material Murgatroyd used for the teaching of English was far less amusing. Contemporary linguistic theory held that all modern languages, English included, were variants of a universal grammar common to all.[66] As Latin syntax was understood to be a better representative of universal structures than was English, school readers presented their mother-tongue to pupils within the same categorical and analytic framework as Latin.[67] There were innovations in English teaching available by the second half of the eighteenth century, and Murgatroyd had a copy of Ann Fisher's *Exercises of Bad English* (or perhaps it was the Leeds publication *Exercises, Instructive and Entertaining, in False English*) in his library. Significantly, it was not kept in his schoolbook collection; perhaps he found it as wasteful of school time as Peter Fogg, who described children legging it up and down the schoolroom to have one painful correction after another to a sentence like 'Thi gospil maiks every man my naibour', approved by the master.[68] Fisher divided her text by the topics of Orthography,

[63] George Holyoake, *Practical Grammar*, orig. pub. 1844 (London: Book Store, 1870), pp. 7–8.

[64] Bailey, *English and Latin Exercises*, p. 107.

[65] Mack, *Elizabethan Rhetoric*, pp. 8, 17. Murgatroyd also possessed Ovid's *Art of Love*, but did not list it as a book useful for teaching.

[66] Hans Aarsleff, *The Study of Language in England, 1780–1860* (Minneapolis: University of Minnesota Press, 1983), pp. 3–43. James Beattie, *The Theory of Language. In Two Parts. Of the Origin and General Nature of Speech . . .* (Edinburgh: Strahan, Cadell and Creech, 1788). David Crystal, *Cambridge Encyclopedia of Language* (Cambridge: Cambridge University Press, 1987), pp. 84, 406.

[67] Michael, *Teaching of English*, pp. 318–30.

[68] Ann Fisher, *A New Grammar, with Exercises of Bad English: or, an easy Guide to Speaking and writing the English Language Properly*, 4th edn (Newcastle upon Tyne: I. Thompson, 1754). For

Prosody, Etymology, Syntax; it is a very thorough – and mighty dull – exposition of the grammar and structure of the English language. When tense agreement was the fault false-English sentences attempted to correct, some small West Riding dialect-speakers may have come to doubt their own speech, but that is the closest the text comes to any language spoken by an actual human being. This is not the case with the homilies and maxims and moral and stories of the *Colloquies* of Erasmus, or even of Culman's *Sententiae Pueriles*, where many of the scenes to be imagined out of the text involve people and animals doing and saying things as they did in 1780s Yorkshire – or in the universal Anywhere.[69]

As for basic instruction in reading and writing, which Slaithwaite Free School was set up to provide, we should not expect to find traces of instructional material in Murgatroyd's library. Very early learners may have copied letters and syllables on to slates; before this, they may have learned the names of letters 'without book', or indeed, without anything at all, except the resources of the catechism and their master's verbal example.[70] Or perhaps – which is more likely – the scholars who, as Murgatroyd noted with pride, 'came in plenty' were past this initial stage. Twenty-nine children registered between 31 May and 31 July 1739 (the only list from half a century of Murgatroyd's teaching that we have), including five groups of brothers and sisters. In these family groups the oldest children must be assumed to have been taught to read at home.[71]

This curriculum – founded on the teaching of Latin, much like that of a grammar school – was what local parents wanted. Education may have been long tailored to commerce: 'the next thing after Learning to be Remark'd in [Halifax], is their manner and way of Trade, into which their Youth, when taken from School are chiefly Educated', noted John Bentley in 1761; 'And this their way of Education hath a principal relation to the Woollen Manufacture, consisting in Making, Buying, & Selling Cloth.'[72] But even descriptions of a modern education for the making of modern commercial man emphasised the

---

Fisher, see Michael, *Teaching of English*, pp. 325–6. Peter Walkden Fogg, *Elementa anglicana; or, the Principles of English Grammar Displayed and Exemplified . . .* (Stockport: J. Clarke, 1796). Cited by Michaels, p. 328.

[69] Murgatroyd put Leonhard Culman's *Sententiae Pueriles* (1639) on his recommendatory 'Authors Useful to be Read at School' list, but does not seem to have possessed a copy.

[70] See Michael, *Teaching of English*, pp. 14–125 for a thorough account of early learning, from the sixteenth century onwards.

[71] Murgatroyd, 'Authors Useful to be Read at School'. Two of these children were noted as being 'free' scholars. As Judith Jago remarks, fee-paying children (who appear to have been the majority in Slaithwaite) would be unlikely to be mentioned on Visitation returns, especially in an establishment set up for free education. Jago, *Aspects of the Georgian Church*, p. 131. The last name on the register – 'Smith, Mary – to pay 2 lessons' – suggests a very great flexibility of provision.

[72] John Bentley, *Halifax and Its Gibbet-law. Placed in a True Light. Together with a Description of the Town, the Nature of the Soil, the Temper and Disposition of the People* (Halifax: P. Darby for the Author, 1761), pp. 9–11.

importance of instruction in Latin. Martin Clare's *Youth's Introduction to Trade and Business* (which Murgatroyd acquired sometime between 1792 and 1799) laid out an entire educational programme for an embryonic man of business, starting with reading and grammar, French, writing, arithmetic, commercial law (enough to understand what a promissory note was, and how to interpret a bill of exchange), book-keeping, drawing, geography, navigation and experimental philosophy. But he must also learn Latin: it would make him a better master of his own tongue, and the frequent use of English translations would transmit a 'Propriety of Stile . . . [that] elegance and good sense requisite for all, that hope to be considerable in the world'.[73] George Fisher's *Young Man's Best Companion*, which Murgatroyd also possessed, promised to 'qualify any person for business, without the aid of a Master'. It described a curriculum much like the one Clare recommended, with the exception of Latin.[74] You could not learn Latin without a master; the teaching of Latin may have been what made and defined a schoolmaster, in parents' understanding.

Murgatroyd taught many of these up-to-date subjects in Slaithwaite. He owned several volumes for teaching arithmetic; Fisher's and Clare's manuals provided a maths curriculum as well.[75] The point of Henry Morehouse's *Village Gleanings*, compiled a hundred years later from Murgatroyd's archive, was to demonstrate that a parochial school like Slaithwaite's could produce a distinguished scientific scholar like James Horsfall (d.1785).[76] But Latin was the foundation for little James's later achievement. Morehouse transcribed a letter from the boy, written under direction to an uncle in London, a product

---

[73] Martin Clare, *Youth's Introduction to Trade and Business*, 18th edn (London: G. Keith, 1769). Clare's emphasis on keeping records and the usefulness of abbreviation in making notes may have promoted Murgatroyd's interest in shorthand. It is certainly something that parents may have asked to be included on the curriculum. He devoted twenty pages of the 'Authors Useful' notebook to either practising shorthand, or making lesson plans for teaching it, probably the latter. He had no shorthand primer in his library; the length of these notes suggests he was working from a borrowed book.

[74] George Fisher (Accomptant), *The Instructor, or Young Man's Best Companion . . . to which is added The Family's Best Companion . . . and a Complete Treatise of Farriery*, 13th edn (London: S. Birt, 1755).

[75] He possessed John Saxton's *The Merchant's Companion, and tradesman's vade mecum: or, Practical Arithmetick, both vulgar and decimal, . . . Together with an appendix for those who are advanced in accompts, . . . The whole necessary for all men of business, teachers of accompts, and their scholars* (Manchester: R. Whitworth, 1737); Edward Cocker's *Cocker's Arithmetic. Being a plain and familiar method, suitable to the meanest capacity, for the full understanding of that incomparable art* (Edinburgh: Walter Ruddiman, 1757); and either Richard Locke's *A Miscellany of Mathematicks, in two parts* (London: Innys and Manby, 1736) or Solomon Lowe's *Arithmetic in Two Parts, containing I. A System of the Art in memorial Verses . . . II. A Collection of Exercises* (London: James Hodges, 1749).

[76] Henry James Morehouse (ed.), *Village Gleanings, or Notes and Jottings from the Manuscripts of the Rev. John Murgatroyd, Master of the Free School at Slaithwaite . . . Including some Account – derived from other Sources – of his distinguished Scholar, James Horsfall, FRS, . . . Son of the Village Blacksmith* (Huddersfield: Parkin, 1886), pp. 18–26.

of Murgatroyd's anxiety to seek for him 'a superior education for his future advancement':

I have, with the leave of my father, taken the opportunity to acquaint you with my progress in the Latin tongue . . . I read these Books . . . Grammar, Latin Testament, Aesop's Fables, and Clarke's Erasmus, and, my master says, with tolerable knowledge. Also I write exercises out of Bailey, and have familiar forms with Cole's Dictionary . . . I was nine years of age, the 18th of this instant . . .[77]

Things went on in Slaithwaite Free School in a way so unlike the way in which the terms of the original deed of endowment proposed that we may even entertain the notion that girls were taught Latin by John Murgatroyd. Of the first entry of twenty-nine children in 1739, seven were girls (and three of these, little sisters of older boys). Perhaps registration of girls stayed at a quarter of the number of boys for the next fifty years, but we are really not to know. In his response to the 1764 Visitation question about teaching at Slaithwaite, the then curate Samuel Furly recorded that '20 children, boys and girls, are taught reading, writing, arithmetic and Latin'.[78] He made no distinction by gender in the acquisition of Latin, and indeed, in a one-room school, where your brother and his friends spend the day getting the *Colloquies* of Cordery and Erasmus by heart and parsing them, it would have been difficult to avoid the Latin tongue, even if you were (as the deeds of trust required, but as probably did not happen) restricted to the syllables on your slate and the Testament. Things went on in this school so oppositional to what was required by deed of trust and conventional and historical expectation that the girls who attended it may well have ended up like Nelly Dean in *Wuthering Heights* (whom, it should be remembered, received her own education in the 1770s Yorkshire of Emily Brontë's historical imagination), able to read any book that took their fancy, 'and got something out of also; unless it be that range of Greek and Latin and that of French – and those . . . know one from another, it is as much as you can expect of a poor man's daughter'.

What also went on, in clear contravention of the deeds, was boarding and fee-paying. Murgatroyd wrote to parents and relatives, acknowledging payments received 'for Learning and Board', reinforcing his regret at termination of study with a little appositely placed (and translated) Latin, so that a Marsden uncle without it could see what the boy was missing: his 'hopeful Nephew' had 'natural talents', he told Mr Haigh; his behaviour had been 'exceedingly commendable', and his 'Diligence becoming'. 'And wn I reflect upon what Horace one of ye greatest of his Times, says, Viz Non progredi, est regredi, that is Not

[77] Morehouse, *Village Gleanings*, pp. 19–20.
[78] Annesley and Hoskin, *Archbishop Drummond's Visitation Returns . . . Yorkshire S–Y*, 'Slaithwaite'.

to go forward, is to go backward, I'm sorry yt ye Thread of his Education must be broken . . .'[79]

The boy had 'ingratiated Himself very much at our House'. Children did board, a problem for one Halifax father, who removed his son in 1753 because of the 'restless plaguey itch' that had invaded the school. On the defensive, Murgatroyd wrote that 'our family' had always been 'remarkably happy for Cleanliness, decency and good order & are so now'; possibly it was the boy's fault?; 'if D — l contracted untoward this plague, & communicated it [to others] & so forwards, who's to be blamed?' Perhaps this 'hellish disorder' could be kept at a distance by letting his son 'lie with me . . .'[80]

Boys also boarded with Slaithwaite householders in the township. Murgatroyd explained to Robert Hamilton's father why the boy had legged it back to Halifax, and what he was like. He had trampled his landlord's 'standing Corn, & pretending to fear some severe punishment from ye old Man who I believe wou'd only have talk'd Him roundly, has made it an Occasion of this Disobedience – '. Robert had upped the ante. Murgatroyd had heard him talking to the other lads about getting his father on his side, 'cou'd he but embrace ye opportunity of telling you his Grievances'. 'Now', said Murgatroyd, 'the true Case is this – his natural Disposition is greatly Averse to Restraint, & pursuant to your Intention in sending him hither, I have kept him up to Scholastic order, by inculcating what he must do, what eschew, & gently restraining his unbecoming Liberties These Lectures thwarting his licentious Schemes, have as I've lately observed, oft made him uneasy, & promise himS[elf]: . . . a very favourable Audience of you.' What his father should do now was 'return him to his Duty & tell him you entirely leave him to my Discretion & gentle Admonitions'.[81] One thing that did go on according to the deeds of trust was 'due admonition', as well as 'moderate correction'.

John Murgatroyd thought about these things, in his last commonplace book. He ruminated on the fact that 'A School . . . Tho' it takes its Denomination from Grammar . . . in its ultimate Effect ought to be . . . a Cure of Souls: tho' Alas! it's not considered by too many . . .' He was at one with that mainstream of Anglican opinion, stretching back two hundred years, that it was 'to those Nurseries of Youth it is yt. Pulpits owe their Success or Disappointment'; moreover, 'if ye greatest Perplexities & most dangerous Convulsions, whch. have at any Time befallen any Government . . . they will be found to spring chiefly fm ye Defect of due Means & proper Methods in ye Education of Youth'. Teaching 'a little

[79] Murgatroyd, 'Book of Records', copy of a letter to Mr Samuel Haigh at Marsden, dated September 1749.

[80] Murgatroyd, 'Book of Records', copy of a letter dated January 1753.

[81] Murgatroyd, 'Book of Records', copy of a letter to Mr Hamilton at Halifax, dated 21 August 1750.

Latin & Greek . . . would not deserve ye Name of Xtian Education was not at ye same Time ye greatest regard had to the subordination of disorderly Passions, ye rectifying of perverse Inclinations ye implanting of virtuous Habits'.[82] He had done this – rectified the perverse passions of his little scholars – he thought, by looking 'on 'em very lovingly' and by cheerful teaching. This form of love, relatively new in the world, which arose in the specific historical conjunction of people, knowledge about the world and social circumstances that is the schoolroom, must await discussion for a little while yet.

---

[82] Murgatroyd, 'Ask, Read, Retain, Teach', KC249/9, p. 3. He did teach Greek, on some occasions, to some children. He possessed three Greek grammars, a Greek *Sententiae*, two Greek *Testaments* and Edward Leigh's *Critica Sacra: or Philologicall and Theologicall Observations upon all the Greek Words of the New Testament in Order alphabeticall, etc.* (London: privately printed, 1646), among others. He listed all of these as 'School Books'.

7   Relations

At the century's close, it was still the law that provided the major means for an employer's understanding of what kind of relationship that of master and servant actually was. Indeed, quite recent common law judgment had reformulated the relationship in consideration of *pregnant* maidservants like Phoebe Beatson. We need the story of this judgment in order to understand the true unusualness of Murgatroyd's behaviour from the end of 1801 until his death in 1806, for in 1777 the Lord Chief Justice, William Mansfield, had found a domestic servant's being with child cause for her lawful dismissal. In February of that year Lord Mansfield and his fellow judges heard the case of Rex v. the Inhabitants of Brampton in Derbyshire. It was a poor law settlement case that had come to King's Bench on appeal. In 1776 Hannah Wright had been removed on the order of two justices from Ashover to Brampton, both of them Derbyshire parishes. Brampton parish had appealed to quarter sessions, where the removal order was confirmed by the magistrates, because Hannah Wright had earned her legal settlement there through a year's hiring and wage-earning. This settlement in Brampton was not really in question, but rather whether or not it might have been superseded by one worked for at Eyam, another Derbyshire village some 15 miles west of Brampton along the Chapel-en-le-Frith road. She had hired herself to Mr Longsdon of that place for a year, and had served under the hiring until just three weeks before the time was up, when 'her master discovering her to be with child, turned her away, and paid her year's wages, and half a crown over; whereupon she went home to her father's at Ashover, from whence she was removed'.[1] Examined at quarter sessions, Hannah Wright said that

---

[1] Thomas Caldecott, *Reports of Cases Relative to the Duty and Office of a Justice of the Peace, from Michaelmas Term 1776, inclusive, to Trinity Term 1785, inclusive* (London: His Majesty's Law Printers for P. Uriel, 1785), p. 11. Quarter Sessions Records, Q/SO 1/9. Translation Sessions, 1776. 'Ashover v. Walton' [Brampton], Derbyshire County Record Office, Matlock. PRO, KB 16/18/1. Records of Orders Files, 17 Geo.III, 1776–1777, The National Archives, Kew. The Order – 'the Writt' – demanding the production of local documents in the case from the Derbyshire magistrates is dated 23 February 1777. This discussion of Hannah Wright's case is taken from the more detailed account in Carolyn Steedman, 'Lord Mansfield's Women', *Past and Present*, 176 (2002), pp. 105–43. See also Paul Craven and Douglas Hay, *Masters, Servants and Magistrates in Britain and the Empire, 1562–1955* (Chapel Hill and London: University of North Carolina Press, 2004), p. 110.

she 'was willing to have staid her year out, if she might; but . . . it was not material to her whether she staid or went, as she had received her whole year's wages; and that she was not half gone with her child when she left her service; and hoped that she could have done the work of her place to the end of the year'.

At Derbyshire quarter sessions, as the parishes of Ashover and Brampton slugged it out, each attempting to rid itself of responsibility for a mother and her bastard child, the case was discussed in terms of the contract between her and her master: whether or not it had been dissolved before the end of the year for which Hannah Wright was hired; whether or not Mr Longsdon had acted 'either arbitrarily or fraudulently'. An employer surely had a right to dismiss his servant if he had 'just and reasonable cause'; there could be no doubt 'but that a criminal conduct like [hers] amounts to a reasonable cause'. To be sure, there was earlier case law to say that 'a maid-servant, got with child can't be dismissed from her service', but that law applied to women who worked as servants in husbandry, surely, and moreover meant they could not be *removed by the parish officers* before the contract was dissolved. In this case, Hannah Wright's misconduct was a very good reason for her master to dissolve contract. There were those who said that a magistrate should have been applied to; 'but in the first place, this [was] not the case of a servant in husbandry, and therefore a justice of the peace had no jurisdiction . . . or if he had, it was in this case unnecessary, as the servant consented [to her own dismissal]', for had she not just said that she really wasn't *very* pregnant and could easily have worked up to her confinement – that 'it was not material to her whether she staid or went, as she had received her whole year's wages'? The question of wages was an important one: did her master give her her full wages (and that extra half a crown) because he assumed that the contract was to last until the end of the year? No; because it has been 'again and again . . . determined that a deduction of wages does not prove a contract *dissolved* within the year'. The arguments on the other side (for Brampton and only incidentally for Hannah Wright) were that 'all the authorities say, that when dismission of a servant is accompanied . . . with the payment of the whole wages, it shall be considered as a . . . constructive continuance of it to the end of the year'. To argue in this way meant denying the servant's consent to the dissolution of the contract, and seeing the extra 2s 6d as a substitute for her board and lodging; indeed, if you followed this train of thought, 'the only object of the master was to defeat the settlement of the servant in his parish'.[2]

When the case came to King's Bench, Mansfield moved with lightning speed from these questions, pondered again by his fellow judges, into the role

---

[2] Caldecott, *Reports*, pp. 1–14.

identified by his first biographer, that of '*custos morum* of the people'.[3] He agreed with the Derbyshire opinion, that her saying that she could have worked out her time was not the point: 'it is not her ability but her criminal conduct that must be the test; or otherwise a master might be obliged to keep a woman in the house for many months, though he were a clergyman, or had a wife and daughters . . .'[4] Derbyshire justices and Mansfield's fellow judges might make the point that Hannah Wright had committed no crime: that 'an unmarried woman by being with child is not guilty of any crime, or even misdemeanour at common law . . .' But the Lord Chief Justice focused on the question of hiring, and referred to 8 & 9 Will.III c.30 (1697) in order to say that 'there must be a hiring for a year, and a continuance for a year in that service, to gain a settlement'.[5] And service, by its very nature he said, 'admits often of questions upon the circumstances . . . but these questions have always been brought to this point. Whether the contract was put an end [to] within the year.' This could not be done by dismissing the servant without good cause, and the solution here to the problem of Hannah Wright rested on asking a quite different question, not about her wrong-doing at all, but rather 'has the master done right or wrong in discharging his servant for this cause?' 'I think he did not do wrong,' Mansfield said. Certainly, if an employer agreed under these circumstances to the continuance of contract (agreed to keep on a pregnant servant) 'the overseers it is true, shall not take her away, because she is with child'.[6] But did this then mean, pursued Mansfield, that 'the master therefore be bound to keep her in his house'? To do this 'would be contra *bonos mores*; and in a family where there are young persons, both scandalous and dangerous'. His fellow judges agreed that 'if the master had daughters, it would not be fit that he should keep such a servant'.[7] The removal orders were affirmed, a point for case law and the justices' manuals, but not for Hannah Wright, or it would seem – in a different

---

[3] Mansfield's role as guardian of the people's morals was identified by his first biographer. John Holliday, *The Life of William Late Earl of Mansfield* (London: P. Elmly and D. Bremner, 1797), p. 214.

[4] Caldecott, *Reports*, pp. 1–14.

[5] 'An Act for Supplying some Defects in the Laws for the Relief of the Poor of this Kingdom'. Mansfield's judgment as described here is taken from Francis Const, *Decisions of the Court of the King's Bench, Upon the Laws Relating to the Poor, Originally Published by Edmund Bott Esq. of the Inner Temple, Barrister at Law. Revised . . . by Francis Const Esq. of the Middle Temple*, 3rd edn, 2 vols. (London: Whieldon and Butterworth, 1793), vol. II, pp. 516–18.

[6] See Keith Snell on this point: 'Pauper Settlements and the Right to Relief in England and Wales', *Continuity and Change*, 6:3 (1991), p. 384. Norma Landau, 'Going Local. The Social History of Stuart and Hanoverian England', *Journal of British Studies*, 24:2 (1985), p. 279. Norma Landau, 'Laws of Settlement and the Surveillance of Immigration in Eighteenth-century Kent', *Continuity and Change*, 3 (1988), pp. 391–420. Norma Landau, 'The Eighteenth-century Context of the Laws of Settlement', *Continuity and Change*, 6:3 (1991), pp. 417–39.

[7] Thomas Waller Williams, *The Whole Law Relative to the Duty Office of a Justice of the Peace*, 4 vols. (London: John Stockdale, 1812), vol. III, pp. 902–3.

modality – for Phoebe Beatson, whose employer was a clergyman and had, if not daughters, nieces of an impressionable age running in and out of the Lingards household on a daily basis, accompanying the heavily pregnant Phoebe on her last trips to Huddersfield, and helping with the housework towards the end of her time.

By the time the Derbyshire case came to Westminster Hall in February 1777, matters – following a different timetable from that of the appeal system – had proceeded apace in Derbyshire. Hannah's daughter Mary had been born and baptised in July 1776 at Ashover, her grandfather's village.[8] This was where, three years later, her second 'Base Dr' was also christened. John Bower, forge man of that parish – easy to track down, unlike the elusive and historically paper-less George Thorp – was named as father of Sarah, as he possibly had been of Mary.[9] Her case was cited as late as 1812 for the benefit of justices of the peace, to show that 'a master may of his own authority, and without the intervention of a magistrate, dismiss [a] servant for moral turpitude; even though it be not such for which the servant may be prosecuted at common law'.[10] In 1825, two former household servants writing a conduct manual for others, stated matter-of-factly that 'Should a woman with child be hired for a term, and her master knew not of it, or should she prove with child during her servitude, he may discharge her, with the concurrence of a magistrate.'[11]

Commenting on the likelihood of dismissal for a pregnant servant (and the contingent, but clearly likely 'new born child murder' in which he is interested), Mark Jackson points out that servants were 'in theory protected by law from summary dismissal'.[12] The protection afforded by 5 Eliz.c.4 extended only to servants in husbandry, but many pregnant women who worked indoors and out found themselves to be domestic servants for the purpose of law and parish ratepayers, who might be dismissed after Mansfield's judgment in the case of Hannah Wright. The judges behaved quite differently a year later, when in the case of Ursula Owens of St Bartholomew's by the Exchange in London, they supported the settlement of a servant seven days short of her year's service (but then, she was not pregnant). Her employer had gone to Manchester to purchase a factory, telling his servants on his return that he would soon be moving there,

---

[8] Ashover Parish Register, 'Christenings at Ashover 1776 July Mary Base Dr of Hannah Wright', Parish Records, M77 Vol. 2, Derbyshire County Record Office, Matlock.

[9] Ashover Parish Register, entry for 4 July 1779, Parish Records, M77 Vol. 2. Quarter Sessions Records, Q/SO 1/9, Order Books, 1774–1780. Easter Sessions 1779, Derbyshire County Record Office, Matlock.

[10] Williams, *Whole Law*, vol. III, pp. 902–3.

[11] Samuel and Sarah Adams, *The Complete Servant; Being a Practical Guide to the peculiar Duties and Business of all Descriptions of Servants from the Housekeeper to the Servant of All-Work, and from the Land Steward to the Footboy; with Useful Receipts and Tables* (London: Knight and Lacey, 1825), p. 11.

[12] Mark Jackson, *New-Born Child Murder. Women, Illegitimacy and the Courts in Eighteenth-century England* (Manchester and New York: Manchester University Press, 1996), pp. 48–9.

'but he did not mention any time & that they might look out for other services if they chuse and might stay with him till he went to Manchester'. One evening in June 1777 he abruptly paid Owens the whole of her wages and half a guinea over, and left for the north. She found a new job two days later, in a different parish, only a year later finding herself removed back to St Bartholomew's. In disagreement with Mansfield, Judges Dunning and Sylvester spoke of her loss of settlement, 'her only one, which she deserves so well', saying that 'Justice as well as reason of the thing are here with the Settlement'. 'Service wanted 7 days of a Year but whole years wages pd gains a Settlement', run the notes on the back of the papers in the case. Indeed; but not for Hannah Wright.[13]

'Pregnancy was grounds for immediate dismissal' of a maidservant, says Bridget Hill. Two of her three example cases are from the period after the Mansfield judgment of 1777.[14] In another case from December 1789, when Julius Hardy, Birmingham button-maker of the Methodistical persuasion, dismissed his pregnant maidservant, he did not think of – probably knew nothing of – this case law; he simply assumed that it was within his capacity as an employer to do so. He had not noticed the girl's condition until an old friend, invited round to smoke a pipe one evening, 'observing the servant girl closely . . . concluded she was pregnant; and in a friendly manner by and bye told his suspicions . . . He spoke pretty confidently.'[15] Hardy got rid of her pretty smartish, though a heavy fall of snow prevented the arrival of the neighbouring matron he had asked to do the actual dismissing. He had to endure what he called two whole 'wearisome nights' full of uneasy sensations, with the girl still in the house. He professed himself 'thunderstruck' at his friend's observation; he was very worried indeed that the situation 'might have involved my reputation in *supposed* guilt beyond the power of remedy'. What would the neighbours think – particularly the Methodist ones? And how might this troubling incident affect his own chances in the marriage market? Would anybody assume that he was the father? When Mrs Stansfield finally arrived to perform the dismissal, equally tuned-in to neighbourly reputation, she told Hardy that he could not turn the girl out there and then into the snow 'lest anyone should impute it a piece of cruelty'.

It was a true crisis for Hardy – 'an affair which had given me the greatest uneasiness, more by far than I ever told any person'. He thought about the maid all the time, running imagined scenes over and over in his mind, especially when he learned that the father was the son of a respectable neighbour and landlord who had entertained the girl ('this abominable creature') at the family house and

[13] Dampier Manuscripts, A. P. B, 19. Easter Term, 1778, Lincoln's Inn Library, London.
[14] Bridget Hill, *Women, Work, and Sexual Politics in Eighteenth-century England* (Oxford: Blackwell, 1989), pp. 136–7.
[15] 'Diary of Julius Hardy (1786–1793) Button-Maker, of Birmingham', transcribed and annotated by A. M. Banks, April 1973, MS 839/53, Birmingham Central Library, Archives Department, Birmingham (28, 29, 30 November, 2 December 1789).

encouraged the relationship between the young pair. He brooded on scenes of love-making taking place under the parents' 'very noses or perhaps frequently in sight . . . [of] freedoms with her, which a modest person should blush to hear named'. Indeed, through the long days and nights he waited to dismiss her (and evidently long after), 'her condition, abominable past practices, and the probable consequences were uppermost, and well-nigh constantly in [his] thoughts'. He finally paid her her wages due (insisting on a receipt); her young man picked her up and presumably took her to his parents' house. Hardy hoped she was ashamed; but there is no indication at all that she was. She and her baby escape all accounting in poor law and legal registers, for this nameless young woman did not need to claim poor relief, having a young man who recognised his child *in utero* and his responsibilities towards the woman (who was evidently well liked by his family).[16]

By the 1790s there were new means available for telling the story of the servant in your house to add to those available from legal process. (It is unlikely that Murgatroyd read any of these new works – they were not in his library. The argument here must rest on the changing nature of circulating plots in the society at large – as indeed, it has done so far in this discussion of the two lives lived out in the Slaithwaite-cum-Lingards household.) Conventional warnings against the servant's insubordination and disobedience that the household advice books had been delivering for nigh on three hundred years, with all their biblical footnotes, were still being delivered in the 1780s. *A Present for Servants* (in its tenth and final edition of 1787) told masters and mistresses that domestic servants were 'Part of every family' and there *'by reason of Poverty . . .* according to the Word of God'; and told servants that they might see the Master of all things in their own.[17] In the same year, in her *Servant's Friend*, Sarah Trimmer had the boy servant who carries her exemplary tale search his Bible 'for the texts that related to the duty of service' on his arrival at a new place, and write them down (commonplace them) 'in a little book, which he made for the purpose'. From these texts he has learned that serving a master faithfully, 'for conscience sake, is esteemed by the Lord as service done to himself'.[18]

The material that Murgatroyd had on his shelves from much earlier in the century had considered service as a social and legal relationship, as well as a godly one (modern commentators often evaded the law as a regulator of a household). Archbishop Tillotson had advised that not only were children 'a

---

[16] I am extremely grateful to Zillah Scott for telling me about this Birmingham incident, and for discussions about Hardy's febrile reaction to pregnancy and the idea of sexual relations.

[17] Anon., *A Present for Servants, from their Ministers, Masters or other Friends*, 10th edn (London: J. F. C. Rivington for the SPCK, 1787), pp. 14–15.

[18] Sarah Trimmer, *The Servant's Friend, an Exemplary Tale; designed to Enforce the Religious Instructions given at Sunday and other Charity Schools, by pointing out the Practical Application of Them, in a State of Service*, 2nd edn (London: T. Longman, 1787), pp. 43–4.

part of our Selves', but so also were a man's household servants: 'common *Humanity* will oblige us to be concerned for their Happiness, as they are *Men* and of the same Nature with our Selves'.[19] William Fleetwood's *Relative Duties* reminded employers (including John Murgatroyd – he had this in his library) of the contract that shaped the relationship, and by way of Col. IV, 1, that it was the duty of the master to pay wages – and to teach any skills that he had promised to deliver at the hiring. This was the law, and might be called the justice of the relationship. There was also a principle of equity at work in it, when the employer treated the servant with fairness, good nature and humanity.[20] Murgatroyd's other guide to this first great relation of private life was William Beveridge's *Private Thoughts*, which counselled its readers not to take up so much of their servants' time that they were unable to serve God: it was 'a Sin, to cumber my Servants, as myself, with too much worldly business'. Servants, who were less likely to read these passages, were told (in a wonderful prolegomenon to the moaning and groaning about servants that eighteenth-century employers brought to a pitch of formal perfection) not to go about the place 'repining at their Master's lawful commandments . . . muttering and maundering at them'.[21]

From the many declarations in this kind of literature, that a master was God's image on earth to the good and faithful servant who might dare to hope for rewards both material and spiritual, there emerged a new account of the female domestic that can be called psychological, in the modern meaning of the term. It was accompanied by a new set of guidelines for understanding her: she was to be read, written and understood in a new way. Thomas Gisborne's *Inquiry into the Duties of Men* (1795) measures the movement of the old advice into the new. Specifically addressed to the middle and higher classes of society, it took into account the ways in which the assertion of contract over status by the law, and modern accounts of the development of civil society, had had the effect of bestowing personhood on the serving classes.[22] Gisborne reiterated the Christian paradox of equality between all of God's creatures, and the social inequalities of this fallen world; he reminded his reader that 'his servants have many claims on him . . . Placed as they are in temporary subordination to him,

---

[19] John Tillotson, *Six Sermons. I. Stedfastness in religion. II. Family-religion III. IV. V. Education of children. VI. The advantages of an early piety* (London: B. Aylmer, 1694), p. 72.

[20] William Fleetwood, *The Relative Duties of Parents and Children, Husbands and Wives, Masters and Servants. Considered in Sixteen Practical Discourses: with Three Sermons upon the Case of Self-Murder*, 3rd edn (London: E. Bell, etc., 1737), Discourse XVI.

[21] William Beveridge, *Private Thoughts in Two Parts Complete. Part I Upon Religion . . . Part II Upon a Christian Life*, 17th edn (London: G. Risk, 1753), pp. 143–4. For the aesthetics of muttering and maundering (the servant joke), see Carolyn Steedman, 'Servants and their Relationship to the Unconscious', *Journal of British Studies*, 42 (2003), pp. 316–50.

[22] Thomas Gisborne, *An Inquiry into the Duties of Men in the Higher and Middle Classes of Society in Great Britain, Resulting from their Respective Stations, Professions and Employments*, 2nd edn, 2 vols. (London: B. & J. White, 1795).

they yet stand on a level with himself in the great family of the universe and before the eye of its impartial sovereign'.[23]

This Christian consideration, said Gisborne, meant that the biblical texts 'strongly inculcat[ed in] servants the duties of conscientious fidelity, respect and obedience'. A master should know about these duties as well, to ensure 'just and humane treatment on his part'. Servants should be allowed to visit their families; they should be taught to read; a gentleman might make them a loan when they got married, or set up in business. Indeed, a very 'strict oeconomy and accountableness should be required from every servant, according to the nature of his place; and should be enforced by a uniform adherence to settled rules and systematic plans'; but this should not be done 'by the master's acting the part of suspicious spy over his kitchen, cellar and stables, and thus incurring the hatred and contempt of his domestics and whetting their ingenuity to impose upon him the more'.[24]

From the early years of the century, guidebooks to service had attempted to find a private psychological stance for adoption by the servant, for the more comfortable occupation of the subordinate's position – for coming to terms with felt resentment and humiliation. 'Humility with respect to servants is a right Sense of their Subjection,' said *The Servant's Calling* of 1725; it was a sense of 'the State of Life to which providence has call'd 'em, for which it has fitted 'em, and is therefore (all Things considered) best for 'em'.[25] A famous (and possibly ironic) footman of the 1740s had found some kind of resignation to the daily round of cat-calling in the streets, rude children and impossible mistresses, in the knowledge that he was 'undergoing the temporal Punishment inflicted upon [him] for Sin, and in the mean Time, serving Others, as Servant . . .'[26]

But new accounts of human subjectivity and social relations had infiltrated this monovocal Christian narrative: what was new in the last decades of the century was, as Gisborne suggests, the attempt to see things from the servant's point of view, to attempt to understand why they did all the things that irritated you so profoundly (never shutting the door; doing everything with a maddening slowness; always making three journeys upstairs when one would do; telling the

---

[23] Gisborne, *Inquiry*, vol. II, pp. 453–7. For other, typically Anglican ways of thinking through this conundrum, see R. A. Soloway, *Prelates and People. Ecclesiastical Social Thought in England, 1783–1852* (London: Routledge and Kegan Paul, 1969), pp. 11–26. And for a guide to its reception on the other side of the door, there's always the insistent, insubordinate voice of Pamela: 'My *soul* is of equal importance with the soul of a princess though in quality I am upon a foot with the meanest slave.' Samuel Richardson, *Pamela, or, Virtue Rewarded*, orig. pub. 1740 (Harmondsworth: Penguin, 1986), p. 197. See below, chapter 11.

[24] Gisborne, *Inquiry*, p. 455.

[25] Anon., *Servant's Calling, With Same Advice to the Apprentice* (London: G. Strahan, 1725) p. 15.

[26] B. J., *The Footman's Looking Glass: or, Proposals to the Livery Servants of London and Westminster etc. for Bettering their Situations in Life, and securing their Credit in the World. To which is added, An Humble Representation to Masters and Mistresses. By J. B. a Brother of the Cloath* (London: M. Cooper, 1747), p. 4.

children completely inappropriate stories).[27] Now, there are attempts to explain
the servant as psychological subject and product of a social order.

Much of the new, psychologised literature was penned by women, rather than
by Church of England clergymen like Gisborne, but they were not the gentry
wives (real or pseudonymous) who had authored much earlier advice about
the management of servants in households.[28] Now, at the turn of the century,
wives of the manufacturing and professional bourgeoisie urged their readers
to *understand* their young domestic servants, advice that involved a serious
attempt to get to grips with working-class psychology, or at least to admit that
there might be such a thing as an attitude of mind shaped by social circumstance.

'We are dinned on every side with the history of bad servants,' said one such
writer in 1800; 'let us not be deaf to the oppressed voice of our inferiors, who
may whisper, though scarcely loud enough to be heard, that there may exist
also bad masters and mistresses . . . I can recollect but few bad servants.'[29]
Young servants were 'in the powers of superiors [with] an infinity of means to
aid . . . a helpless female'; her master's house need not 'appear like a prison
to her, but a welcome asylum'. They could be given books as presents, the
Bible and a Testament of course, but also Knox's *Essays*, Stretch's *Beauties of
History*, Ogden on prayer, and Watts's *Improvement of the Mind*.[30] The mistress
should improve the girl's writing skills, 'which will be very useful to her, in a
married state'. Ann Taylor presented herself as a mother to servants, in her book
of 1816. Its audience was intended to be 'young girls at their first setting out
in life' and its problematic was the trouble 'plain families' found in 'forming
such for higher situations' and making 'good wives and mothers among the
poor'.[31] Above all, the girls needed 'a minute mode of instruction', as their
class background had not given them the means to 'reason from the general to
the particular'.[32]

---

[27] Steedman, 'Servants'.

[28] Nancy Armstrong, *Desire and Domestic Fiction. A Political History of the Novel* (Oxford and
New York: Oxford University Press, 1987), pp. 59–95. Mitzi Myers, '"Servants as They are
Now Educated". Women Writers and Georgian Pedagogy', *Essays in Literature*, 16:1 (1989),
pp. 51–69.

[29] Anon., *Hints to Masters and Mistresses, Respecting Female Servants* (London: Darnton and
Harvey, 1800), p. 5.

[30] The Knox was more likely to have been Hugh Knox's *The Moral and Religious Miscellany, or
Sixty-one aphoretical Essays on the Christian Doctrines and Virtues* (Hertford: privately printed,
1790) than Vicesimus Knox, *Essays, Moral and Literary*, 14th edn, 2 vols. (London: Charles
Dilly, 1800). Recommended as well were L. M. Stretch, *The Beauties of History, or, Pictures
of Virtue and Vice*, 5th edn (Springfield: privately printed, 1794); Samuel Ogden, *Sermons on
the Efficacy of Prayers and Intercession* (Cambridge: privately printed, 1770); Isaac Watts, *The
Improvement of the Mind. To which is added, a Discourse on the Education of Children and
Youth* (London: privately printed, 1795).

[31] Ann Taylor, *The Present of a Mother for a Young Servant: Consisting of Friendly Advice and
Real Histories*, 2nd edn (London: Taylor and Hessey, 1816), pp. v–vi.

[32] Taylor, *Present*, pp. 69–70.

In the peculiar manner of these texts, the implied reader shifts second by second, wildly oscillating between anxious employer and truculent servant, often in the same sentence. Indeed, a text like John Trusler's *Domestic Management* (he was not a middle-class lady, nor a gentry wife, but a clergyman dispenser of life-style advice and mail-order supplier of pre-written sermons to his brethren) quite implodes the concept of the implied reader.[33] Trusler would have preferred the categories of servants named on his contents page to go straight to their section and 'get their job by heart'; though he thought that a housemaid, for example, might well read 'To a Footman' if none were kept at her place, for 'it comprises many of her duties'. Trusler hoped to police reading rather in the way he supported employers in policing a family. But servants who did obey him would have missed a laugh, especially the housemaid reading diligently in order to transform herself into a footman: 'To the Footman . . . If at dinner-time, he be ordered to break the claw of a lobster, he will not crack it between the hinges of the dining-room door, but will take it into the kitchen'! It would have been rumbustious and Swiftian (after Swift's inverted, or looking-glass instructions to servants of 1745) laughter.[34] Trusler's long moan *about* servants directed *at* servants warns in its Preface that 'the subject of *watchfulness*, to which the master or mistress of a family will find it at all times to be particularly attentive', is going to be very high on the agenda.[35] It thus allows the servant to watch the master or mistress trying not to be *too* obvious about watching them (for that 'would betray all confidence in those we employ') and desperately trying to avoid setting them traps, where dishonesty was suspected. However, its most unpleasant anecdote of domestic policing involves no such subtlety or restraint. Knowing it to be the duty of a mistress to curb servants' persistent tendencies in 'dressing beyond the line of life in which they are placed', an anonymous Domestic Panopticon, noting that hers has sewn a flounce and a pair of epaulettes to her dress, sends her out on an errand, enters the girl's room and plucks off the offending haberdashery. The young woman is 'astonished and displeased', but soon works out that the lady of the house must have done it. 'Nothing was said on either

---

[33] John Trusler, *Trusler's Domestic Management, or the Art of Conducting a Family, with Economy, Frugality and Method, the Result of long Experience; with full Instructions to Servants of Various Denominations, How to Time and Execute their Work Well, Necessary for every Mistress to know, and the best Present she can make Them, even for her own Comfort and Interest* (London: J. Souter, 1819).

[34] Swift's *Directions* had an extraordinarily long run right through to the nineteenth century. See Steedman, 'Servants'; Janet Thaddeus, 'Swift's Directions to Servants', *Studies in Eighteenth-Century Culture*, 16 (1986): pp. 107–23. See in particular the inverted instructions to all sorts of female servant in Jonathan Swift, *Polite Conversation, consisting of smart, witty, droll, and whimsical Sayings collected for his Amusement, and made into a regular Dialogue* (London: Joseph Wenman, 1783).

[35] Trusler, *Domestic Management*, pp. 4–5, 149–59.

side, the rebuke was powerful, and it had the desired effect,' noted Trusler with satisfaction.[36]

Across turn-of-the-century literature, the servant was counselled not to waste provisions, not to cut more bread than was needed for a meal; to bring everything from the day before out of the pantry, systematically, every morning, and to eat her share of the leftovers; then, without a pause, the mistress is told that 'it is probable that [these leavings] are better than what she has been accustomed to taste at her mother's cottage, or what she may taste again when she gets one of her own'. And then it is the servant being addressed: 'a neat and careful servant, may almost be known by the way she manages her bread'; 'it's been expensive for years; – make bread pudding! Don't give to the chickens and the pigs! – You can save 30s a year by not wasting bread'; 'Say not, my young friend, that it is *only* a bit of bread, *only* a slice of meat, *only* a shovel of coal, *only* a small piece of soap . . .'[37]

The age-old practice of going-slow – the way some servants had acquired the habits of 'being slow in their motions' – learned across all forms of servitude, is 'unspeakably tiresome where there is much to do'.[38] But relatively new habits of empathy and, indeed, new forms of child psychology . . . could be inculcated in the girl: Be kind to animals! How to kill a fish! ('they feel as much as you would do in such a case') . . . Play with the children! 'All young things are playful . . . The colt, the lamb, the puppy, the kitten, can help themselves, almost as soon as born; but an infant requires assistance, even in play, and those who love infants will be amused by playing with them'. If you didn't do so, then you were 'unfit to be a nursemaid'. Carrying toddlers around is not *caring* for them! The best way to learn the habits of caring is to retrieve your own childhood and relate it to the child in your arms.[39]

A year before this, Mrs Taylor had attempted a more linear depiction of working-class psychology, one made up not so much of what the girl lacked, as of how she had been formed as a psychological subject. Women like her shouldn't wonder at what happened when they admitted into their households children of the careless poor, 'incapable of using either their eyes, their ears, or understandings: Why should we expect to gather grapes of thorns, or figs of thistles?' She wrote of the 'sudden change' experienced by those who had 'passed their childhood in want and wretchedness', who now, in a decently appointed house, are only capable of annexing 'the idea of *riches* and suppose that any, and everything can be afforded'. She asked for empathy from

[36] Trusler, *Domestic Management*, p. xii.
[37] Taylor, *Present*, pp. 69–77.   [38] Taylor, *Present*, p. 85.
[39] Taylor, *Present*, pp. 116–17. For the odd trajectory of the servant-figure as the first type of character in English literature to possess a childhood, see Carolyn Steedman, 'Enforced Narratives. Stories of Another Self', in Tess Cosslett, Celia Lury and Penny Summerfield (eds.), *Feminism and Autobiography. Texts, Theories, Methods* (London: Routledge, 2000), pp. 25–39.

her readers in the very moment she acknowledged the impossibility of it in maidservants: 'a master can scarcely appear to them other than a being of a different species, with whom they are totally unqualified to sympathise, and in whose welfare they can scarcely be expected to take much interest'.[40]

Much more radical women than Mrs Taylor had thought of servants as good for empathy (their own, in the relationship between them and their maids, and in regard to children) for thirty years past. Mary Wollstonecraft thought that the presence of servants in a modest household helped children to learn sympathy for radically different beings, in much the same way that animals kept as pets did.[41] She had Emilia in *Young Grandison* (1790) shame her brother Edward first, by treating a sick servant 'as if the poor girl had been her own sister', and then by drawing from her own conduct the precept that 'a servant is a human being; we are differently educated, I cannot make them my companions but will ever try to treat them humanely – and remember they are fellow creatures'.[42] In her dealings with her own little girl (or at least, in her plans for the second child), as in much of her fiction, Wollstonecraft had been keen to alert the child to her reliance on servants. A little girl repeats a kind of catechism of empathy: '"I button my gown myself. I do not want a maid to assist me, when I am dressing." "But you have not yet got sense enough to do it properly, and must beg someone to help you, till you are older."'[43] In some of the new fiction for children, the audience of little readers is warned against rudeness to servants (and given some of the lessons in the political philosophy of labour that were discussed in chapter 3). An appallingly behaved child, who has just been extremely disagreeable to her nursemaid, is castigated thus by her mother in Dorothy Kilner's *Perambulations of a Mouse* (1783): '"And who do you think will do anything for you, if you are not good, and do not speak civilly! Not *I*, I promise you, neither shall nurse or any of the servants, for though I pay her wages to do my business for me, I never want them to do anything, unless they are desired in a pretty manner."'[44]

---

[40] Ann Taylor, *Practical Hints to Young Females on the Duties of a Wife, a Mother and a Mistress of a Family* (London: Taylor and Hessey, 1815), pp. 36–44.

[41] Mary Wollstonecraft, *Original Stories from Real Life. With Conversations Calculated to regulate the Affections and Form the Mind to Truth and Goodness*, orig. pub. 1796, in Janet Todd and Marilyn Butler (eds.), *The Works of Mary Wollstonecraft*, 6 vols. (London: William Pickering, 1989), vol. IV, pp. 353–450.

[42] Mary Wollstonecraft, *Young Grandison. A Series of Letters from Young Persons to their Friends. Translated from the Dutch of Madame de Cambon. With Alterations and Improvements*, orig. pub. 1790, in Todd and Butler, *Works of Mary Wollstonecraft*, vol. II, pp. 214–35, 237, 220. See also her *Elements of Morality for the Use of Children, with an Introductory Address to Parents. Translated from the German of the Rev. C. G. Salzman*, orig. pub. 1790, in Todd and Butler, *Works of Mary Wollstonecraft*, vol. II, pp. 4–210; 144. See also Myers, 'Servants'.

[43] Mary Wollstonecraft, *Lessons. From the Posthumous Works of the Author of a Vindication of the Rights of Woman* (1798), Todd and Butler, *Works of Mary Wollstonecraft*, vol. IV, pp. 466–74.

[44] Dorothy Kilner, *Life and Perambulations of a Mouse*, 1st edn (London: John Marshall, 1783), p. 31.

Across forty years or so of this kind of literature, from the 1780s to the 1820s, there is something present of the comic writing that developed out of Swift's *Instructions*, in which servant psychology is explored through a series of ironic orders to them, to do the things that drove their employers insane, in a much earlier attempt to explore a mind so very different from one's own. And female employers had sometimes pleaded with their maids to understand *them*, particularly over the question of how they felt seeing a domestic dressed in a replica of their new frock.[45] What is new about the advice of the new century is the serious attempt to explain the maidservant's mind by analysis – however rudimentary – of her class background. That is why you should bear with 'all their little complaints', said Mrs Parkes in 1825, for 'there is not any class of people more fanciful, or inclined to imagine themselves more indisposed than they really are'.[46] But you could still turn back what you saw in them, as a form of accusation. 'Muttering', said John Trusler, to his intended audience of servants, 'only shows opposition and ill-humour.' How would they like a muttering servant, if they were master or mistress? 'Keep this in mind . . . this simple question – How should I like to be so served? And depend on it, you will never act wrong.'[47] Empathy was still cut to one side of the cloth, and all of this literature still served its old-established function, of ritualising moaning and groaning about the servant problem. 'When I hear an indolent footman, if asked to drive in a nail, say "Ill [*sic*] go for a carpenter;" or a pert wench, if desired to shut the stable door, reply "I don't understand horses," I am ready to brain the fools,' said Trusler.[48] Nevertheless, in the conduct literature of the new century, the servant had both voice and persona, both of which emerged out of some dimly perceived social matrix. Moreover, the comedy that had dictated the words and behaviour of servants from earlier texts slips away between the lines of the new. There is an indication, as well, that the servant's labour was slipping away from the master or mistress, that he or she who served was no longer the contracted-for prosthesis or extra limb of Lockean prescription. This sense of loss is what we perhaps see at work in Mrs Taylor's complaints about teaching everything you know to servants who will, shortly, just get up and go – true enactment of their separation from you – and certainly present in the 1770s, in Jonas Hanway's 'monstrous pile of piety', his *Virtue in Humble Life*. Here, Hanway's doppelganger Father Trueman reports on how he has

[45] Ann Walker, *A Complete Guide for a Servant Maid; or the Sure Means of Gaining Love and Esteem*, 5th edn (London: T. Sabine, 1787), pp. 20–1.

[46] Mrs William Parkes, *Domestic Duties; or Instructions to Young Married Ladies on the Management of their Households, and the Regulation of their Conduct in the Various Relations and Duties of Married Life* (London: Longman, 1825), pp. 118–19.

[47] Trusler, *Domestic Management*, pp. 36–7.   [48] Trusler, *Domestic Management*, p. 38.

frequently stood amazed at the patience, or rather the folly of some masters when I have heard servants answer to reasonable and necessary commands, *Yes, if I have time*; or *I will do it, when I have time*; and this in a tone of voice, which seemed to signify in plain *English* 'I have certain duties to perform. You, Sir, do not understand what you say. I am the best judge whether it might be done or not; and if I find it necessary, or it pleases me to do it, it shall be done when I think proper . . .'[49]

All these accounts of the master–servant relationship are part of the tale of English conduct literature; they also indicate very large changes indeed, in legal and political understandings, of labour, the location of labour in persons as a kind of possession, and of the way in which determined enforcement of contract law by the courts, in the case of service, from the 1760s onwards, had made servants into persons – or at the very least, people. The invented voices of these texts, the exasperations of employers embodied in servants remembered and servants quoted, the attempts to spell out the eighteenth century's great lessons in moral sympathy, in front of stable doors and over deeply contested bread-boards ('I have heard servants say, it is *only* a little broken dry bread, *only* a little bit of soap, *only* a few ends of candle,' wrote Trusler, echoing Mrs Taylor; and then, in a fine fury, flinging at the servant, 'How do *you* [my italics] know what [the master] can afford?'[50]), are all acknowledgement of these changes taking place in the organisation of social relations in civil society (or in the class structures of emergent industrial capitalism).

The story of the conduct books is, in any case, a story of class and class rela-tions, at least in the view of Nancy Armstrong. In *Desire and Domestic Fiction* she made the startling proposition (one not yet fully absorbed by historians) that in the earlier versions of conduct literature, a middle class was imagined and written before it existed socially, that is to say, the *idea* of a household as a unit of the polity and supported by actually existing class relations was brought into being from the seventeenth century onwards, between the lines of books of household management. In this genre of literature, it is argued, a middle class existed *avant la lettre sociale*.[51] These propositions are useful for current purposes, if only for emphasising that ways of imagining, thinking and writing have some kind of social existence and force. And that is about all we can say, in relation to these books of household management and John Murgatroyd's own. It is purposeless to surmise that he read any of them (at least three of the ones discussed here were published after his death) and pointless to speculate about how the fantasies of a Jonas Hanway or a Mrs Taylor may have structured

---

[49] Jonas Hanway, *Virtue in Humble Life: containing Reflections on the Reciprocal Duties of the Wealthy and the Indigent, the Master and the Servant . . .* 2 vols. (London: J. Dodley Brotherton and Sewel, 1774), vol. I, p. 360. Hanway himself labelled his work the 'monstrous pile', putting this pre-emptive judgement into the mouth of a lady reader: '"Lord what *good* will you do, by taking so much pains to build this *monstrous pile* of piety."' A great deal, he thought.

[50] Trusler, *Domestic Management*, p. 43.   [51] Armstrong, *Desire*, pp. 59–69.

his relationship with Phoebe Beatson. He had not seemed to notice, back in the 1750s, that le Sage's Gil Blas was a servant, and had the character of a victim *because* that is what he was.[52] We can say that, in the wider society, it was possible to imagine, write and read domestic servants in the ways suggested by this literature, that their fantasies embody discernible shifts in the legal and political understandings that ordered the service relationship (these shifts had been largely *brought about* by changes in the law regulating services). Servants were, indeed, 'good to think with', specifically to think through the great questions of moral sentiment, sympathy and the social order, rank, class and personhood, as they had been since John Locke had first provided the means and metaphors for doing so, at the end of the seventeenth century.[53]

What is not quite so pointless, in speculating about John Murgatroyd and his cultural and print context, is that these conduct book writers would have disapproved very much indeed of his final and most antinomian treatment of Phoebe Beatson, in making her financially independent. There were severe doubts about the servant's independence expressed in contemporary advice literature. The anonymous author of *Hints to Masters and Mistresses* (1800) opened her (or his) discussion with the absolutist statement that 'The proud expression of a fellow creature "I am independent" to me has ever been ungrateful; for I never knew that sublunary being, who could claim a moral right to this assumption', and went on to opine that

independence is an unsocial, and in the strict sense of moral obligation, an unfounded sentiment; whilst a due conviction of mutual dependence, and mutual obligation, tends to humanise the mind, and begets those dignified sympathies, which not only move the heart to feel for, but likewise to administer to, every human woe.[54]

The old gods haunt early nineteenth-century conduct literature: the God of the Old Testament, who commands complete fidelity and obedience from the servant, and the God of the New Testament, with His injunctions for the servant to do with all his or her heart what they had to do anyway (the Apostle Paul's condemnation of eye-servants, those who only behaved well when they believed they were being watched, did indeed involve a psychologised attitude on the part of the servant[55]). An old God lingers, in their account of a social world in which (in the words of a footman from the 1740s) some were 'undergoing the temporal Punishment inflicted upon men for Sin, and in the mean Time, serving others as servants'; or in the words of the more up-to-date *Present for*

---

[52] See above, chapter 3. Malcolm Cook, *Le Sage. Gil Blas* (London: Grant and Cutler, 1988), pp. 16–17, 49–53.

[53] For the other creatures being 'good to think with', see Claude Levi-Strauss, *Totemism* (Boston: Beacon Press, 1963).

[54] Anon., *Hints*, pp. 3–4.

[55] Tim Meldrum, 'Domestic Service in London, 1660–1750. Gender, Life Cycle, Work and Household Relations', PhD, University of London, 1996, chapter 6.

Servants of 1787, where He has rendered 'all Persons in this Inequality of their Conduct . . . mutually helpful to each other, yea, necessary to each other in this lapsed State'. This God is still present in the reiteration of the same biblical texts (I Cor. 7.22; Ephes. 6.6, 9; Coloss. 4.1; Titus 2. 9–10). But none of them dealt with the God who was a palpable presence in Murgatroyd's household, and in his understanding of Phoebe Beatson.

Murgatroyd's love of God – indeed, his God – will be discussed further in a later chapter, but here, as far as His household presence is concerned, there is something to say in relation to a wider ideology of service and domestic management. Murgatroyd's was a God of sociability and hospitality. He enjoyed the times he could record neighbourliness: a neighbouring cleric 'came to our House a little before Noon, & din'd with Us – we spent a few Hours very agreeably like friendly neighbours'.[56] Drink flowed through the house, from Phoebe's brewing (though that, presumably, was for ordinary mealtime consumption) and from the elaborate arrangements noted for collecting spirits from Huddersfield and Rochdale.[57] Drinking was an aspect of sociability and good relationships. Drink was involved in all kinds of social and professional dealings: 'This morn I rode to Salterhebble Hannah Mellor [one of his nieces] walk'd having had 1 pint of warm Ale as Prevention. Hannah return'd with ye Mare, and got safely Home – She was ill wet. I went to Halifax & was ill wet. I slept at Joseph Bentley's . . . had 6d in Ale – J Banton help'd to drink it . . .'[58] Murgatroyd might comment on his builder's time in the alehouse with an exasperated 'Joseph Pogson went a drinking today – well – some will not learn wit', but that was because a day on the booze meant no progress on the new house. He and his sister enjoyed their glass: one night in Halifax in 1790 he had to stay over rather than walk back because he and sister Ann had got a-drinking after dinner.[59] At Lingards, company dined, and was astonished at the efficacy of Murgatroyd's cure for tainted meat. ('My Company praised it & when I told them wht had happened, would not believe Me.')[60] Anyway, a good minister of Christ could only proceed by analogy with the good householder. A minister should be

like a Man, that is a Householder, which bringeth forth out of his Treasure, Things old and new: He is a Householder, who for the Maintenance of his Family and the Entertainment of his Guests all the year long, is supposed to have a repository for Provisions and there [to] have laid in a great Store, and Abundance of all Sorts and Kinds in order to keep a well-furnished Table for all Comers.[61]

---

[56] Murgatroyd Diaries, KC 242/1 (31 December 1788).
[57] Murgatroyd Diaries, KC 242/5 (22 July 1800); KC 242/7 (3 April 1804).
[58] KC 242/6 (26 April 1802).
[59] KC 242/1 (21 March 1786, 9 May 1790). For the pleasures of drink, see Roy Porter, *Enlightenment. Britain and the Creation of the Modern World* (London: Penguin, 2001), pp. 270–1.
[60] Murgatroyd, 'Ask, Read, Retain, Teach', KC 242/9, p. 8, 'Cure for Tainted meat'.
[61] Murgatroyd, 'The Qualifications of a Minister of Christ', KC 242/8, p. 4.

Murgatroyd knew the contents of his pantry (off or not) and of the kitchen garden, as we have seen. And his maidservant span, much as she might have done in the time of Abraham. (Or as in the time before the imposition of the Norman Yoke. The worsted field produced varieties of Golden Age fantasy in regard to spinning.[62]) Such a man must be 'wise especially in the Government of his Family, for . . . if a man know not how to rule his own House, how shall he take care of the Church of God'.[63]

Even at this late date, a strict application of the law of service might involve the declaration that a servant was part of a man's family, though interpretation by the courts since the middle of the century had emphasised the practical consequences of this (the servant's right to care and sustenance in sickness, for example) rather than the godly principle of the matter. Indeed, the principle had not really been mentioned, in magistrates' dealings nor in high court judgment, for many decades. Tim Meldrum has suggested that 'the script for patriarchal household management' had always been a 'rhetorical resource, available to masters . . . a set of ideal devices', albeit a very powerful one.[64] But it seems that even the script stopped being referred to, in the second half of the eighteenth century. Modern legal guidebooks continued to refer to seventeenth-century law abridgements over many aspects of the service relationship, well into the eighteenth century; but the master as a father and the servant as a kind of child simply disappeared from the discourse. Probably the last cry of the earlier rhetoric came in the anonymous *Servant's Calling* of 1785 which declares that 'a Servant when affectionate, differeth little from a Son. Affection improves the relationship, and becomes a sort of Adoption.'[65] But a contracted employee in your household speaks against a patriarchal structure, however much a patriarchal system of family management might continue to be referred to, in sermons and godly advice books.[66] In naming the servant first in his discussion of the

---

[62] See Anon., *An Essay on Halifax* (Halifax: P. Darby, 1761); Ebenezer Hunt, *The Rush-Bearing. A Poem. With a Probable Account of the Rise of Wakes* (Huddersfield: Joseph Brook, 1784); John Bentley, *The History of the Town and Parish of Halifax, containing a Description of the Town, the Nature of the Soil &c &c. An Account of the Gentry and Other Eminent Persons born in the said Town . . . Also the Antient Customs and Modern Improvements . . .* (Halifax: E. Jacob, 1789); and below, chapter 8.

[63] Murgatroyd, 'Qualifications', KC 242/8, p. 5.

[64] Tim Meldrum, *Domestic Service and Gender, 1660–1750. Life and Work in the London Household* (London: Longman, 2000), pp. 34–40. The ideal of the Abrahamic family, translated to capitalist England, was always, indeed, 'shot through with ambiguity'. Meldrum, quoting Keith Wrightson, 'Politics of the Parish', in Paul Griffiths, Adam Fox and Steve Hindle (eds.), *The Experience of Authority in Early Modern England* (Basingstoke: Macmillan, 1996), pp. 10–46.

[65] Anon, *Servant's Calling*, p. 52. See Richard Lucas, *The Duty of Servants. Containing I Their Preparation for, and Choice of Service. II Their Duty in Service*, 3rd edn (London: William Ineys, 1710), p. 7: 'in a word, if you would prove *good Servants*, you must first prove *good Children*'.

[66] Pavla Miller, *Transformations of Patriarchy in the West, 1500–1900* (Bloomington: Indiana University Press, 1998), pp. 41–74.

family, Blackstone underscored this point: the servant's relationship with the householder was regulated by contract; it was the most telling relationship – the first sort – because those of husband and wife and father and child were (perhaps unhappily) not so regulated. Patriarchalism is challenged not only by the intrusions of state institutions into households, but by everyday practices within them, especially when they are performed by a contracted employee whose presence is noticed by the law not just as a putative child enjoined to honour and obey a father (or master) but as a worker, with some legal rights recognised by the higher and lower courts.[67] And in commercial society, kitchens and cooking and housekeeping dissolve forms of control, authority and management, on a daily basis. The person – the female servant – in charge of daily life possesses a knowledge that erodes authority. In November 1804, when Phoebe had gone down into Slaithwaite, 'a man called & phebe gone . . . left ½ lb tea – unpaid for'.[68] Murgatroyd did not know the man's name or what tea-buying arrangements for his household were; he certainly didn't think it his job to pay him. Phoebe Beatson was in charge of all of this.

Indeed, William Blackstone set the tone for later discussions of the place of servants within families. He said that the relationship between master and servant 'was founded in convenience', whereby a man is directed to call in the assistance of others, when his own skill and labour will not be sufficient to answer the cares incumbent on him.[69] What happened between them depended on contract, on the formal agreement to serve on one side and to maintain on the other. 'Servitude', said Taylor in 1767, 'is nothing else but plain Contract, and to be guided by the Rules and Conditions of that Bargain Invariably.'[70] As far as I can see, the anonymous author of *Laws Concerning Master and Servants* of 1785 was the last to quote something like 'Sheppard's Grand Abridgement of the Common and Statute Law of England' (1675) to the effect that 'Master and Servants are Relatives; And a Servant in the Intendment of our Law seems to be such a one as by Agreement and retainer oweth Duty and Service to another, who therefore is called Master.'[71] This was an old quotation, from a different social and legal world.

Phoebe dwelt in the Murgatroyd household as a contracted employee; family relations developed out of a quite different set of circumstances, and out of a

---

[67] Miller, *Transformations of Patriarchy*, pp. 41–74.

[68] Murgatroyd Diaries, KC 242/7 (16 November 1804).

[69] William Blackstone, *Commentaries on the Laws of England. In Four Books*, orig. pub. 1765, 6th edn (Dublin: Company of Booksellers, 1775), Book 1, p. 422.

[70] Taylor, *Elements*, p. 413.

[71] Gentleman of the Inner Temple, *Law Concerning Master and Servants, Viz Clerks to Attornies and Solicitors . . . Apprentices . . . Menial Servants . . . Labourers, Journeymen, Artificers, Handicraftmen and other Workmen* (London: His Majesty's Law Printer, 1785), p. 1. But he went immediately on to quote Blackstone, as above, who was himself referring to Bacon's *New Abridgement* of 1736.

different kind of love from the one the law had once had in mind. And anyone who did read their own household in the light of an Abrahamic one may have been disturbed by the very modern paradox that William Alexander noted, in his *History of Women*, that 'When Abraham entertained the angels sent to denounce the destruction of Sodom, he appears to have treated his wife as a menial servant: "Make ready quickly", said he, "three measures of fine meal, knead it, and make cakes for the hearth". And from the sequel of the story it is plain, that she was not permitted to partake of the entertainment she had dressed.' He was puzzled and offended by this, but 'In ages so remote as those we are now considering, the imperfect and mutilated accounts from which alone we can draw information, sometime relate incidents which have so little resemblance to the manners and customs of our times, that we are altogether at a loss how to account for them.' He was particularly puzzled by the role of the servants here: 'though Sarah officiated as a servant . . . she had at the same time one, or rather, perhaps, several hand-maids . . . under her, but in what they were employed or how they served their mistress we can only conjecture'. Not so in West Yorkshire, where Phoebe brewed and baked along with the two Anns, whilst they had their health and strength.[72]

In 1825, Sarah and Samuel Adams saw a gap in the domestic service advice market, and attempted to plug it. *The Complete Servant* was written out of the fifty years' experience they had both had in 'Different Families' from the 1770s onwards, when fresh from an endowed grammar school, he had gone to service as a footboy, and she had started the upward climb from maid-of-all-work to housekeeper.[73] All those years they had been making notes about the way these households had gone about the reproduction of everyday life, and they had very clear ideas about how things might be managed is a different way. There were two reasons for writing their book. First was the old-fashioned literature that had been directed at the households they knew: 'We have had Sermons on the moral obligations of masters and servants, and many books of religious advice, addressed to the latter, all good in their way, but we have had no work, which like the present, addresses itself to the actual personal practice of their duties.'[74] The other prompt to writing was their understanding of the full implications of William Blackstone's legal formulation (though they may have never set eyes on the *Commentaries on the Laws of England*), that the master–servant relationship was the first relationship of private life, which provided the pattern

[72] William Alexander, *The History of Women, from the Earliest Antiquity, to the Present Time; giving some Account of almost every interesting Particular concerning that Sex, among all Nations, ancient and modern*, 2 vols. (London: Strahan and Cadell, 1779), vol. I, p. 104.

[73] Samuel and Sarah Adams, *The Complete Servant; Being a Practical Guide to the Peculiar Duties and Business of all Descriptions of Servants from the Housekeeper to the Servant of All-Work, and from the Land Steward to the Footboy; with Useful Receipts and Tables* (London: Knight and Lacey, 1825), p. iv.

[74] Adams, *Complete Servant*, p. iii.

for all others. What the Adams said was that 'No relations in society are so numerous and universal as those of Master and Servant . . . it is proportionately important that they should be well defined and understood.' Their book does, indeed, give a clear and accurate summary of the law of master and domestic servant, as it stood in the early nineteenth century, all the more interesting – and precise – for being the first penned from the employee's side of the relationship.

The Adams dealt with the social division, the ordering of society by rank and ownership, in what, on the face of it, looks like advice from the godly conduct books of a century before, telling their servant readers that 'The Supreme Lord of the Universe, in his wisdom rendered the various conditions of mankind necessary to our individual happiness – some are rich, others are poor – some are masters and others are servants. Subordination, indeed, attaches to your rank in life, but not *disgrace*.'[75] This was very old comfort, to be sure; but new was the advice to the servant to construct a kind of serving personality – the persona of a domestic – as if he or she might finally detach from the master, no longer a prosthesis of the employer's labouring body, but now, a kind of automaton, whose cooking and dusting and knife-cleaning masked some other, real person. Mrs Parkes and Mrs Taylor had apprehended the maidservant in masquerade, in their worrying-away at where she came from, what her home life had been like, what had made her what she was. It had not been possible to conceive of servants in this way when the relationship had been divinely ordered, and man and maid and mistress and master had all been one. Indeed, Parker and Taylor struggled with this sudden efflorescence of personhood (or rather, their anticipation of such a thing) in the teenage girls fetching water and chopping cabbage in the kitchen. However, interesting and important developments in social thought apart, what the Adams were really up to was the definition and understanding of the servant's labour – 'the actual personal practice of their duties' – that they could provide for their readers. This was instruction for servants and their employers, and it focused, above all other rooms in a house, on the kitchen and on cooking.

Twenty, forty years before this, the Lingards kitchen, and the provision and production of food, was the place where the service relationship in John Murgatroyd's household was made most apparent, at least in the pages of his diary. When Phoebe Beatson acts in its pages (apart from the immense work of walking to and from the putter-out), it is in or near the kitchen, putting down the peas and the beans in its garden, brewing and baking. The conduct literature for men that Murgatroyd had in his library assumed that a gentleman (or one who aspired to that estate) would take great interest in the kitchen and the kitchen garden. Rider's *British Merlin* (Murgatroyd had the 1775 edition of this gazetteer) told a man everything he needed to know, from the going down of

75 Adams, *Complete Servant*, p. 17.

the sun, to the arrival of stage coaches in different towns, but actually devoted its largest number of pages to 'Notes on Husbandry', which told, in poetic and practical detail, how to manage vegetable and fruit production throughout the year.[76] Beveridge's *Thoughts* did indeed present its advice to the woman of the Christian household, but she was the godly master in disguise, taking an interest not only in its good ordering, but in remedies for sore throats.[77]

All over England, in the recesses of family archives, are the letters of employers frantic at the disappearance of their cook, committed to Bedlam perhaps, gone home to mother, or simply not there, pleading with friends, family and employment agencies to let them have another one soon.[78] The records of grander households than Murgatroyd's, with hierarchies of servants, show that certain kinds of status might be acquired in this period, and in this region, through the act of feeding others – at least among fellow servants.[79] As for Slaithwaite-cum-Lingards, and the Murgatroyd kitchen, all we know is that Phoebe was most apparent to her employer in and around it. (As indeed, she must actually have been.) It may have been a stage for the domestic enactment of a much larger political-legal development: the place where she (thousands of other domestics) stopped being conceptualised as a servant of God and a relation of the master who represented Him on earth, and became a person, wearing the persona of a maidservant, as twenty years later, Samuel and Sarah Adams were to advise women like her to do.

[76] Cardanus Rider, *The Court and City Register, or Gentleman's Complete Annual Calendar. Rider's British Merlin* (London: J. Joliffe, 1775).

[77] Murgatroyd's one listed cookery book was 'A Closet for Ladies', possibly Anon., *A Closet for Ladies and Gentlewomen. Or, the Art of preserving, conserving, and candying. With the manner how to make diverse kindes of sirups, and all kinde of banquetting stuffs. Also diverse soveraigh medicines and salves for sundry diseases* (London: R. H., 1656). Kept on the parlour shelves and not in the kitchen, it had probably belonged to his wife or his sister. It tells you how to feed a sweet tooth using a cuisine based on pastry-making.

[78] Thomas Cooper of New Place Farm in Guestling, 1788–1824, Household Account Book, AMS 6191, East Sussex County Record Office, Lewes (4 July 1799). Norfolk Country Record Office, BOL/2/115. Leathes Family Papers. Letter dated 1794. L. G. Mitchell (ed.), *The Purefoy Letters, 1735–1753*, 2 vols. (London: Sidgwick and Jackson, 1973), vol. I, pp. 148–9.

[79] Jane Holmes, 'Domestic Servitude in Yorkshire, 1650–1780', PhD, University of York, 1989, p. 98. This question is pursued in Carolyn Steedman, 'Poetical Maids and Cooks Who Wrote', *Eighteenth-century Studies*, 39:1 (2005), pp. 1–27.

8   The Gods

Given the number of social and cultural historians who have roamed the worsted field from the early eighteenth century onwards, we should expect to know a good deal about the ideological context to the life of its people. Belief systems of the West Riding, both official and personal, have been described by many kinds of historian, not only those who have focused on the Anglican Church. It was among these hills and valleys that Edward Thompson located his making of the English working class, in the years between 1780 and 1830. According to Callum Brown, he and other social historians of the 1960s and 1970s were forced to concede the power of religion in the making of popular political consciousness (and perhaps in the making of class), but only by concentrating on Methodism, and then by placing Methodism's fervent adherents in ideological opposition to those who planted the Liberty Tree.[1] For the Methodists there was the chiliasm of despair, a febrile escape from the social and political circumstances that produced it; for other, less godly men and women, the making of class consciousness through a rational apprehension of the meaning of their experience, as both workers and political subjects.[2]

It is indeed difficult to square the religious formation of your historical subjects with the politically conscious men whom you now – in 1963 – represent as their historians. Clothiers rehearsing the catechism through their schooldays, wool combers lisping the creed from the cradle, now crowding Huddersfield parish church to receive the bishop's blessing for a second or third time, an obligation to attend divine service so deeply inculcated and felt that they went even after a morning in the pub and blind drunk – difficult to square this version of the West Riding worker with the man who protested, and marched, and petitioned and struck, for political liberty and against the deterioration of working

---

[1] E. P. Thompson, *The Making of the English Working Class*, orig. pub. 1963 (Harmondsworth: Penguin, 1968), chapter 5, 'Planting the Liberty Tree'; chapter 11, 'The Transforming Power of the Cross'. Callum G. Brown, *The Death of Christian Britain. Understanding Secularisation, 1800–2000* (London and New York: Routledge, 2000), pp. 16–34.

[2] Thompson, *Making*, pp. 411–40, for the chiliasm of despair.

conditions and the rising price of food.[3] Thompson had deep sympathy and admiration for the men who made a class society out of their experience of life and labour in the Calder and Colne valleys during these years of revolution and counter-revolution. Their story, made into history, became a foundational form of political analysis for modern British society; one of the effects of continued recourse to it has been to make it even more embarrassing to talk about the god of the West Riding than it was for Thompson himself. Indeed, an Anglican God and his manifestation in the institutional activities of the church were what had been struggled against and rejected, through the century or more of demystification that produced Thompson's socialist humanism (and that of many more of us, who were schooled by *The Making of the English Working Class* in the 1960s). As a result the army of redressers meeting under cover of darkness on the moors five miles beyond Halifax in order to swear the creation of 'a Spirit of Love, Brotherhood & Affection among the friends of freedom' and to await the landing of the French revolutionary army have not been seen as formed by a faith and a devotional practice; these have not been recognised as part of their experience, however 'experience' is described.[4]

Other, equally compelling social histories of the Pennine district have told of 'Churches . . . [and] the people who attended churches and what they did there'.[5] In accounts like Mark Smith's, of religious practice in an industrialising society, confessional developments are given intimate connection with the process of secularisation, or de-Christianisation, from the perspective of their full nineteenth-century development. As Smith does, other historians of the region frequently connect these long-term developments with the terrain (as did Murgatroyd's first historian, Canon Hulbert writing in the 1860s, albeit from a different ideological perspective).[6] Smith argues that in its non-traditional communities (new, and rapidly expanding old ones) a social space was opened up, in which 'perhaps for the first time . . . a class segregated, dechristianised culture might develop, claiming the allegiance of the mass of an unchurched population'.[7] In these accounts, wool, worsted, cotton – and the means of their production – make such cultural spaces; they provide an aperture for new religious forms, as well as for irreligion.

---

[3] Barry Reay has several times pointed out that agricultural rioters in 1830s Kent were Church of England communicants and members of the church choir. Barry Reay, *The Last Rising of the Agricultural Labourers. Rural Life and Protest in Nineteenth-century England* (Oxford: Clarendon Press, 1990), pp. 64–8, 177–9.

[4] Thompson, *Making*, pp. 515–659, for 'An Army of Redressers', and these incidents. William H. Sewell, 'How Classes are Made. Critical Reflections on E. P. Thompson's Theory of Working-class Formation', in Harvey J. Kaye and Keith McClelland (eds.), *E. P. Thompson. Critical Perspectives* (Cambridge: Polity Press, 1990), pp. 50–77 for a discussion of Thompson's category 'experience'.

[5] Mark Smith, *Religion in an Industrial Society. Oldham and Saddleworth, 1740–1865* (Oxford: Clarendon Press, 1994), p. 1.

[6] See above, chapter 1.   [7] Smith, *Religion in an Industrial Society*, p. 32.

Where the Church of England was weak, in sprawling upland parishes, with few or no chapelries, Methodism took hold.[8] ('Pretty numerous in the remoter parts of the parish,' the Reverend Rishton said of Almondbury Methodists in 1764, 'but such a vagrant sect that it is impossible to give any account of them.'[9]) In the Slaithwaite district the Methodists were in fact preceded by the Baptists, who opened a chapel in 1790 on the high ground above the settlement of Pole Moor. It was established by members of the Reverend Wilson's congregation whose Evangelical sermons had whetted an appetite for a more rigorous discussion of the doctrine of special election than he was prepared to deliver.[10] The Pole Moor chapel is an example of the way in which, across the region, the Evangelical revival in the Church of England gave rise to radical dissent, from the 1760s onwards. Some argue, however, that there has been far too much emphasis on this revival, on Evangelicals and their beliefs, by twentieth-century historians, and that the weight of their writing has obscured the everyday practices of the majority of moderate Anglican preachers and laity.[11] Evangelicals have certainly exercised the same kind of historical fascination as the Methodists did over Thompson, in *The Making of the English Working Class*.[12]

We know a good deal about what was delivered from pulpits and in some cases, like the Pole Moor Baptist one, the reactions of a congregation to preaching during a period of war, invasion scares and conspiracy theories of revolution. After Particular Baptism had organised itself on a trans-Pennine basis, local printers and publishers provided many accounts for those who cared to read them. Much of the output of the local press during Murgatroyd's later life constituted a running commentary on personal devotional dramas and the organisation of religious schism.[13] These years of Baptist and Methodist expansion were the ones in which the Church of England delivered its most consistent

---

[8] Edward Royle, 'The Church of England and Methodism in Yorkshire, c.1750–1850. From Monopoly to Free Market', *Northern History*, 33 (1997), pp. 137–61; 137.

[9] Cressida Annesley and Philippa Hoskin (eds.), *Archbishop Drummond's Visitation Returns 1764 I: Yorkshire A–G*, Borthwick Texts and Calendars 23 (York: University of York, 1998), 'Almondbury'.

[10] Royle, 'Church of England', p. 144.

[11] Robert Hole, *Pulpits, Politics and Public Order in England, 1760–1832* (Cambridge: Cambridge University Press, 1989), 'Introduction'.

[12] See, for example, Leonore Davidoff and Catherine Hall, *Family Fortunes. Men and Women of the English Middle Class, 1780–1850* (London: Hutchinson, 1987).

[13] Particular Baptist Church, Yorkshire and Lancashire Association, *The Nature and Importance of Repentance. The Ministers of the Denomination of Particular Baptists, assembled in Association at Hebden-Bridge, near Halifax, the eleventh and twelfth of June, 1794, send Christian Salutation to the several Churches they represent* (Halifax: privately printed, 1794). Particular Baptist Church, Yorkshire and Lancashire Association, *Christian Communion. The Ministers of the Denomination of Particular Baptists, assembled in Association at Halifax, on the 30th and 31st of May, 1798, send Christian salutation . . .* (Halifax: privately printed, 1798). Alexander Disney, *Reasons for Methodism, briefly Stated, in three Letters to a Friend* (Halifax: J. Nicholson, 1793).

arguments for social morality and social hierarchy.[14] What the Anglican pulpit had delivered by way of explanation and comfort during the trauma of the American Revolution has been particularly well explored.[15] This has been seen as fostering of national identity by the Church of England in the same period of war and revolution. William Gibson suggests that 'national identity in eighteenth-century England was indivisible from Anglicanism', for 'government was a religious construct and Anglicanism was welded into the structure of the establishment'. When war was waged, it was an English church and state indivisible that waged it.[16]

The union of church and state became a more present social reality in the last years of the century. The way of life of an Anglican clergyman came much more to resemble that of the gentry and the solid, respectable middle classes than it had hitherto done. Moreover, the number of clerical magistrates increased in the period under discussion here, linking the administration of local communities to the established church. The profile of the Church of England clergyman changed as part of a complex response to the French Revolution: financial pressures on the landed classes, the traditional source for justices of the peace, forced the abandonment of estates by some of them, leaving Church of England incumbents as the only available and qualified occupants of the bench.[17] Local echoes of the Revolution in France provoked the particularly Evangelical call for the church's increased presence in the laity's mind, or at least in its weekly calendar: the practice of double Sunday service was urged as a bulwark against seditious and irreligious ideas.[18] (The Slaithwaite curate – the chapelry was in the gift of successive Evangelical vicars of Huddersfield – had been holding two services on Sunday from at least the 1760s.[19]) The church's strategy of making of new members by catechising children, and by their general

[14] Hole, *Pulpits*, pp. 97, 108, 128–9, 136–7, 177.

[15] James E. Bradley, 'The Anglican Pulpit, the Social Order and the Resurgence of Toryism during the American Revolution', *Albion*, 21:3 (1989), pp. 361–88. The only work of politics, or contemporary history, that John Murgatroyd had in his library was James Murray's *An Impartial History of the War in America; from its first Commencement to the present Times*, 2 vols. (Newcastle: T. Robson, 1778). This was written in support of the rebels, but in acknowledgement of the necessary happiness of all Protestants 'where a Prince [rules] by law'.

[16] William Gibson, *The Church of England, 1688–1832* (London and New York: Routledge, 2001), p. 2.

[17] John Walsh and Stephen Taylor, 'The Church and Anglicanism in the "Long" Eighteenth Century', in John Walsh, Colin Haydon and Stephen Taylor, *The Church of England, c.1689–1883. From Toleration to Tractarianism* (Cambridge: Cambridge University Press, 1993), pp. 1–64; 28. Hole, *Pulpits*, pp. 251–3. Anthony Russell, *The Clerical Profession* (London: SPCK, 1980), p. 11. For further discussion of the increased union of church and state within parishes, see William Gibson, *Church, State and Society, 1760–1850* (Basingstoke: Macmillan, 1994), pp. 191–2, 195.

[18] Hole, *Pulpits*, pp. 58–9.

[19] Cressida Annesley and Philippa Hoskin (eds.), *Archbishop Drummond's Visitation Returns 1764 III: Yorkshire S–Y*, Borthwick Texts and Calendars 23 (York: University of York, 1998), 'Slaithwaite'.

education in parochial schools, was apparent in the West Riding. Educational activity here was evidence, as Jago and Royle put it, of an intention to make and sustain parishioners in the national faith.[20] The increase in enthusiasm and Evangelicalism, and the formation of Methodist and Baptist congregations across the district, is understood by Edward Royle to be a consequence of the Church of England's success in raising expectations of something from the pulpit and a minister that might speak directly to congregations' spiritual and social circumstances.[21]

It is a very long time indeed since historians accounted for the late eighteenth-century church in terms of its outward forms: 'the ornaments of the church and of the ministers, the design of church interiors, the pattern of services . . .'[22] Recent consensus of historical opinion about the Anglican Church has been arrived at by considering what the clergy and laity actually *did*, how they behaved and acted in particular places and social circumstances, and by what was said by its priests, particularly those whose words were preserved by publication. The piety of the age, rather than its theology, has been emphasised. It has been proposed that Anglicanism was a cultural form and a means of identification 'linking rich and poor' in a common world view.[23]

As for what people believed and the itinerary of an individual and collective faith, historians have generally proceeded by looking at the articles of that faith, the forms and formularies and liturgy of the Church of England, and using them as a measure of what must have been a personal appropriation of cognitive content held to be true, or to be dissented from. What people did on Sundays, the number of times they sought the bishop's blessing, or deserted the church for a Baptist chapel, comprise a checklist that allows a historian to determine what was the religious doctrine held to be true by late eighteenth-century people of differing sorts. In doing this, some historians of the church have, like William Cobbett, seen it 'everywhere', as an institution providing a world view and a set of cultural norms, outside which there was no place to be, or to think.

This book has proceeded in something of the same manner in its assumption that what you tell children about a god, their means of approaching that god and the implications of that information for the child's individuality and personhood, all offer some kind of access to the beliefs of the adult doing the

---

[20] Judith Jago, *Aspects of the Georgian Church. Visitation of the Diocese of York, 1761–1776* (London: Associated University Press, 1997), pp. 120–30. Judith Jago and Edward Royle, *The Eighteenth-century Church in Yorkshire. Archbishop Drummond's Primary Visitation of 1764*, Borthwick Papers 95 (York: University of York, 1999), p. 14.

[21] Royle, 'Church of England', pp. 159–61.

[22] F. C. Mather, 'Georgian Churchmanship Reconsidered. Some Variations in Anglican Public Worship, 1714–1830', *Journal of Ecclesiastical History*, 36:2 (1985), pp. 255–83; 256.

[23] Walsh and Taylor, 'Church and Anglicanism', p. 27.

teaching. This is a broadly sociological view, which understands the socialisa-
tion, training and general treatment of its children as providing access to the
deep structure of a society's belief system.[24] We certainly need to take into
account the ways in which information for children is selected and tailored to
their perceived needs (seventeenth- and eighteenth-century Anglicans thought
a good deal about this, as we have seen), all the means of obfuscation available
to the adult, and all the information that might be held in reserve. And yet,
what was taught in Slaithwaite Free School closely reflected the Trinitarianism
of the Anglican theologians, and their views on original sin and atonement;
it emphasised biblical knowledge; the works of seventeenth-century Anglican
divines crowded the shelves of its schoolmaster. Nigel Aston has argued that
there is strong evidence for a kind of counter-Enlightenment in the Church of
England in the later eighteenth century, an anti-philosophical movement that
worked by reviving the founding texts of the seventeenth-century Anglican revolution.[25] On the evidence of John Murgatroyd's book inventories many works
like these (with seventeenth-century imprints; no later editions were published)
came into his possession between 1792 and 1799, not through the purchase of
new (counter-revolutionary) editions, but because the originals he listed were
part of his deceased wife's and sister's estate. His then was a personal version
of a wider philosophical and political strategy of the Church of England; divinity like this came into his possession long after he had finished teaching in
Slaithwaite school.

Given what we know about all of these developments in Anglican thought
in the last quarter of the century, to proceed as if Murgatroyd believed in what
he taught does not seem an entirely unproductive course of action. Barbara
Taylor's recent work on Mary Wollstonecraft's religious imagination suggests
an additional way of understanding what these beliefs meant to John Murgatroyd. *Mary Wollstonecraft and the Feminist Imagination* involves a sustained
attempt to understand Wollstonecraft's thinking and feeling in relationship to
the Church of England, her adherence to and her dissent from its teaching and
doctrines.[26] It is unusual in modern intellectual biography in the attention given
to religious belief in the making of individual imagination – and for its several
index references to 'God'. Indeed, the Anglican God is actually a presence, or
event, in its pages, at least in regard to Wollstonecraft's belief in His existence
and presence. Nothing here of the embarrassment and weariness of spirit felt
by social historians schooled in the post-Thompsonian era when confronting

---

[24] Paul Connerton, *How Societies Remember* (Cambridge: Cambridge University Press, 1989),
pp. 10–13, 72–104.
[25] Nigel Aston, 'Horne and Heterodoxy. The Defence of Anglican Beliefs in the Late Enlightenment', *English Historical Review*, 108 (1993), pp. 895–919.
[26] Barbara Taylor, *Mary Wollstonecraft and the Feminist Imagination* (Cambridge: Cambridge
University Press, 2003).

that idea (or belief, or presence), rejection of which is the very mark of our modernity as historians. That sacred history belongs to God and that the history of civil society, which was made by men and women, belongs to the historian, was declared by Giambattista Vico in the early eighteenth century (though the import of *La Scienza Nuova* took a century to come to prominence). The distinction between the world of civil society, which was made by human beings and is therefore knowable by them, and the world of nature, made by God and only knowable to Him, was a founding principle of the profession, and one of the most profound ideological shifts of Western modernity.[27] Taylor's acceptance of Wollstonecraft's God (her acceptance that he existed for her, and that he had discernible effects on her) is a profound and exhilarating achievement. It is particularly exhilarating given the fact that in Wollstonecraft's case so many layers of twentieth-century iconisation of her as the first modern feminist and as a 'woman before her time' have to be stripped away, in order to see plain her ambition of the 1780s and 1790s, that women might attain virtue and the freedom to act rightly according to God's design for them.[28]

However, it is an achievement made within the inescapable confines of a modern world view and the practices of history that have helped shape it. It relies on the assumption (we can probably have no other) that any god is the creation of humankind; that 'god' is another name for the structures of belief and meaning that people develop in particular social and material circumstances. Taylor repeats William James's founding lesson in the sociology of religion, that 'the gods we stand by are the gods we need and can use . . . the gods whose demands on us are reinforcements of our demands on ourselves and on one another'. This formulation is particularly important for Taylor because it allows her to interpret Wollstonecraft's need for God as a demand for 'a self-identity that [was] psychically and culturally viable'. With her historian using the working principles of psycho-analytic theory, Wollstonecraft is then seen to take part in a universal psychic process: she shapes the fulfilment of her need on the model of her own parents, in the way that 'as children we turn to our father and mother with an idealising passion that moulds our fantasised contours'. It is out of this 'worshipful identification with deified parents' that

---

[27] Giambattista Vico, *The New Science of Giambattista Vico*, orig. pub. 1744, trans. Thomas Goddard Bergin and Max Harold Fisch (New York: Doubleday, 1961), pp. 401–2. See the discussion in Roger Smith, *The Human Sciences* (New York: Norton, 1997), pp. 340–5. On the distinction between sacred and secular history, see Edward Gibbon, *The Decline and Fall of the Roman Empire*, vol. I, orig. pub. 1776 (Chicago and London: Encyclopaedia Britannica, 1990), p. 79 (chapter 15). In arguing that historians can only look at secondary causes, not the first causes of events and happenings (as first causes are the province of 'the great Author'), he says pretty much the same as Vico.

[28] Taylor, *Mary Wollstonecraft*, pp. 12, 95–142.

our subjectivity is woven, and our gods – like Mary Wollstonecraft's Anglican God – are made.[29]

Not the least result of these procedures is a detailed and convincing account of Wollstonecraft's making of selfhood and subjectivity out of her religious belief. The role of Protestant Christianity in the making of the modern Western self has been very well explored, by historians and sociologists over the past century.[30] In a large number of cases this has been done by identifying the places in an autobiographical text where items of a general theology or belief system turn up. Taylor's study of the same processes in Wollstonecraft has been productive and innovative, in beginning with what Wollstonecraft *actually wrote* about her God and her faith – looking outward from the text, as it were, towards the Church of England and radical dissent from it, not the other way round. Given that it is impossible for the historian (certainly this historian) to *believe in* an Anglican God, this seems not only a productive, but also the only possible way of proceeding.

The God of Murgatroyd's writing and contemplation is linked to other contemporary ways of thinking, about individual selves and the social order. (He may be another name for that thinking; or as Roger Smith has put it, Christian faith and knowledge have been integral to thought about human nature, since at least the medieval period.[31]) And the God of Murgatroyd's personal writing may help answer the question this book is shaped by: how were these people able to do as they did: bear an illegitimate baby in a clergyman's house, leave a little bastard girl and her mother a small fortune (and the whole world, in compass of a globe), when most of the accounts we have of them, and of the prescriptions and prohibitions of their religious faith, suggest that they should have behaved quite otherwise?

The Anglican God was not the only deity present in the eighteenth-century West Riding. It was something of a convention among local literary men to see the old gods of classical antiquity move among the hills and cottages of the worsted field, to find 'Ceres and [the] country Gods' present at the people's

[29] Taylor, *Mary Wollstonecraft*, p. 128.
[30] William Haller, *The Rise of Puritanism* (New York: Harper, 1958). Paul Delaney, *British Autobiography in the Seventeenth Century* (London: Routledge and Kegan Paul, 1969). Owen Watkins, *The Puritan Experience. Studies in Spiritual Autobiography* (London: Routledge and Kegan Paul, 1972). Dean Ebner, *Autobiography in Seventeenth-century England. Theology and the Self* (The Hague: Mouton, 1971). Miriam J. Benknovitz, 'Some Observations on Women's Concept of Self in the Eighteenth Century', in Paul Fritz (ed.), *Woman in the Eighteenth Century and other Essays* (Toronto: Hakkert, 1976). Margaret P. Hannay, *Silent But for the Word. Tudor Women as Patrons, Translators, and Writers of Religious Works* (Ohio: Kent State University Press, 1985). Felicity Nussbaum, *The Autobiographical Subject* (Baltimore: The Johns Hopkins University Press, 1989).
[31] Smith, *Human Sciences*, p. 20.

feasts and wakes.[32] The pagan gods had been in West Yorkshire for a very long time: wakes was in origin a ploughman's feast, said one authority, first adopted by Christians 'under Constantine'. The rush-bearing festival involved worship of some kind of goddess figure made out of rushes; crowds of spinners in brand-new shoes and stockings were noted as claiming her as their own. Now in the 1780s, this occasion could only be viewed as 'bad in its Institution, and hurtful in its consequences to Morality'; for Bacchus, who had not metamorphosed into a northern and homely deity at all, but who was alive and well in the ale house in his original form, was cause of the great numbers of finely shod maidens being lustfully pursued during the festival, abused, and then abandoned.

The gods of classical antiquity are something of a problem for any historian describing the schooling in Christianity that John Murgatroyd provided for the Colne Valley, particularly in its Slaithwaite schoolroom. How were they under-stood in relation to the God of Christianity, who was promoted through the same teaching process? Latin language was a necessary foundation of any education beyond the rudimentary. It provided access to a sum of human knowledge, and in some views, to a universal structure, or grammar that underlay all languages. Its acquisition made understanding and use of the English tongue effective and more complete. It was taught, as we have seen, by means of a curriculum that took children through simple moral sentences, through fables, stories and colloquies, to the more extended narratives provided by – an example from Murgatroyd's schoolbook collection – Lucius Florus' *Roman History*.[33]

Among the sixty or so books that made up his teaching library, Murgatroyd had two copies of Ovid's *Metamorphoses*, a very old one dated 1664 and a modern edition with John Minellius's notes, in Bailey's translation and with his additional commentary.[34] Schoolboys had been encouraged to reach a compe-tence in Latin that allowed them access to Ovid for a least a century before Mur-gatroyd came to teach, but also, and for longer than that, his *Metamorphoses* had been culled for inclusion in *sententiae* and other teaching anthologies.[35] Thus

---

[32] Ebenezer Hunt, *The Rush-Bearing: A Poem. With a Probable Account of the Rise of Wakes* (Huddersfield: Joseph Brook, 1784), pp. 1–6.

[33] There was 'a Duodecimo Lucius Florus' in Murgatroyd's schoolbook collection – so possibly Lucius Annaeus Florus, *Epitome Rerum Romarum. Lucius Floruss his Epitome of Roman His-tory . . . made into English from the best editions and corrections of learned men. Illustrated with CXXVI cuts . . .* (London: John Nicholson, 1714).

[34] *Ovid's Metamorphoses in English by George Sandys*, London: X. Tomlines, 1664. Ovid, *Ovid's Metamorphoses, in fifteen books, with the arguments and notes of John Minellius translated into English. To which is marginally added, a prose version, . . . For the use of schools. By Nathan Bailey* (London: J. Rivington and Sons; G. Keith; T. Lowndes; T. Longman; W. Strahan, etc., 1778).

[35] Jean Seznec, *The Survival of the Pagan Gods. The Mythological Tradition and its Place in Renaissance Humanism and Art*, orig. pub. 1940 (New York: Harper, 1953), pp. 84–121. M. L. Clarke, *Classical Education in Britain, 1500–1900* (Cambridge: Cambridge University Press, 1959), pp. 5–20, 46–60.

they taught moral lessons, and the Greek myths that children might encounter later, in Latin poetry. *The Metamorphoses* was also valued as a resource book for history and geography.[36] But in its pages children also learned of the pagan gods, behaving in highly disreputable ways to protect their own honour, with nary a thought for the human beings they used, traduced and turned into trees along the way. The narrator is as ethically indifferent to the deceit, seduction and betrayal enacted by these gods, as they are indifferent to the human beings who are their occasional playthings.

If John Murgatroyd ever got round to using his copy of Hesiod with Slaithwaite schoolboys (probably *Work and Days*, though he gave no details in his inventory), they may have learned something useful about the organisation of the agricultural year on a small-time clothier's farm plot (not so very different from how you went about things in eighth-century BC Boetia). They may have recognised the paranoid uncertainty of any mortal who relies on weather and water (on the gods) to produce a crop, or a fleece for combing. Deep suspicion and resentment of the high-ups, of men who own more land than you, is a feature of its pages. By the time you came to Hesiod, if you did in Slaithwaite school, you would know *how* to read its weird and compelling mixture of domestic advice and propitiatory proposals for living with the fickleness and frank disinterest of the gods, for this was the way in which the Latin colloquies of Erasmus and Corderius proceeded.[37] Hesiod also taught the supremely important lesson of good neighbourliness among those whose livelihood was insecure; but this was not the injunction of the catechism, to love a neighbour – made like you in God's image – as you love yourself, and to do as you would be done by in regard to Him. Hesiod's good neighbour was the product of a shame culture, in which the chief reason for behaving decently is what others will think of you. By way of contrast, in a guilt culture, a God who takes a personal interest in you and all your doings in the world, who has enjoined you to learn and labour to get your own living, is a measure of how well you have fulfilled his commandments, and how far fallen short of them.[38]

The gods of the *Iliad* and the *Odyssey* (Murgatroyd simply recorded 'Homer' in his schoolbook inventory) are considerably more elegant and refined than Hesiod's, but no nearer to humankind and no more like it than his. They provide

---

[36] Peter Mack, *Elizabethan Rhetoric. Theory and Practice* (Cambridge: Cambridge University Press, 2002), p. 17.

[37] Murgatroyd must have taught Greek to at least some of his generations of schoolboys. He lists several Greek grammars, commentaries and works of literature in his 1790s inventories, and devotes some space in his 'Book of Records' to transcribing Greek – probably for teaching purposes. Perhaps he owned Hesiod, *The Works of Hesiod translated from the Greek. By Mr Cooke*, 2 vols. (London: T. Green, 1728). This was the earliest eighteenth-century edition.

[38] The catechism asked, 'What is thy Duty towards thy Neighbour?', to which the answer was 'to love him as thyself, and to do to all men as I would they should do unto me . . . to learn and labour truly to get my own living . . .'

a model of what life might be like were mortals blessed with immortality and ease, but there is no direct communication with them to be had, only an anxious search for what might be a carelessly left sign or portent.[39] Odysseus experiences the intervention of the gods as benevolent on some occasions, and justice is delivered in a way that can be interpreted as ethical, as is not the case with Hesiod. But the gods still lie and cheat, as they do in Virgil's account of them (four Virgils in Murgatroyd's collection, two seventeenth-century editions, two more modern ones.)[40] The Olympian gods may have forgotten the incest, genital mutilation and child-eating that gave them birth (about which Hesiod is quite frank), but most of their sexual relations are adulterous at best and forced at worse. They are figured more like characters – are anthropomorphised and civilised to some degree – compared with Hesiod's crew, who are abstractly inexplicable. Virgil's gods eat and drink and get dressed up, as human beings do in texts. Yet their limited and capricious interest in humankind remains their central characteristic. The world was not made for poor, bare forked creatures, and their existence in it is merely tolerated by the gods, when they deign to notice it. Because of this indifference, a reader's attention is perhaps drawn to the human figures of the *Aeneid*: it is possible to make a hero out of Aeneas, using other theologies, and much later texts of Christian humanism.

Nearly all of John Murgatroyd's classical literature was in very old editions, dating from the seventeenth century. In all probability they were the ones he had acquired as a schoolboy. His copies of Ovid, for example, had been produced during a period when the gods were thoroughly allegorised as aspects of Christian doctrine and belief. Ancient mythology had been endowed with moral meaning through the labours of scholars, from the eleventh century onwards.[41] The schoolbooks had allowed boys 'to pass away their youth among the gods' in a relative degree of safety for a very long time indeed.[42] There were some clerical and educational thinkers who worried about a childhood spent 'wallowing in "a continual series of wanton sports",'[43] but as schoolbooks have such an extraordinarily long and economical life, boys went on doing so,

[39] Mary Lefkowitz, *Greek Gods, Human Lives. What We Can Learn from Myths* (New Haven and London: Yale University Press, 2003), p. 84.

[40] The 1664 edition (Murgatroyd noted this date) which included the Aeneid, the Ecologues and the Georgics must have been Virgil, *Opera. Variorum autorum annotationibus illustrata* (London: J. M. for the Society of Stationers, 1664). I have not been able to trace the others.

[41] Seznec, *Survival*, pp. 84–121.

[42] Frank E. Manuel, *The Eighteenth Century Confronts the Gods* (Cambridge, Mass.: Harvard University Press, 1959), p. 5 quoting Abbé Pluché, *Histoire du ciel considéré selon les idées des poètes, des philosophes et de Moyse*, 2 vols. (Paris: La Veuve Estienne, 1739) vol. II, p. 387. Abbé Pluché, *The History of the Heavens, considered according to the Notions of the Poets and Philosophers, compared with the Doctrines of Moses*, trans. J. B. de Freval, 2 vols. (London: J. Osborn, 1740), vol. II, p. 269. Pluché actually said that 'Ainsi l'enfance se passe parmi les dieux' – more to the point for the Slaithwaite schoolroom.

[43] Manuel, *Eighteenth Century*, p. 5, quoting Pluché, *Histoire*, vol. 2, p. 387.

willy-nilly, right through the eighteenth century. Most of Murgatroyd's eighteenth-century editions of Latin and Greek literature were reprints of works originally published in the previous century. They came for the main part with editorial comment and prolegomena that still placed them firmly within the Christian tradition.

There was no echo in any of them of the new (anachronistically named) anthropology and sociology of religion. Travel writing, reports home from the contact zones by missionaries and gentlemen soldiers, had allowed comparison between Graeco-Roman paganism and religious practices in New World heathen societies. This provided a new view of the world of classical antiquity: it was made pagan, primitive and historical in the new eighteenth-century mythologies and natural histories of religion. From the Stoic philosophers themselves, modern ones learned what William James was later to formulate, that the pagans had 'copied their divinities after themselves'.[44]

But none of this was for the Slaithwaite schoolroom, if its master's teaching books are anything to go by. These gods came to the West Riding still clothed by Renaissance humanism, as virtues, attributes, aspects of the Christian soul seeking its God. Children's appropriation of these texts was in any case partial: classical literature was studied in order to learn a language, and to acquire a vocabulary for later conversation and composition. (Greek was probably only ever studied for reading competence.) Ovid, or Virgil – or the satires of Juvenal and Persius – were delivered much like the *Sententiae Pueriles* or Bailey's *Exercises* had been at an earlier stage of this schooling. Short extracts were learned by heart, and then analysed word by word. Most children did not venture very far into a text, and it was unlikely that they had direct access to it – actually held in their hands. It was linguistic knowledge parcelled up and kept at a distance from its literary form and story content. Centuries of teaching in this way had smoothed the violent, old gods into literary tropes, figures of speech, rhetorical terms and aphorisms. The gods had been made ideas, forms of thinking, and ways of using a language, by the time they entered the Slaithwaite schoolroom.

Also available in the Latin and Greek literature that Murgatroyd taught was the political philosophy of the societies that gave rise to it, particularly that of the late Roman empire. A quietly confident detachment from the hustle and ambition of the world was predicated on retirement from some metropolis – Rome, or London, or Halifax. In the satires of Persius, the view is from a country place, where men live on their own harvest and mill their own grain. It may be biting in its analysis of the economic order, but cynicism comes in a voice vastly more secure than that of Hesiod's farmer, with his curmudgeonly suspicions of

---

[44] Manuel, *Eighteenth Century*, p. 45, quoting Bernard Le Bovier de Fontenelle, *De l'origine des fables*, orig. pub. 1724 (Paris: Felix Alcan, 1932), pp. 17–18.

the troublesome people around him.[45] The gods were very distant in Persius' poetry, not forces of inevitability, but intellectual propositions that might be discussed over dinner. Stoicism inscribed the civic virtues, told of the use that men might be to each other in the organisation of community and everyday life. It has been said that Stoical moral thought was expressed in regard to a subjective self 'as the distinct home of what is good'; this may also have been the way it was read.[46] If so, his was a self that might act in order to achieve a good and honourable life in this world, particularly by subduing its own unruly passions, in acts of self-control.

Murgatroyd made many notes on neighbourliness, and on the duties of friends towards each other. But in his view of the small farming and weaving communities of the West Riding he made a distinction between the comeliness of a public life as it was figured in the pages of Juvenal or Horace, and the Christian virtues. He called the responsibilities of civil society 'Moral Duties, as taught by Nature, namely Justice, Temperance, Chastity . . .' 'Gospel duties', on the other hand, consisted of 'doing good for evil, forgiving enemies'.[47] What others thought of you, the praise and approbation you might gain from behaving well towards those around you was subordinate to the doing of it; indeed 'the Nature of Hypocrisy is to study more to seem religious in Man's sight yn be truly religious before God – A hypocrite counts ye World's Acceptn more than God's Favour & Approbatn'.[48] This was a Christian perspective, far removed from the classical one he read, translated and taught.

He made notes of guidance on the way in which God was to be known within individual souls. There was the enormousness of Creation, to be sure: 'God governs ye World in infinite Wisdm., ye Creatures & all their Actns, and always under His Eye ye Eye of Providce. is quick sighted . . . is intent, reaches far thro' ye whole World; ev'rymost dark & distant Corner & his Eye directs his hand, & power ∼ He governs for our good, does all in pursuance of ye Counsels of his Love concern.g our Salvation . . . Wisdom & might are his. . .'[49] But relationship with this God was through the narrow passage of an individual soul. Those who kept close to Him would know His presence, but only through consistent individual perseverance in seeking it: 'The Lord is with you, whilst

[45] 'Horace, Juvenal, Persius bound together . . . Bonds Persius', noted Murgatroyd in his inventory. John Murgatroyd, 'Authors Useful to be Read at School', 1745–1802, 082.2 MUR, Special Collections, Slaithwaite Parish Collection, University of York, York. '1792 October 25th School Books', notes Murgatroyd. He may have purchased Bond's edition of Persius after he finished school teaching. Persius, *Auli Persii Flacci satyrae sex. Cum posthumis commentariis Joannis Bond, quibis recens accessit index verborum*, 2nd edn (Dublin: William M'Kensie, 1787). But it is more likely that his copy was Persius, *Auli Persii Flacci satyrae sex. Cum posthumis commentariis Joannis Bond* (London: Nathaniel Butteriij, 1614, acquired sometime in the 1730s).
[46] Smith, *Human Sciences*, p. 70.
[47] Murgatroyd, 'Ask, Read, Retain, Teach', KC249/9, p. 7.
[48] Murgatroyd,'Ask, Read, Retain, Teach', KC249/9, p. 91.
[49] Murgatroyd, 'Ask, Read, Retain, Teach', KC249/9, p. 98.

you be with Him ∼ if you seek Him, He will be found of you ∼ if you forsake Him, He will forsake you ∼ On such terms we stand with God,' he noted (he may have started many sermons in this way – with a good example of a theology that was clearly not Evangelical). Those who kept 'close to God, shall know his lov.g presence'. Indeed, 'all Service to God terminates in Ourselves', he wrote under the heading of 'Examples Necessary'. In this precise example what ended up in the individual human soul was a purchase of 'ye Benefits of Xt's satisfactn by servg. God'.[50] Indeed, the individual in relationship with his God was the very definition of religion:

Religion consider'd in its foundation is yt Sense we have of God's Being & Power & of ye relation in wch we stand to Him, as Creatures & Subjects – This Sense is ye. very Bond wch ties to God. Ye first Conseqce arising hence is we must love fear & trust in God as Creator and Governour ∼ these are religious Acts of a ration.l Mind ∼ it is religion to love God, also, our Neighbours ∼ for any branch of Relign immed.y refelcti.g either God, ourselve or Neighbrs may be term'd Religion.[51]

Murgatroyd inventoried none of the works that might allow us to trace the linear movement of John Locke's natural history of the soul through eighteenth-century faculty psychology to a fully fledged nineteenth-century philosophy of mind and self – none of the works of Hume, nor Hartley (though he had read and made twenty pages of notes on the *Essay concerning Human Understanding* in the 1740s). Nevertheless, this psychology, and its broadly physiological under-standing of mind–body relations, framed at least one of the books of advice Murgatroyd possessed. The clergyman Wetenhall Wilkes's *Advice to a Young Lady* was proceeded by entirely modern notions of the body and its workings, and Wilkes used an overtly Lockean psychology to explain to her the relation-ship between body and mind.[52] The natural philosophy of the mid-century – what later came to be called 'faculty psychology' – described the soul's nature, its attributes, its purpose, its ways of working. What a soul was, and what it could do, were itemised under the headings of cognition (what it could know) and affection (what it could feel) and what it could will, or determine. These faculties were understood as the powers of the soul.[53]

The notes and jottings of a broadly Latitudinarian West Riding clergyman gave expression to a wider 'science of man', part of a European movement towards 'Enlightenment' that had its roots in 'reformist Christianity, either

---

[50] Murgatroyd, 'Ask, Read, Retain, Teach', KC249/9, p. 7.

[51] Murgatroyd, 'Ask, Read, Retain, Teach', KC249/9, pp. 101–2, 'Printed 1787 Remarks on Bp Sherlock's Argumts agt repealing ye Corporatn and Test Acts'.

[52] Wetenhall Wilkes, *A Letter of Genteel and Moral Advice to a Young Lady*, 8th edn (London: L. Haws, 1766), pp. 18–34.

[53] Smith, *Human Sciences*, pp. 203–5.

Catholic or Protestant'.[54] Perhaps we should find it unsurprising that Murgatroyd's personal writing gave expression to a version of this 'science', though it is certainly the case that conventional Christianity has usually been omitted from the lists of texts that conveyed it, and that have been the most consulted by modern scholars describing its history. In fact, John Murgatroyd owned books that show the lines of transmission to have been religious as well as scientific. Some time between 1792 and 1799 he acquired the American Jonathan Edward's *Treatise on Religious Affections* (1746), which asked 'what is the nature of true Religion?' It found its answer in 'the Affections . . . the Affections are no other, than the most vigorous and sensible Exercises of the Inclination and the Will of the Soul'.[55] God has endowed souls with two faculties, perception and speculation. This is how souls gain knowledge of the world and ideas, and assess them. Perception allows you to apprehend things, and decide whether you are 'inclin'd to 'em, or . . . disinclin'd, and adverse from 'em'. Edwards admitted that his terminology was confusing (and even more confusing to twenty-first-century readers, who have learned their vocabulary from a much later psychology), for this first faculty 'is called by various Names: it is sometimes called the Inclination'. And then, because it is connected to 'the Actions that are determined and governed by it, [it] is called the Will: And the Mind, with regard to the Exercises of this Faculty, is often called the Heart'. In any case, there are two sorts of affections. The ones that go by the names of love, desire, joy, gratitude, complacence, carry the soul towards something – towards God; whilst 'hatred, fear, anger and grief' move the soul away from the thing perceived and contemplated. Religion is itself 'holy affection'.[56] It is not so much that this itemisation of the individual, this assessment of capacities, abilities and aptitudes inscribes the deep, interior and 'true' self of a much later subjectivity. Rather, this is an attempt to describe the dimensions of the creature that God created in order to know Him. This schema of knowing, or apprehension, or feeling (after reading Edwards, you know how legion are the words to describe the capacity to know God), is probably what John Murgatroyd had in mind when he concluded that 'religion . . . in its foundation' was 'yt Sense we have of God's Being & Power & of ye relation in wch we stand to Him, as Creatures & Subjects – This Sense is ye. very Bond wch ties to God . . .'[57] It was by using this model of the human soul, or self, that Murgatroyd could write that 'Xtianity . . . [is] an operative Principle in ye Mind, regulating ye affectns, & leading. Us to obey ye Precepts

---

54 Though the case was different in France. See Nigel Aston on 'The Church and the Enlightenment', in his *Religion and Revolution in France, 1780–1804* (Washington: Catholic University of America Press, 2000), pp. 81–99.

55 Jonathan Edwards, *A Treatise on Religious Affections* (Boston: S. Kneeland, 1746), p. 4. See Smith, *Human Sciences*, p. 217. Edwards was published locally in the 1790s. Jonathan Edwards, *Some remarkable Narratives . . .* (Huddersfield: J. Brook, Huddersfield, 1791).

56 Edwards, *Treatise*, pp. 7–9.

57 Murgatroyd, 'Ask, Read, Retain, Teach', KC249/9, pp. 101–2.

of ye Gospel – this Love, in ye Heart, is ye Root whence evr'y virtuous action springs, always look ye to actions, to find ye real Xtian – who is, considering natl. Infirmity, unblameable in his morals . . .'[58]

John Murgatroyd dwelt much on judgment. He was required to believe in it: it is the substance of Article four of the Thirty-Nine. One of the characteristics of the unfaithful and negligent minister, he said, was his failure to believe in 'Xt's com.g to Judgement'; this is what the bad minister muttered in his heart – that there would be no such thing; and yet 'It's writn yre shall, necessar.y shou'd be a Day of Judgemt. wh Everyone must be examd by ye Judge – Jesus Xt – whom ye wealthiest cannot bribe ye mightiest cannot daunt ye wisest cannot delude – fm. wm. no appeal & no repealig his sentence.' We were to be 'judged in ye same Bodies we died, of course'; a Resurrection would necessarily involve 'ever so many improbable Circumstances', but nevertheless everywhere – 'all places' – 'shall give up yr dead – by ye powr of God, they must be restored'.[59] He noted that 'the Sentence will be, as ev'ry one's Work is – as ye Sincereity, not Imperfecn of ye Work' (another example of a clearly non-Evangelical theology) and earlier that 'Xt alone is ye only Person to show doctrine & precepts wh are absolute Truth & Obedce.' But really, there is little attention to Christ shown in his notebooks, not to the personhood of Christ, nor to the Atonement, which on my reading of his notes, he does not mention once. John Murgatroyd spent half his life covering for the incumbents of Huddersfield parish, preaching in their churches and chapels, and exchanging sermons and conviviality with an increasingly Evangelical professional body. From 1759 to 1771, the vicar of Huddersfield, Henry Venn, had promoted the 'scheme of salvation' to be found in his *Complete Duty of Man* (1763).[60] Moreover, the local publishing industry kept West Riding readers up-to-date on the theology of Atonement, from the 1760s onwards. There was an account of it in verse, designed for 'unlearned . . . and poor readers', and numerous more intellectually demanding tracts available.[61] Faith in this schema *was* faith in the Atonement; justification came through that faith. Priests and sacraments were of very little importance – mere intermediaries between the individual and his Maker. Neither were goodness, good works and godliness likely to purchase the Evangelical

---

[58] Murgatroyd, 'Ask, Read, Retain, Teach', KC249/9, p. 35.

[59] Murgatroyd, 'Ask, Read, Retain, Teach', KC249/9, p. 104.

[60] Henry Venn, *The Complete Duty of Man; or a system of Doctrinal and practical Christianity. To which are added Forms of Prayer*, orig. pub. 1763 (London: S. Crowder, etc., 1779). See also Henry Venn (ed.), *The Life and a Selection from the Letters of the late Henry Venn*, MA, 4th edn (London: John Hatchard, 1836).

[61] Philaganthus, *A Practical Improvement of the Divinity and Atonement of Jesus, attempted in Verse; humbly offered as a Supplement to the Tracts lately published* (Halifax: E. Jacob, 1772). Philaganthus does not raise one's hopes as a reader. He lists several local tracts in which we might find proper arguments about these 'glorious doctrines'; the poetry in your hands was merely for the 'faint purpose' of pointing out their 'Importance and excellency'; he pretends to 'little skill in *Poetry* . . . a subject on which he seldom employs a single thought'.

eternal salvation; salvation lay in the way of *knowing* that Christ had purchased your soul for you, through his sacrifice. In Boyd Hilton's trenchant summary of this brand of Evangelicalism, Christ had purchased salvation on the Cross; thus was ransom paid for the sins of all humankind. From the 1780s onwards (and certainly in Huddersfield parish) Evangelical Christian faith was faith in the Atonement.[62] But Murgatroyd did not contemplate the Atonement in his commonplace books, though if he used other men's sermons as frequently as Canon Hulbert thought he did, he may sometimes have preached it.

The relationship that Murgatroyd described, between minister, God and the individuals who made up his flock, was not the same as the one promoted by the new, 'vital' Christianity of the Colne Valley. Murgatroyd was interested in the office and behaviour of ministers, whilst many Evangelicals thought priests to be relatively insignificant intermediaries between individuals and God. Sacraments are minor factors in the Evangelical relationship, an interruption of the arrangement between soul and maker (though Wesley regarded Holy Communion as a means by which people might come to know the grace of God). Murgatroyd dwelt on the form and meaning of the sacraments of the Church of England. The Day of Judgment was a certainty for Murgatroyd as much as it was for his Evangelical colleagues, but in his notes on it, he emphasised, as we have seen, that intention rather than outcome would be judged ('Sentence will be, as ev'ry one's Work is – as ye Sincereity, not imperfection of ye Work'[63]), whilst many Evangelicals were extremely doubtful about the ultimate value of good works in purchasing salvation. For them, good works were the mere outward sign of faith and a sense of grace. Neither were Murgatroyd's neighbours and congregations loaded down and saturated with original sin, as they were in Henry Venn's scheme of things. In fact, as we have seen, Murgatroyd made considerable efforts to explore the ways in which fears of its consequences might be allayed. Or, at least, he did this in writing. He may also have delivered his advice from pulpits. In this, he was closer to Wesley than to the theology of a Henry Venn: neither he nor his 'people' were weighed down by sin; rather they had the means to liberation from it. The individual human conscience was the way and means of salvation; in Evangelicalism the 'all-important contractual relationship is directly between each soul and its maker'.[64] So it was in Murgatroyd's musings and jottings, though his notes on the relationship do not

---

[62] Boyd Hilton, *The Age of Atonement. The Influence of Evangelicalism on Social and Economic Thought, 1785–1865* (Oxford: Clarendon Press, 1988), pp. 1–35; 8–9. The other main doctrine which distinguished Methodists from Evangelicals concerned the Holy Spirit. Churchmen believed that the Holy Spirit had operated freely in New Testament times, but subsequently only through the church. Methodists thought that the Holy Spirit continued to operate in the old way – a clear threat to ecclesiastical and clerical order. I am grateful to Ted Royle for pointing this distinction out, as it operated in late eighteenth- and early nineteenth-century Yorkshire.

[63] Murgatroyd, 'Ask, Read, Retain, Teach', KC249/9, p. 104.

[64] Hilton, *Age of Atonement*, p. 8.

evoke the negotiated and enforceable arrangement that 'contract' does. When he taught of God, and of Christ, he told people (or maybe just himself, if these were nothing more than random notes taken from his reading) about their nature: what kind of thing a human individual was, and how it was organised.

We may use Murgatroyd and the Evangelical West Riding clergymen he differed from as examples of the development that so much twentieth-century history testifies to: the making of the modern self through a wide variety of Protestant theologies and practices, from the sixteenth century onwards. What is interesting about the 'Ourselves' that Murgatroyd deals with in his notes is the way in which it uses the broad categories of contemporary psychology and physiology. Ideas about a self made so that it might know itself had been developed in religious discourse, as much as in scientific thinking. This self was located in a body that divines of the seventeenth century had understood to belong to a soul that sought connection with God. This theology was part of Murgatroyd's library and his thinking. In his last years, he obtained from somewhere (probably it was his sister's; she died in 1801) Thomas Fuller's *Good Thoughts in Bad Times* (1680), which took as its epigraph 'Commune with your own heart, and in your Chamber, and be still' (Psalms 4.4). It delivers – among the meditations and scriptural observations – a compelling account of the state of sickness, and of that state of being neither well, nor ill, nor in any recognisable somatic state: conversations with yourself, a third party present, which is both your God and your very self.[65]

In the kind of literature that advised on teaching children about the Angli-can God, the opportunities for experiencing this selfhood, its expression by affection, knowledge and determination towards God, were opened up in the 1790s, in detailed advice about where and how to pray. James Stonhouse pro-vided prayers for many categories of people, of all ages; prayers you could say silently when riding, or at a party in a crowded room, or just walking along a road: commune with your own heart, and be still. This was old advice, rewrought, telling you that you did not need a private chamber in which to be with God and your self.[66] This schema was formalised at the century's end, again most obviously, in the kind of literature that Murgatroyd did not possess. This space of individual privacy could be accessed outside the closet – or so the advice went, by the 1790s.[67] It is not so much that God was this space, or that

---

[65] Thomas Fuller, *Good Thoughts in Bad Times: Together with Bad Thoughts in Good Times* (London: John Williams, 1680), pp. 2, 84–5. If Murgatroyd obtained this book after his sister's death, he did not have it to refer to during his own period of illness during October and November 1789. The language he recorded it in, though, is much like Fuller's: he wrote in the fevered state in which boundaries between body and spirit are lost. It is not clear what was wrong with him, though he mentioned several times a 'pricking in the Bowels'.

[66] James Stonhouse, *Prayers for the Use of Private Persons, Families, Children and Servants*, 14th edn (London: J. F. & C. Rivington, 1800), p. 40.

[67] Stonhouse, *Prayers for the Use of Private Persons*.

he was to be found in it, for he was a Spirit, not to be found present. Rather, his Creation was to make that space and place, increasingly conceived as both within and portable, where He could be spoken to.

Following the course of Murgatroyd's reading through the notebooks he kept for sixty years reveals the God of a West Riding Enlightenment. He first emerged during Murgatroyd's early years in Slaithwaite, when he read Thomas Nettleton's *Some Thoughts Concerning Virtue and Happiness*. When his lifetime's note-taking can be traced to its source, Nettleton's (1683–1742) cheerful and rational account of God's Creation is the one that reverberates more than any other, through his diaries and the last commonplace book, still in use some forty years after he had noted that Nettleton was a Halifax medical man.[68] Murgatroyd probably used the second or third edition of Nettleton's work, which expanded the original *Thoughts . . . in a Letter to a Clergyman* of 1729 into something three times as long, with the status of a 'treatise'.[69] The first little book had been written by Nettleton as a token of thanks for a friendship with which an anonymous clergyman had honoured the author for 'many years', and also because the addressee was 'not afraid of any *Freedom* or *Debate*', and would listen to 'anything that can be advanced, provided it is not contrary to Religion and Good Manners'.[70] This kind of epistolary exchange of enlightenment was familiar to Murgatroyd (perhaps it was common across the West Riding, for many clergymen and their friends), for in 1749 he copied out into his 'Book of Records' a letter received from Daniel Eagland (son of the churchwarden who had introduced him to the Slaithwaite schoolroom ten years before), 'About Human Reason'. 'Bro' Jno', Eagland wrote, 'These Thoughts occur'd to me upon ye July 1, I write 'em to you wth ye utmost Freedom, not in a dictatorial Way, you're entirely at Liberty ei'r to approve or reject . . .'[71] This kind of exchange went on until the end of Murgatroyd's life. On New Year's Eve 1802 ('Some Rain and Darkish') he sat companionably with Revd Falcon, who 'din'd, drank Tea, sup'd and spent Eveng with me – I read 2 sermons, & we were very instructive & agreeable to one another – his Mothr & Family are tolerably in Health – He would have Moonlight – & I hope, got well Home.'[72] Alexander Disney explained his going over to the West Riding Methodists in

---

[68] John Murgatroyd, 'A Cornucopia: or Collection of weighty Extracts transcribed out of the scarcest, most necessary & best chosen Books &c according to this proper Maxim, that every Man shou'd take down in Writing what He learns for fear of forgetting any useful Circumstance. By John Murgatroyd, Master of Slaithwaite School. Anno Domini 1742', 082.2 MUR, Special Collections, Slaithwaite Parish Collection, University of York, York, pp. 625–30 for the notes on Nettleton.

[69] Thomas Nettleton, *Some Thoughts Concerning Virtue and Happiness, in a Letter to a Clergyman* (London: Jeremiah Batley, 1729). *A Treatise on Virtue and Happiness*, 2nd edn (London: J. Batley and J. Wood, 1736).

[70] Nettleton, *Some Thoughts*, pp. i, vi.   [71] Murgatroyd, 'Book of Records'.

[72] Murgatroyd Diaries, KC 242/6 (31 December 1802).

1793, in 'three letters to a friend', and gave as a major motivating factor the increased opportunities for 'human happiness' among them. His friend and addressee was a gloomy kind of man who believed life to be one long series of calamities and a vale of tears; 'Real and experimental Religion' might cheer him up; Methodism was much misunderstood; the congregation with which Disney had found himself at home was not against gaiety and 'chearful intercourse'.[73]

Thomas Nettleton's *Letter* and his vastly expanded *Treatise* tell how to be happy, in the light of what recent developments in the philosophy of the human subject told of God's Creatures, as physiological and psychological entities, for there could be 'none but who would desire to pass through the world as easily as they can, and to give themselves as little pain as possible: And how we may learn to do this, and also obtain the greatest and most lasting pleasure, is the subject of [my] inquiry'.[74] 'The eighteenth century engaged in obsessional talk about happiness . . .'[75] The method Nettleton proposed for attaining it was 'attended with some trouble', for it 'required some degree of self-denial'. It was not for everyone, but of particular use to the reader who understood that the 'chief business in life was to promote his own happiness, and that of others'. Doing this would have discernible effects on civil society, in particular putting an end to the abuses of power and to corruption. To be virtuous was the only way to be happy and free. Using the same physiology and psychology of perception as Edwards in his *Treatise on the Religious Affections*, Nettleton explained in some detail the way in which modes of grief and joy were excited by external phenomena and happenings operating on our senses, or 'powers of affection'. 'A STATE of *uninterrupted* felicity was not to be expected', for the 'wise author of our beings' having 'endowed us with a power of self and motion, and designated them for action and employment' had also 'in order to put us into motion, subjected us to many unavoidable *pains*, and *uneasiness*; and such

---

[73] Disney, *Reasons for Methodism*, pp. 9, 64–73.   [74] Nettleton, *Treatise*, p. 11.

[75] S. A. Grave, 'Some Eighteenth-century Attempts to Use the Notion of Happiness', in R. F. Brissenden (ed.), *Studies in the Eighteenth Century. Papers presented at the David Nichol Memorial Seminar* (Canberra: Australian National University Press, 1968), pp. 155–69. Nettleton, *Treatise*, p. ii. For Nettleton's discussion of the social realm, see pp. 132–73. For the dangers of benevolence run riot, p. 265. The *Treatise* was enormously popular, running through fourteen editions before the century's end. Nettleton's arguments bear some resemblance to Francis Hutcheson's and his philosophy of universal benevolence. See T. A. Roberts, *The Concept of Benevolence. Aspects of Eighteenth-century Moral Philosophy* (London: Macmillan, 1973); Thomas Mautner (ed.), *Francis Hutcheson. On Human Nature. Reflections on our Common Systems of Morality. On the Social Nature of Man* (Cambridge: Cambridge University Press, 1993). Nettleton may have shared a background and education with Hutcheson in Ireland. His doctoral thesis was published as Thomas Nettleton, *Resp. Desputatio de Inflammatione Praes. H. A. Roell* (Trajecti ad Rhenum, 1706). He also published on inoculation for smallpox. Thomas Nettleton, *An Account of Inoculating the Small-pox: in a Letter to Dr William Whitaker* (London: J. Batley, 1722). When Nettleton and his work are fully investigated, it will be important to defend the *Treatise* from charges of Panglossianism.

is our make and constitution, that whenever we feel any uneasy sensation, we are determined to get quit of it, as soon as possible'.[76]

The great author had also endowed his human creatures 'with *reason*, to be our guide and director . . . has given us those *powers* and *faculties*, to judge of what relates to ourselves, which will lead us so much the nearer to our happiness'.[77] Moreover, it was 'highly requisite that, in order to be happy . . . we employ that natural talent of thinking, which GOD almighty has given us . . .'[78] He also advocated laughter, and the pleasures of looking – at the infinite variety of the natural world, at the sky – as a great promoter of happiness.[79] But the God he described was no mere reflection of his Creatures – not their invention, but rather, radically other: 'the perfectly reasonable, just god . . . the *sovereign ruler* of the world' is not like us, influenced by 'weak passions'; neither does this God 'act in partial and capricious manner, but governs by general, steady and inviolable Laws . . . he is not favourable to some of his creatures, and cruel to the rest'.[80] In the earlier version, Nettleton had satirised the Christian God in his Roman Catholic and Calvinist aspects, a God supposed to be an 'arbitrary, angry and vindictive being, revenging himself when offended on others than those who gave the Provocation, or like some Eastern Monarch, pleased with Flattery, Cringing and mean prostration, partial to a few of [their] Creatures and cruel to all the rest'.[81] He further observed to his clergyman friend that it was 'no less true than [it was] seriously affecting, that at this very Day, in the greater part of *Europe*, where the reform'd Religion has not obtain'd, Rewards and Punishments are almost entirely misapply'd . . . in those Countries, by suppressing or perverting the Scriptures, the Clergy seldom fail to make their own Will the Will of God'.[82]

'True religion' was the greatest support of the programme of moral virtue that he laid out; as John Murgatroyd was to note – or to remember – so many years later, Christianity asked for particular procedures that aided the general scheme of virtue: returning good for evil, suppressing resentment at others and their actions, loving your neighbour as yourself. Indeed, 'the commands of our *holy religion* will from their own just authority . . . claim an implicit obedience'.[83] The thinking, feeling, acting and reacting creature made by a wise and just God had been given the faculty to know Him; His existence was to be known within each individual: Nettleton urged his readers to have good and appropriate conceptions of a good and appropriate God, making '*free and impartial use* of those natural powers he has given them'.[84]

---

[76] Nettleton, *Treatise*, p. 26.   [77] Nettleton, *Treatise*, p. 75.   [78] Nettleton, *Treatise*, p. 118.
[79] Nettleton, *Treatise*, pp. 179, 190–1.   [80] Nettleton, *Treatise*, pp. 260–1.
[81] Nettleton, *Thoughts*, p. 107.   [82] Nettleton, *Thoughts*, p. 110.
[83] Nettleton's first mention of Christianity is on p. 265 of a 300-page treatise.
[84] Nettleton, *Thoughts*, p. 296.

Above all the other aspects and versions of God and Christianity available to Murgatroyd, this, I think, was the one that allowed the events of 1801–6 to fall out as they did. In Nettleton's account and in Murgatroyd's notes, he had established the same organisation of body and mind in all men and women. Their actions – 'motions' in Nettleton's terminology – were determined by either an uneasiness arising from the apprehension of a present evil, representation of an absent good or an approaching evil. These were the mainsprings of human action; in Nettleton's nice example, it was just the same for the day labourer as it was for Alexander the Great.[85] Of course, much depended on given 'genius and capacity' and even more on what 'rank and station will admit of'; but there is some space here for Murgatroyd to be able to understand Phoebe Beatson as a creature something like himself, and to act to make her happier than not.[86]

But John Murgatroyd did not look at the sky in the way that Thomas Nettleton recommended; or at least, there is no record in his journals and other notebooks of his gazing at cloud formation in awe and aesthetic wonder. He must have taken note of it, in order to write his daily weather reports, but the particular sense of wonder at the 'Immensity of Nature' that it promoted in some gentleman scholars, their imagining of that 'Infinite Variety of Creatures, which in all probability swarm through these immeasurable Regions of Matter', was not his.[87] For Joseph Addison in the early years of the century, night sky-gazing had been the most effective route to his 'Omniscient God': the enormity of the sky, the smallness of Joseph Addison in comparison with it, was the very metaphor of His regard for 'every thing that has Being, especially such of his Creatures who fear they are not regarded by him . . . It is impossible he should overlook any of his Creatures . . .' Addison knew all of this, as a small figure on a hill, looking at the stars. But this was not John Murgatroyd's way of seeing. His imagination, and the deep structure of his responses to God's creation, was made by the word, and by the book; by the echoing voices of the seventeenth-century saints and churchmen (and their eighteenth-century editors) whose works lined his parlour; by the words of scholars from ancient Rome and seventeenth-century England. If he *saw* the natural or supernatural world, with that minute vision and impulse to detail beauty, that Lorraine Daston has described as the capacity for attention in the European Enlightenment, then he did not record *looking* or *paying attention* to the natural world in the thousands of words he wrote.[88] He did not botanise, or search for the leaf forms and the habits of insects that might express the divine and the aesthetic, as well as the moral,

[85] Nettleton, *Treatise*, p. 11.   [86] Nettleton, *Treatise*, p. 39.
[87] Joseph Addison, 'No. 565, Friday July 9, 1714', *The Spectator*, ed. Donald F. Bond (Oxford: Clarendon Press, 1965), vol. IV, pp. 529–33.
[88] Lorraine Daston, 'Attention and the Values of Nature in the Enlightenment', in Lorraine Daston and Fernando Vidal (eds.), *The Moral Authority of Nature* (Chicago and London: University of Chicago Press, 2004), pp. 100–26.

purposes of God. This was not the register of his thought, or of his ethics. He could many times have seen the gentleman botanist Mr Bolton of Stannary mushroom-gathering in the woods and spinneys around Halifax. Indeed, on the occasions when Murgatroyd walked to his home township of Ovenden, Halifax, he *must* have seen James Bolton in the distance, peering at rotten logs in Bracken-Bed-Wood, or spied him finding 'the Red Agaric' in 'the little wood near Shibden Hall . . . October 29th, 1786', or 'the Noble Agaric at Millsbridge near Huddersfield . . .' (As both these men dated absolutely everything they did or found, it is possible that they did meet on the road, or missed each other by a few hours.[89]) Bolton collected his fungi for the most beautiful expression of what Daston has called a minute attention to the detail of a whole: the hand-coloured plates of his *History of Fungusses growing about Halifax* (published in Huddersfield) are quite stunning in their loveliness, and a fine West Riding example of a European-wide detailing of the natural world. Indeed, so beautiful are these plates, so minute the description of the circumstances in which 'the Red Agaric', the 'Flat Agaric', 'the Noble Agaric' were acquired, that one suspects Bolton felt something of the same guilt as many of the Christian naturalists of the period, who knew they were paying more attention to the structure and the form of the mushroom, or the bee hive, or the aphid – their great importance and loveliness – than they were to the mushroom's Creator.[90] But John Murgatroyd encountered Nature only as 'a very plashy winterly day'. His God was a god of words – was the Word – transmitted through the writings of the previous century's churchmen and the rational, abstract version of that God, inscribed by the West Riding *philosophe*, Thomas Nettleton.

This may be Murgatroyd's God (I think it is); but the only way to discern Phoebe Beatson's beliefs about these matters is through Murgatroyd. There is much written on irreligion among the poorer sort; some historians of the English working class writing over the past thirty years have entertained the suggestion that Christianity never had much of a foothold among them.[91] Paganism, folk-belief, ghost-belief, witchcraft, even into the nineteenth century, are currently under much scrutiny. A major account of religion in industrial society, based on two communities not very far from Slaithwaite, suggests the changes experienced in Oldham and Saddleworth between 1740 and the 1860s to be best described as de-Christianisation going hand in hand with belief.[92] There is no

---

[89] James Bolton, *A History of Fungusses, growing about Halifax* . . ., 4 vols. (Huddersfield: J. Brook, 1788–91), vol. I, p. 36; vol. II, pp. 46, 73.

[90] Daston, 'Attention and the Values of Nature', p. 108.

[91] This is not Michael Snape's contention; but on the slow decline of Anglicanism as a habit of everyday life and a structure of belief among the laity, from the 1770s onwards, see his *The Church in an Industrial Society. The Lancashire Parish of Whalley in the Eighteenth Century* (Woodbridge: Boydell Press, 2003), pp. 23–5. For irreligion, Jim Obelkevich, *Religion and Rural Society. South Lindsay 1825–1875* (Oxford: Oxford University Press, 1976).

[92] Smith, *Religion in an Industrial Society*; Snape, *Church in an Industrial Society*, pp. 42–71.

way of using this history or these perspectives in regard to Phoebe Beatson: there is nothing to know of her religious beliefs, given that Murgatroyd writes nothing of them. We can only assume that, because her lack of church attendance on the Sundays after Elizabeth's birth was a matter of note, she had previously been a regular attender. Perhaps she was confirmed rather late; we can speculate about this – sixteen was the usual age, noted by Murgatroyd as fitting. She was nineteen or twenty when she went off to Huddersfield to receive the bishop's blessing; perhaps this had something to do with her new residence in a clergyman's household, or more probably because confirmation depended on when the bishop was available: this was her first opportunity to be confirmed. When Murgatroyd gave communion to his wife and a group of neighbours in his parlour in August 1790, Phoebe was included in the gathering, and took the sacrament. But we can discern nothing of a private and individual faith from this, as a domestic servant had no real power to refuse the ministrations of her employer. There seems no more to say about Phoebe Beatson and an Enlightenment Anglican God: only that she was part of a religious culture and the practice of a faith that – so its historians say – was pervasive and encompassing and should be taken for granted.[93]

---

[93] But see Snape, *Church in an Industrial Society*, pp. 27–41; and the remarks of Jan Albers, '"Papist Traitors" and "Presbyterian Rogues". Religious Identities in Eighteenth-century Lancashire', in John Walsh, John Haydon and Stephen Taylor (eds.), *The Church of England, c.1689–1883. From Toleration to Tractarianism* (Cambridge: Cambridge University Press, 1993), p. 333.

9   Love

Phoebe Beatson's baby was born on 29 August 1802, so she must have had sexual intercourse with George Thorp (and it was he: no doubts here about his being the father) during the pre-Christmas period of 1801. How much more than this is there to say? She was thirty-seven or thirty-eight years old when these events took place, and had been in service to the Murgatroyds for some seventeen years. There is no way of telling whether the holiday season of 1801 brought the two together for the first time, or whether theirs was a relationship of longer standing. (Murgatroyd's diary for 1801 is not extant; there is no mention of the Thorp family of Stockcarhead (Stocker Head) before 1802, though Murgatroyd appears to have known them well.) He cannot have known about her pregnancy on New Year's Day 1802 (she can scarcely have known herself), but his diary entry was uncannily prescient. 'God for Christ's sake, bless me & my Family thro' this month & this year if Life is continued', he wrote; 'we are by Nature prone to do what we should not do but, ye Blessing of thy Grace will be a restraint on Nature so as ye Soul shall not be hurt thereby . . .'[1] (Perhaps he did know about what had happened between Phoebe and George.) It is not at all clear what Phoebe's expectations were during her pregnancy and after the child's birth, but very clear indeed what Murgatroyd's were, regarding George Thorp. He expected the man to marry her.

He made extraordinary and determined efforts to bring such an event about. On 19 May (he had known about the pregnancy for at least a month) he was 'agate this afternoon to Stockcarhead & George being gone . . . talked to his mother abt Ph. being with Child & that an end must be made . . .'[2] He involved his solicitor John Bentley of Huddersfield, who had a practical solution ('he proposed letting 'em have Parloes'),[3] but Bentley too 'could get nothing from him to good purpose'. Neither of them could get a satisfactory answer from

---

[1] John Murgatroyd Diaries, KC 242/7, West Yorkshire Archive Service, Kirklees District, Huddersfield (1 January 1802).

[2] Murgatroyd Diaries, KC242/6 and 7. All references in this chapter are to the 1802 and 1804 volumes.

[3] Parloes sounds like a farmhouse, the kind of property that Murgatroyd did not own. However, I have been unable to find any trace of it – whatever it was.

Thorp: 'He appears unwilling to marry.' Now Murgatroyd was determined that Thorp 'must make an end of it tonight at my house', still hoping, perhaps, that seeing Phoebe might change Thorp's mind.[4] But he did not come, 'so there will be no marriage', noted Murgatroyd.

'He must pay something to her,' added Murgatroyd later on that day. 'He must pay according to Law.' But he did not give up. Two days later he was back at Stockcarhead talking to Thorp's mother 'about his Behaviour to Phoebe'. He sent his neighbour and brother-in-law Edmund Mellor over, but the answer was the same: 'He will not marry.' Then, a couple of weeks later, 'George came to Phoebe last Night'; both of them, it seems, were reluctant to make an end of it. Thorp was back again on 30 June: 'G. Thorp wth Phoebe in ye Kitchin last Night. He will not marry Her. I went this morng . . . to Stockcarhead, I wanted an answer whether she must bear a Bastard or no – I talked with his Mothr about it.' Thorp then disappears from the account until the end of October, when baby Elizabeth was two months old: 'I got hold of G. Thorp at our Door about 10 – but he forced himself from me . . .'

How may we read a love story from this? At this end of historical inquiry, after fifty years of social and cultural history and the attempt to retrieve the plebeian experience of living in the past, we know – or presume to know – much more about Phoebe Beatson's feelings and attitudes than we do about George Thorp's. Women's history and feminist scholarship have made us a template for eighteenth-century female sexuality, two parts passivity, one part victimhood, one part rape, by which we might depict a pregnant serving maid. We may add to this other serious and illuminating research on plebeian sexual practices, and even newer investigations into eighteenth-century masculinity and sexuality among the poorer sort.[5] We emerge, then, with an account of sex, love and desire that proclaims (much like the eighteenth-century sentimental novel did, and like the historians do, who have learned their plot lines and conclusions from those novels) female virtue in distress, coercive masculinity and a yielding (mind-less, and certainly body-less) femininity, which acts against its own best interests. (My point is that these are the interests of historians, not of their historical subjects. As, indeed, what I write now is in my interest.)

This historical work, constructed for the main part out of rape trial evidence, and settlement and bastardy examinations, gives us one account (in fact, authored by a man) which may stand in for the rest. It is from a highly respected

---

[4] This entry for 19 May 1802 is very heavily scored through, as is the entry for 20 May.

[5] Jeremy Gregory is illuminating on religion and masculinity, but the connections he makes have to be assumed for the poorer sort of men. His *homo religiosus* is textually middle class (which, of course, is no argument that the structures of feeling and faith that he describes were not available to men like George Thorp). See Jeremy Gregory, '*Homo religiosus*: Masculinity and Religion in the Long Eighteenth Century', in Tim Hitchcock and Michèle Cohen (eds.), *English Masculinities, 1660–1800* (London and New York: Longman, 1999), pp. 85–110.

edited collection of women's history, in which Richard Connors writes about 'Poor Women, the Parish and the Politics of Poverty'. He tells the story of Elizabeth Elless, who, sometime in 1756, either killed herself, or was murdered – or in any case, suffered a fatally late abortion – after being dragged around the county of Sussex by the overseers of her home parish, trying to find a magistrate before whom she could swear the father of her child. (If she would name the father of her child, as Phoebe Beatson did in the summer of 1802, and the magistrates recognise her testimony, they could then make an affiliation order that made him, not the parish and its ratepayers, responsible for her and her baby. This happened in the Beatson case in October 1802, six weeks after the baby was born.) Elless's story is meant to illustrate – it does illustrate – that the poor, and poor women in particular, 'were most susceptible to a harsh morality regime', and to describe the power relationship that pertained in general 'between paupers and their social and political superiors'. With a glance at the rare (but always-to-be-found) benevolent magistrate, it paints the most depressing picture of an eighteenth-century poor woman's life, with Janet Todd quoted to remind us that 'at the bottom levels of the rural population where most women existed, life was a remorseless struggle against poverty, a foraging for food and firewood, and unremitting war against disease and lice'.[6]

It is the remorselessness, the struggle – and above all, *the lice* – that brings forward the insistent and irritated question: *How do you know?* And who among us will not be seen as lice-ridden (or the equivalent of lice-ridden) by our future historians, if they should ever be interested enough to give an account of us? We too, one day, will be subjected – of this I am sure – to the subordinating gaze of sympathy, by someone attempting to place us in a history of the world's suffering. I am not denying the extraordinary difficulties of this woman's life; I am not denying real hunger, real cold – real lice. And I certainly concur with the view that eighteenth-century law enforced a brutal morality, as far as poor men and women were concerned. But I have written elsewhere about the ways in which the sympathies and empathies of twentieth-century social history can be read as part of a long-standing project of modernity (originating in the eighteenth century and given its most elegant exposition by Adam Smith in *The Theory of the Moral Sentiments*) of finding your own soul finer in its ability to feel the pain of others.[7] We can feel Elless's pain, but perhaps only

---

[6] Richard Connors, 'Poor Women, the Parish and the Politics of Poverty', in Elaine Chalus and Hannah Barker (eds.), *Gender in Eighteenth-century England. Roles, Representations and Responsibilities* (London: Longman, 1997), pp. 126–47.

[7] Desire for the poor's story of suffering on the part of middle-class writers and readers was a fundamental affective development of modernity and of a class society. It had the same roots as eighteenth-century theories of the moral sentiments (see note 5). Or at least that's what I argue in 'Enforced Narratives. Stories of Another Self', in Tess Cosslett, Celia Lury and Penny Summerfield (eds.), *Feminism and Autobiography. Texts, Theories, Methods* (London: Routledge, 2000), pp. 25–39.

by ignoring the wider context to her experience. Did she never fall in love, nor long *very much* for the new painted silk gown, that if she'd been luckier and living as a domestic in a different kind of household, up at Ponden Hall near Haworth in the 1790s for example, her mistress might have bought her?[8] Did she never enjoy a drink? Nor the man who fathered the baby? Nor look at the sky?

To counteract the lice, the miscarriage, the unremitting victimhood of Elless that her historian has given her, and in order to say something about Phoebe Beatson and George Thorp (that he was an archetypal bad lot, and certainly irresponsible, must be taken as read), we may consider the structures of romance, passion and love that pertained in West Yorkshire, round about the turn of the century (at least allow that they may have existed). We could, for instance, as I have suggested, look at worsted spinning, and all the erotic connections that George Thorp and Phoebe Beatson might have been able to make out of it, from the culture around them and from what they may (just possibly) have read. Watching the spinners and knitters in the sun, I'm on very shaky evidential ground indeed; but then George Thorp could have scarce moved along the Huddersfield road nor approached any Colne Valley township without seeing hundreds of women at work. (Stocker Head is in Linthwaite, just up from the Baptist chapel at Pole Moor and on the footpath which still rises from Linthwaite into Lingards.) And soon I shall establish that spinning was sexier in its operations than was knitting. The opportunities offered by spinning for alluring display of the female form were noted at the time. 'Come, muses to yonder cot a while retire', invites the anonymous poet of *An Essay on Halifax* as he sings of 'Social Commerce, that improves Mankind'. This cottage

> Though humble, neat, the bow'r of industry;
> There with sweet frugality and care she dwells;
> The lovely maid her auburn tresses loose
> And beaut'ous bosom open to the day,
> Incessant whirls the speedy circling wheel . . .

'Let not the feet of lewdness tread this way,' the poet hastily adds: both his gaze and the flame-haired beauty's carelessness of dress are entirely ingenuous:

> Here innocence, sequestered from the world,
> In modest negligence, and purest mind,
> Performs her daily task, well satisfy'd.[9]

---

[8] Carolyn Steedman, 'Englishness, Clothes and Little Things. Towards a Political Economy of the Corset', Christopher Breward et al (eds.), *The Englishness of English Dress* (Oxford and New York: Berg, 2002), pp. 29–44.

[9] Anon., *An Essay on Halifax* (Halifax: P. Darby, 1761), pp. 8–9.

Phoebe Beatson and George Thorp's relationship defied many a norm, at least those norms established by historians investigating plebeian sexual attitudes and arrangements in the later eighteenth century. But not all of the trends, of course, for the period was one of rapidly increasing prenuptial pregnancy and illegitimacy, both of which 'accelerated at a rate unprecedented in the known history of the British population', from the 1750s onwards. The Beatson case is but a tiny statistical flotsam of the great changes in affective life and its organisation that occurred as a result of industrialisation. John Gillis has asked us to note changing sexual relationships in this period, particularly among the young, the long and the short of it being that men and women were more likely now to have intercourse, rather than other forms of sexual contact.[10] The mean age of first marriage dropped by two years for men and three for women between 1700 and 1850; the average age at prenuptial conception in 1799 has been estimated at twenty-six years.[11] But now, in this case, Phoebe and Elizabeth Beatson and George Thorp detach themselves from these averages, before our very eyes. Phoebe's was not a prenuptial pregnancy, she was in her late thirties when she conceived her child, and when she married – not the father of her child, but John Sykes the Golcar wool comber – in January 1807, she was in her early forties.[12]

Guided by the historiography of eighteenth-century sexual practice, we might suppose that Phoebe did what she did in order to secure a husband. 'Couples were less likely to abstain from sexual intercourse, in part because this was one of the ways in which a woman could be sure of enticing, and if pregnant, holding a man,' says Gillis.[13] Tim Hitchcock has discerned a spreading pattern of courting in which penetrative sex before betrothal became increasingly common in the middle years of the century, though he attributes these developments to 'changing patterns and discourses of consumption' rather than to the reorganisation of emotional life under industrialisation.[14] In the new centres of rural industrialisation, a pregnant daughter was not the shameful liability she may once have been, and perhaps still was, in the agricultural regions of the south and east. In places like the Calder and Colne valleys, families might be relatively independent – in spirit, and financially – of local structures of authority and morality. The new, mechanising industries increasingly sought out the labour of children, to say nothing of their mothers, pregnant or not. Parents were not so keen to get children off their hands in the Pennine villages: a pregnant twenty-four year old could still spin; independence of housing might mean

---

[10] John R. Gillis, *For Better, For Worse. British Marriages 1600 to the Present* (Oxford: Oxford University Press, 1985), pp. 110, 114–15.

[11] Gillis, *Better, Worse*, pp. 109–10.

[12] Marriage Bonds, John Sykes, Golcar and Phebe Beatson, Halifax, Jan. 1807, MBS 1807, Borthwick Institute of Historical Research, York.

[13] Gillis, *Better, Worse*, p. 115.

[14] Tim Hitchcock, *English Sexualities, 1700–1800* (Basingstoke: Macmillan, 1997), pp. 24–41.

that the father – husband-at-the-last-minute – could move in with his partner and child. In other words, 'the new industrial proletariat expanded the notion of legitimate love relationships to include those outside as well as within marriage. Their definition of family also expanded, as did their idea of parenthood.'[15]

There were sexual arrangements that both effected and reflected these new attitudes. The practice of night visiting emerged, wherever 'there was industry in the countryside', observes Gillis. A young man, a potential lover and husband, was invited over by the family, who contrived to leave the couple alone at bedtime, sometimes making a sleeping place for them before the fire – the only warm place in the house – before the rest of them disappeared. The couple then had time and space in which to decide if they fancied each other, and what they were going to do about it, if they did. Employers of maidservants understood the conventions of night visiting as well, had to countenance it, turn a blind eye to what happened before the kitchen fire after dark, or give up the idea of keeping female servants altogether.[16]

The couple courted in this manner. The woman 'proved' herself, that is, proved that she was capable of bearing a child, with a man she wanted. (But Phoebe Beatson, proving herself? At thirty-seven?) Contemporary notions of honour and decency dictated that the man marry the woman if she did become pregnant, at some point before the baby's birth. (George Thorp signally failed to follow this code of honour.) In an older, more traditional world, some two hundred miles away in the agricultural south, many a clergyman involved himself in 'negotiations with putative fathers' just as John Murgatroyd did, though we have no other account in such detail, of the immense efforts Murgatroyd went to, to get Thorp to marry his servant.[17] His lack of success owes something to the fact that this was West Yorkshire, 'raw frontier country' of the industrial age, with lines of authority, both ecclesiastical and secular, much attenuated. Certainly, John Murgatroyd was not able to use poor law and other parish officials to force a marriage, as did happen in other parts of the country. Indeed, the local administrative state in its operation of the poor laws was as distant and mysterious to him as it appears to have been to Phoebe Beatson – or at least, that is how he presents the arrival of parish officers at his door, and Phoebe's frustrating journeys to declare and affiliate: a bemused old man, sharing something of the experience with her. And he was, of course, ecclesiastical authority himself, but an authority that seems not to have had a moment's doubts about allowing Phoebe to live out her pregnancy and early motherhood in his house.[18] Long

---

[15] Gillis, *Better, Worse*, pp. 116, 126.
[16] Gillis, *Better, Worse*, p. 121.   [17] Gillis, *Better, Worse*, pp. 115–16.
[18] In Almondbury forty years before, when Murgatroyd had served Edward Rishton as curate, 'Thomas Kirkshaw and Elizabeth Bradley were presented by our churchwardens . . . for the crime of fornication together she having fathered a bastard child upon him [*sic*]. The woman performed public penance in the church . . .' Cressida Annesley and Philippa Hoskin (eds.), *Archbishop*

ago (I think a long time before 1802, probably when he was preparing to take orders in 1752) he had written an essay, which may have been part of a putative training programme, on 'The Qualifications of a Minister'. It was then either the distilled wisdom of the church, or Murgatroyd's own opinion, or both, that a clergyman must 'be wise in the Government of his Carriage and Actions, distinguishing especially between Lawfulness and Expediency, and shunning, not only that which is directly sinful, but whatsoever is scandalous and offensive'.[19] He did not seem to care about scandalous and offensive reputation now.

None of these accounts, neither the contemporary nor the historical, gives us much insight into Thorp's feelings in the matter. All we are left with is his steadfast refusal to marry, and some sense of the legal and economic circumstances of the West Riding in 1802 that allowed him to resist the pressures on him to do so. He is, in this way, and as is shortly to be discussed, a faint but actual echo of the passionate question of *Wuthering Heights* – who and what is Heathcliff? – and an echo (or a foreshadowing) of Emily Brontë's response to the formation of an extraordinary masculinity in a particular geographical terrain and set of economic circumstances (and confirmation of the belief I have held for years, that there is nothing mysterious or uncanny about Heathcliff at all, and we are meant to know it: he is just one more bloody-minded Yorkshireman). George Thorp was an unusual man – at least unusual in the context of historical depiction of working-class masculinity in the later eighteenth century. This is especially the case when it is compared with the detailed attribution of feeling and motive to women like Phoebe Beatson. More things happen to a woman's body in the physiological sense than they do to a man's in the course of the life-cycle, of course, and the state is particularly interested in the pregnancies and parturitions that involve so very much interaction with the officials and institutions which are obliged, by law, to note the troublesome passing of women like Phoebe Beatson. All of this means that there is a good deal more to work with in the historical retrieval of a woman like her than there is with a man like George Thorp. And contemporaries speculated more about women like her than they ever did about the society's men. Samuel Bamford, for example, wrote about the sturdy sexual and spiritual independence of Pennine girls.[20]

Drummond's Visitation Returns 1764 I: Yorkshire A–G, Borthwick Texts and Calendars 23 (York: University of York, 1998), 'Almondbury'.

[19] Reverend John Murgatroyd, 'The Qualifications of a Minister of Christ', KC242/8, West Yorkshire Archive Service, Kirklees District, Huddersfield.

[20] His Mima is actually from Lancashire, but it is her clear independence of mind and spirit that he presents and that we are invited to admire, not her county of origin. Samuel Bamford, *Early Days* (London: Simpkin and Marshall, 1849), especially p. 294, where their baby is put into his arms at their wedding feast. Bamford was no George Thorp. See also *Passages in the Life of a Radical*, orig. pub. 1844 (London: McGibbon Kee, 1967), pp. 356–8, where Jemima is

We can be much more certain about the other forms of love that developed in this tumultuous year of 1801–2, in the Murgatroyd household. John Murgatroyd noted the progress of Phoebe's pregnancy in some detail. It was possibly the first he had lived through at such close proximity, though he had paid attention to the birth of his brother-in-law's children. He stood as godfather to two of the five who survived their early days.[21] With Phoebe, he recorded her morning sickness ('Phoebe queased') and noted that a week before her confinement she was 'still on her legs'.[22] He noted all the household arrangements that had to be adjusted because of her condition (help with the brewing, Richard Walker calling for the yarn instead of her going to him, the tiny amount she span). All through May and June, Phoebe did not attend church on Sundays. Murgatroyd defended himself against the neighbours who were shocked at the imminent birth of a bastard in a clergyman's house: 'Miss Shaw arg'd wth me abt. Phebe bearing her Child at my House, in ye Hearg. of ye Manchester Ladies . . .'[23] When the baby came, he did not write anything in his journal for a whole day, recording the next that 'My Servant Phoebe bore her Child a Girl yesterday about 8 o'clock in the morning. John Dyson's mother was her midwife All/Thank God/ went well forward.' That evening he 'gave Phoebe's child private Baptism . . . & call'd it at her choosing Elizabeth ye midwife handed it to me'.[24] Elizabeth was formally christened when her mother was churched, at the end of September.[25] Which form of churching did the Revd Wilson choose? There were two in the Book of Common Prayer, one by which a woman might contemplate the thesis that 'children and the fruit of the womb: are an heritage and gift that cometh of the Lord. Like as the arrows in the hand of the giant: even so are the young children.' Or perhaps, under the rubric of Psalm 126, Wilson gave her the opportunity to think about George Thorp, as he uttered: 'thou hast delivered my soul from death: mine eyes from tears, and my feet from falling . . . I believed, and therefore will I speak; but I was sore troubled: I said in my haste, All men are liars.'

And then a new love grew. 'Phoebe & Elizabeth are in good order/thank almighty God –' Murgatroyd recorded on 10 October. For a whole series of Sundays, not so much to excuse Phoebe as to note what he felt for the baby, he wrote that she was 'at Home, taking care of beloved Elizabeth'; 'Phebe at

---

discussed as the only woman in the world capable of seeing the Spirit of Life move across the sky towards them, as the couple walked from Derbyshire into Yorkshire.

[21] Murgatroyd, 'Ask, Read, Retain, Teach', KC 242/9, pp. 88–9.

[22] Murgatroyd Diaries (5 May, 22 August 1802).

[23] Entries for 27 July, 4 August 1802. He was much taken with these ladies, staying with friends on a visit to Slaithwaite, who were so free and easy in their manner with him, who would always stop for conversation when he went down into Slaithwaite, and who lent him the Manchester newspapers and books: 'went for News – talk'd wth ye Ladies – They were open and free.'

[24] Murgatroyd Diaries (31 August 1802).   [25] Murgatroyd Diaries (24 September 1802).

Home takg care of her hopeful Child'; 'her lovely Child'; 'her hopeful Child'.[26] There were models for his feelings available from a lifetime's reading. He may have remembered *The History of Tom Jones A Foundling* (he had read it and commonplaced it sixty years before): the little bastard child found on Squire Allworthy's bed, the Squire's rapt attention to the infant, entranced by the insistent grip of baby fingers round his own.[27] Visitors arrived with 'stuff for frock for Elizabeth brought at Hudd:'; he noted other events like this in her small life.[28] He was able to do this because the child was evidently living in the house. One October evening when the baby was two he stayed at home whilst 'Phebe went . . . with Elizabeth to Joseph Pogson's Even'g Entertainment'.[29] Phoebe started to spin her usual quantity of worsted thread; Sally Pogson was brought in to clean the house.

As a young, ardent and loving lad just arrived in Slaithwaite in the 1740s, Murgatroyd had learned much from his reading of literature about the passions, the affections, and about love. From the London journals, he copied out striking passages about the nature and attributes of women. Most conduct-book writers of the mid-century recommended an 'Equanimity of Temper . . . uniform & harmonious Disposition of the Passions' to young women, as the very best cosmetic; these qualities diffused 'a Grace & Sweetn: o'er the Counten. infinit: Surpassing all ye Standard Arts of Coquetry', and this is what Murgatroyd noted in his 'Cornucopia' in 1742.[30] *Avant la lettre* of Rousseau's injunction to Sophie (and all of us) to keep ourselves clean, Murgatroyd wrote that 'neatness & Simplicity' of dress was the best fashion advice. He extracted the same principles from his reading of *Gil Blas*, which he finished in December 1751, that 'a Woman polite & good natur'd may inspire Love without ye help of Beauty'.[31] At the same time he wrote serious memoranda to himself, concerning the 'Rules to be observed in the choice of Wife & affections I ought to bear towards her'. This passage, if the form of abbreviation (the relative lack of it) is anything to go by, was his own composition, not copied out from somewhere else. He must – he would – always endeavour 'to make a Choice of such a Woman who has fst Choice of Christ as a Spouse for herS[elf]:'. This formulation allowed him to

---

[26] Murgatroyd Diaries (4 and 21 November, 12 December 1802).

[27] Henry Fielding, *The History of Tom Jones*, orig. pub. 1749 (Harmondsworth: Penguin, 1985), p. 29.

[28] Murgatroyd Diaries (18 May 1804).

[29] Entry for 26 October 1804. Joseph Pogson was extremely versatile: delver, gravedigger, maddening builder. His wife Sally was one of the Lingards household's regular helpers, or charwomen.

[30] John Murgatroyd, 'A Cornucopia: or Collection of weighty Extracts transcribed out of the scarcest, most necessary & best chosen Books &c according to this proper Maxim, that every Man shou'd take down in Writing what He learns for fear of forgetting any useful Circumstance. By John Murgatroyd, Master of Slaithwaite School. Anno Domini 1742', 082.2 MUR, Special Collections, Slaithwaite Parish Collection, University of York, York, 'Memoirs transcrib'd from the London Magazines beg: wth January 1742/3', p. 781. Also p. 636, 'Of a Woman'.

[31] Murgatroyd, 'Cornucopia', p. 781.

think about physical love: 'none may be made one Flesh wth Her who's not made one Spirit wth Christ my Saviour'. The making of one body – one person – out of two was not just a theological or legal formulary; it precisely described the divine prescription for marriage – its point and purpose – as discussed in *Paradise Lost*, for example.[32] Moreover, in these ponderings and ambitions, the young John Murgatroyd (he was perhaps twenty-two when he made these notes) was gratified at the affective providentialism of these arrangements, for if he should be so lucky as to encounter a woman whose love of Christ was her 'Mark of Beauty', and whose portion was 'the Grace of God', how could he help but love her? – 'it wd be impossible for me not to be hearty & sincere in my Affections twds her'. Such qualities in a woman would prevent the temptation to love anyone else: 'thus to love her, will not only be my Duty, but my Happiness'. Then – 'Ephesians 5: 5, 8, 33', he noted, which reminded him that no whoremonger would have any inheritance in the kingdom of God, and that he was enjoined to love his wife 'even as himself'.[33] Such a course of action would ensure happiness in a way that marriage for wealth could not: 'oh! the Happiness of the Couple whose Inclinations to each other are as mutual as their Duties, whose Affections as well as Persons are link'd together with the same Ties. This is the chief Conception for a happy & desirable Matrimony.' It would be the 'chief motivation' to induce him into that state.[34]

Then there was Ovid, for very long-standing and wry advice on how to fall in and out of love. There was not only the cynicism of *The Art of Love*, or ways of reading the *Metamorphoses* as a rough guide to sexual philandering, but also Ovid in role as 'the West's first champion of true and lasting love between man and woman'.[35] In the *Metamorphoses* there was also the means to learn (and to teach, to generations of boys, parsing and construing in Slaithwaite Free School) *what it is like* to feel desire and fall in love. The swift, physiological intensity of Apollo's falling for Daphne ('Phoebus caught sight of her, fell in love and longed to possess her') or of Hermes struck in an instant by Herse ('Her beauty dumfounded Jupiter's son . . . he burned with the flames of desire, like a bullet of lead shot, launched by a Baleraic sling') was what he noted in much more modern literature.[36] Among the novels, satires and magazine literature he

[32] He made extensive notes on *Paradise Lost* in his 'Book of Records', probably in 1750.
[33] 'Cornucopia', p. 697. Colossians 3.19, which he also noted here, enjoined 'Husbands, love your wives, and be not bitter against them.'
[34] Murgatroyd, 'Cornucopia', p. 697.
[35] He had Ovid's *Art of Love* (edition unspecified) in his private, that is, non-schoolbook collection. For Ovid's many roles, see Irving Singer, *The Nature of Love, 2. Courtly and Romantic* (Chicago and London: University of Chicago Press, 1984), pp. 30–1.
[36] Ovid, *Ovid's Metamorphoses, in fifteen books, with the arguments and notes of John Minellius translated into English. To which is marginally added, a prose version, . . . For the Use of Schools. By Nathan Bailey* (London: J. Rivington and Sons; G. Keith; T. Lowndes; T. Longman; W. Strahan, etc., 1778), I, 9; II, 5, 6. Here I have used Ovid, *Ovid, Metamorphoses. A New Verse Translation*, trans. David Raeburn (London: Penguin, 2004).

read in his first years at Slaithwaite was that archetypal text of the West Riding Enlightenment, Thomas Nettleton's *Treatise on Virtue and Happiness*, which, as we have seen, Murgatroyd copied from extensively.[37] Most readers take the majority of their notes from a book's beginning anyway, but Murgatroyd extracted and underlined from Nettleton's measured advice about the regulation of the passions, a description of states of desire and arousal much like Apollo's, the way in which 'ye Lovr pursues his Mistress . . . because ye Passion it glows in his Breast, will not let him be at Ease'.[38] The edition of 1736 (which is the one probably read) is in the less emphatic conditional tense: 'The common labourer would not toil for his daily bread, if he was not prompted by hunger . . . neither would the lover pursue his mistress with so much ardour, if the passion which glows in his breast would let him be at ease'.[39] As John Mullen has remarked, in a culture in which the new art of becoming an individual involved learning to have feelings, literature was an excellent tutor.[40] Mullen is writing about the 1770s, the decade in which, in English, the word 'feelings' was first used to mean 'emotions', and about the novel, which was 'where you went to have those feelings'.[41] But Murgatroyd, in his concentrated note-taking from Nettleton in the 1750s, adds much to this insight, showing that a wide range of literature might be used for self-instruction in the art of feeling yourself to be in love, and that the language of classical antiquity was still available for its appropriation and expression. And young John Murgatroyd was lonely, and longing for love. What he noted from his reading of *Tom Jones* in regard to Sophia and Tom was that 'Such generous passion merits a return of the same Passion, nor her Frowns & Scorn . . .'[42] In these years, he tried out three 'English'd' versions of a Latin maxim (he headed the page 'Of Love'), running through 'Venus alone makes Life serenely move; oh! May I Die e'er I'm unfit to Love!'; and 'Anothr Life venus only blesses frm Above, O! Let me cease at once to live & love', and 'Ano. Without Love's balmy Sweets, & soft delights, Tedious ye Days & joyless are ye Nights'. Then there followed the extraordinary

> This I really Know–
> That since in years I find I grow
> 'Tis bettr far tho' late to live yn ne'er to know w Love can give.
> 'Tis hard Love's passion not to know . . .[43]

---

[37] Murgatroyd, 'Cornucopia', pp. 625–30.   [38] Murgatroyd, 'Cornucopia', p. 625.

[39] Thomas Nettleton, *A Treatise on Virtue and Happiness*, 2nd edn (London: J. Batley and J. Wood, 1736), pp. 15–16.

[40] John Mullan, 'Feelings and Novels', in Roy Porter (ed.), *Rewriting the Self. Histories from the Renaissance to the Present* (London: Routledge, 1997), pp. 119–31.

[41] Mullan, 'Feelings', p. 120.

[42] John Murgatroyd, 'Book of Records', 082.2 MUR, Special Collections, Slaithwaite Parish Collection, University of York, York.

[43] Murgatroyd, 'Book of Records', translating 'Quid Vitae esto Quid dulce, Venus quando absit, habemuso Spiritis hoc fugit pectus, ut exit Amor.'

Murgatroyd thought it noteworthy that Nettleton's thesis concerning embodied human happiness (which happiness derives from behaving virtuously, in the giving and receiving of pleasure) was penned by a medical man. Forty years later he used the language of another medical treatise to explore the passions, and the route from mourning to melancholia, as we have seen. His observations on grief and the violence of passion in the 'Ask, Read, Retain, Teach' notebook are taken almost word for word from William Buchan's *Domestic Medicine*, one of the several home-doctors he had in his library.[44]

Despite all the appearances and symptoms of love that he noted with such very great assiduity and at such length in his early commonplace book, the relationship between him and Ann Murgatroyd, whom he married in his forty-eighth year, is as obscure as the one between Phoebe and George (though the obvious difference is that the Murgatroyds had no children). Except that now, in his last years, as little Elizabeth Beatson enters his household, something is revealed. The day before the Lingards overseer came to collect Phoebe for her settlement examination, back in March 1802, he had written of his departed wife:

Now 5 years are passed from my dearly beloved Wife's Leaving this world. She was much afflicted in Body several years all whereof She, with God's gracious help, bore patiently. She put it to his Will either to depart, or be longer Times in this world. She spent her allow'd Time in reading ye word of God & ye notes upon its meditation . . . She is gone, whither I am with God's gracious Help following after her. . .[45]

(It was a Sunday. Before his memorial note he recorded that 'Phoebe at Home on Account of Weather. Spring Quarter begins this morning . . .')

At the very beginning of her final illness, in 1789, he had called Ann Murgatroyd his child:

My Dear Child Mrs Murgatroyd was abt. 8 o'clock this Evening very suddenly seiz'd with a Sick=Fit She fell back from her Chair . . . I immediately took her in my Arms. She was a considerable Time before she recover'd her Understanding – it threw Me into an Agony of Sorrow.[46]

Who and what John Murgatroyd loved *had to be* a child of some sort to him, just as he was a child of God. He had learned these impulses of the affections through his long involvement with children, perhaps during the course of teaching them the lessons of great ontological security and pleasure in being contained in God's sight and love. In modern times an impulse of love towards those who are dependent on you, and whose future course you understand to be

[44] William Buchan, *Domestic Medicine, or, a Treatise on the Prevention and Cure of Disease by Regime and Simple Medicine* (London: W. Strahan, T. Cadell, London, 1772), pp. 145–7.
[45] Murgatroyd Diaries, KC242/6 (21 March 1802).
[46] Murgatroyd Diaries, KC242/1 (14 February 1789).

shaped by your intervention, is a sentiment that was partially learned in relation to children gathered together for the purposes of schooling. In this learned impulse of the heart, it has mattered very much that you believe the content of *what* you teach to be of importance, whether it be the principles imparted by the catechism, or the great grammar of the world that the Latin tongue gave access to. As Archbishop Tillotson had pointed out at the end of the previous century, when parents and preachers taught children to read, listened to them rehearse the creed – whatever – children were, in this endeavour, conceived of as part of the self, a self that also knows and rehearses these things. Protestantism, piety and pedagogy had brought together children in places like Slaithwaite school, and provided the circumstances for this kind of love to grow. It was a partial expression of *caritas*: an affection that is *to do* with a movement of the heart towards those who are, in some way, smaller than you, or subordinate to, or dependent on you, just as you are small, and held in God's sight. All of this apart, and in any case, most babies are winning; or they can win most people. But a child in a godly household could be a most affecting and potent reminder of one's own delight and security in God's eye and care: a little lamb, indeed, in Yorkshire parlance.[47] The long and short of it is that a very old man fell in love with a baby and left her the whole world (hers to choose), in the shape of the globe he bequeathed her in his will.

And quite apart from the visceral tenderness and pleasure felt in relationship to what was evidently an appealing, happy and healthy child, Murgatroyd possessed certain beliefs about childhood – in relation to Christian theology – that may have enabled and sustained his love. On the question of original sin he had made notes in 1789 by which he perhaps planned to tell one of his many congregations that 'Sin lies in the Will and Choice of ye Agent acting', and that the original transgression was not binding on each individual soul. Thus – though he did not put it like this – a baby did not come into the world stained by Adam's and Eve's first trespass: 'we had not Will or Choice when Adam sin'd. Consequently Adam sin'd personally, & ye Guilt was *so too*.' Those who saw Adam's sin as the innate and general human inheritance were just plain wrong: 'Adam's Stand'g as a federal Head or representative of moral Actions, is a false way of reasoning & unscriptural, it's vastly contrary to the perfectly good, wise & just Being, whom we serve.' Much earlier, when he read *Paradise Lost*, he had written 'Eve was perverted by Satan's false Guile – & Adam by her – whose Fault was his own; Ingrateful man! He had of God all he cou'd have – who made him just, & right; suffict. to ha' Stood, tho' free to fall.'[48]

---

[47] Feeling little – safe and childlike – in God's (or some substitute for God's) eye is discussed in Carolyn Steedman, 'Inside, Outside, Other. Accounts of National Identity in the 19th Century', *History of the Human Sciences*, 8:4 (1995), pp. 59–76.

[48] Murgatroyd, 'Read, Ask, Retain, Teach', KC 242/9, p. 12, 'The Love of God Displayed'. For his reading of *Paradise Lost*, Murgatroyd, 'Book of Records'.

Later, on the question of the parents' sins being visited upon the children, he was very clear that though 'It is a righteous Thing with God to Punish good Persons for their Parents' Sin', that happened only when 'Childn. follow their parents' Sins, instead of abhor.g 'em, & being humbled for 'em'. He reiterated the point about individual responsibility for sinful actions in relation to the doctrine of original sin:

> furth.r it's meant of, of temporal Evil not Eternal punishment no one shall for ye. parents' Sins be etern.ly punished . . . neither will their Sins bring Us to Hell Evr'y one at Judgmt Day [will] be separately consider'd accord'g to their Deeds . . . Sinners' Ruin is wholly chargeable on their own Obstinacy . . .[49]

Baby Eliza was without sin. He gave her private baptism not to drive out sin, but to receive her into a community.

These varieties of love, old and new, that developed in the Lingards household as the century turned can be mapped on to many existing histories. The very least offered by a narrative of Phoebe's pregnancy and Elizabeth's coming into the world is a contribution to the underwritten history of the role religion has played in the history of the human sciences. During the course of the century, immense attention was paid to the question of humanity: to what kind of thing a human being was, how it operated, what its history might have been. The irreducible fact of God and His act of creation – which frames the thought of René Descartes, John Locke, and provincial men of the Enlightenment like John Nettleton of Halifax – was part of the eighteenth-century 'invention' of that very science. Their reformulations of humanity, their accounts of how human creatures developed as physiological and psychic entities, were thought through in the private writing, the teaching, and perhaps the preaching, of one obscure West Riding clergyman. Medical literature, which would now be labelled psychological in import, was particularly important for John Murgatroyd: it mapped the human body and soul in terms of its capacities, affects and passions. In his reading and note-taking, we have also seen how very much was available to him, linguistically and imaginatively, in the classical literature that many besides him may have used for the turning of old propositions about individual selves into new ones, and into personal knowledge about self and other.

As for love, and for disinterring its ways and means in his household during the Phoebe Beatson crisis, we are hampered as much as we are helped by its twentieth-century historians. Perceptive and wide-ranging work has given us the distinction between *amor passion* and romantic love in European modernity that Anthony Giddens is able to make in *Transformations of Intimacy*.[50] A Christian God has certainly been seen playing a full historical role in the

[49] Murgatroyd, 'Read, Ask, Retain, Teach', pp. 91–2, 'Minsters &C'.
[50] Anthony Giddens, *The Transformation of Intimacy. Sexuality, Love and Eroticism in Modern Societies* (Cambridge: Polity Press, 1992).

development of modern, sexual passion. Irving Singer has argued convincingly
that a harmonisation between Christian *caritas* and human striving for the happiness of erotic fulfilment was effected in many different turns of divinity and
literature, from the medieval period onwards.[51] As all creation – or all reality –
emanates from God and is sustained by his love, the love of human beings one
for the other might be conceived of as a return, or paying back to the Him who
loves them.[52] Then, as new forms of feeling, and techniques and methods for
discerning feeling in others, were inscribed in all sorts of eighteenth-century
cultural form, the intimacy, longing and desire for 'interpersonal oneness' that
are the hallmarks of modern romantic love come into being. The literature,
theology and teaching materials that end up on the Lingards parlour shelves
in the 1790s carry many of these ideas about and reformulations of the human
subject, and there is the extraordinary good fortune here, of being able to follow their course through the reading and note-taking of one Church of England
clergyman.

But the trouble with our modern histories of love is that, for the main part,
they stay within the conceptual confines of *agape* and *eros*, laid down so many
centuries ago, seeking to understand how people in the past reconciled the one
with the other, or to chart the course of how the love of God lost out to the love
of men and women. There is no place in their scheme for the other kinds of
love so discernible in this story (and in the mythic Pennine tale that is about
to be discussed with *Wuthering Heights*): no account of new forms of love
for children: for those who are smaller but who will grow; or those who are
subordinate, and likely to stay that way.[53] Modern histories of love and intimacy
remain within the delighted contours of the equality of spirit and sexual desire
that Milton wrested from the biblical story in order to depict the first marriage
in *Paradise Lost* (a book which Murgatroyd did indeed have in his library, and
which echoes throughout his sober and loving assessment of Ann Murgatroyd's
relationship to her God).[54]

Modern histories of love can take us only so far, then, in discerning what it
was that happened in Murgatroyd's household between 1802 and 1806 (or in
a longer frame, between 1785, when Phoebe Beatson first came to his service,
and 1806), for they deal only with adult, erotic love. But the very least we
can do, after reading Murgatroyd's notes and the books he read, and above
all, by considering his behaviour, is give weight to that sentiment of delight in
children, in their appealing littleness and tenderness. It underpins much of the
modern material, secular and divine, that Murgatroyd worked with, and that he
taught through his long career. Babies and small children were good to think

---

[51] Singer, *Nature of Love. 2*, pp. 23–6.   [52] Singer, *Nature of Love. 2*, pp. 23–5.
[53] Carolyn Steedman, *Strange Dislocations. Childhood and the Idea of Human Interiority, 1780–
1930* (Cambridge, Mass.: Harvard University Press, 1995).
[54] For the Miltonic marriage, see Singer, *Nature of Love. 2*, pp. 241–56.

with – above all, to feel with – in this new society of sentiment, a reminder of one's own status in the eye of the Creator, and a means for developing the understanding that the first thing to seek was the welfare and happiness of others.

However, in political and legal terms, servants were even better to think with, and much more overtly so. Obsessed about, laughed and litigated over, legislated for, and massively represented, they were living embodiments of great constitutional and legal questions, and of ordinary, everyday deliberations about human and social relationships. Staying close to the matter in question – a godly household, a Church of England clergyman, religion in the new industrial age – we can see John Murgatroyd's love for the baby (and for Phoebe Beatson, though that was love in a different register) as part of a relatively modern conception of an Anglican God, who besides playing His major role in constitutional-philosophical thinking as He had long done, was now also to be used as the outline of a social theory and the 'science of man'.[55]

Understanding this, though, will not take us very far into reading the relationship between master and servant in this particular household. I fall back on a kind of common-sense social history: Phoebe Beatson had been with the Murgatroyds since girlhood; she did not leave, nor flit over the valley to another place; she nursed first her master's wife, and then his sister, through their final illnesses. She was rewarded, on this earth, as good and faithful servants ought to be. Her master showed great charity, care and forethought in regard to her (and worried dreadfully all those years, when she was late home from Forrest with her worsted bundles). Perhaps there is no further to go than this, in determining what his feelings towards her were: whether or not he loved her.

For the illustrations to her biography of Samuel Pepys, Claire Tomalin was – of course! – unable to find a portrait of Jane Birch, the Pepys's maid who figures so prominently in the diary, her life threaded through that of Sam and Elizabeth, for so many years. Instead Tomalin uses a charming contemporary drawing of another London maidservant, Susan Gill.[56] Contemplating the servant's fetching and carrying, scrubbing, cleaning and chopping, the thousand dinners cooked, the fumbling under Jane Birch's skirts by her master, the long years, the bonds of affection, Tomalin remarks simply that 'Pepys loved Jane as you love someone who becomes part of your life'.[57] With Phoebe Beatson, there is no better – no greater thing – to do than this: repeat this fertile and intelligent assessment. (I refuse to have Phoebe Beatson represented by the ubiquitous one-thread worsted spinner in Yorkshire dress from 1814.[58]) Historians of love (whether they are dealing with *eros* or *agape*) tell us that during the course of

[55] See, for example, Robert Hole, *Pulpits, Politics and Public Order in England, 1760–1832* (Cambridge: Cambridge University Press, 1989), p. 84, and *passim*.
[56] Claire Tomalin, *Samuel Pepys. The Unequalled Self* (London: Penguin, 2003), Plate 23.
[57] Tomalin, *Samuel Pepys*, p. 251.   [58] See chapter 2.

the eighteenth century it became possible to love someone else not because all love was a reciprocal arrangement with God, whereby you pay Him back for the love of His Creation, but rather, because they were themselves. It became possible to love others 'just as the human beings they are, combinations of body and soul, ends in themselves and not mere instrumentalities for loving God'.[59] One small note here, perhaps, up in Lingards, of the vast movement of modernity. And achieved, in this case, against the rather large odds of another birth in the Pennine district, that of class society, and the restratification in these years of war and revolution, hardship and repressive state action, of relationships between owners and dispossessed, servants and masters, workers and capitalist bourgeoisie.

And Tomalin is surely correct in seeing *action* as the shaping force in the development of the kind of feeling that pertained between Samuel Pepys and Jane Birch: living together, managing a household, washing, scrubbing, preparing food and eating it, the bonds of affect are spun tighter, even across the vast social and legal spaces that divide both these masters and both these maids. It was a twentieth-century perception that love grows through doing, as in the iconic process of childcare and the growth of love.[60] Love for babies is born in washing and feeding – and loving them. A baby was deeply implicated in what went on in Lingards-cum-Slaithwaite in 1802; the lovableness of that baby provided a structure by which to express other forms of love.

[59] Singer, *Nature of Love, 2*, p. 36.
[60] John Bowlby, *Child Care and the Growth of Love* (London: Penguin, 1953).

10   Nelly's version

Emily Brontë's *Wuthering Heights* (1847) has been read as a form of history before. In *Heathcliff and the Great Hunger* Terry Eagleton's purpose is to make Heathcliff a 'fragment of Ireland', some kind of embodiment of the Brontës' own Irish inheritance and of a modern history of Anglo-Irish relations.[1] The project is to make visible the material and historical realities that are the sinews of the novel. 'What governs interpersonal relations in *Wuthering Heights*', says Eagleton, 'is a tightly material economy of labour, kinship and inheritance. For all the critical blather about transcendent and Romantic love, few more tenaciously materialist fictions have flowed from an English pen than this genealogically obsessed work, in which law and property and inheritance are the very stuff of the plot . . .'[2] I suggest that the blather about transcendence is part of the material history that Emily Brontë penned; but I would not have been able to do this without Eagleton's noticing what is really there, in the text. You cannot just do any old thing with *Wuthering Heights*, but you can use Heathcliff to write a history of the tortured hunger endured by England's first colonial possession, and you can let one of its narrators, Nelly Dean, speak of the service relationship and of being a servant, because those histories are there, embedded in her as figure and in the story she tells.

A plot summary of the novel is almost certainly in order. It is notoriously difficult to remember its sequence of events, even if you know it really well, partly because of confusion of names among the generations of its characters (two Catherines, men with strange, animal-like names – Hindley, Hareton, Lindley – that elide each other as you read); and partly because of the elaborate narrative layering of the text, which makes it difficult to work out whether you are reading its narrative 'now', which is 1801–4, or its historic past, which stretches back to the middle years of the eighteenth century. Accomplished readers of *Wuthering Heights*, offended perhaps at the idea that they may not know their Earnshaws one from the other, may pass over this summary, a

---

[1] Terry Eagleton, *Heathcliff and the Great Hunger* (London: Verso, 1995). See also Edward Chitham, *The Birth of* Wuthering Heights. *Emily Brontë at Work* (Basingstoke: Palgrave, 2001), pp. 117–21.

[2] Eagleton, *Heathcliff*, pp. 17–18.

version of which is in any case to be found on some 200 internet websites, or in any companion to English literature. Many modern editions of the novel also provide trees for the family relations the novel depicts, and they are probably more useful than any plot summary.

Somewhere in West Yorkshire, near a village called Gimmerton, there are two properties. There is the working hill farm Wuthering Heights, occupied by the Earnshaw family, and Thrushcross Grange, occupied by the more genteel Lintons. There are a son and a daughter at Wuthering Heights – Catherine and Hindley Earnshaw – and a son and daughter at the Grange – Edgar and Isabella Linton. Heathcliff (he has no other name) is picked up from the streets of Liverpool by Mr Earnshaw, brought back to the Heights to be reared with his own children, who are then six (Catherine) and thirteen (Hindley) years old. Ellen (Nelly) Dean, a young servant, is also a member of the household into which Heathcliff is introduced.

Two of the children, Catherine and Heathcliff, wander the moors and make connection with the Linton family at the Grange. Catherine is (superficially) seduced by them and their genteel civility; Heathcliff remains an outsider, watching his companion's absorption into their refined and cultured life through the window. Catherine Earnshaw is transformed by her time at the Grange. This transformation into a (somewhat uncertain) lady prepares for her marriage, some years later, to the son of the house, young Edgar Linton.

After old Earnshaw's death, Heathcliff is bullied, exploited and degraded by Hindley Earnshaw, who is now married and head of the household. Passionately and ferociously, Heathcliff falls in love with Catherine. She returns his love, but says that it would be humiliating and degrading for her to marry him, a mere labourer on the Heights farm. Heathcliff overhears this, and in rejection and despair slips away – no one knows where. He will not return for three years. Meanwhile, Hindley Earnshaw's wife, Frances, has borne him a son, Hareton, and died. Catherine Earnshaw has become Catherine Linton by her marriage to Edgar, now master of Thrushcross Grange. Heathcliff returns to the Heights. He has somehow acquired wealth, the presence and persona of a gentleman, a ferocious kind of dignity and a compelling masculinity. He makes contact with his former childhood companion, Catherine, and asserts his natural claims on her, over the artificial claims of her husband, Edgar Linton. He begins to take revenge on the Lintons and the Grange for what he sees as the alienation of Catherine's affections. Heathcliff's first victim is Catherine herself; he hastens her death by incessant accusations of betrayal. She is, in any case, weakened by pregnancy; she dies giving birth to a girl, another Catherine (Linton).

Meanwhile, Isabella Linton (Edgar's sister) has become infatuated with Heathcliff. He, determined in his revenge against her family, takes advantage of her feelings in a runaway marriage; this is a cunning plan to gain possession of the Linton property. Isabella is driven by coldness and violence to run away

to 'the South'. Her son by Heathcliff, Linton Heathcliff, is returned to the full
horrors of Wuthering Heights, to be brought up by his father. Heathcliff simultaneously effects the degradation of Hindley Earnshaw, who dies an alcoholic
death at the age of twenty-seven, deeply in debt. Heathcliff is then revealed to
be the mortgagee of the Heights. It is now in his possession. Hindley leaves
behind his boy Hareton, who is not allowed by Heathcliff to be taught to read
and write. He is reduced to the level of a beast (or a feral child, or brutish
country lout) by the treatment he receives at Heathcliff's hands. Heathcliff's
two obsessions throughout all of this are, first, acquisition of Linton land and
property; and second, hopes of reunion with the dead Catherine.

He wreaks further revenge in engineering a marriage between young
Catherine Linton and his own son, Linton Heathcliff. He thus secures the
family property. The 'ailing, peevish creature' Linton Heathcliff soon dies;
young widow Catherine Heathcliff (as she now is) develops an interest in the
loutish Hareton. Soon she will civilise him into fitness to be her husband. By
now Heathcliff thinks of nothing but union (in body and in spirit) with the dead
Catherine. He refuses to eat; he is visited by spectres and visions of Catherine;
he dies. In fact, he has failed to disintegrate or eliminate the Earnshaw and
Linton families. There will be a new Catherine Earnshaw; together with her
husband, they will unite the capital value of the Grange and the Heights. The
younger generation (Catherine and Hareton) inherit not only substantial property but also hope of a happier future. This story – this shocking story – is told
for the main part by the servant Nelly Dean. She has worked all her life either
at the Heights or at the Grange. She tells it – though not chronologically, as it
is given here – to a visitor to Yorkshire, a Mr Lockwood, temporary tenant of
Thrushcross Grange, from the later part of 1801 onwards.

Paying attention to Ellen Dean's voice cannot disperse Phoebe's silence.
Phoebe was there once; she did speak; if it were not for the unfortunate absence –
a technical problem – of certain kinds of record, I would be able to reconstruct
something of it. Rather, by having Nelly Dean here in this book, I want to recognise properly, and have others recognise, the full implications of the proposition
that 'history' is a form of writing, a particular genre of literary production that
came into being in its modern form during the course of the long eighteenth
century. Emily Brontë's novel is part of a history of narrative forms, and thus
of the ways of thinking and feeling attendant on them. Of course, among all the
things *Wuthering Heights* is, and probably the least of them, is a social history
of service and a psychology of servitude; but that is what I must take from it,
compelled to do so by the rank and status of its principal narrator, its historical
setting, and its date structure, which almost exactly matches the one of the story
I have told.

Characters in books, plot structures and literary devices have historical existence, because they are brought into the world, where they were not before.

They are thus events; and as such, they go on to do work in the world: they are read, reimagined; characters are named and evoked for a thousand purposes never dreamed of by their author. They *happen*. I must make it very clear that *I* am clear that Heathcliff and Nelly Dean did not have the same *kind* of historical existence as Phoebe Beatson and her employer, but in the tale I tell they have the same meaning, for they come to embody (I make them, not unreasonably, embody) the same historical processes.

To recognise that characters in books, and plot structures and literary devices have historical existence, and can be made to do the work of historical analysis, is not to blur the boundaries between fiction and fact, and it is not a denial of 'history' – whatever that denial might be. The past *was* there, whilst history *is* here. Things indubitably happened, in one way rather than another, and it is that one way (rather than the other, might-have-been) with which we deal. In the past tense, however, whatever it was, has gone. 'History' in the historian's writing exists only in the narrative or account extracted from the Everything of the past: it exists in the head of the historian, in the words on the page where it is written down, and in the realm of other imaginations when it comes to be read. The indeterminacy and speculative nature of any historical account does not derive only from the historian's great distance from the time, place and people she recounts and interprets. It derives from the fact that it did not happen – cannot have happened – *like* this: it cannot have happened as it is told, here by me, nor by anybody else. History (the written history) depends on a double absence, says Jacques Rancière: the 'absence of the "thing itself"' that is *no longer there* – that is in the past, and is gone; and that never was – because it never was *such as it was told*'.[3] I shall be strict in my procedures in discussing *Wuthering Heights*, as I have been straightforward about the lacunae that I believe helped structure the preceding pages. I shall not pretend that Nelly Dean walked the Pennine Hills with bundles of worsted for spinning into thread, or that her passion was the same as Phoebe Beatson's; but Nelly *has* walked here, because she means something of the same thing as pregnant Phoebe.

In another meditation on writing, different from his account of the great, strandless river of Everything from which he precipitated *The General in His Labyrinth*, García Márquez says that 'one of the most useful secrets for writing is to learn to read the hieroglyphs of reality without knocking or asking anything'.[4] Historians, though, have to knock on doors and ask questions: it is their professional obligation; it is what we are paid to do. But we can shift the focus too, look disaligned, like other writers do, see *something else* that's really there, like the faun García Márquez saw once on a Bogotá tramcar. It may have been a

---

[3] Jacques Rancière, *The Names of History. On the Poetics of Knowledge* (Minneapolis: University of Minnesota Press, 1994), p. 63.

[4] Gabriel García Márquez, *Living to Tell the Tale*, orig. pub. 2002 (London: Jonathan Cape, 2003), p. 405.

dream, he says, a startling materiality aroused in a moment of nodding off. But it was 'so clear that [he] could not separate it from reality'. He continues: 'In the end, the essential thing for me was not if the faun was real, but that I had lived the experience as if he were . . .'[5] Nelly Dean has been in this history, which I have written out of other ones, composed long ago, and calling themselves by other names ('the novel'; *Wuthering Heights*). She cannot be extricated now, for she is *about something*. She is about real historical processes experienced in actual social circumstances and in already-mapped terrains and topographies. Like Phoebe Beatson, she – Nelly – (and the rest of the mad crew at the Grange and the Heights) happen now, in this piece of writing. Nelly is a faun on a Bogotá streetcar; she is what Phoebe was pregnant with.

This place, these people who have been the subject of this book, have already been mythologised: all that was solid melted into air here, first. Twentieth-century novelists explored the relationship between land and loom, economic structures and human affect in the West Riding, in something of the manner of modern social history, long before E. P. Thompson restructured the telling according to a Marxist plot-line, making its protesting wool combers and weavers representative of a proletarianised workforce.[6] By the time Thompson gave detail to the founding myth of English industrial society, these Pennine Hills were already an Attica, a Thrace, an Olympus – wherever – where the stories of gods and men explained something coming into being. That is one reason for seeing the Huddersfield–Halifax district in the later eighteenth century in relationship with another, further north up the Pennine Ridge. *Wuthering Heights* is frequently referred to as mythic, in its depiction of human love and immortal passion – all told prosaically among the porridge pots and cow byres of the hill-farming district round Haworth.

But in *Wuthering Heights* it is not actually Nelly Dean who translates the Lancashire–Yorkshire border district into a realm of myth. Love, Passion, Sin and Death move among these hills; men devour their children (in spirit, if not actually dining off them in the manner of Cronus); the children taunt and maim those beneath them, hanging puppies and teaching toddlers to lisp curses; Fate repeats her lesson, about the visitation of sin upon the generations, with

---

[5] García Márquez, *Living to Tell the Tale*, p. 270.

[6] For a novel dealing with 'Machines and Men', 'Loss' and 'Reparation' in the Colne and Calder valleys, see Phyllis Bentley, *Inheritance* (London: Gollancz, 1932). See also Thomas Armstrong, *The Crowthers of Bankdean* (London: Collins, 1941), especially for a fine version of the enduring West Yorkshire *mise-en-scène*, used in nineteenth-century novel and twentieth-century film: 'And a picture of the West Riding rose before him – its sombre mass of hills and locking valleys, its wild moors, its cold dark streams, its lonely cottages, its busy lighted towns, the machinery in the mills whirring, the looms clattering, the long chimneys smoking, lorries rushing up and down hills with loads of cloth . . .' (590). Brightly lit towns and lorries apart, this could serve for the Halifax–Huddersfield region, *c.*1800. I am grateful to Professor Ted Royle for introducing me to these two novels.

a monstrous indifference to the Christian testaments from which she takes her strictures; a man loves seventeen years beyond a woman's death and beyond the ability of a mortal frame to sustain such feeling. But all of the powerful and satisfactory insights we gain by believing stolid and sensible Ellen Dean – a cant Yorkshire lass, who says of herself that 'I certainly esteem myself a steady, reasonable kind of body' – to be one of the West Pennine Eumenedes, Brontë makes it many times as plain as a pikestaff that it is, in fact, young Mr Lockwood's tale.[7] The cautious, effete young townie who is Heathcliff's tenant at Thrushcross Grange listens to her narrative told over a two-year period between November 1801 and January 1803 and writes it down.

Lockwood's voice encloses Ellen Dean's; his is the beginning of the tale, and appears to be its end. He sits by the fire in November 1801 (he has caught cold, on his way back from a first visit to Wuthering Heights) and listens to his housekeeper tell a story stretching back thirty years from the novel's precisely inscribed opening moment.[8] She sews; he urges her on: 'you've done just right to tell the story leisurely. That is the method I like' (102).[9] Nelly's voice, the one he purportedly transcribes, is, in turn, made up of multiple narratives: the wild, passionate cries of the Earnshaw children and all those they damage along the way, and significantly, for the perspective of this book, the voices of two other servants. There is the almost-impenetrable dialect of Joseph, the mean, misanthropic, Evangelical Joseph (Methodist, Baptist – no one cares to know which[10]), hired servant in the husbandry way at the Heights, and Zillah, the housekeeper there after Nelly's exile to the Grange – Zillah, she of the

---

[7] The Eumenedes, 'the kindly ones', are so called because their actual name is too terrible to utter aloud. See Mary Lefkowitz, *Greek Gods, Human Lives: What We Can Learn from Myths* (New Haven and London: Yale University Press, 2003), pp. 124–6. For Nelly fulfilling the function of a chorus, and Emily Brontë's use of her in this role by reference to Horace, see Chitham, *The Birth of* Wuthering Heights, pp. 29–31.

[8] Nelly starts to tell her story in the very month – in the wilder reaches of my historical imagination, at the very hour – when Eliza Beatson was conceived.

[9] Emily Brontë, *Wuthering Heights* (1847). Page references in the text are to the Penguin edition, 1965, Intro. David Daiches.

[10] Brontë is careful to show that nobody knows or cares much what is the denomination of the reader of 'Seventy Times Seven, and the First of the Seventy-First. A Pious Discourse delivered by the Reverend Jabes Branderham, in the Chapel of Gimmerton Sough' (64). It is mysterious out of his boringness – and Zillah's (she is one of the other Heights servants) flightiness: 'Joseph and I generally go to chapel on Sundays,' says Zillah to Mrs Dean, who reports this to Lockwood, explaining that 'the Kirk you know, has no minister now . . . and they call the Methodists' or Baptists' place, I can't say which it is, at Gimmerton, a chapel'. (326) This has not prevented a busy historical industry of the past fifty years working hard to tell us exactly what Joseph's religious affiliation was. For its beginnings, see John Dixon Walsh, 'The Yorkshire Evangelicals in the Eighteenth Century, with Especial Reference to Methodism', PhD thesis, University of Cambridge, 1956. Whilst Baptist and Methodist places of worship were called 'chapels', so too were those places of Anglican worship subordinate to a parish and its church. Building chapels in West Yorkshire was one solution to the Church of England's problems with very large parishes, increasing population, want of personnel, and financial barriers to erecting new churches. See F. C. Mather, 'Georgian Churchmanship Reconsidered. Some Variations in Anglican Public

scarlet cloak and black silk bonnet for gadding off to Gimmerton in (270, 310). Zillah is noisy and self-assured, no better than she ought to be, and of rather narrow psychological perception, in Ellen Dean's eyes. (Nelly dislikes noise, loud speech, an improper mode of discourse – 'a clamorous manner' (169) – but only in her fellow servants. She would have been hard pressed to endure her thirty-year service to the Earnshaws and the Lintons had she cared half as much about weeping and wailing and the gnashing of teeth among her employers.)

Thus is both the refinement and the complexity of Nelly's own voice explained. It is accounted for, not by an uncertainty on Brontë's part over how to render in modified orthography the language of the Pennine serving class (she can do Joseph's dialect to the pitch of the impassable: there are places you simply cannot go, as reader of Joseph's gloomy interjections), nor by reference to Lockwood's genteel circumlocutions, that he may be imagined to insert somewhere in the space between the telling of a story and writing it down. Rather, Nelly's narrative voice is explained by self-characterisation, which occurs emphatically and early on in the novel: 'Excepting a few provincialisms of slight consequence', Lockwood tells her, 'you have no marks of the manners which I am habituated to consider as peculiar to your class. I am sure you have thought a great deal more than the generality of servants think.' She replies that she has read more than he might fancy. She opens an aperture on to what on earth it was she did in the spaces between tending the elemental passions of her employers and the blazing fires with which she is continually associated, and putting her Christmas cakes in the oven (95). 'You could not open a book in this library that I have not looked in to,' she continues. 'And got something out of also; unless it be that range of Greek and Latin and that of French – and those I know one from another, it is as much as you can expect of a poor man's daughter' (103).

We may want to add Ellen Dean to the list of great servant-narrators – Richardson's Pamela and Godwin's Caleb Williams are two already-mentioned eighteenth-century English examples – but the text actually prevents us from doing so. Richardson's novel of 1740 *was* known to Haworth parsonage, or at the very least, turns up in the kitchen at Gateshead Hall where Betty and the other maids tell an eight-year-old the story of the servant Pamela, so that we might be sure exactly what kind of story *we* are in, reading *Jane Eyre*.[11] But Nelly is not another Pamela; her consciousness is not the unambiguous container of the story, as is that of the earlier fictional servant. Rather, Ellen Dean is made in the image of that 'archaic fate' that Bruce Robbins has discerned across world literature when a servant is figured in a text – a Fate that

Worship, 1714–1830', *Journal of Ecclesiastical History*, 36:2 (1985), pp. 255–83; and Judith Jago and Edward Royle, *The Eighteenth-century Church in Yorkshire. Archbishop Drummond's Primary Visitation of 1764*, Borthwick Papers 95 (York: University of York, 1999), p. 30.

[11] Charlotte Brontë, *Jane Eyre*, orig. pub. 1847 (Harmondsworth: Penguin, 1966), p. 41.

'asserts the ultimate power of community and presses obscurely towards social inclusiveness'.[12]

We never learn where Ellen Dean came from, or who she is; the manner of her hiring (annual? as a servant in husbandry or in housewifery? apprenticed by the parish to old Earnshaw?) is obscure. Her mother was nurse to the oldest Earnshaw child, taking Ellen with her – 'I was almost always at Wuthering Heights'; or maybe the little girl lodged at Gimmerton and came over often (76). There is only one period of time in which Nelly disappears from the story – when we don't know where she is – and that is on the night of Heathcliff's arrival at the Heights in the summer of 1771, when, like Hindley and Cathy, she refuses to have the little black thing in her bed. Finding the new arrival shivering on the landing outside his chamber door, Mr Earnshaw sends Nelly away 'in recompense for [her] cowardice and inhumanity' (78). She cannot go far – has somewhere to go – she is back in a few days ('I did not consider my banishment perpetual'). She grows up with the Earnshaw children, is clearly a servant but also a kind of foster sister as well, eating her porridge with them: 'I got used to playing with the children – I ran errands too, and helped to make hay, and hung about the farm ready for anything that anyone would send me to' (76). When the three children fall ill of the measles, Ellen Dean takes on the 'cares of a woman' in nursing them. (Mrs Earnshaw dies in the early part of 1773.) She is the same age as Hindley Earnshaw whom we know to have been born in 1757 (the novel, as many have remarked, is absolutely insistent that we know precisely the date of everything that happens).[13]

Nelly's mirror Heathcliff's mysterious origins (hers are more resistant to speculation than his; nobody does speculate about them in the text). There have been half-spoken attempts to make both of them illegitimate children of Mr Earnshaw.[14] But in the way that Robbins notes, Nelly remains still a poor man's daughter, asserting the wider economic and social structures of the Pennine district by the mere fact of her existence. Indeed, she has the power – textually speaking – to make all of them servants by her presence. In a formulation of sexual, household and contractual relations that would indeed have been the understanding of any substantial gentleman farmer of the later eighteenth century, Heathcliff explains what he is up to in letting Thrushcross Grange and keeping his daughter-in-law and son (the feeble Linton, now married under

---

[12] Bruce Robbins, *The Servant's Hand. English Fiction from Below*, orig. pub. 1986 (Durham and London: Duke University Press, 1993), p. 29.

[13] For Nelly's age, see Chitham, *The Birth of* Wuthering Heights, pp. 161–2. And it is, perhaps, noteworthy that it is Doctor Kenneth who imparts this information to the reader. Kenneth the medical man (a servant, in his own way) operates rather like Joseph, in his overview and knowledge of circumstances.

[14] Susan M. Gilbert and Susan Gubar, *The Madwoman in the Attic. The Woman Writer and the Nineteenth-century Literary Imagination*, 2nd edn (New Haven: Yale University Press, 2000), pp. 264–90.

some duress to the younger Catherine) at the Heights, thus: 'I'm seeking a tenant for the Grange . . . and I want my children about me, to be sure – beside, the lass owes me her services for her bread; I'm not going to nurture her in luxury and idleness after Linton has gone . . .' (318). Joseph several times emphasises that the younger Catherine should be working in the household and husbandry way – just like him and Nelly Dean. And, as if to sustain a perception to be achieved sixty years later by Sigmund Freud, Ellen Dean makes Lockwood her amanuensis, or mere secretary: a kind of servant who writes down her long tale.[15]

It was an important legal fiction – or fantasy – of the second half of the eighteenth century that the service relationship might stand as the model and pattern for relationships between husband and wife, and parent and child. William Blackstone called service a '*private* oeconomical relation', a domestic arrangement 'founded in convenience, whereby a man is directed to call in the assistance of others, where his own skill and labour will not be sufficient to answer the cares incumbent on him', a relationship happily and satisfyingly regulated by contract law.[16] There really was no such thing as a sexual contract, despite the efforts of twentieth-century political scientists to write the past as if there were,[17] and no body of law that dictated in minute detail the lived relationship between children and their parents as there existed for the service relationship.[18] Servants stood as the example of how things might be, if only there were such law; if only all relationships could be contracted for and managed in that way.

Ellen Dean represents the social order in ways other than the legal and the metaphoric. It is her voice that draws attention to the absence of ecclesiastical authority in the area. She remarks on the local livings and curacies left unfilled in the area on more than one occasion. In introducing Lockwood to the social

---

[15] For Freud's understanding of the psycho-analyst as a secretary and servant, and for the variety of jokes sustained out of this perception (long before Freud had it), see Carolyn Steedman, 'Servants and their Relationship to the Unconscious', *Journal of British Studies*, 42 (2003), pp. 316–50.

[16] William Blackstone, *Commentaries on the Laws of England. In Four Books*, orig. pub. 1765, 6th edn (Dublin: Company of Booksellers, 1775), Book 1, p. 422. For a fuller discussion of service and contract in this period, see Carolyn Steedman, 'Lord Mansfield's Women', *Past and Present*, 176 (2002), pp. 105–43, and 'The Servant's Labour. The Business of Life, England, 1760–1820', *Social History*, 29:1 (2004), pp. 1–29. See Paul Craven and Douglas Hay, *Masters, Servants and Magistrates in Britain and the Empire, 1562–1955* (Chapel Hill and London: University of North Carolina Press, 2004), pp. 59–116; S. F. Deakin and Frank Wilkinson, *The Law of the Labour Market. Industrialization, Employment and Legal Evolution* (Oxford and New York: Oxford University Press, 2005).

[17] Carole Pateman, *The Sexual Contract* (Cambridge: Polity Press, 1988), pp. 116–53.

[18] As Pavla Miller remarks, there was a great body of law that related to infancy and minority across early modern Europe, but it was equity law for the main part, devised for those with property. It did not govern the lived relationship of parent and child, or assign duties and obligations to the parties as did the law of master and servant. *Transformations of Patriarchy in the West, 1500–1900* (Bloomington: Indiana University Press, 1998), p. 17.

setting of the Yorkshire myth she is about to tell, she is careful indeed to hearken back to the 1770s when 'we had a curate . . . who made the living by teaching the little Lintons and Earnshaws, and farming his bit of land himself . . .' (82). She is Heathcliff's good and last confessor: he talks to her in the last frenzies of his passion, about his degradation, pride, happiness, anguish; the way in which 'the entire world is a dreadful collection of memoranda that she did exist, and that I have lost her!' (353–6). She questions him closely about the state of his soul, and his fear – or lack of fear – of death. She has done this before, delivering more conventional Christian strictures when he digs up the departed Catherine's coffin (319). She tells him on one occasion that he has lived an unchristian life, and that the time has come to repent. But as Lockwood remarks, her religious opinions are 'something heterodox'. This is after she has told him about her happiness in watching in a chamber of death (as long as there's no one else with her, a-weeping and a-wailing; 'no frenzied or despairing mourner to share the duty with me'). At this moment, Nelly prefigures the last lines of the novel, where Lockwood (in an observation that many readers have believed can only be ironic) ponders the graves of Catherine and Heathcliff, and their quiet slumbers in a quiet earth. These are probably not Lockwood's feelings at all, for three years before, rising to her full stature as Moros of the Moors, Nelly had discussed the same questions with him, indicating someplace beyond, or outwith the Christian hierarchies of afterlife, telling him that watching a corpse shows her 'a repose that neither earth nor hell can break; [I] feel an assurance of the endless and shadowless hereafter – the Eternity they have entered – where life is boundless in its duration, and love in its sympathy, and joy in its fulness'.[19] This is a complicated theological position: for Ellen, a corpse asserts 'its own tranquillity', even though reflection in the cold light of day might suggest that Catherine Linton's 'wayward and impatient existence' merited no such 'haven of peace at last' (201–2). Lockwood doesn't really understand, though Ellen's beliefs and her thoughts provide him with the very last words of the novel, to do with those quiet slumbers in a quiet earth.

She draws attention, as well, to a dearth of law in the area. (How different in Pamela's case. Her problem is too much law, for in fictional 1740s Bedfordshire and Lincolnshire, Mr B. is the local magistrate, has several livings in his gift, controls, in various ways, the turnpike roads and post office. He is the entire epitome of the administrative and confessional state for her.) In drawing attention to its absences in West Yorkshire, Ellen Dean becomes the law. When Heathcliff suggests something very like a forced marriage between the younger Catherine and his son Linton, Nelly cries out: 'Let him dare to force you . . . There's law in the land, thank God there is! though we *be* in an out-of-the-way place. I'd inform, if he were my own son, and it's felony without benefit of clergy' (305).

---

[19] Heterodox it may seem to Lockwood, but it was possibly also the position of the Reverend John Murgatroyd. See above, chapter 8.

But inform whom? There is a corrupt and high-handed attorney in the picture, but only one resident magistrate in the entire narrative, and that is Mr Linton himself (211). It is Joseph who points this out. As will be discussed later, his is an even more sociologically informed account of the district than is Nelly's.

To whom else could Heathcliff have said those things? – made his confession? It is structurally impossible for any other character to act as his confessor. Nelly grew up with the Earnshaw children, and with him. She has been nurse, mother, sister to him, not only during the time of his great degradation at Hindley's hands, when she was the only one to do the neglected child 'the kindness to call him a dirty boy, and bid him wash himself once a week' (94). Tending him in his infancy, watching him grow to youth, tracking his existence over and over again in her mind (355), she learns her child psychology from the play of his expressions, his fierce rages, his reaction to humiliation: to all the ways ill-treatment and neglect nourished the child's 'pride and black temper' (82). During one of her absences from the Heights, the new housekeeper's account of the way in which Heathcliff treats his son Linton is given from the same perspective, and Nelly divines that 'utter lack of sympathy had rendered young Heathcliff selfish and disagreeable, if he were not so originally . . .' (246). Years before she had seen the five-year-old Hareton corrupted into cursing, his baby features distorted 'into a shocking expression of malignity', taught profanity and obscenity in the battle between his alcoholic father Hindley and Heathcliff (147–9).

Deeply implicated in the structures of child abuse, child care, and the growth of love and hate that her narrative reveals, her place among the three children of the Earnshaw household does indeed mirror Heathcliff's. For if a ruined nest of baby birds high on the moors represents the sexual connection between Catherine and Heathcliff that took place – that may have taken place – in the lost realm of childhood when they still shared a bed, then the little pit near the Heights 'still full of [the] snail shells and pebbles' that she and Hindley had put there, playing together 'twenty years before', is the same topos of a relationship between them, in the manner of the little heap of lapwing skeletons (147, 160).[20]

Nelly is not another Pamela, but she does repeat one of Pamela's most important assertions: that once we were all the same, all on a foot, in a lost realm of community when there were no masters and their maids and men, no country gentlemen, no hierarchies . . . Nelly is a device for both the assertion and the

---

[20] The snail shells are Nelly's emblem: 'She goeth softly, but she goeth sure/She stumbles not as stronger creatures do./Her journey's shorter, so she may endure/Better than they which do much further go./ She makes no noise, but stilly seizeth on/The flower or herb appointed for her food,/The which she doth feed upon/While others range and are, but find no good./And though she doth but very softly go,/However, 'tis not fast nor slow, but sure;/And certainly they that do travel so,/The prize they do aim at they do procure.' 'Upon a Snail' was known to the Brontë children. John Bunyan, *A Book for Boys and Girls, or, Temporal Things Spiritualised* (London: R. Tookey, 1701), Verse No. 43.

dissolution of the social and economic structures of Yorkshire society, 1771–1804, and has the figurative means to make master and mistress, and all the rest of them, the same as her. Except for Lockwood, who, it seems, cannot be removed from his place as narrator and for whom she cannot perform this textual and political function.

There are other resonances, too, between Pamela and Nelly. Both of them commit the servant's original sin, of making known outside the household what goes on within it.[21] (Nelly's tale – *Wuthering Heights* – is one long enactment of this sin.) She also repeats, a century on from the time of *Pamela*'s writing, Pamela's irreducible intermediariness, which, according to Robbins, distorts the fourteen-year-old Pamela's style (that is to say, Pamela does not always sound like your actual Bedfordshire cottager's girl) in a way that we may see Ellen Dean's style and language distorted. Robbins explains Pamela's wildly shifting registers, her rapid move from one voice to another, as arising from 'the structural ambivalence of an intermediary between two powers . . . The words of such a mediator cannot avoid duplicity. Their middleness is structural and irreducible.'[22] Middleness is connected to the liminality of the servant figure. Robbins comments on servants' connection with lintels, doors and windows, across great swathes of text and culture. He notes in particular Virginia Woolf's Mrs Ramsay, musing as she mends stockings for the lighthouse keeper's child, that 'children and servants are forever leaving the door of the house open'.[23] This was a twentieth-century echo of the eighteenth-century's major moan and groan about servants: households rang with the cry, after departing servants, of 'Shut that door!'[24] Liminal places, window-frames in particular, are important in *Wuthering Heights*; Nelly frequently opens windows; and one key turn of the plot, when Heathcliff visits Catherine Earnshaw on the eve of her child's birth and her own death, occurs because the servant leaves open the door. It is deliberately done. As she explains to Lockwood, it was a Sunday:

> There was a man servant left to keep the house with me, and we generally made a practice of locking the doors during the hours of service; but on that occasion, the weather was so warm and pleasant that I set them wide open, and to fulfill my engagement, as I knew who would be coming, I told my companion that the mistress wished very much for some oranges, and he must run over to the village and get a few, to be paid for on the morrow . . . (192)[25]

---

[21] Robbins, *Servant's Hand*, p. 83. Richardson, *Pamela*, p. 62.

[22] Robbins, *Servant's Hand*, p. 103.   [23] Robbins, *Servant's Hand*, p. 50.

[24] Anon., *Domestic Management, or the Art of Conducting a Family* (London: H. D. Symonds, 1800), p. 18. Janet Thaddeus, "Swift's Directions to Servants', *Studies in Eighteenth-century Culture*, 16 (1986), pp. 107–23; 108–9. John Trusler, *Domestic Management, or the Art of Conducting a Family* (London: J. Souter, 1819), p. 65.

[25] By the early nineteenth century, the time of divine service was believed to be the housebreaker's golden opportunity, and householders were conventionally advised to lock up, even if (as usual) they had left a servant behind.

There are indeed many connections, as there must be, for in Robbins's view, liminality, intermediariness, unreliability and the pressure of Fate (the insistent pressure of how stories *must be*, and *must* be told) are what the servant figure is *for*.

But Pamela is *seen*; her voice records the reactions of others to her prettiness, her figure, her funniness; to her stays and petticoats and gowns. Not so with Nelly, who remains as visually obscure as does her real-life counterpart, the actually existing Slaithwaite maidservant Phoebe Beatson (same dates, fifteen miles down the road; turbulent romantic career; passion in a different register). Nelly is twenty, perhaps, when the story of Wuthering Heights opens, and in her forties when it closes. A poor man's daughter, she tells us that, and that she's a 'stirring, active body' (271). She presumably doesn't go in for maidservant's glad-rags (no scarlet cloaks and black silk bonnets for her); but the only account of her as a person is buried deep in Joseph's discourse when, at a moment of great trauma for him (which will be discussed later), he lets loose with 'Shoo wer niver soa handsome, bud what a body mud look at her 'baht winking' (349). (Typically impenetrable: is she good looking only when you blink? Handsome enough? Or not at all?) Anyway, he thinks she's past it, for earlier he has shown her up when she invites Lockwood into the Heights kitchen for a mug of ale and he hears Joseph 'asking, whether "it wasn't a crying scandal that she should have fellies at her time of life?"' (340). She's in her early forties, not too late for a fellow, or a follower; Phoebe Beatson was thirty-seven when her follower fathered a bastard child on her. And there is something perspicacious in Joseph's rudeness here, or coquettish in Nelly's behaviour (or erotically charged in Lockwood's reporting of it), as she welcomes him to Wuthering Heights as if it were for all the world her domain and she its mistress. This part is told not by her, but by the sexually insecure Lockwood, who is eager to deny the meaning of the moment by

pressing a remembrance into the hand of Mrs Dean, and disregarding her expostulations at my rudeness . . . [vanishing] through the kitchen, as they opened the house-door, and so, should have confirmed Joseph in his opinion of his fellow-servant's gay indiscretions, had he not, fortunately, recognised me for a respectable character, by the sweet ring of a sovereign at his feet (267).

It is possible – just possible – that in some realm of fantasy outside the text, Nelly might have landed Lockwood, and he have married the woman who had cooked his meals, stoked up his fires, who had given him a tale to tell and the language with which to do it – and whose own had become more refined in his presence. Such a partnership was not unheard of, either in 1800, or forty years on: my fantasy is not constructed in reference to Pamela's amazing netting of Mr B. All the servants in *Wuthering Heights* enact the domestic plot of the new-ish bourgeois domesticity of the period. They *make* the haven in a heartless world that found early poetic expression in the safely curtained, glowing parlour of William Cowper's *The Task* (1785); they keep the fires going (now blazing, now smouldering); they perform all welcomes at all doors, brew the coffee that comforts after punishing walks over the moors. They scour the pewter and polish the fire brass that give its interiors the sensory depth and comfort of a home. It is not unlikely that a sexually diffident young man might be aroused to confidence and comfort with a woman who has been a weird combination of Scheherazade and Angel in the House to him. (Coventry Patmore's summation of these developments in the ideology of conjugal love and Evangelical domesticity will start to be published in 1854.) Especially if they can keep to an out-of-the-way place like Gimmerton. And she can't be *that* much older than him.

But we cannot make Ellen Dean a Pamela Andrews; we cannot have Nelly in those ways (though many have found it helpful to see her mediating between two nodal points of power: the Heights/the Grange; the Earnshaws/the Lintons; Heathcliff/Catherine). We can have her, and what she represents though, if we discard Lockwood and his role as superordinate narrator, rely on his transcription as accurate (historians perform this act of trust every day), and reckon that Nelly is telling a story that he does not hear, or understand; a story that is not about herself, but the others, whose plots she forwards according to the arbitrary movements of a malign destiny. Seeing her as a Pennine Fate, we may then hear what it is she is saying. Personally, I have always thought that Lockwood was written to be dispensed with.

I shall do this (I have already have done this) – marry him to Nelly Dean. This will produce two effects. First, in English law as it pertained (in 1848 and 1804), her story becomes Lockwood's, his property (so, in fact, by discarding him, we restore him to his purported position in the text).[26] Second, we can deal with *Wuthering Heights* as a historical novel that takes as one of its many topics a history of service in the West Riding districts, 1777–1804. Doing this will answer questions about what Nelly Dean is doing in a historical account of the Huddersfield–Halifax district, the human relations attendant on proto-industrialisation and domestic service, and the pregnant serving maid of the Reverend John Murgatroyd.

Why should – how can – a historian do this? Because Emily Brontë gives permission. She is a historian *avant l'emergence* of the modern, university-trained, professional; but she is one, nevertheless. Her material makes her one. She suffered from – or needed – the same chronological fix as we do; she was a trainspotter of dates, in the modern manner.[27] Dates appear to be our

[26] Susan Staves, *Married Women's Separate Property in England, 1660–1833* (Cambridge, Mass.: Harvard University Press, 1990). Bridget Hill, *Women, Work and Sexual Politics in Eighteenth-century England* (Oxford: Blackwell, 1989), pp. 196–220.

[27] Bonnie G. Smith, *The Gender of History. Men, Women and Historical Practice* (Cambridge, Mass.: Harvard University Press, 1998), pp. 103–56. Mary Poovey, *A History of the Modern Fact.*

obsession, or even our fetish. Give me a date! you cry, to anyone who tells you about anything; I can't think about it without a date! Which means that you cannot interpret whatever it is that has been told without reference to a wider political and social context already established in some other historian's previous narrative. Dates are not the mere markers of a chronology; they are, in fact, the deep structure of our narrative explanations and make up a philosophy of event and causation, albeit a rarely articulated one.[28] The peculiar 'telling of what has been' that is *Wuthering Heights* (as another novelist-historian of the nineteenth century described her task[29]) retains something of the fetish about it. Some version of a modern mode of historical thinking and historical narrative was clearly available to a genteelly and privately educated young woman of the 1840s. Given what the current history of history writing and historical thinking has to say, we should expect no less. Emily Brontë simply shared in a cognitive development of modernity.

None of this, however, explains the peculiar fix of *Wuthering Heights*, in dating absolutely everything. It has frequently been observed that 'it is possible to work out the date of significant events in the story, including the dates of nearly everybody's birth, marriage and death'.[30] (Clio was the muse of the 'unique historical fact', according to W. H. Auden; he was too polite to speculate about the structures of boredom and inconsequentiality of the fact's conventional embodiment in a date.[31]) My attention was first caught by the way in which the detailed chronology of the novel can be mapped on to the date structure of the Murgatroyd–Beatson–Thorp story. But why has no one yet produced a convincing answer to *why*, in regard to *Wuthering Heights*? Why 1801? – the first line of the novel? Why 1500 carved on the Earnshaw lintel? Why does the first Catherine die, and is the second born, on 20 March 1784? The dates of birth and of death of everyone in the novel are pedantically noted – an accounting escaped only by Nelly, Joseph and – of course – Lockwood, though there are many clues as to what these must have been. Why this period, 1757–1801 (1757 is the year of Hindley's birth) – or, more conventionally, from 1771 when Heathcliff arrives, tumbled on to the kitchen floor from Mr Earnshaw's greatcoat, to 1804?

Problems of Knowledge in the Sciences of Wealth and Society (Chicago: University of Chicago Press, 1998), does not deal with dates as 'facts'. The eighteenth-century historians discussed in this book were for the main part the conjectural Enlightenment kind, whose narratives of the move from barbarity to modern refinement did not need to be – could not be – structured in this way. See James William Johnson, 'Chronological Writing. Its Concept and Development', *History and Theory*, 2:2 (1962), pp. 124–35; and Louis O. Mink, 'Everyman His or Her Own Annalist', *Critical Inquiry*, 7:4 (1981), pp. 777–83.

[28] P. A. Roth, 'Narrative Explanation. The Case of History', *History and Theory*, 27 (1988), pp. 1–13.

[29] George Eliot, *Middlemarch*, orig. pub. 1871–2 (Harmondsworth: Penguin, 1965), p. 122.

[30] Brontë, *Wuthering Heights*, Intro. Daiches, p. 15.

[31] W. H. Auden, 'Homage to Clio', in *Homage to Clio* (London: Faber, 1960). See Carolyn Steedman, *Dust* (Manchester: Manchester University Press, 2001), pp. 142–6.

Why?[32] The social historian (child of modernity) must conclude that Emily Brontë was a creature like her, with the same interest in the great drama of the modern world: the development of industrial capitalism (a development that, in England, took place at a time of revolutionary and counter-revolutionary turmoil) and the irreversible changes in human subjectivity attendant on it. And if, like me, you think that domestic service, and the political thinking and legal attention it provoked in these years, is one key to writing a new version of a well-worn history of the making of a class society, then you read *Wuthering Heights*, its insistent, opaque attention to *that* period, *that* place, all in a setting of 'Sixty Years Since',[33] in this light.

Emily Brontë's sister Charlotte said something like this – or at least, something that allows the novel to be read in the way it is read here – when she described the working method that resulted in *Wuthering Heights*. 'My sister's disposition was not naturally gregarious,' she wrote in the 1850 Preface. 'Except to go to church or take a walk on the hills, she rarely crossed the threshold of home':

Though her feeling for the people round was benevolent, intercourse with them she never sought; nor with few exceptions, ever experienced. And yet she knew them; knew their ways, their language; their family histories; she could hear of them with interest and talk of them in detail, minute, graphic, and accurate; but *with* them she rarely exchanged a word . . . It ensued that what her mind had gathered of the real (*sic*) concerning them, was too exclusively confined to more tragic and terrible traits of which, in listening to the secret annals of every rude vicarage, the memory is sometimes compelled to receive the impress . . . (38–9)

It would be illuminating to know about those 'very few exceptions'; but under the circumstances, we must posit kitchens as her major source.[34] Haworth Parsonage kitchen was the egress for Richardson's *Pamela*; it is the place – the only warm place in the house – where servants dwell and children 'help', and each tells tales to the others. *Wuthering Heights* opens in a kitchen, and ends there. Not the back kitchen – the scullery – where insubordinate servants and naughty children are sometimes banished, but the spacious, glittering, cleanly

[32] Chitham's argument, which follows the progress of a narrative conceived and written in two parts, is highly convincing on Brontë's need to make the events of Nelly's narrative match the story already written, which did not contain her. Chitham, *The Birth of* Wuthering Heights, pp. 158–67. But this explanation does not deal with the broader date structure of the final version.

[33] Sir Walter Scott thought that this distance of time was the precisely appropriate setting for a historical novel. The subtitle of *Waverley* (1814) is *'Tis Sixty Years Since*. See Steedman, *Dust*, pp. 90–1. See also James Chandler, *England in 1819. The Politics of Literary Culture and the Case of Romantic Historicism* (Chicago and London: University of Chicago Press, 1998).

[34] For Emily Brontë in the kitchen at Ponden Hall, three miles west of Haworth on the Pennine Way, home to the cotton and worsted manufacturing Heatons, see Mary A. Butterworth, *The Heatons of Ponden Hall and the Legendary Link with Thrushcross Grange in Emily Brontë's* Wuthering Heights (Keighley: Roderick and Brenda Taylor, 1976).

room that is – we must note this – Joseph's inheritance, and where the story ends: 'Why, Joseph will take care of the house, and, perhaps, a lad to keep him company. They will live in the kitchen, and the rest will be shut up.' (If you want to know what's really going on here, you should look to Joseph, not to Nelly Dean. We shall come to this, by and by.)

Emily Brontë knew a good deal about domestic service in her chosen historical period, though the accumulated social history of a century and a half has much to add to it. She did not know, for example, that after 1777, when a whole range of goods and services were taxed to fund, first, the American and then the French (or Revolutionary) Wars, first Mr Earnshaw, then Hindley would have been liable for the servant tax in respect of Joseph, and that between 1785 and 1794 Heathcliff would have been liable for Nelly Dean. Joseph would have presented a particularly satisfying catch for the local assessor and the crown surveyor, for though he was – assume this – originally hired as a servant in husbandry back in the distant 1740s, and though the legislation specifically exempted servants kept for the purposes of husbandry, manufacture or trade, 'whereby the master earns a livelihood or profit', the boundaries between house and field were permeable ones, as commissioners sitting to listen to appeals against assessment by local employers quickly learned. All over the country, properly hired servants in husbandry were used as Joseph was, to mind the children (the three-hour sermon in the garret delivered to the little Earnshaws and Heathcliff in the autumn of 1777, so that Hindley and Frances might canoodle by the fire downstairs, was a highly effective form of child-minding, right on tap); to fetch and carry; to cook (Joseph's culinary *élan* in regard to porridge has already been noted); waiting at table; carrying trays of food upstairs; performing the services of a valet for Hindley, for Linton, for Heathcliff . . . The appeals committee meeting would have been most interested in the porridge question (and in Joseph's involvement with the Heights horses: seeing a farm worker perform the work of a groom or stable boy netted many a gentleman farmer's payment); they may well have declared Joseph 'a servant, within the meaning of the Act'. His master (whoever) may have protested; the case may have gone to King's Bench, for determination by the judges . . . Hindley or Heathcliff protesting the while that Joseph *really* was a servant in husbandry, and that they simply could not carry on the Wuthering Heights business without a man like Joseph. At least they didn't dress him up in powdered wig and silk knee-breeches to wait at table as many enterprising householders did with their ploughmen, protesting the while that they didn't do it very often, and he was *really* a servant in husbandry.[35] (Though the thought is irresistibly comic, despite the want of elegant company to dine at the Heights. Charlotte Brontë

---

[35] Commissioners of Excise, *Abstract of Cases and Decisions on Appeals Relating to the Tax on Servants* (London: Mount and Page for T. Longman and T. Cadell, 1781).

believed that Joseph was there for the purposes of 'dry saturnine humour'.[36])
Gimmerton – or Haworth – or Luddenham – was an out-of-the-way place, and
the Heights' masters may have been as surprised as the Reverend Murgatroyd
was one day in July 1791 when 'Mr Wilkingson, ye Window looker counted our
Windows . . . & charged for ym – & our servt. – & left me a printed Paper – ye
first payment will be about old Michaelmas'.[37] (The fiscal-military state moved
slowly up here, even in the dynamic Colne Valley: the legislation extending the
servant tax to women had been in effect for nearly five years.) But, remote or
not, commissioners' appeal meetings were held regularly at Leeds, Wakefield,
Skipton and Staincliff in these years. Staincliff would have been the most convenient for Heathcliff (it was where Phoebe Beatson was to have one of her
own bruising encounters with the administrative state in 1802); but not that
convenient: gentlemen had to travel many miles and stay overnight to attend
these meetings.[38]

This want of knowledge about the local structures of the developing fiscal-
administrative state, its encroachments into kitchens and domestic relations, is
of a piece with the absence of ecclesiastical and legal authority in the novel, as
has already been noted. Yet Joseph, serving at Wuthering Heights since 1742,
does know about these things. He knows who is the local magistrate (211);
knows that the doctor and the parson must come running together over the
fields in their black coats on the day that old Earnshaw dies (84); he knows
what a coroner's inquest is, and such a thing is his first thought in describing an almost-deadly fight between Hindley and Heathcliff (142); he knows
about the assizes, the travelling circuit of common-law judges (126). He is
hard-wired into an actual history of law and society, in a way that Ellen Dean
is not.

Perhaps Nelly's ambivalence of position (you never know the terms of her
various hirings, not at the Heights, nor at the Grange, nor indeed whether she
hired at all) comes from a similar want of knowledge on Emily Brontë's part.
How, in the late 1840s, when the Poor Law Amendment Act (1834) has long
removed the right to settlement by domestic service, would you know about
the importance of settlement to English female domestics in the second half
of the eighteenth century? Working as a menial had carried one of the most
important rights to parish settlement and attendant welfare rights for women,
from the seventeenth century onwards. Zillah and Nelly (had they been real)
would have spent a lot of time demonstrating to local magistrates where their
last place of legal settlement actually was. Textually speaking at least, we can

---

[36] Brontë, *Wuthering Heights*, p. 39.

[37] Murgatroyd Diaries, KC 242/1 (7 July 1791). The servant tax legislation used the same administrative structure as the much older window tax legislation.

[38] Twelve West Riding appeal meetings were held between 1777 and 1781. Blackburn in Lancashire
would have been easier from Gimmerton (or Haworth; or wherever). But Haworth fell under
Yorkshire jurisdiction. Commissioners of Excise, *Cases*.

say that this absence of history from the characterisation of Nelly Dean adds to her intermediariness, to her function of liminality.

And there are more absences still, from socio-historical West Yorkshire, 1740–1804. Where are the wool combers and carders, the worsted spinners and weavers of worsted and woollen, whose cottages and shops and manufacturies littered these hills? Where are the likes of the Heatons, whose manufactory at Ponden Mill, Stanbury (just three miles from Haworth Parsonage, Ponden Hall often visited by Emily Brontë) produced both worsted and cotton textiles in the late eighteenth century?[39] The maidservants at the Hall were as keen on scarlet cloaks and silk hats as Zillah was (and paper boxes for the hats, one of which the actually existing Nancy Holmes had during her second year of service with the Heatons in 1783), and on new painted silk gowns (18s was laid out on one for another maid the year before).[40] Where are the likes of Phoebe Beatson, and many others across the Pennines, taking part in the most finely tuned putting-out system, so that a domestic servant like her spent half her life spinning worsted thread? But here, in fictional Gimmerton, no one spins, no one weaves. Nelly sews and knits, but never puts a foot to a one-thread wheel. This, we must conclude, is the restructuring of Haworth district c.1840 for the fictional imagination, not 1780s Haworth. And indeed, more recent histories of this borderland, the triangle between Colne, Burnley and Clitheroe, have been produced, in which looms do not clatter incessantly, nor wheels turn, and the rapidly shifting labour relations of proto-industrialisation are only a dim backdrop.[41] It has always been possible, then, to tell how it was in the area, to write good histories of it, without foregrounding its economic base. But perhaps we should pay more attention to the knitting, for this was the oldest and most widespread of proto-industries, utilising 'the slack periods of the pastoral-farming year', and with a highly developed putting-out system (though it *was* most highly developed on the Westmorland edges of the North Riding).[42] Nelly may actually be a proto-industrial aperture in the text of *Wuthering Heights*, behind whose needles' clacking *can* be heard the hum of the wheel and the clatter of the loom . . .

[39] Ponden Hall was long thought to be one of the sources for the fictional Wuthering Heights farmhouse. See Chitham, *The Birth of* Wuthering Heights, pp. 97–8, 101. Butterworth, *Heatons of Ponden Hall*. See John Styles, 'Involuntary Consumers? Servants and their Clothes in Eighteenth-century England', *Textile History*, 33:1 (2002), pp. 9–21.

[40] For the Heatons and their finely got-up serving maids, see Robert Heaton, Account Book, giving names of servants employed and wages paid, HEATON B149, West Yorkshire Archive Service, Bradford District, Bradford. See also Carolyn Steedman, 'Englishness, Clothes and Little Things. Towards a Political Economy of the Corset', in Christopher Breward et al. (eds), *The Englishness of English Dress* (Oxford and New York: Berg, 2002), pp. 29–44. Styles, 'Involuntary Consumers'.

[41] Amanda Vickery, *The Gentleman's Daughter. Women's Lives in Georgian England* (New Haven and London: Yale University Press, 1998).

[42] Christine Hallas, *Rural Responses to Industrialisation. The North Yorkshire Pennines 1790–1914* (Bern: Peter Lang, 1999), pp. 194–207.

Listing the socio-historical lacunae in a novel is a sorry thing to do, and does not begin to show what *is* in *Wuthering Heights* concerning domestic service and the kind of human relationship it involved. It confirms arguments already made, about changes in subjectivity and social relations that accompanied the later eighteenth-century regulation and reformulation of service. What kind of human relationship was this? We may be sure, along with William Blackstone, that relationship was what it was, even if we disagree that it was actually the first and primary one, on which all others could be patterned. In some ways, Emily Brontë has answers to this question, though I do not suggest that that is what she set out to do in *Wuthering Heights*. Only that an intelligent, observant and rather odd child of the early 1800s understood what may have been heard and observed in a lot of kitchens, and that these observations and understandings play some role in the characterisation of Joseph and Nelly Dean. (And of course Zillah. She has to be, in some way, a much more conscious repetition of the 'Who *does* she think she is?' that greeted most dressing-up and swinging of brand new willow baskets by servants. It came from fellow servants as well as employers.[43])

Forty years ago, David Daiches asked of Nelly Dean why she shows 'no sense of the real oddness of [the] goings-on' at the Heights. Why does she never 'throw . . . up her hands and exclaim: "for God's sake, what is going on here? What kind of people *are* they?"'[44] Of course, she is more deeply implicated in the turn of events – in the narrative inevitability – of the novel than earlier critics noticed: at several points events proceed towards their various tragedies because of what Nelly does (or does not do).[45] And she has nursed these children of the storm: fed them, washed them, told them off; sung lullabies to them, taught them their letters; nurtured their passions as they hurtle through her hands to perdition. Her love for them originates as love for children does under conditions of modernity, in the daily and habitual care of them.

Zillah has an answer to Daiches's question. She provides it towards the end of the novel when she and Nelly meet on the moors (she housekeeper at the Heights, Nelly undergoing one of her spells at the Grange). Zillah's attitude towards the daily madness she has been witnessing is as matter-of-fact as Ellen Dean's, and at one point she briefly indicates why she just gets on with it, as Mrs Dean has done all her life: 'I'll be bound you're saving', she says; '– and I'm doing my little all, that road.' It's a job; a way of getting by in the world and a little nest-egg together (and a settlement, if only Emily Brontë had known the history of the poor laws; Phoebe Beatson got her earthly rewards in a different

---

[43] For 'who *does* she think she is?', see Carolyn Steedman, *Past Tenses. Essays on Writing, Autobiography and History* (London: Rivers Oram Press, 1992), pp. 1–18.

[44] Brontë, *Wuthering Heights*, Intro. Daiches, p. 11.

[45] James Hafley, 'Nelly as Villain in *Wuthering Heights*', *Nineteenth-Century Fiction*, 13 (1958), pp. 199–215.

manner, as we have seen). They are not mothers, daughters, sisters, wives, but domestic servants, hired hands, doing the best they can with what their employers hand out to them. This must be why Cervantes' *Don Quixote* was so popular among English servants (Hester Thrale's domestic sociological survey of 1778 suggested that, at any one time, you could rely on 30 per cent of them knowing it really well[46]). Your master is quite mad, and spends 900 pages telling you to do inexplicably crazy things. You don't ask questions, or even have them to ask; you concern yourself with getting your dinner and a dry place to sleep (but not, in this case, saving, for wages do not appear to be part of the arrangement between Sancho Panza and the Don). You just get on with it, in a stunned and amiable kind of way; that's the deal; the way things are. This is the disaligned, disconnected stoicism of Nelly and Zillah. And that is why, to those modern critics who might name Nelly as agent of the patriarchy, she will reply: Well; someone's got to do it. It's just a job. It's part of the contract.

Not that Nelly hasn't *studied* them all, in that particular Lancashire–Yorkshire border meaning of the word. Older women from this region still speak of studying their husbands: watching, working out what motivates them, delineating their personalities; knowing them – having their number – in the common psychological perception of subordinates everywhere. Nelly has a fine line in the psychology of loss and knows how presence may torture. She reveals this particularly in her last long talk with Heathcliff. She is extremely perspicacious and knowing about the Earnshaws and Heathcliff, about what made them as psychological subjects. And she does, in fact, throw up her hands as Daiches wanted her to do on more than one occasion, notably when the traumatic meeting between Heathcliff and the dying Catherine Linton – the meeting she opened the door for – is interrupted by the return of Catherine's husband. They've been at it for hours; Nelly, frantic at the return of the household from divine service, enters the discourse (shows she can do high-horse Gothic as well as any of the gentry), cries passionately (her word) to Heathcliff: '"Are you going to listen to her ravings? . . . She does not know what she says. Will you ruin her, because she has not wit to help herself? Get up! You could be free instantly. This is the most diabolical deed that ever you did. We are all done for – master, mistress, and servant."' Then, she just lets it go; wishes Catherine dead, in a fine depiction of the psychology of service:

I wrung my hands, and cried out; and Mr Linton hastened his step at the noise. In the midst of my agitation, I was sincerely glad to observe that Catherine's arms had fallen relaxed, and her head hung down. 'She's fainted or dead,' I thought; so much the better. 'Far better that she should be dead, than lingering a burden and a misery-maker to all about her' (193).

46 Hester Thrale, *Thraliana. The Diary of Mrs Hester Lynch Thrale (Later Mrs Piozzi)*, ed. Katherine Balderson, 2 vols. (Oxford: Clarendon Press, 1951), vol. I, pp. 354–5. See Carolyn Steedman, 'Don Quixote in England', forthcoming.

These are the limits to her love, and to her complicated emotional ties to the story she finds herself in, to her involvement and investment in these people, for all of that has been bought. Judges and clergymen may have been averring for nigh on two centuries that master and servant are really relations, that they are each part of each other; but you're not: not daughter, not mother, not wife. You're a servant, hired to bake and brew, wash children and love them. It's just a job; she's only a hired hand.

Joseph complicates and deepens this resonant account of the service relationship, for, as a figure, he is constructed on a much more traditional model. He is a live-in servant in husbandry, who – he tells us towards the end – came to live at the Heights 'sixty years since' (347). There is no hint at all about where he came from, and the text does not ask us to speculate on his origins, as it does in Nelly's case. He may have come to turn his hand to anything – to do all those bits and pieces in the household way ('other little matters for the use of the master's family'), as one employer put it at his local assessed taxes appeal meeting; but farm servant is what he is.[47] The Heights is his home. He sits in the kitchen as in 'a sort of elysium . . . beside a roaring fire; a quart of ale on the table near him, bristling with large pieces of toasted oatcake; and his black, short pipe in his mouth . . .' (269). He rises to the full stature of tragedy when this home is threatened, when the younger Catherine has Hareton pull up his currant bushes to make a flower garden. Nelly knows what the effect of this will be, telling Lockwood that 'I was devastated at the devastation which had been accomplished in a brief half hour; the black currant trees were the apple of Joseph's eye . . .'[48] He is more than upset. 'Aw mun hev my wage, and Aw mun goa!' he says to Heathcliff.

'Aw *hed* aimed tuh dee, wheare Aw'd sarved for sixty years; un' Aw thowt Aw'd lug my books up intuh t'garret, 'un all my bits uh stuff, un' they sud hev the kitchen tuh theirseln; fur t'sake uh quietness. It wur hard tuh gie up my awn heathstun, bud I thowt Aw *could* do that! Bud, nah, shoo's taan my garden frough me, un by th'heart! Maister, Aw cannot stand it! Yah must bend tuh th'yoak, an ye will – *Aw* noan used to't and an ow'd man doesn't ooin get used tuh new barthens – Aw'd rayther arn my bite, an' my sup, wi' a hammer in th'road!'

'Now, now, idiot!' interrupted Heathcliff, 'cut it short! What's your grievance? I'll interfere in no quarrels between you and Nelly – she can thrust you in the coal-hole for anything I care.'

---

[47] Commissioners of Excise, *Cases*, Northamptonshire, Commissioners' Meeting, 1 July 1778. Ann Kussmaul, *Servants in Husbandry in Early Modern England* (Cambridge: Cambridge University Press, 1981).

[48] Who can doubt that these servants are present in the novel for the purposes of comedy? The long-running joke about the servant's malapropisms is repeated here in Nelly's clumsy repetition of the (hyperbolic) 'devastated'. (Working-class speakers are still laughed at for their use of 'I'm devastated' in response to the journalist's 'How do you feel about . . .?')

Joseph's response tells of the social history of his class, and of its mythology, of a *then*, before the imposition of a Norman Yoke; it tells of commoners becoming hired hands, of enclosure and expropriation, the spread of industry over the land of small hill farmers; the soil (or is it 'soul'? Let the ambiguity stand) stolen by *them*[49] – whatever species of gentry happens to inhabit the Heights or the Grange:

'It's noan Nelly! . . . Aw sudn't shift fur Nelly – Nasty, ill nowt as shoo is, Thank God! *shoo* cannot steal t'sowl uh nob'dy!! . . . It's yon falysome, graceless quaen, ut's witched ahr lad, wi' her bold een, un' her forrard ways – till – Nay! it fair brust my heart! He's forgotten all E done for him, and made on him, un goan un' rivenup a whole row ut t' grandest currant trees, i't' garden!' (347)

He is there in the beginning, and he will be there at the end, alone, when all passion is spent, when the story has worked itself out, and most of his family are lying under the sod in Gimmerton Kirkyard.[50] He, as much as the love Catherine and Heathcliff bear each other, is 'the eternal rocks beneath'. He is a very old servant, and a very old servant-type (which is perhaps why he *must* be called Joseph). Nelly is the modern type, flitting over the hills from one hiring to another, calculating her wages with a very nice reckoning of what she will and will not do, and when and whom she'll love. We will stay with Nelly from now on: this book has been about a modern servant, and a modern household arrangement, just down the road. But the Pennine Ridge must be kept in mind as a barrier; it is as impassable in winter as the snowy route Lockwood followed back from Wuthering Heights in November 1801, 'on one side of the road, at intervals of six or seven yards, a line of upright stones, continued through the whole length of the barren . . . erected, and daubed with lime on purpose to serve as guides in the dark and also, when a fall . . . confounded the deep swamps on either hand with the firmer path: but, excepting a dirty dot pointing up, here and there, all traces of their existence . . . vanished . . .' (73). The Pennines must serve as the limit between two economic systems and systems of land tenure, and between literature and history. But as this *is* a history, we are allowed – indeed, obliged – to take our evidence where we can.

And there is a material and economic reality that allows the Pennine pathways to be kept open, that even dissolves such limits and limitations, for Amanda

---

[49] Jeanette Neeson, *Commoners. Common Right, Enclosure and Social Change in England, 1700–1820* (Cambridge: Cambridge University Press, 1993). E. P. Thompson, *The Making of the English Working Class*, orig. pub. 1963 (Harmondsworth: Penguin, 1968), pp. 94–5.

[50] See Naomi Tadmor, 'The Concept of the Household Family in Eighteenth-century England', *Past and Present*, 151 (1996), pp. 111–40; Naomi Tadmor, *Family and Friends in Eighteenth-century England. Household, Kinship, and Patronage* (Cambridge: Cambridge University Press, 2001), pp. 21–2 for Murgatroyd's meaning in using 'family' to describe Phoebe Beatson and himself.

Vickery has pointed out that histories of early textile production in north-east Lancashire and the border parishes show it to be 'an offshoot of the Yorkshire worsted field'.[51] Moreover, there are new and (to my mind) entirely convincing accounts of the genesis of *Wuthering Heights* that have one of its points of origin in the area around Hipperholme, High Sunderland and Shibden Hall just outside Halifax to the north, not Haworth at all, and only two or three miles further on from Phoebe Beatson's spinning master's place, and her parents' house in Halifax town.[52]

Once, E. P. Thompson evoked *Wuthering Heights* as a history of the years he was most interested in. He described a social 'field-of-force' during the eighteenth century, in which patricians and plebs organised themselves, their beliefs and their actions, along the lines of power and ideology, 'the crowd at one pole, the aristocracy at the other'.[53] From about 1790 onwards, former relationships of reciprocity (crowd playing knowing counter-theatre to a local magistracy's knowing and ostentatious display of force) 'snapped', in his words, and a new world, in which there was a structural reordering of class relations and class ideology, was born. It became – and becomes for the historian – possible to understand the society in terms of class, and to speak of the plebeian crowd as a working class.[54] He evoked *Wuthering Heights* in these passages, as a counterblast to some historians' fantasies about a cosy paternalism in the earlier century (he had been keen to replace 'paternalism' with 'patrician' as a term of economic and social analysis), when in reasonably modest household enterprises like the Heights farm, 'the whole of life' was seen to go forward 'in the family, in a circle of loved and familiar faces, known and fondled objects, all to human size'.[55] He went on to remark that 'it would be unfair to meet this with the reminder that *Wuthering Heights* is presented in exactly such a familial situation'. There has been a similar unfairness here, in reading Nelly's narrative as a guide to the private terrors of a world we have lost (a world we never had), but also as contrapuntal to the great story of *The Making of the English Working Class*.

---

[51] Vickery, *Gentleman's Daughter*, p. 299, note 8. See, in addition to references in chapter 1, A. P. Wadsworth and J. de Lacey Mann, *The Cotton Trade and Industrial Lancashire, 1660–1770* (Manchester: Manchester University Press, 1931).

[52] Chitham, *The Birth of* Wuthering Heights, pp. 175–6, 185–7. For another account of Emily Brontë's time at Law Hill School, near Hipperholme and Luddenham, in 1838–9, see Juliet Barker, *The Brontës* (London: Weidenfeld and Nicholson, 1994), pp. 293–6, 306–7.

[53] E. P. Thompson, 'The Patricians and the Plebs', in Thompson (ed.), *Customs in Common* (London: Penguin, 1993), pp. 16–96; 73.

[54] Thompson, 'Patricians and Plebs', pp. 95–6.

[55] Thompson, 'Patricians and Plebs', p. 22, quoting Peter Laslett, *The World We Have Lost* (London: Methuen, 1965), p. 21.

11   Conclusion: Phoebe in Arcadia

Arcadian tales are hard-luck stories too.

W. H. Auden, 'Words' (1960)[1]

In his *History of Tom Jones A Foundling*, long after the little bastard child has been found on Squire Allworthy's bed, and Henry Fielding has had the servant Deborah Wilkins pause in her enumeration of hussies in the village who may have placed evidence of their shame in the Squire's chamber, to notice that he is not listening to her so rapt is his attention to the baby – long after all of this, the author discusses the relationship between 'the marvellous' and the writing of history. (By 'history' he meant 'explanatory narrative'.)[2] Fielding ponders the way in which, were the historian to confine himself 'to what really happened' and to reject utterly any circumstance 'which tho' never so well attested, he must be well assured is false', then he might well 'fall into the marvellous, but never into the incredible'. He might raise 'the wonder and surprise of his reader, but never the incredulous hatred mentioned by Horace'.[3] Horace has been important in Fielding's leading up to this point, for he had taken pains to urge writers (historians) not to introduce supernatural agents into their accounts. Had his advice been followed, observed Fielding, then we should not, for example, have seen Homer's gods and goddesses 'coming on trivial errands . . . behaving themselves so as not only to forfeit all title to respect, but to become objects of scorn and derision'. So derisory and ridiculous were the activities of Homer's deities that perhaps he had had 'an intent to burlesque the superstitious faith of his own age and country'? But these speculations are not to the point, Fielding concludes: he has 'rested too long on a doctrine which can be of no use to a Christian writer: for he cannot introduce into his works any of that heavenly host which make a part of his creed; so it is horrible puerility to search the heathen theology for any of those deities who have been long since dethroned . . .'[4]

---

[1] W. H. Auden, 'Words', *Homage to Clio* (London: Faber, 1960), p. 28.

[2] See chapter 9 for Murgatroyd's reading of *Tom Jones* and the possible model it offered for loving – or at least an attitude towards – Elizabeth Beatson.

[3] Henry Fielding, *The History of Tom Jones A Foundling*, orig pub. 1749 (Harmondsworth: Penguin, 1985), pp. 325–6.

[4] Fielding, *Tom Jones*, p. 324.

We have seen Fielding's correctness of judgement on this point: a modern writer simply cannot make the items of Christian theology into characters in a narrative. Neither does this impossibility of characterisation depend on the historian being either a Christian or an (eighteenth-century) gentleman. The Trinity and the heavenly host are not available for narrativisation in the way of Homer's deities.

But this is not to deny that there were other Phoebes here in late eighteenth-century Slaithwaite, in the books gathered on the Lingards parlour shelves, and in John Murgatroyd's imagination – though he probably did not know, or know much about, the first one: the original Phoebe. The Phoebe he must have known best was the Ovidian one, Phoebe-Diana, who was sister to Apollo. She makes her elegant and virginal way through the *Metamorphoses*, changing those who see her bathing into stags, and other women (sometimes goddesses) into guinea fowl and mountain springs.[5] Sometimes, in the Roman versions of the Greek myths, she is the Moon, partner to her brother as the Sun. But there is a much older Phoebe, a daughter, sister, mother (not at all virginal), in the bloodier creation story that Hesiod tells, of the overthrow of the old gods – the original ones, the Titans (if gods are what they were) – by the Olympians.

Hesiod's *Theogony* tells of how, from vast and dark Chaos, there emerged Gaea, the Earth, and Eros, which was Love. So also from Chaos came black Night, and Erebos, who gave birth to Day and Space.[6] Two (or maybe just one, depending on your authority) incestuous generations along, Earth lay with Heaven, and gave birth to the race of Titans, including Phoebe, their first-born daughter. Hesiod has not much to say of Phoebe, except that she was 'golden-crowned', and later, that she was loved. Cronus (devourer of his own children) was one of her brothers; but it was with a second, Koios (Coeus), that she conceived her child Leto (known to Ovid as Latona).[7] Leto was later to be ravished by Zeus, long after he had defeated the Titans. He would father on her both Artemis and Apollo, making Phoebe, in this case, Apollo's grandmother. (In some later versions of this genealogy, Artemis replaces Phoebe-Diana as Apollo's sister.) When Zeus begat Artemis on Phoebe's daughter Leto, he made them both quails for the occasion, and engendered a story that any classically educated gentleman might think of as he contemplated what happened to the unfortunate Elizabeth Elless (though emphatically not to the West Riding Phoebe).[8] For Zeus' wife, the jealous Hera, sent the Python to pursue Latona

---

[5] The most recent translation of the *Metamorphoses* is used here, trans. David Raeburn (London: Penguin, 2004).

[6] Murgatroyd did not specify his edition of Hesiod. He may have possessed a contemporary translation, perhaps Thomas Cooke, *The Works of Hesiod. Translated from the Greek. Volume II. The Theogony, or the Generation of the Gods* (London: T. Green, 1728).

[7] Robert Graves, *The Greek Myths*, orig. pub. 1960, 2 vols. (London: Folio Society, 1996), vol. I, pp. 60–1.

[8] See chapter 9.

all over the wide world, so that nowhere might she deliver her child in safety. Some of this was in Ovid, the disdain, for example, of the mortal Niobe for this girl 'born to some Titan called Cöéns – Latona, who couldn't obtain/ the meanest refuge on earth when about to give birth to her children'.[9] Ovid does not mention the children's grandmother, and the older Phoebe, the Titaness Phoebe, does not figure in his tale. In Hesiod 'Phoebe came to Koios' longed-for bed/ Loved by the god, the goddess conceived and bore' – three girls in this version, Leto, Asteria and Hekate – lovely, kind Hekate, to be particularly honoured and favoured by the Olympian gods.[10] There is no more than this about Phoebe her mother.

The race of Titans was defeated. In some versions those who are defeated are called gods; in others, because they were deposed by the Olympians, they are no longer and never were gods; rather they are a particular Creation of their own, each a half-way creature, neither god nor man. However the race of Giants is named, these were hard and terrible times: by means of rape, incest, child-eating and genital mutilation a new Olympian order was enthroned and the defeated Titans were banished. (For Phoebe, about whom so little is said – only that incest gave her birth and produced her own daughters, and that she wore a golden crown – there was also her aspect as the Moon, fixed eternally in the firmament, as life after defeat.[11])

Hard times in the West Riding too, for the making of our modern myths. The larger conflicts of revolution and counter-revolution were played out in the register of the 'oppressive relationships intrinsic to industrial capitalism'.[12] Dearth, 'distressing poverty', short pay, 'Hard Times', were recorded by John Murgatroyd (though not an army of redressers meeting by moonlight to effect the alteration of the world). Defeat is the end-point, perhaps the very structuring device of *The Making of the English Working Class*, particularly when it concerns the years after 1832, when the Reform Act so signally prevented the people from entering the polity.[13] In the very last lines of his book, Thompson thanks these men of the West Riding for those years, stretching from the 1780s, that produced such a heroic culture. This place, these times, made the men and women who resisted being turned into an industrial proletariat. Thus is written an elegy of defeat that is also a creation myth: defeat is also these people's

---

[9] Ovid, *Metamorphoses*, trans. Raeburn, pp. 528–9. Graves, *Greek Myths*, vol. I, p. 60.

[10] Hesiod, *Hesiod. Theogony. Work and Days. Theognis. Elegies*, trans. Dorothea Wender (Harmondsworth: Penguin, 1972), p. 36. Cooke had this coupling more elegantly, as 'Phoebe with Fondness, to her Coeus cleav'd/And she a Godess, by a God conceiv'd;/Latona, fable-veil'd,/the Produce proves,/Pleasing to all, of their connubial Loves,/Sweetly engaging from her natal Hour/The most delightful in th'olympian Bow'r'. Cooke, *Works of Hesiod*, p. 55.

[11] Graves, *Greek Myths*, vol. I, p. 35.

[12] E. P. Thompson, *The Making of the English Working Class*, orig. pub 1963 (Harmondsworth: Penguin, 1968), p. 915.

[13] Thompson, *Making*, pp. 781–915.

triumph; the triumph consists of *knowing* what had happened, and understanding all the ways in which they had been bastardised by the new machine and political age.

In the wake of *The Making of the English Working Class*, many historians have attempted to understand and work with Thompson's category of 'experience'; new techniques have been developed for uncovering it, in a very wide range of social situations in the past. At the same time, its contradictions as a term of historical analysis – in its Thompsonian meaning – have been thoroughly explored. In the industrialising Calder and Colne valleys between 1790 and 1830, did experience *mediate* between productive relations and class consciousness, as Thompson said it did? Was your consciousness of yourself as a worker, with interests in common with other workers forged by doing these things (combing your wool, collecting your bundles, spinning your thread), and reflecting on them, for yourself and others? As William Sewell has said, the term slips between your fingers: surely 'productive relations' (the arrangement between Phoebe Beatson and the spinning master, his with the men who combed the wool he supplied her with) and 'consciousness' can't exist *outside* experience? And if 'experience' mediates between productive relations and consciousness of them, does that not imply that those relationships to the mode of production are already *there*, as some kind of pre-existent reality, maybe even as a structure – when class as a structure (as a mere 'thing', in his famous condemnation) is what Thompson is seeking to deny?[14] 'Thompson's claims about experience as a theoretical category are so incoherent that one is tempted to discard the term entirely,' says Sewell in despair.[15] But he does not, no more than the historians who have chosen the more straightforward route of attempting the reconstruction 'not so much of the actual events people lived through, as the way people construed events as they were living through them . . .'[16]

The great achievement of *The Making of the English Working Class* is to show people knowing what had happened to them; though we have observed that not all that they knew of the world (believed they knew of the world) was brought to bear on Thompson's reconstruction of their experience, between 1790 and 1830; not what they had been taught as children, nor what they did and did not retain of their religious formation, for example. Indeed, in none of the work done with the category of 'experience' since the 1960s has a life story been reckoned, the history of the self and of personhood that individuals might bring to a moment of consciousness, revelation or revolution. 'Experience' has been construed as

---

[14] 'Class is a relationship, and not a thing . . . "It" does not exist, either to have an ideal interest or consciousness, or to lie as a patient on the Adjustor's table . . .' Thompson, *Making*, p. 11.
[15] William H. Sewell, 'How Classes are Made. Critical Reflections on E. P. Thompson's Theory of Working-class Formation', in Harvey J. Kaye and Keith McClelland (eds.), *E. P. Thompson. Critical Perspectives* (Cambridge: Polity Press, 1990), pp. 50–77; 63.
[16] Sewell, 'How Classes are Made', p. 64.

a momentary thing, a reaction to and reflection on immediate circumstances: the news from France, the militia stationed at Halifax, short pay, wool combers forced from workshop to home; dearth now, this week, in Huddersfield. These things happen; they are experienced; men and women reflect on them, work out what is going on. They are for the main part men and women without histories, and without experiences of different kinds, and of longer standing. The machine is stopped (stopped by the historian) for a seditious and secret meeting; for a day, a week; for forty years (the time-span of this class's formation), and experience is seen to do its work on consciousness. This is strange indeed, for Thompson (in one of the many contradictory statements about class structure and class consciousness that Sewell has noted) thought that if you stopped the machine (if you stopped time) there were no classes, only a flux of individuality and individual experiences. Class could only happen with and in history, he said.[17] (Perhaps he meant: in the writing of historians, in received or known histories; or perhaps he naturalised 'history' here as *time*.[18]) Anyway, what we should notice is that this time, or history, is a moment of *nowness*, that the historian watches, and in which he or she sees the agency of these people, as they process and understand what is happening to them.

In a wider frame, the historical account of the English industrial revolution has been naturalised as the inevitable way in which industrial capitalism does, and has done, the work of class formation, even in circumstances radically different from those that pertained in the British Isles from the early sixteenth century onwards, and in societies where industrialisation and social restructuring came much later and took a much shorter time. The historical prototype for all industrial revolutions was probably given its first modelling by Marx and Engels in the 1840s and 1850s. Since the 1960s and Thompson's revised blueprint of class formation, historians of the nineteenth century in particular have pursued the 'experience' of the European working class, brought into being by the processes of industrial capitalism. They have seen, for example, how 'the propertyless have always laid claim to . . . their own forms in which. . . . they [appropriated] various "colonizing" inroads into their lives (ranging from "education" to "hygiene")'.[19] Used to the paucity of direct documentation concerning the propertyless, we have become adept at using the reports of – Alf

---

[17] 'If we stop history at a given point, then there are no classes but simply a multitude of individuals with a multitude of experiences . . .' Thompson, *Making*, p. 11. See Sewell, 'How Classes Are Made', p. 52.

[18] The conventional distinction between 'the past and 'history', the past as the Everything of past times out of which, by means of narrative, the historian precipitates 'history', which is now taught to undergraduate historians was not available to, certainly not used by, Thompson in the 1960s.

[19] Alf Lüdtke (ed.), *The History of Everyday Life. Reconstructing Historical Experiences and Ways of Life*, trans. William Templar (Princeton, N.J.: Princeton University Press, 1995). 'Introduction', pp. 3–40; 17.

Lüdtke's examples – police, domestic missionaries and social investigators, converting their voices of disapproval, in order to find something like the people's 'form of living', and even how they reflected on it whilst living it. This technique could not work for Phoebe Beatson. Here we have a paradigmatic absence of direct documentation (I have written an entire book around this absence); and even were it found, a settlement or bastardy examination produced a required, or enforced, or at least highly formulaic narrative.[20] It might tell us a little more about *what happened* in November and December 1801, but could scarcely help reconstruct experience of it. John Murgatroyd's is the pen of the social, spiritual and cultural superior that records Phoebe's doings, but he never wrote of her with disapprobation: here, there is no voice of disapproval to invert.

Further techniques of inquiry into 'experience' have been developed in relation to the mode of production that made an industrial proletariat. Alf Lüdtke's *Eigensinn*, which is a kind of wilfulness, a self-affirmation, expresses itself in prankishness *on a shop-floor*, or in a factory: it is a way of reappropriating alienated social relations, of carving out a little space, a little place of your own, within the monolith of industrial capitalism.[21] It can be made available to the historian to work on. Robert Darnton's account of what went on in a Paris print-shop in the 1740s – prankishness run riot in a wholesale massacre of the master's cats – could be seen as following the lines of *Eigensinn*, though that was not at all Darnton's intention in writing 'The Great Cat Massacre'.[22] We can note, however, that this form of analysis seems to need an industrial (or proto-industrial) setting for its historians to see it in operation.

Historians of the European working class like Alf Lüdtke have taken seriously E. P. Thompson's teachings on what he sometimes called 'the discipline of context'.[23] Lüdtke urges us to devote ourselves to it, and to miniatures and micro-histories.[24] Often in the absence of direct testimony, it is, indeed, the only thing to do, as we have seen. But 'context' comes no more unmediated than 'experience' does: it is a thing made by its historians. 'Historians are always talking about "putting things in context,"' complain Keith Jenkins and Alan Munslow in *The Nature of History*. For them, it is no discipline at all. 'Context' is an epistemologically impossible thing: 'no "context" is ever exhaustive; you

[20] Carolyn Steedman, 'Enforced Narratives. Stories of Another Self', in Tess Cosslett, Celia Lury and Penny Summerfield (eds.), *Feminism and Autobiography. Texts, Theories, Methods* (London: Routledge, 2000), pp. 25–39.

[21] Lutz Niethammer, 'Zeroing in on Change. In Search of Popular Experience in the Industrial Province in the German Democratic Republic', in Lüdtke, *History of Everyday Life*, pp. 252–311.

[22] Robert Darnton, *The Great Cat Massacre and other Episodes in French Cultural History* (Harmondsworth: Penguin, 1985), pp. 75–104.

[23] Craig Calhoun, 'E. P. Thompson and the Discipline of Historical Context', *Social Research*, 61:2 (1994), pp. 223–44.

[24] Lüdtke, *History of Everyday Life*, pp. 3–40.

can always get another (arbitrary) set of circumstances . . .'[25] Edward Thompson would scarcely have approved my attention to Anglicanism as a context to Phoebe Beatson's life or as an attempt to explain her, though he would not – could not – have thought that it was an *arbitrary* attention. But he believed that the eighteenth-century church in England was so 'profoundly Erastian' that it was incapable of making a difference to plebeian lives, or to the histories have been or will come to be written about them.[26] This judgement depends on understanding the attitude of men and women like Phoebe Beatson and George Thorp as a felt and articulated resentment of the union of church and state, enacted every time they encountered a clerical magistrate, or heard the prayer for the preservation of the sovereign. And so they did, many of them. But that experience and that context is of a different order from what might have been deposited in a consciousness, imagination and language during a long and still relatively common education, which I have argued here provides some access to how (some of) these people understood their world and their place in it. The measure of its failure as a technique is that most of what I have told here concerns John Murgatroyd rather than Phoebe Beatson.

Advances in understanding 'experience' in recent years have centred not only on the industrial workplace, but on overt ideological systems in which workers struggled not only to realise themselves as workers, but also and at the same time, to find a place to be and to think as themselves (who were both workers and not-workers, at the same time). In Lutz Niethammer's German Democratic Republic and in Stephen Kotkin's study of the Soviet industrial complex of Magnitogorsk during the Stalinist era, people live through and attempt to make sense of the official interpretation of their being. Belief and non-belief in the Soviet system co-existed within the same individual, Kotkin concludes. The discrepancies between lived experience and revolutionary interpretation 'appear to have given rise to a dual reality: observational truth based on experience, and a higher revolutionary truth, based partly on experience but ultimately on theory'.[27] This may be a way of understanding the experiential relationship of someone like Phoebe Beatson to her ideological formation and experience, not by comparing eighteenth-century Anglicanism with Stalinism, but by allowing us to note the gaps and spaces in any ideological system that allow people to find their own thoughts on the difference between what *is*, and what is asserted *to be*. In the case of Anglican Christianity in the eighteenth century, this gap or space (the sign that hegemony, of its nature, can never be total) is perfectly noted in

---

[25] Keith Jenkins and Alun Munslow, *The Nature of History Reader* (London and New York: Routledge, 2004), p. 3.

[26] E. P. Thompson, 'The Patricians and the Plebs', in Thompson (ed.), *Customs in Common* (London: Perguin, 1993), p. 49.

[27] Stephen Kotkin, *Magnetic Mountain. Stalinism as a Civilization* (Berkeley, Los Angeles and London: University of California Press, 1995), pp. 184, 229.

Maureen Lawrence's recent play about Samuel Johnson's relationship with his black servant (and, in childhood at least, when he was passed on to Johnson by a friend, briefly his slave) Francis Barber.[28] The ghost of Dr Johnson visits Barber in the mad-ward of Lichfield Poor House, where the terrible pressures of Barber's own experience and his own story have driven him, and which all of Sam's care and love and foresight in providing for him (a kindness and a legacy to rival Murgatroyd's in regard to Phoebe Beatson) cannot obviate. Come, Frank, says Johnson's ghost, attempting to rally him to sanity and piety. We are all brothers in Christ. But, as Frank observes, we are not; not brothers and sisters in this fallen world, but rather, owner and slave, master and servant, employer and worker. These histories of loss, expropriation and subordination, a life spent buckling someone else's shoes, and cooking someone else's dinner, cannot be done away with; what Frank Barber brought to that moment in the Lichfield madhouse could not be undone.[29]

At least one contemporary thinker believed that domestic servants like Francis Barber and Phoebe Beatson were in the best position to develop at least an individual consciousness of class position, if not the full-blown class consciousness that Thompson understood to lie at the end of the historical process he described. William Godwin thought hard about servants (fictional and real), and was a severer critic than was even his wife, Mary Wollstonecraft, of polite parents' insulting anxieties about their domestics, their long-standing and nagging doubts about the 'degrees of intercourse which is to be allowed between children and servants'.[30] According to Godwin, parents would 'caution their offspring against the intercourse of menials and explicitly tell them that the company of servants is by no means a suitable relaxation for the children of a family'. This practice outraged him:

---

[28] Maureen Lawrence, *Resurrection* (prod. Bush Theatre London, 1996; Garrick Theatre Lichfield, 2005). For Francis Barber, see Peter Fryer, *Staying Power. The History of Black People in Britain* (London: Pluto, 1984), pp. 424–6; Aleyn Lyell Reade, *Johnsonian Gleanings. Part II. Francis Barber, the Doctor's Negro Servant* (London: privately printed, 1952), p. 15; and Hester Lynch Piozzi, *Anecdotes of the Late Samuel Johnson, LLD during the last Twenty Years of his Life* (Dublin: Moncrieffe, White, Byrne etc., 1786), p. 210.

[29] On the shoe-buckling, which Dr Johnson thought hard about, and we may presume so did Frank Barber, see Fryer, *Staying Power*, p. 425, quoting the *Gentleman's Magazine*, 63:2 (1793), p. 620: 'If Francis offered to buckle the shoe, &c. "No, Francis, time enough yet! When I can do it no longer, then you may."' He did not like Barber kneeling in front of him.

[30] See William Godwin, 'Of Servants', orig. pub. 1797, Essay IV, *The Enquirer. Reflections on Education, Manners and Literature. Political and Philosophical Writings of William Godwin, Volume 5, Educational and Literary Writings*, ed. Pamela Clemit (London: Pickering and Chatto, 1993), pp. 167–71. For Wollstonecraft's observations on parents' suspicion of servants, see Mary Wollstonecraft, *Lessons from the Posthumous Works of the Author of a Vindication of the Rights of Woman*, orig. pub 1798, in Janet Todd and Marilyn Butler (eds.), *The Collected Works of Mary Wollstonecraft* (London: Pickering London, 1989), vol. VI. For her earlier, more conventional position on this question, see *Thoughts on the Education of Daughters* (1788).

It is a lesson of the most insufferable insolence and magisterial aristocracy, that it is possible for language to convey. We teach them that they are themselves a precious species of creatures, that must not be touched too rudely . . . Come not near me! In the exuberance of our humanity perhaps, we inform our children, that these creatures are to be tenderly treated, that we neither scratch nor bite them, and that, poisonous and degraded as they are, we must rather soothe than aggravate their calamity. We may shake our heads in arrogant compassion of their lot; but we must think of them as the puppy-dog in the hall, who is not to be touched because he has got the mange. – This lesson of separation, mixing with the unformed notions of childhood, will almost necessarily produce the most injurious effects.[31]

He thought of the spatial hierarchies of modern houses, and the social hierarchies deposited in modern society by the historical process. The house was 'inhabited by two classes of being, or, more accurately speaking, by two sets of men drawn from two distinct stages of barbarism and refinement'.[32] He admires the airy apartments on the upper floors; and then, 'the fancy strikes me of viewing the servants' offices'. He descends by a narrow staircase (he will soon observe that whilst, so far, he has been describing the household arrangements of the rich, exactly the same topography of subordination is to be found in modest middle-class households; we should note that, in any case, he describes a household in which there are more than two servants who can gather together at least in their sleeping quarters, not a one-servant household like the Lingards one). And then Godwin creeps 'cautiously along passages . . . everywhere is gloom. The light of day never fully enters the apartments . . . there is something in the very air that feels musty and stagnant.' Entering a servant's room, he perceives

---

[31] Godwin, 'Of Servants', pp. 168–9.

[32] He used the century's social theory and cultural history here, a history of the 'rise' of modern (commercial and refined) society from the discarded husks of former modes of production: savagery, barbarism, pastoralism, agriculture. For conjectural history and the four- (or five-) stage model of the past, see Adam Smith, *Lectures on Jurisprudence. Glasgow Edition of the Works and Correspondence of Adam Smith*, ed. R. L. Meek, D. D. Raphael and P. G. Stein (Oxford: Clarendon Press, 1978), vol. V, pp. 76–8; 175–9. Adam Ferguson, *An Essay on the History of Civil Society*, orig. pub. 1767 (Edinburgh: Edinburgh University Press, 1966). John Millar, *The Origin of the Distinction of Ranks; or, An Inquiry into the Circumstances which give Rise to Influence and Authority in the Different Members of Society*, orig. pub. 1771, 3rd edn (London: J. Murray, 1779). See also J. G. A. Pocock, 'The Mobility of Property and the Rise of Eighteenth-century Sociology', in Anthony Parel and Thomas Flanagan (eds.), *Theories of Property. Aristotle to the Present* (Waterloo, Ontario: Wilfrid Laurier for the Calgary Institute for the Humanities, 1979). See Robert Wokler, 'Anthropology and Conjectural History in the Enlightenment', in Christopher Fox, Roy Porter and Robert Wokler (eds.), *Inventing Human Science. Eighteenth-century Domains* (Berkeley: University of California Press, 1995), pp. 31–52. The century's most famous conjectural history was Rousseau's: Jean-Jacques Rousseau, *A Discourse on Inequality*, orig. pub. 1755 (Harmondsworth: Penguin, 1984), pp. 118–37; Jean-Jacques Rousseau, *On the Origin of Language. Two Essays. Jean-Jacques Rousseau and Johann Gottfried Herder*, Rousseau orig. pub. 1781 (Chicago: University of Chicago Press, 1966), pp. 1–74. The point for Godwin was that in modern, polite, commercial society, you could still see the traces of earlier economic eras.

'a general air of slovenliness and negligence, that amply represents to [him] the depression and humiliated state of mind of its tenant'. What Godwin has seen is 'a monstrous association and union of wealth and poverty together'; it exercises him much, and the thought of a wealthy man maintaining a household inhabited by 'two different classes of being' enrages. He observes that 'if we were told of a man who appropriated a considerable portion of his house to the habitation of rats, and pole-cats, and serpents and wolves, we certainly should not applaud his taste or judgement' (169).

The servant's depression – of social being, and of mind and spirit – was palpable for Godwin; he brooded on how servants must either develop a consciousness of their position as subordinates, of that 'monstrous . . . union of wealth and poverty . . .', or – this was the more likely – introject their depression:

Servants . . . must either cherish a burning envy in their bosoms, an inextinguishable abhorrence against the injustice of society; or, guided by the hopelessness of their condition, they must blunt every finer feeling of the mind, and sit down in their obscure retreat, having for the constant habits of their reflections, slavery and contentment. They can scarcely expect to emerge from their depression. They must expect to spend the best years of their existence in a miserable dependence.[33]

For Godwin it was the obscene conjunction of great wealth and poverty that might produce the servant's consciousness of class difference. His household of depressed footmen beneath stairs was a substantial one. But advice manual writer Ann Taylor surmised that the same reaction would take place in any kind of household that employed a servant. Teenage girls who had 'passed their childhood in want and wretchedness' now wielding a broom in a modest, one-servant dwelling saw only '*riches* and suppose that any, and everything can be afforded', and that their master was 'a being of a different species . . .'[34]

Godwin was not the only metropolitan commentator of the 1790s to understand servants in this way, though he wrote from a different political position from the anonymous author of *Reflections on the Relative Situations of Master and Servant, Historically Considered . . .* of 1800.[35] These were troubling times, especially if you believed that half the footmen and postillions in London were French *émigrés* fomenting revolution among their brethren. 'They have patriotic meetings,' he wrote, sorry that he had to use this dignified phrase ('as I must call them') for he thought them nothing of the kind. 'They have . . . corresponding clubs . . . [and] were the daemons of Discord . . . to quit the Paris Pandemonium and cross the British Channel, the menial servants of this

[33] Godwin, 'Of Servants', p. 170.

[34] Ann Taylor, *Practical Hints to Young Females on the Duties of a Wife, a Mother and a Mistress of a Family* (London: Taylor and Hessey, 1815), pp. 36–44.

[35] Anon., *Reflections on the Relative Situations of Masters and Servants, Historically and Politically Considered; the Irregularities of Servants; the Employment of Foreigners; and the General Inconveniences Resulting from the Want of Regulations* (London: W. Miller, 1800).

country . . . would form no inconsiderable cohort in the armies of rebellion.'[36] He saw domestic servants in communication with each other and organised in meetings about seditious topics and dangerous ideas.[37] In his political imagination they were not the depressed, broodingly resentful, atomistic individuals of William Godwin, but rather, 'a large body of men' who could combine, 'actuated by the impulse of a common interest'.[38] Their depravity was of an old sort, for did they not know too much? They discussed their employing families at their meetings, committing in brotherhood Pamela's original sin, which was to make known outside it, what went on within a household. But it was the modern trade combination that was truly alarming: their benefit funds were not benefit funds at all, but were used to pay legal fees in cases against their employers.[39] In short, servants were a large *body* of men who could *combine*, 'actuated by the impulse of a common interest'. At this very moment (probably 1799) they were 'forming clubs of the most pernicious tendency'.[40] In the vastly complex productive relationship into which these men had entered voluntarily, both his and Godwin's depressed, alienated and resentful footmen possessed a consciousness of their position and of class relations. Neither commentator assumed that the footman's allegiance lay with his employer. Both had abandoned the fantasy (if they ever entertained it) that the servant was at one with the master.

'Modern commercial', 'modern refined' society had developed out of earlier stages of human history, defined by their dominant mode of production.[41] Footmen played a role in the active production of refinement and civilisation, as contemporaneously defined. Their household might stand at the crossroad of domesticity and the commercial polity. Handing the dish of beans round at table, even cleaning the knives and forks in the kitchen and whitewashing the necessary house, their contracted labour ordered, sweetened and refined the commercial, capitalist and cultural relations enacted round the dining table where clients and friends were entertained (and that the footman had earlier polished). We could make him fit into the great drama of class society if we used contemporary social theory and the understanding of political commentators like William Godwin in this way. But why should we bother, really? The history to which we are seeking entry for them is actually about their absence, their irreducible *not-thereness*. Thompson's account of class formation and class consciousness does, in fact, measure the presence of domestic servants on several occasions, noting that right through to the end of the nineteenth century

---

[36] Anon., *Reflections*, p. 13.

[37] For networking – perhaps organisation – among London servants, see A Gentleman of the Inner Temple, *Laws Concerning Masters and Servants* (London: His Majesty's Law Printer, 1785). He suggests the possibility of networks among black servants. See also, p. 15.

[38] Anon., *Reflections*, p. 4.   [39] Anon., *Reflections*, p. 14.   [40] Anon., *Reflections*, p. 5.

[41] For conjectural history used to explain the development of modern society, see note 32.

they comprised one of the largest occupational categories in the society, and that the majority of them were women.[42] But they play no role in the making of their class, for the very obvious reason that they are not *already in* the story that is being told, which is one about resistance to industrial capitalism, thought through and understood in relation to an industrial (or industrialising) mode of production.[43]

The great triumph of Thompson's telling of the making of a working class is that the wool combers and weavers who enact the drama in the Calder Valley and Wharfedale did what Thompson set out to show them doing: they were present, in body and in intelligence, at their own making. I have not done here what I believed it was my task to do: to *explain* why things fell out as they did, in Slaithwaite-cum-Lingards in the autumn of 1802. (Though I have shown Phoebe Beatson to be a proto-industrial worker as well as a domestic worker. She may be allowed to at least complicate the other histories we have of this time and place, in which servants must forever be a non-industrial, unradical, non-productive footnote.) I have also made Nelly Dean a historian of the West Riding, and I have made her (or Emily Brontë) a historian in a highly appropriate manner for the later eighteenth century, casting her (whichever her you choose) in the Herderian mode.[44] That is to say, reading *Wuthering Heights* with the historical protocols laid down by Johann Herder in mind, we can see that the explanation for things is that they are – or were – *as they are*; the explanation for them is that they are as they *must be*; events carry with them their own eventuality. They happen and pass when their own time has come. There is no answer to the persistent question of *Wuthering Heights* – who and what is Heathcliff? – except that he *is* in life, and *is* later in death, under the sod in Gimmerton Kirkyard. And I cannot explain what happened in this history – the one I have written – except by reference to those happenings, contained within themselves. I cannot make this story enter *The Making of the English Working Class*. Of course, I am elated to find that you can still do this, write like this, make events carry their own eventuality, after the passage of two centuries; that this narrative form is still available to me. (There is also the highly pertinent point to make, that no one will notice what I have done; apart from the eccentricity of using a novel of 1847 to tell a piece of eighteenth-century social history, and the true weirdness of my identification with Nelly Dean, who will notice that this is not just another social history of life, love, labour and religion in the West Riding of Yorkshire, 1786–1806?)

I may have a fantasy that I can simply by-pass the nineteenth century and all the forms of narrative explanation it devised, including formal, academic history writing; that I can use a form and model of time, event and written narrative that

---

[42] Thompson, *Making*, pp. 231, 259, 344.   [43] See above, chapter 4.

[44] For the model of causation in Johann Herder's history writing, see Hayden White, *Metahistory. The Historical Imagination in Nineteenth-century Europe* (Baltimore and London: The Johns Hopkins University Press, 1973), pp. 69–79.

belongs to the period I have investigated, the turn of the eighteenth century into the new. But I can't, of course; I am a social historian in the modern, twentieth-century mode, my allegiance (like E. P. Thompson's allegiance, and in W. H. Auden's view from the 1960s, the allegiance of the Muse of History herself) is to those who bred *their* horses, combed *their* wool, span *their* worsted thread, put down the peas and bean seeds in *their* kitchen garden; made *their* myths for them.[45]

Thompson's West Riding myth was not made at the time, by the people who are its subject, but rather, by their twentieth-century historians; it did not circulate like the creation stories translated, parsed and rehearsed in Murgatroyd's Slaithwaite schoolroom. He had no access to the modern, Thompsonian one; neither do I think he used the Hesiodian or the Ovidian myths to think through his own and Phoebe's life course, for the Titaness Phoebe is as much of a cipher and an enigma as is the West Riding one. But the West Riding Phoebe does actually do something to the myth, then and now, in this land of origins, beginnings, metamorphoses. For a start, she can show us another version of the labour theory of value that underpins the post-eighteenth-century accounts of this place we have been discussing. What she inscribes is the poetic version that has lain hidden beneath the formulations of John Locke, Adam Smith, Karl Marx and E. P. Thompson. Or perhaps, she merely tells us that poetry will be made out of the historical process and all our theorising about it. The things that Thompson tells of really happened: men and women lost much of the control they had exercised over the means of production; they pawned, sold, or burned for fuel the implements and machinery they had once owned; they were proletarianised, became a working class. Poetry tells of processes like these, quite as much as history does. In *The Poetics of Space*, Gaston Bachelard contemplates housework, though he does not call it that. He is concerned with the sudden, visceral sense that a reader of poetry has, of seeing or knowing something *for the first time*. For Bachelard the way in which quite ordinary objects are marked 'with the sign of "the first time"' by the writer is the highest form of poetic expression.[46] By reference to Rilke's *Fragments of an Intimate Diary*, he suggests that when objects are lit in this way *as for the first time*, they transmit a light to their surroundings. According to Bachelard, this intimate light is particularly manifest in things 'that are cherished', and he suggests that polishing, the giving of a bright appearance to things, is the best mark of cherishing:

Objects that are cherished in this way really are born of an intimate light, and they attain to a higher degree of reality than indifferent objects, or those that are defined by geometric reality. For they produce a new reality of being, and take their place not only in an order but in a community of order. . .[47]

---

[45] Auden, 'Makers of History', in *Homage to Clio*, pp. 30–1.
[46] Gaston Bachelard, *The Poetics of Space*, orig. pub. 1958 (Boston: Beacon Press, 1994), p. 27.
[47] Bachelard, *Poetics*, p. 68.

He does not propose the startling image of Rainer Maria Rilke with a duster in his hand, and quite effaces the servant who did, in fact, invest her labour and her labour power in his (and indeed, in Bachelard's) furniture and kickshaws. Neither does he relate whether or not in their wills, either man gave these anonymous women the things they had made their own by their mingling of their labour with them (walnut table, 'dressing box with five drawers', 'corner cupboard', 'Bookcase above stairs', 'little round table in common use'). But Phoebe got the things she had burnished, and mingled her labour with, and that she thus made enter into a community of order – into the world of goods and men.

We do not know what happened to her, to her new husband and little girl, in the far worse years to come. Her good health and the 'competent estate' that Thomas Nettleton said were the prerequisites for happiness may have seen them through the first decades of the new century. This West Riding myth should probably not leave her in Arcadia, which in poetic fantasy is irreducibly a *pastoral* paradise. Here in West Yorkshire, woollen and worsted had united land and loom to efface singing shepherds and purling rills in a new topography of industrialisation, long before this story begins. Emily Brontë put the servant Joseph into Elysium at the end of *Wuthering Heights*, a figurative realm that is more to our point. Elysium is at the ends of the earth; the Elysian Fields are where the gods convey those who are favoured by them, and whom they have exempted from death. Of course, Joseph's Elysian Fields were made out of paltry things, in the face of the much larger gains of property and capital made in the novel, and in these historical times: just a warm fire and a few pieces of toasted oatcake. No more than Phoebe Beatson's gains do these comforts obviate the larger drama of profit, accumulation and class, by which both servants, fictional and real, are bastardised. All of this story is only about getting by.

Nevertheless, *this* Phoebe is not banished, or left palely gleaming in the night sky: the West Riding Phoebe triumphs; she wins: a houseful of furniture, a fortune, a beautiful child, a respectable husband. Somewhere, from the other side of the hills, you may hear Joseph – who was there in the beginning and is here at the end – cackle, blithely ignoring, even now, that this really is Nelly's Version.[48]

---

[48] That is, it is the tale that Nelly Dean (really; really might have) told, not the development in stream-of-consciousness technique that Eva Figes's novel of the same title represents. Eva Figes, *Nelly's Version* (London: Secker and Warburg, 1977). However, some may be interested to note that the narrator who checks into a hotel and signs the register as 'Nelly Dean' *has lost her memory.*

Bibliography

ARCHIVAL DOCUMENTS

BIRMINGHAM CENTRAL LIBRARY, ARCHIVES DEPARTMENT,
BIRMINGHAM

MS 839/53, 'Diary of Julius Hardy (1786–1793) Button-Maker, of Birmingham.' Transcribed and annotated by A. M. Banks, April 1973.

BORTHWICK INSTITUTE OF HISTORICAL RESEARCH, UNIVERSITY
OF YORK, YORK

MBS 1807. Marriage Bonds, John Sykes, Golcar and Phebe Beatson, Halifax, Jan. 1807.
Will of the Reverend John Murgatroyd of Lingards, p.Almondbury, 1806.

BRITISH LIBRARY, LONDON

Add. Mss. 4260, 42598, 42599, 42599du, Brockman Papers, vols. XIII–XV. Three Justices' Diaries, kept by the Brockman Family of Beachborough, Newington, Kent.

DERBYSHIRE COUNTY RECORD OFFICE, MATLOCK

Q/SO 1/9, Quarter Sessions Records, Order Books, 1774–1780.
Parish Record Offices, Parish Records, M77 Vol. II, Ashover Parish Register.

DONCASTER METROPOLITAN BOROUGH COUNCIL
ARCHIVES, DONCASTER

DD.DC/H7/1/1, Davies-Cooke of Ouston. Mrs Mary Cooke, Copy Letter Book, 1763–1767.
AB6/2/17, 'Doncaster Window Duty 1789.'

EAST SUSSEX COUNTY RECORD OFFICE, LEWES

AMS 6191, Household Account Book of Thomas Cooper of New Place Farm in Guestling, 1788–1824.

LINCOLN'S INN LIBRARY, LONDON

Dampier Manuscripts, A. P. B, 19. Easter Term, 1778.

THE MANOR HOUSE, SLAITHWAITE

Dartmouth Estate Papers, I Rentals, 1803.
Dartmouth Estate Papers, Register, Survey and Rentals. 'Slaithwaite and Lingards, General Information.'

THE NATIONAL ARCHIVES (PUBLIC RECORD OFFICE), KEW

PRO, KB 16/18/1, Records of Orders Files, 17 Geo III, 1776–1777.
PRO, IR 70/1, 'Assessed Taxes and Inhabited Houses Duties. Judges Opinions, 1805–1830', vol. I, July 1805–1 May 1807.
PRO, IR 70/3, 'Assessed Taxes and Inhabited Houses Duties. Judges Opinions, 1805–1830', vol. III, February 1810–June 1830.
PRO, IR 83/131, 'Appeals before Commissioners, 1770–1785 . . . Hastings, Sussex'; 'Appeals heard determined at Meeting of the Commissioners held at the George Inn Battel the 21st day of January 1785.'
PRO, T 22/8, Letter Book, 1777–1805.

NOTTINGHAMSHIRE RECORD OFFICE, NOTTINGHAM

M8050, Notebooks of Sir Gervase Clifton JP, 1772–1812.

SHROPSHIRE RECORDS AND RESEARCH, SHREWSBURY

3365/374, 'An Assessment of the Township . . . for the Taxes on Male, Female Servants, Coaching Horses, Waggons, Carts, April 1786.'

SOMERSET COUNTRY RECORD OFFICE, TAUNTON

DD/FS 5–7, Bishops Lydeard Household and Farm Account Books, kept by Frances Hamilton.

WARWICKSHIRE COUNTY RECORD OFFICE, WARWICK

CR 1707/120, Heber-Percy of Guy's Cliffe, Diary of Bertie Greatheed.

WEST YORKSHIRE ARCHIVES SERVICE, BRADFORD DISTRICT, BRADFORD

HEATON B149, Account Book of Robert Heaton, giving names of servants employed and wages paid.

WEST YORKSHIRE ARCHIVE SERVICE, CALDERDALE DISTRICT, HALIFAX

D 531/11, Halifax Parish Records, St John's Parish Register.
Valuations 1735–1852, 155; Valuation 1797, 'General Regulation or Rate of Assessment of All the Lands and Houses within the Township of Halifax; Rev. John Murgatroyd, Weathercock Fold'; Folio 6.

WEST YORKSHIRE ARCHIVE SERVICE, KIRKLEES DISTRICT, HUDDERSFIELD

KC242/1–7, Reverend John Murgatroyd, Diaries, KC242/1 (1781–2, 1786, 1788, 1789, 1790, 1791); KC242/2 (1794); KC242/3 (1796); KC242/4 (1797); KC242/5 (1800); KC242/6 (1802); KC242/7 (1804).
KC242/8, Reverend John Murgatroyd, Notebook, 'The Qualifications of a Minister of Christ', nd.
KC249/9, Reverend John Murgatroyd, Notebook, 'Ask, Read, Retain, Teach', Notebook containing miscellaneous observations.

WEST YORKSHIRE ARCHIVE SERVICE, LEEDS DISTRICT, LEEDS

Radcliffe MSS 50, 'Survey of Sir John Radcliffe's Estate and Linthwaite and Golcar, made by Joshua Biran, 1786.'
Radcliffe MSS 309 ©/12, 'Names of the Acting Magistrates and Principal Officers within the West Riding of County of Yorkshire.'

WEST YORKSHIRE ARCHIVE SERVICE, WAKEFIELD DISTRICT, WAKEFIELD

D120/2, Slaithwaite Parish Records, Slaithwaite Chapel, Baptism and Burials, 1755–1812.
QD 552, Quarter Sessions Records, 1805, 'The Opinion of G. B. Holroyd, Grays Inn, on Bastardy Cases.'

UNIVERSITY OF YORK, YORK

082.2 MUR, John Murgatroyd, 'Authors Useful to be Read at School', Notebook, 1745–1802, unpaginated; Special Collections, Raymond Burton Library, Slaithwaite Parish Collection.
082.2 MUR, John Murgatroyd, 'A Book of Records'; Special Collections, Raymond Burton Library, Slaithwaite Parish Collection.
082.2 MUR, John Murgatroyd, 'A Cornucopia: or Collection of weighty Extracts transcribed out of the scarcest, most necessary & best chosen Books &c according to this proper Maxim, that every Man shou'd take down in Writing what He learns for fear of forgetting any useful Circumstance. By John Murgatroyd, Master of Slaithwaite School. Anno Domini 1742', quarto Notebook, nd, unpaginated; Special Collections, Raymond Burton Library, Slaithwaite Parish Collection.

GOVERNMENT REPORTS, PARLIAMENTARY PAPERS AND OTHER REPORTS OF PARLIAMENTARY PROCEEDINGS

Parliamentary History of England.
Hansard's Parliamentary History.
Minutes of Evidence taken before the Commissioners, to whom the Bill, respecting the Laws relating to the Woollen Trade, is committed, Parliamentary Papers, 1803 III (Part 3).

FICTION, POETRY AND PLAYS

Anon., *An Essay on Halifax* (Halifax: P. Darby, 1761).

Anon., *The Widow of Kent; or, the History of Mrs Rowley. A Novel in Two Volumes*, 2 vols. (London: F. Noble, 1788).

Armstrong, Thomas, *The Crowthers of Bankdean* (London: Collins, 1941).

Auden, W. H., *Homage to Clio* (London: Faber, 1960).

Bentley, Phyllis, *Inheritance* (London: Gollancz, 1932).

Brontë, Charlotte, *Jane Eyre*, orig. pub. 1847 (Harmondsworth: Penguin, 1966).

Brontë, Emily, *Wuthering Heights*, orig. pub. 1847 (Harmondsworth: Penguin, 1965).

Bunyan, John, *A Book for Boys and Girls, or, Temporal Things Spiritualised* (London: R. Tookey, 1701).

Duck, Stephen and Mary Collier, *Stephen Duck, 'The Thresher's Labour', Mary Collier, 'The Woman's Labour', Two Eighteenth Century Poems*, ed. E. P. Thompson and Marian Sugden (London: Merlin Press, 1989).

Eliot, George, *Adam Bede* (Edinburgh and London: Blackwood, 1859).

  Middlemarch, orig. pub. 1871–2 (Harmondsworth: Penguin, 1965).

Fielding, Henry, *The History of Tom Jones A Foundling*, orig. pub. 1749 (Harmondsworth: Penguin, 1985).

Figes, Eva, *Nelly's Version* (London: Secker and Warburg, 1977).

Hunt, Ebenezer, *The Rush-Bearing: A Poem. With a Probable Account of the Rise of Wakes* (Huddersfield: Joseph Brook, 1784).

Kilner, Dorothy, *Life and Perambulations of a Mouse* (London: John Marshall, 1783).

  Life and Perambulations of a Mouse, 2nd edn (London: John Marshall, 1787).

Lawrence, Maureen, *Resurrection* (prod. Bush Theatre London, 1996; Garrick Theatre Lichfield, 2005).

Le Sage, Alain René, *The History and Adventures of Gil Blas of Santillane*, orig. pub. 1716 (New York: Garland, 1972).

Márquez, Gabriel García, *The General in His Labyrinth*, orig. pub. 1990 (London: Jonathan Cape, 1991).

Miller, Joseph, *A Choice Collection of Family Prayers for every Day of the Week. To which are added a few Divine Poems by the Collector, Jos. Miller, Schoolmaster, Halifax* (Halifax: P. Darby for the author, 1760).

Ovid, *Ovid's Metamorphoses in English by George Sandys* (London: X. Tomlines, 1664).

  Ovid's Metamorphoses, in fifteen books, with the arguments and notes of John Minellius translated into English. To which is marginally added, a prose version, . . . For the use of schools. By Nathan Bailey (London: J. Rivington and Sons; G. Keith; T. Lowndes; T. Longman; W. Strahan, etc., 1778).

  Ovid, Metamorphoses. A New Verse Translation, trans. David Raeburn (London: Penguin, 2004).

Reed, J., *The Register-Office; A Farce in Two Acts. Acted at the Theatre Royal in Drury Lane* (Dublin: H. Saunders, 1761).

Richardson, Samuel, *Pamela, or, Virtue Rewarded*, orig. pub. 1740 (Harmondsworth: Penguin, 1986).

Thomson, Katherine, *Constance. A Novel. In Three Volumes* (London: Richard Bentley, 1833).

PRIMARY TRACTS, TREATISES AND OTHER
PUBLICATIONS, PRE-1900

Adam, Thomas, *Practical Lectures on the Church Catechism* (London: C. Hitch and L. Hawes, 1755).

Adams, Samuel and Sarah, *The Complete Servant; Being a Practical Guide to the Peculiar Duties and Business of all Descriptions of Servants from the Housekeeper to the Servant of All-Work, and from the Land Steward to the Footboy; with Useful Receipts and Tables* (London: Knight and Lacey, 1825).

Addison, Joseph, 'No. 565, Friday July 9, 1714', *Spectator*, ed. Donald F. Bond (Oxford: Clarendon Press, 1965), vol. IV, pp. 529–33.

Aikin, John, *A Description of the Country from Thirty to Forty Miles Around Manchester*, orig. pub. 1795 (Newton Abbot: David and Charles, 1968).

Alexander, William, *The History of Women, from the Earliest Antiquity, to the Present Time; giving some Account of almost every interesting Particular concerning that Sex, among all Nations, ancient and modern*, 2 vols. (London: Strahan and Cadell, 1779).

Anon., *Bishop Sherlock's Arguments against a Repeal of the Test and Corporations Acts; wherein most of the Pleas advanced in a Paper now circulating styled The Case of the Protestant Dissenters etc are discussed* (London: privately printed, 1787).

Anon., *A Closet for Ladies and Gentlewomen. Or, the Art of preserving, conserving, and candying. With the manner how to make diverse kindes of sirups, and all kinde of banquetting stuffs. Also diverse soveraign medicines and salves for sundry diseases* (London: R. H., 1656).

Anon., *Domestic Management, or the Art of Conducting a Family* (London: H. D. Symonds at the Literary Press, 1800).

Anon., *A Familiar Summary of the Laws respecting Masters and Servants* (London: Henry Washbourne, 1831).

Anon., *Hints to Masters and Mistresses, Respecting Female Servants* (London: Darnton and Harvey, 1800).

Anon., *The Laws Relating to Master and Servant: With Brief Notes and Explanations, to render them easy and intelligible to the meanest Capacity* (London: Henry Lintot, 1755).

Anon., *A Present for Servants, from their Ministers, Masters, or other Friends*, 10th edn (London: J. F. and C. Rivington for the SPCK, 1787).

Anon., *Reflections on the Relative Situations of Master and Servant, Historically Considered* (London: W. Miller, 1800).

Anon., *The Servant's Calling, With Some Advice to the Apprentice* (London: G. Strahan, 1725).

B. J., *The Footman's Looking Glass: or, Proposals to the Livery Servants of London and Westminster etc. for Bettering their Situations in Life, and securing their Credit in the World. To which is added, An Humble Representation to Masters and Mistresses. By J. B. a Brother of the Cloath* (London: M. Cooper, 1747).

Bailey, Nathan, *English and Latin Exercises for School-Boys: Comprising the Rules of Syntax, with Explanations, and other necessary Observations on each Rule*, 11th edn (London: R. Ware, 1744).

Bamford, Samuel, *Early Days* (London: Simpkin and Marshall, 1849).

    Passages in the Life of a Radical, orig. pub. 1844 (London: McGibbon, Kee, 1967).

Bentley, John, *Halifax and Its Gibbet-law. Placed in a True Light. Together with a Description of the Town, the Nature of the Soil, the Temper and Disposition of the People* (Halifax: P. Darby for the author, 1761).

    The History of the Town and Parish of Halifax, containing a Description of the Town, the Nature of the Soil &c &c. An Account of the Gentry and Other Eminent Persons born in the said Town . . . Also the Antient Customs and Modern Improvements . . . (Halifax: E. Jacob, 1789).

Beattie, James, *The Theory of Language. In Two Parts. Of the Origin and General Nature of Speech. . . .* (Edinburgh: Strahan, Cadell and Creech, 1788).

Beveridge, William, *Private Thoughts in Two Parts Complete. Part I Upon Religion . . . Part II Upon a Christian Life*, 17th edn (London: G. Risk, 1753).

    The Works of the Right Reverend Father in God, Dr William Beveridge, . . . Containining [sic] all his Sermons, as well those publishd by Himself, as those since his Death, 2nd edn, 2 vols. (London: William Innys, 1729).

Bird, James Barry, *The Laws Respecting Masters and Servants*, 3rd edn (London: W. Clarke, 1799).

Blackstone, William, *Commentaries on the Laws of England. In Four Books*, orig. pub. 1765, 6th edn (Dublin: Company of Booksellers, 1775).

Bolton, James, *A History of Fungusses, growing about Halifax . . .*, 4 vols. (Huddersfield: J. Brook, 1788–91).

Buchan, William, *Domestic Medicine, or, a Treatise on the Prevention and Cure of Disease by Regime and Simple Medicine* (London: W. Strahan, T. Cadell, 1772).

Burchill, Joseph, *Arrangement and Digest of the Law in Cases Adjudged in the King's Bench and Common Pleas from the Year 1756 to 1794, inclusive* (London: J. Jones, 1796).

Burn, Richard, *Ecclesiastical Law*, 6th edn, 4 vols. (London: T. Cadell and W. Davies, 1799).

    Ecclesiastical Law. Corrected by Robert Philip Tyrwhitt, 8th edn, 4 vols. (London: A. Strahan, etc., 1824).

    The History of the Poor Laws: With Observations (London: H. Woodfall and N. Strahan, 1764).

    The Justice of the Peace and Parish Officer, 15th edn, 4 vols. (London: T. Cadell, 1785).

    The Justice of the Peace and Parish Officer. Continued to the Present Time by John Burn, Esq. his Son, 17th edn, 4 vols. (London: A. Strahan and W. Woodfall, 1793).

Caldecott, Thomas, *Reports of Cases Relative to the Duty and Office of a Justice of the Peace, from Michaelmas Term 1776, inclusive, to Trinity Term 1785, inclusive* (London: His Majesty's Law Printers for P. Uriel, 1785).

Challoner, Richard, *The Young Gentleman Instructed in the Grounds of the Christian Religion. In Three Dialogues between a Young Gentleman and his Tutor* (London: T. Meighan, 1755).

Chambers, E. *Cyclopaedia: or, a Universal Dictionary of Arts and Sciences . . . with the Supplement and Modern Improvements Incorporated in One Alphabet, by Abraham Rees* (London: J. F.& C. Rivington, 1778).

Clare, Martin, *Youth's Introduction to Trade and Business*, 18th edn (London: G. Keith, 1769).

Clarke, John, *A Compendius History of Rome by L. Florus with an English Translation*, 6th edn (London: Hawes, Clarke and Collins, 1763).

Clarke, John, *Corderii Colloquior mu Centuria Selecta, or, a Century of Cordery's Colloquies*, 15th edn (London: W. Smith, 1773).

Corderii Colloquiorum. Centura Selecta. A select Century of Corderius's Colloquies; with an English Translation, as Literal as Possible; designed for the Use of Beginners in the Latin Tongue. A New Edition. Corrected (Huddersfield: Brook and Lancashire, 1798).

Dissertation upon the Usefulness of Translations of Classick Authors, both literal and free, for the easy and expeditious Attainment of the Latin Tongue, being an Extract from the Essay upon Education (London: privately printed, 1734).

Erasmi Colloquia Selecta: or, the Select Colloquies of Erasmus, 22nd edn (London: J. F. C. Rivington, 1789).

An Essay upon the Education of Youth in Grammar-Schools, 3rd edn (London: Charles Hitch, 1740).

Cocker, Edward, *Cocker's Arithmetic. Being a plain and familiar Method, suitable to the meanest Capacity, for the full Understanding of that incomparable Art* (Edinburgh: Walter Ruddiman, 1757).

Collinson, Burton & Co., *The West Riding Worsted Directory containing the History of the Worsted Trade* (Bradford: Collinson, Burton, 1851).

Colquhoun, Patrick, *A Treatise on Indigence; Exhibiting a General View of the National Resource for Productive Labour . . .* (London: J. Hatchard, 1806).

Commissioners of Excise, *Abstract of Cases and Decisions on Appeals Relating to the Tax on Servants* (London: Mount and Page for T. Longman and T. Cadell, 1781).

Const, Francis, *Decisions of the Court of the King's Bench, Upon the Laws Relating to the Poor, Originally Published by Edmund Bott Esq. of the Inner Temple, Barrister at Law. Revised . . . by Francis Const Esq. of the Middle Temple*, 3rd edn, 2 vols. (London: Whieldon and Butterworth, 1793).

Defoe, Daniel, *A Tour thro' the whole Island of Great Britain*, orig. pub. 1742 (London: Dent, 1928).

Disney, Alexander, *Reasons for Methodism, briefly Stated, in three Letters to a Friend* (Halifax: J. Nicholson, 1793).

Doddridge, Peter, *Sermons on the Education of Children. Preached at Northampton. With a Recommendatory Preface by the Reverend Mr David Stone*, 3rd edn (London: M. Fenner, 1743).

Edwards, Jonathan, *Some remarkable Narratives. . . .* (Huddersfield: J. Brook, 1791).

A Treatise on Religious Affections (Boston: S. Kneeland, 1746).

Farnaby, Thomas, *Index Rhetoricus et Oratorius. Scholis, & institutioni Aeatis accomodatus* (London: G. Conyers and J. Clarke, 1728).

Ferguson, Adam, *An Essay on the History of Civil Society*, orig. pub. 1767 (Edinburgh: Edinburgh University Press, 1966).

Fisher, Ann, *A New Grammar, with Exercises of Bad English: or, an easy Guide to Speaking and writing the English Language Properly*, 4th edn (Newcastle upon Tyne: I. Thompson, 1754).

Fisher, George (Accomptant), *The Instructor, or Young Man's Best Companion . . . to which is added The Family's Best Companion . . . and a Complete Treatise of Farriery*, 13th edn (London: S. Birt, 1755).

Fleetwood, William, *The Relative Duties of Parents and Children, Husbands and Wives, Masters and Servants. Considered in Sixteen Practical Discourses: with Three Sermons upon the Case of Self-Murder*, 3rd edn (London: E. Bell, etc., 1737).

Florus, Lucius Annaeus, *Epitome Rerum Romarum. Lucius Floruss his Epitome of Roman History . . . made into English from the best editions and corrections of learned men. Illustrated with CXXVI cuts . . .* (London: John Nicholson, 1714).

Fogg, Peter Walkden, *Elementa anglicana; or, the Principles of English Grammar Displayed and Exemplified . . .* (Stockport: J. Clarke, 1796).

de Fontenelle, Bernard Le Bovier, *De l'origine des fables*, orig. pub. 1724 (Paris: Felix Alcan, 1932).

Forbes, Henry, *Rise, Progress and Present State of the Worsted Manufacture of England. Lectures on the Result of the Exhibition delivered before the Society of Arts, Manufactures and Commerce. Lecture XXI* (London: David Bogue, 1852).

Fuller, Thomas, *Good Thoughts in Bad Times: Together with Bad Thoughts in Good Times* (London: John Williams, 1680).

Gardiner, William, *Music and Friends: or, Pleasant Recollections of a Dilettante*, 3 vols. (London: privately printed, 1838).

Gentleman of the Inner Temple, *Law Concerning Master and Servants, viz Clerks to Attornies and Solicitors . . . Apprentices . . . Menial Servants . . . Labourers, Journeymen, Artificers, Handicraftmen and other Workmen* (London: His Majesty's Law Printer, 1785).

Gibbon, Edward, *The Decline and Fall of the Roman Empire*, vol. I, orig. pub. 1776 (Chicago and London: Encyclopaedia Britannica, 1990).

Gisborne, Thomas, *An Inquiry into the Duties of Men in the Higher and Middle Classes of Society in Great Britain, Resulting from their Respective Stations, Professions and Employments*, 2nd edn, 2 vols. (London: B. and J. White, 1795).

Godwin, William, 'Of Servants', orig. pub. 1797, Essay IV, *The Enquirer. Reflections on Education, Manners and Literature. Political and Philosophical Writings of William Godwin. Volume V, Educational and Literary Writings*, ed. Pamela Clemit (London: Pickering and Chatto, 1993).

Greenwood, James, *The London Vocabulary. English and Latin put into a new Method, proper to acquaint the Learner with Things, as well as Pure Latin Words. Adorned with Twenty-six Pictures*, 11th edn (London: C. Hitch, 1749).

Haller, Albrecht von, *Letters from Baron Haller to his Daughter on the Truths of the Christian Religion. Translated from the German* (London: J. Murray, 1780).

Hanway, Jonas, *Virtue in Humble Life: containing Reflections on the Reciprocal Duties of the Wealthy and the Indigent, the Master and the Servant . . .*, 2 vols. (London: Dodley Brotherton and Sewell, 1774).

Henry, Matthew, *The Beauties of Henry. A Selection of the most striking Passages in the Exposition of that celebrated Commentator. To which is prefixed a brief Account of the Life . . . of the Author, by John Geard*, 3 vols. (London: privately printed, 1793–1803).

Hesiod, *The Works of Hesiod translated from the Greek. By Mr Cooke*, 2 vols. (London: T. Green, 1728).

Holliday, John, *The Life of William Late Earl of Mansfield* (London: P. Elmly and D. Bremner, 1797).

The Holy Bible Abridged, or the History of the Old and New System. Illustrated with Notes, and adorned with Cuts. For the Use of Children (London: T. Carnan, 1782).

Holyoake, George, *Practical Grammar*, orig. pub. 1844 (London: Book Store, 1870), pp. 7–8.

Hoole, Charles, *The Common Accidence Explained by Short Questions and Answers. According to the very Words of the Book* (London: A. Armstrong, 1697).

Hulbert, Charles Augustus, *Annals of the Church in Slaithwaite (near Huddersfield) West Riding of Yorkshire from 1793–1864, in Five Lectures* (London: Longman, 1864).

Huntingford, J., *An Account of the Proceedings, Intentions, Rules, and Orders of the Society for the Encouragement of Agriculture and Industry, instituted at Odiham in Hampshire . . .* (London: Frys and Couchman, 1785).

The Laws of Masters and Servants Considered (London: privately printed, 1792).

James, John, *History of the Worsted Manufacture in England*, orig. pub. 1857 (London: Frank Cass, 1968).

Jones, Charles, *The Story of Charles Jones, the Footman. Written by Himself* (London: J. Marshall, 1796).

Kilner, Dorothy, *A Clear and Concise Account of the Origin and Design of Christianity Intended as a second Part to the Work entitled 'The First Principles of Religion and the Existence of a Deity, explained in a Series of Dialogues adapted to the capacity of the Infant Mind'*, 2 vols. (London: John Marshall, 1783).

Knox, Hugh, *The Moral and Religious Miscellany, or Sixty-one aphoretical Essays on the Christian Doctrines and Virtues* (Hertford: privately printed, 1790).

Knox, Vicesimus, *Essays, Moral and Literary*, 14th edn, 2 vols. (privately printed: London, 1800).

Leigh, Edward, *Critica Sacra: or Philologicall and Theologicall Observations upon all the Greek Words of the New Testament in Order alphabeticall, etc.* (London: privately printed, 1646).

Lewis, John, *The Church Catechism Explained, By Way of Question and Answer; and Confirmed by Scriptural Proofs*, 13th edn (London: John Rivington, 1766).

Lily, William, *The Royal Grammar Reformed . . . for the better Understanding of the English and the more speedy Attainment of the Latin Tongue* (London: A. and J. Churchill, 1695).

Locke, John *Two Treatises of Government*, orig. pub. 1689 (London: Dent, 1993).

Locke, Richard, *A Miscellany of Mathematicks, in two parts* (London: Innys and Manby, 1736).

Lowe, Solomon, *Arithmetic in Two Parts, containing I. A System of the Art in memorial Verses . . . II. A Collection of Excercise* (London: James Hodges, 1749).

Lucas, Richard, *The Duty of Servants. Containing I Their Preparation for, and Choice of Service. II Their Duty in Service*, 3rd edn (London: William Ineys, 1710).

March, R. *A Treatise on Wool, Worsted, Cotton, and Thread, describing their Nature, Properties and Qualities* (London: privately printed, 1779).

Marx, Karl, *Capital I*, orig. pub. 1867 (Harmondsworth: Penguin, 1976).

'Wage Labour and Capital', *Neue Rheinische Zeitung*, 5–8 (Apr. 1849).

Millar, John, *The Origin of the Distinction of Ranks; or, An Inquiry into the Circum-stances which give Rise to Influence and Authority in the Different Members of Society*, orig. pub. 1771, 3rd edn (London: J. Murray, 1779).

Morehouse, Henry James, *Extracts from the Diary of the Rev. Robert Meeke . . . Also a Continuation of the History of Slaithwaite Free School and an Account of the Educational Establishments in Slaithwaite-cum-Lingards, by the Rev. Charles Augustus Hulbert* (Huddersfield: *Daily Chronicle* Steam Press; London: Bohn, 1874).

Village Gleanings, or Notes and Jottings from the Manuscripts of the Rev. John Murgatroyd, Master of the Free School of Slaithwaite . . . Including some Account of his distinguished Scholar, James Horsfall, Born at Slaithwaite, the Son of the Village Blacksmith (Huddersfield: Parkin, 1886).

Murray, James, *An Impartial History of the War in America; from its first Commencement to the present Times*, 2 vols. (Newcastle: T. Robson, 1778).

Murrell, Henry, 'On a New Washing Machine', *Letters and Papers on Agriculture*, vol. V (Bath: Bath and West of England Society, 1793).

Nettleton, Thomas, *An Account of Inoculating the Small-pox: in a Letter to Dr William Whitaker* (London: J. Batley, 1722).

Resp. Desputatio de Inflammatione. Praes. H. A. Roell (Trajecti ad Rhenum, 1706).

Some Thoughts Concerning Virtue and Happiness, in a Letter to a Clergyman (London: Jeremiah Batley, 1729).

A Treatise on Virtue and Happiness, 2nd edn (London: J. Batley and J. Wood, 1736).

Newcome, Peter, *A Catechetical Course of Sermons for the Whole Year. Being an Expla-nation of the Church Catechism. In Fifty Two distinct Discourses. In two Volumes* (London: J. R., 1702).

Ogden, Samuel, *Sermons on the Efficacy of Prayers and Intercession* (Cambridge: pri-vately printed, 1770).

Owen, Henry, *Directions to Young Students in Divinity, with regard to Those Attainments which are necessary to Qualify them for Holy Orders*, 2nd edn (London: privately printed, 1773).

Parkes, Mrs William, *Domestic Duties; or Instructions to Young Married Ladies on the Management of their Households, and the Regulation of their Conduct in the Various Relations and Duties of Married Life* (London: Longman, 1825).

Parkyns, Thomas, *A Method Proposed, for the Recording of Servants in Husbandry, Arts, Mysteries, & etc. Offer'd by Sir Thomas Parkyns, Bart., One of His Majesty's Justices of the Peace for the Counties of Nottingham and Leicester* (London: pri-vately printed, 1724).

Particular Baptist Church, Yorkshire and Lancashire Association, *Christian Communion. The Ministers of the Denomination of Particular Baptists, assembled in Association at Halifax, on the 30th and 31st of May, 1798, send Christian salutation . . .* (Halifax: privately printed, 1798).

The Nature and Importance of Repentance. The Ministers of the Denomination of Particular Baptists, assembled in Association at Hebden-Bridge, near Halifax, the eleventh and twelfth of June, 1794, send Christian Salutation to the several Churches they represent (Halifax: privately printed, 1794).

Pashley, Robert, *Pauperism and Poor Laws* (London: Longman, Brown, Green and Longman, 1852).

Persius, *Auli Persii Flacci satyrae sex. Cum posthumis commentariis Joannis Bond* (London: Nathaniel Butteriij, 1614).

Auli Persii Flacci satyrae sex. Cum posthumis commentariis Joannis Bond, quibis recens accessit index verborum, 2nd edn (Dublin: William M'Kensie, 1787).

Philangathus, *Practical Improvement of the Divinity and Atonement of Jesus, attempted in Verse; humbly offered as a Supplement to the Tracts lately published* (Halifax: E. Jacob, 1772).

Piozzi, Hester Lynch, *Anecdotes of the Late Samuel Johnson, LLD during the last Twenty Years of his Life* (Dublin: Moncrieffe, White, Byrne etc., 1786).

Pluché, Abbé, *Histoire du ciel considéré selon les idées des poètes, des philosophes et de Moyse*, 2 vols. (Paris: La Veuve Estienne, 1739).

The History of the Heavens, considered according to the Notions of the Poets and Philosophers, compared with the Doctrines of Moses, trans. J. B. de Freval, 2 vols. (London: J. Osborn, 1740).

Potter, R., *Observations on the Poor Laws, on the Present State of the Poor, and on Houses of Industry* (London: J. Wilkie, 1775).

Richards, Reverend Mr, *Hints for Religious Conversation with the Afflicted in Mind, Body or Estate, and with such as stand in need of Spiritual Assistance* (London: Williams and Smith, 1807).

Rider, Cardanus, *The Court and City Register, or Gentleman's Complete Annual Calendar. Rider's British Merlin* (London: J. Joliffe, 1775).

Rousseau, Jean-Jacques, *A Discourse on Inequality*, orig. pub. 1755 (Harmondsworth: Penguin, 1984).

On the Origin of Language. Two Essays. Jean-Jacques Rousseau and Johann Gottfried Herder (Chicago: University of Chicago Press, 1966).

Ruggles, Thomas, *The History of the Poor; their Rights, Duties, and the Laws respecting Them*, 2 vols. (London: J. Deighton, 1793).

Saxton, John, *The Merchant's Companion, and tradesman's vade mecum: or, Practical Arithmetick, both vulgar and decimal, . . . Together with an appendix for those who are advanced in accompts, . . . The whole necessary for all men of business, teachers of accompts, and their scholars* (Manchester: R. Whitworth, 1737).

Smee, John, *A Complete Collection of Abstracts of Acts of Parliament and Cases with Opinions sought of the Judges upon the following Taxes, viz, upon Houses, Windows, Servants . . .*, 2 vols. (London: J. Butterworth, 1797).

Smith, Adam, *Lectures on Jurisprudence. Glasgow Edition of the Works and Correspondence of Adam Smith*, ed. R. L. Meek, D. D. Raphael and P. G. Stein (Oxford: Clarendon Press, 1978).

Smith, Adam, *The Wealth of Nations. Books I–III*, orig. pub. 1776 (London: Penguin, 1986).

Smith, John, *The Mystery of Rhetorick Unveiled* (London: George Eversden, 1693).

Society for the Promotion of Industry, *An Account of the Origin, Proceedings, and Intentions of the Society . . . in the Southern Districts of the Parts of Lindsey in the Country of Lincoln*, 3rd edn (London: R. Sheardown, 1791).

Sprat, Thomas, *A Discourse made by the Lord Bishop of Rochester to the Clergy of his Diocese on the Occasion of his Visitation in the year 1695; published at their request* (London: Edward Jones, 1696).

Stirling, John, *Phaedri Fabulae: or, Phaedrus's Fables with . . . Improvements . . . in a Method entirely new*, 9th edn (London: J. Rivington, 1771).

Stonhouse, James, *The Most Important Truths and Duties of Christianity. Designed for those in the lower Stations of Life. Particularly for the Instruction of Those who cannot read* (London: J. F. & C. Rivington, 1796).

Prayers for the Use of Private Persons, Families, Children and Servants, 14th edn (London: J. F. & C. Rivington, 1800).

The Religious Instruction of Children Recommended (London: J. F. C. Rivington, 1791).

Stretch, L. M., *The Beauties of History, or, Pictures of Virtue and Vice*, 5th edn (Springfield: privately printed, 1794).

Swift, Jonathan, *Polite Conversation, consisting of smart, witty, droll, and whimsical Sayings collected for his Amusement, and made into a regular Dialogue* (London: Joseph Wenman, 1783).

Sykes, D. F. E., *The History of the Colne Valley* (Slaithwaite: F. Walker, 1896).

Huddersfield and its Vicinity (Huddersfield: Advertiser Press, 1898).

Taylor, Ann, *Practical Hints to Young Females on the Duties of a Wife, a Mother and a Mistress of a Family* (London: Taylor and Hessey, 1815).

Taylor, Ann, *The Present of a Mother for a Young Servant: Consisting of Friendly Advice and Real Histories*, 2nd edn (London: Taylor and Hessey, 1816).

Taylor, John, *Elements of the Civil Law* (Cambridge: privately printed, 1767).

Tillotson, John, *Six Sermons. I. Stedfastness in religion. II. Family-religion. III. IV. V. Education of children. VI. The advantages of an early piety* (London: B. Aylmer, 1694).

Tomlins, T. E., *The Law-Dictionary, Explaining the Rise, Progress and Present State of the English Law . . . originally compiled by Giles Jacob*, 2 vols. (London: Strahan, 1797).

Trimmer, Sarah, *The Servant's Friend, an Exemplary Tale; Designed to Enforce the Religious Instructions given at Sunday and other Charity Schools, by Pointing Out the Practical Application of Them in a State of Servitude*, 2nd edn (London: T. Longman, 1787).

Trusler, John, *Domestic Management, or the Art of Conducting a Family* (London: J. Souter, 1819).

Memoirs of the Life of the Rev. John Trusler. With his Opinions on a Variety of Interesting Subjects and his Remarks through a long Life, on Men and Manners. Written by Himself. Replete with Humorous, Useful and Entertaining Anecdote. Part I (Bath: John Brown, 1806).

Venn, Henry, *The Complete Duty of Man; or a system of doctrinal and practical Christianity. To which are added Forms of Prayer* (London: privately printed, 1763).

(ed.), *The Life and a Selection from the Letters of the late Henry Venn, MA*, 4th edn (London: John Hatchard, 1836).

Virgil, *Opera. Variorum autorum annotationibus illustrata* (London: J. M. for the Society of Stationers, 1664).

Waldo, Peter, *An Essay on the Holy Sacrament* (London: J. F. and C. Rivington, 1821).

Walker, Ann, *A Complete Guide for a Servant Maid; or the Sure Means of Gaining Love and Esteem*, 5th edn (London: T. Sabine, 1787).

Walker, George, *The Costume of Yorkshire, illustrated by a Series of forty Engravings, being fac-similies of original Drawings, with Descriptions in English and French* (London: Longman, Hurst, etc.; Leeds: Robinson, etc., 1814).

Warren, Robert, *Practical Discourses on Various Subjects. Proper for all Families. In two volumes* (London: Edmund Parker, 1723).

Wase, Christopher, *Methodi Practae Specimen. An Essay of Practical Grammar, or an Inquiry after a more easie Help to the Construing . . . of Authors and the making and speaking of Latin* (London: privately printed, 1660).

Watson, William, *The Clergyman's Law; or, the Complete Incumbent*, 4th edn (London: privately printed, 1747).

Watts, Isaac, *The Improvement of the Mind. To which is added, a Discourse on the Education of Children and Youth* (London: privately printed, 1795).

Wilkes, Wetenhall, *A Letter of Genteel and Moral Advice to a Young Lady*, 8th edn (London: L. Hawes, 1766).

Williams, Thomas Waller, *The Practice of the Commissioners, Surveyors, Collectors and Other Officers, under the Authority of the several Acts relating to the Assessed Taxes* (London: W. Clarke, 1804).

The Whole Law Relative to the Duty Office of a Justice of the Peace, 4 vols. (London: John Stockdale, 1812).

Willis, James, *On the poor laws of England* (London: John Lambert, 1808).

Wollstonecraft, Mary, *Elements of Morality for the Use of Children, with an Introductory Address to Parents. Translated from the German of the Rev. C. G. Salzman*, orig. pub. 1790, in Janet Todd and Marilyn Butler (eds.), *The Works of Mary Wollstonecraft*, vol. II (London: William Pickering, 1989).

Lessons. From the Posthumous Works of the Author of a Vindication of the Rights of Woman, orig. pub. 1798, in Janet Todd and Marilyn Butler (eds.), *The Works of Mary Wollstonecraft*, vol. IV (London: William Pickering, 1989).

Original Stories from Real Life. With Conversations Calculated to regulate the Affections and Form the Mind to Truth and Goodness, orig. pub. 1796, in Janet Todd and Marilyn Butler (eds.), *The Works of Mary Wollstonecraft* 6 vols. (London: William Pickering, 1989), vol. IV, pp. 353–450.

Young Grandison. A Series of Letters from Young Persons to their Friends. Translated from the Dutch of Madame de Cambon. With Alterations and Improvements, orig. pub. 1790, in Janet Todd and Marilyn Butler (eds.), *The Works of Mary Wollstonecraft*, vol. II (London: William Pickering, 1989).

Wotton, William, *Some Thoughts concerning a Proper Method of Studying Divinity* (London: William Bowyer, 1734).

SECONDARY SOURCES

Aarsleff, Hans, *The Study of Language in England, 1780–1860* (Minneapolis: University of Minnesota Press, 1983).

Albers, Jan, '"Papist Traitors" and "Presbyterian Rogues". Religious Identities in Eighteenth-century Lancashire', in John Walsh, John Haydon and Stephen Taylor (eds.), *The Church of England, c.1689–1883. From Toleration to Tractarianism* (Cambridge: Cambridge University Press, 1993).

Allen, Margaret, 'Frances Hamilton of Bishops Lydeard', *Notes and Queries for Somerset and Dorset*, 31: Part 317 (March 1983), pp. 259–72.

Annesley, Cressida and Philippa Hoskin (eds.), *Archbishop Drummond's Visitation Returns 1764 I: Yorkshire A–G*, Borthwick Texts and Calendars 23 (York: University of York, 1998).

(eds.), *Archbishop Drummond's Visitation Returns 1764 III: Yorkshire S–Y*, Borthwick Texts and Calendars 23 (York: University of York, 1998).

Arkinson, Frank (ed.), *Some Aspects of the Eighteenth-century Woollen Trade in Halifax* (Halifax: Halifax Museums, 1951).

Armstrong, Nancy, *Desire and Domestic Fiction. A Political History of the Novel* (Oxford and New York: Oxford University Press, 1987).

Ayres, Jack (ed.), *Paupers and Pig Killers. The Diary of William Holland, a Somerset Parson, 1799–1818*, orig. pub. 1984 (Stroud: Sutton, 1997).

Aston, Nigel, 'Horne and Heterodoxy. The Defence of Anglican Beliefs in the Late Enlightenment', *English Historical Review*, 108 (1993), pp. 895–919.

Religion and Revolution in France, 1780–1804 (Washington: Catholic University of America Press, 2000).

Axtell, James L., *The Educational Writings of John Locke. A Critical Edition with Introduction and Notes* (Cambridge: Cambridge University Press, 1968).

Bachelard, Gaston, *The Poetics of Space*, orig. pub. 1958 (Boston: Beacon Press, 1994).

Baigent, E., 'Assessed Taxes as Sources for a Study of Urban Wealth', *Urban History Year Book*, 7 (1988), pp. 31–48.

Barker, Juliet, *The Brontës* (London: Weidenfeld and Nicholson, 1994).

Barker-Benfield, G. J., *The Culture of Sensibility. Sex and Society in Eighteenth-century Britain* (Chicago and London: University of Chicago Press, 1992).

Barnes, Bernard, 'Early Factories in a Pennine Parish', *Local Historian*, 15:5 (1983), pp. 277–87.

Beckett, J. V., 'Land Tax or Excise. The Levying of Taxation in Seventeenth- and Eighteenth-century England', *English Historical Review*, 100 (1985), pp. 285–308.

Beckett, J. V. and Michael Turner, 'Taxation and Economic Growth in Eighteenth-century England', *Economic History Review*, 43:3 (1990), pp. 377–403.

Benknovitz, Miriam J., 'Some Observations on Women's Concept of Self in the Eighteenth Century', in Paul Fritz (ed.), *Woman in the Eighteenth Century and other Essays* (Toronto: Hakkert, 1976).

Berg, Maxine, *The Age of Manufactures* (London: Fontana, 1985).

Berkhofer, Robert F., *Beyond the Great Story. History as Text and Discourse* (Cambridge, Mass.: Belknap Press of Harvard University Press, 1995).

Biernacki, Richard, *The Fabrication of Labour. Germany and Britain, 1640–1914* (Berkeley, Los Angeles and London: University of California Press, 1995).

Bloom, Edward A. and Lilian D. Bloom (eds.), *The Piozzi Letters. Correspondence of Hester Lynch Piozzi, 1784–1821. Volume 1, 1784–1791* (London and Toronto: Delaware University Press, 1989).

Blunt, John Henry, *The Book of Church Law*, 11th edn (London: Longman Green, 1921).

Bowlby, John, *Child Care and the Growth of Love* (London: Penguin, 1953).

Bradley, James E., 'The Anglican Pulpit, the Social Order and the Resurgence of Toryism during the American Revolution', *Albion*, 21:3 (1989), pp. 361–88.

Braverman, Harry, *Labour and Monopoly Capitalism. The Degradation of Work in the Twentieth Century* (New York and London: Monthly Review Press, 1974).

Brewer, John, *The Sinews of Power. War, Money and the English State, 1688–1793* (Cambridge, Mass.: Harvard University Press, 1990).

Brissenden, R. F., *Virtue in Distress. Studies in the Novel of Sentiment from Richardson to Sade* (London and Basingstoke: Macmillan, 1974).

Brown, Callum G., *The Death of Christian Britain. Understanding Secularisation, 1800–2000* (London and New York: Routledge, 2000).

Butterworth, Mary A., *The Heatons of Ponden Hall and the Legendary Link with Thrushcross Grange in Emily Brontë's* Wuthering Heights (Keighley: Roderick and Brenda Taylor, 1976).

Calhoun, Craig, 'E. P. Thompson and the Discipline of Historical Context', *Social Research*, 61:2 (1994), pp. 223–44.

Carpenter, Edward, *Thomas Sherlock, 1678–1761. Bishop of Bangor 1728; of Salisbury 1734; of London 1748* (London: SPCK, 1936).

Caverero, Adriana, *Relating Narratives. Storytelling and Selfhood*, orig. pub 1997 (London: Routledge, 2000).

Chandler, James, *England in 1819. The Politics of Literary Culture and the Case of Romantic Historicism* (Chicago and London: University of Chicago Press, 1998).

Chapman, S. D., 'The Pioneers of Worsted Spinning by Power', *Business History*, 7:2 (1965), pp. 97–116.

Chitham, Edward, *The Birth of* Wuthering Heights. *Emily Brontë at Work* (Basingstoke: Palgrave, 2001).

Clapham, J. H., *The Woollen and Worsted Industries* (London: Methuen, 1907).

Clark, Anna, *The Struggle for the Breeches. Gender and the Making of the British Working Class* (Berkeley, Los Angeles and London: University of California Press, 1995).

Clark, J. C. D., 'England's Ancien Regime as a Confessional State', *Albion*, 21:3 (1989), pp. 450–75.

Clarke, M. L., *Classical Education in Britain, 1500–1900* (Cambridge: Cambridge University Press, 1959).

Clarke, W. K. Lawther, *Eighteenth-century Piety* (London: SPCK, 1944).

Cocksworth, Christopher J., 'The Presence of Christ in the Eucharist and the Formularies of the Church of England', *Journal of Ecumenical Studies*, 35:2 (1998), pp. 197–209.

Connerton, Paul, *How Societies Remember* (Cambridge: Cambridge University Press, 1989).

Connors, Richard, 'Poor Women, the Parish and the Politics of Poverty', in Elaine Chalus and Hannah Barker (eds.), *Gender in Eighteenth-century England. Roles, Representations and Responsibilities* (London: Longman, 1997), pp. 126–47.

Cook, Malcolm, *Le Sage. Gil Blas* (London: Grant and Cuttler, 1988).

Cornwall, Robert, 'The Right of Confirmation in Anglican Thought during the Eighteenth Century', *Church History*, 68 (1999), pp. 359–72.

Craven, Paul and Douglas Hay, *Masters, Servants and Magistrates in Britain and the Empire, 1562–1955* (Chapel Hill and London: University of North Carolina Press, 2004).

Cressy, David, *Literacy and the Social Order. Reading and Writing in Tudor and Stuart England* (Cambridge: Cambridge University Press, 1980).

Croft, Andy, 'Walthamstow, Little Gidding and Middlesbrough. Edward Thompson the Literature Tutor', in Richard Taylor (ed.), *Beyond the Walls. Fifty Years of Adult Education at the University of Leeds, 1946–1966* (Leeds: Leeds Studies in Continuing Education, 1995), pp. 144–56.

Crump, W. B., *Huddersfield Highways Down the Ages*, orig. pub. 1949, Kirklees Historical Reprints 3 (Huddersfield: Kirklees Historical Reprints, 1988).

Crump, W. B. and Gertrude Ghorbal, *History of the Huddersfield Woollen Industry* (Huddersfield: Tolson Memorial Museum Publications, 1935).

Crystal, David, *Cambridge Encyclopedia of Language* (Cambridge: Cambridge University Press, 1987).

Darnton, Robert, *The Great Cat Massacre and other Episodes in French Cultural History* (Harmondsworth: Penguin, 1985).

Daston, Lorraine, 'Attention and the Values of Nature in the Enlightenment', in Lorraine Daston and Fernando Vidal (eds.), *The Moral Authority of Nature* (Chicago and London: University of Chicago Press, 2004), pp. 100–26.

Daunton, Martin, *Trusting Leviathan. The Politics of Taxation in Britain, 1799–1914* (Cambridge: Cambridge University Press, 2001).

Davidoff, Lee, 'Mastered for Life. Servant and Wife in Victorian and Edwardian England', *Journal of Social History*, 7:4 (1974), pp. 406–28.

Davidoff, Leonore, and Catherine Hall, *Family Fortunes. Men and Women of the English Middle Class, 1780–1850* (London: Hutchinson, 1987).

Davidson, Caroline, *A Woman's Work is Never Done. A History of Housework in the British Isles, 1650–1950* (London: Chatto and Windus, 1982).

Davis, Lennard, *Factual Fictions. The Origins of the English Novel* (New York and Guildford: Columbia University Press, 1988).

Deakin, S. F. and Frank Wilkinson, *The Law of the Labour Market. Industrialization, Employment and Legal Evolution* (Oxford and New York: Oxford University Press, 2005).

Deconinck-Brossard, Françoise, *Dr John Sharp. An Eighteenth-Century Northumbrian Preacher* (Durham: St Mary's College, 1995).

'"We Live so far North". The Church in the North East of England', in Jeremy Gregory and Jeffrey S. Chamberlain (eds.), *The National Church in Local Perspective. The Church of England and the Regions, 1660–1800* (Woodbridge: Boydell Press, 2003), pp. 223–42.

Delaney, Paul, *British Autobiography in the Seventeenth Century* (London: Routledge and Kegan Paul, 1969).

Ditchfield, G. M., 'The Parliamentary Struggle over the Repeal of the Test and Corporation Acts, 1787–1790', *English Historical Review*, 89 (1974), pp. 551–77.

Donaldson, Ian, *The Rapes of Lucretia. A Myth and its Transformations* (Oxford: Clarendon Press, 1982).

Downey, James, *The Eighteenth Century Pulpit. A Study in the Sermons of Butler, Berkeley, Secker, Sterne, Whitefield and Wesley* (Oxford: Clarendon Press, 1969).

Duffy, Eamon (ed.), *Challoner and his Church. A Catholic Bishop in Georgian England* (London: Darton, Longman and Todd, 1981).

The Voices of Morebath. Reformation and Rebellion in an English Village (New Haven and London: Yale University Press, 2001).

Eagleton, Terry, *Heathcliff and the Great Hunger* (London: Verso, 1995).

Earle, Peter, *A City Full of People. Men and Women of London, 1650–1750* (London: Methuen, 1994).

The Making of the English Middle Class. Business, Society and Family Life in London, 1660–1730 (London: Methuen, 1989).

Ebner, Dean, *Autobiography in Seventeenth-century England. Theology and the Self* (The Hague: Mouton, 1971).

Eland, G. (ed.), *The Purefoy Letters 1735–1753*, 2 vols. (London: Sidgwick and Jackson, 1931).

Elbaz, Robert, *The Changing Nature of the Self* (London: Croom Helm, 1988).

Eley, Geoff, *A Crooked Line. From Cultural History to the History of Society* (Ann Arbor: University of Michigan Press, 2005).

Emsley, Clive, *British Society and the French Wars, 1793–1815* (Basingstoke: Macmillan, 1979).

Evans, E. J., 'The Anglican Clergy of Northern England', in Clyve Jones (ed.), *Britain in the First Age of Party, 1680–1750. Essays presented to Geoffrey Holmes* (London and Rounceverte: Hambledon, 1987), pp. 221–40.

Fairchilds, Cissie, *Domestic Enemies. Servants and their Masters in Old Regime France* (Baltimore and London: The Johns Hopkins University Press, 1984).

Finn, Margot, *The Character of Credit. Personal Debt in English Culture, 1740–1914* (Cambridge: Cambridge University Press, 2003).

Fryer, Peter, *Staying Power. The History of Black People in Britain* (London: Pluto, 1984).

Gibson, William, *The Achievement of the Anglican Church, 1689–1800. The Confessional State in Eighteenth-century England* (Lewiston, N.Y.: E. Mellen, 1995).

The Church of England, 1688–1832 (London and New York: Routledge, 2001).

Church, State and Society, 1760–1850 (London: Macmillan, 1994).

Giddens, Anthony, *Modernity and Self-Identity. Self and Society in the Late Modern Age* (Cambridge: Polity Press, 1991).

The Transformation of Intimacy. Sexuality, Love and Eroticism in Modern Societies (Cambridge: Polity Press, 1992).

Gilbert, Susan M. and Susan Gubar, *The Madwoman in the Attic. The Woman Writer and the Nineteenth-century Literary Imagination*, 2nd edn (New Haven: Yale University Press, 2000).

Giles, Colum and Ian H. Goodhall (Royal Commission on the Historical Monuments of England), *Yorkshire Textile Mills* (London: HMSO, 1992).

Gillis, John R., *For Better, For Worse. British Marriages 1600 to the Present* (Oxford: Oxford University Press, 1985).

Glanville, Phillipa and Hilary Young (eds.), *The Art of Elegant Eating. Four Hundred Years of Dining in Style* (London: V&A Publications, 2002).

Goodway, David, 'E. P. Thompson and *The Making of the English Working Class*', in Richard Taylor (ed.), *Beyond the Walls. Fifty Years of Adult Education at the University of Leeds, 1946–1966* (Leeds: Leeds Studies in Continuing Education, 1995), pp. 144–56.

Graff, Harvey J. (ed.), *Literacy and Social Development in the West. A Reader* (Cambridge: Cambridge University Press, 1981).

Grave, S. A., 'Some Eighteenth-century Attempts to Use the Notion of Happiness', in R. F. Brissenden (ed.), *Studies in the Eighteenth Century. Papers presented at the*

David Nichol Memorial Seminar (Canberra: Australian National University Press, 1968), pp. 155–69.

Graves, Robert, *The Greek Myths*, orig. pub. 1960, 2 vols. (London: Folio Society, 1996).

Gregory, Jeremy, '*Homo religiosus*. Masculinity and Religion in the Long Eighteenth Century', in Tim Hitchcock and Michèle Cohen (eds.), *English Masculinities, 1660–1800* (London and New York: Longman, 1999), pp. 85–110.

Restoration, Reformation and Reform, 1660–1828. Archbishops of Canterbury and their Diocese (Oxford: Clarendon Press, 2000).

Gregory, Jeremy and Jeffrey Chamberlain (eds.), *The National Church in Local Perspective. The Church of England and the Regions, 1660–1800* (Woodbridge: Boydell Press, 2003).

Hafley, James, 'Nelly as Villain in *Wuthering Heights*', *Nineteenth-Century Fiction*, 13 (1958), pp. 199–215.

Hall, Catherine, 'The Tale of Samuel and Jemima. Gender and Working Class Culture in Nineteenth-century England', in Harvey J. Kaye and Keith McClelland (eds.), *E. P. Thompson. Critical Perspectives* (Polity Press: Cambridge, 1990), pp. 78–102.

Hall, Richard and Sarah Richardson, *The Anglican Clergy and Yorkshire Politics in the Eighteenth Century*, Borthwick Paper 94 (York: University of York, 1998).

Hallas, Christine, *Rural Responses to Industrialisation. The North Yorkshire Pennines 1790–1914* (Bern: Peter Lang, 1999).

Haller, William, *The Rise of Puritanism* (New York: Harper, 1958).

Hannay, Margaret P., *Silent But for the Word. Tudor Women as Patrons, Translators, and Writers of Religious Works* (Ohio: Kent State University Press, 1985).

Harber, Julian, 'Edward Thompson (1924–1993)', *Transaction of the Halifax Antiquarian Society*, 2 (New Series) (1994), pp. 125–8.

Hardy, Mary, *Mary Hardy's Diary. With an Introduction by B. Cozent Hardy*, Norfolk Record Society, vol. XXXVII (1968).

Harvey, David, *The Limits to Capital* (London: Verso, 1999).

Hecht, J. Jean, *The Domestic Servant Class in Eighteenth Century England* (London: Routledge Kegan Paul, 1956).

Hesiod, *Hesiod. Theogony. Work and Days. Theognis. Elegies*, trans. Dorothea Wender (Harmondsworth: Penguin, 1972).

Higgs, Edward, 'Women, Occupations and Work in the Nineteenth-century Censuses', *History Workshop Journal*, 23 (1987), pp. 59–80.

Hill, Bridget, *Servants. English Domestics in the Eighteenth Century* (Oxford: Clarendon Press, 1996).

Women, Work, and Sexual Politics in Eighteenth-century England (Oxford: Blackwell, 1989).

Hilton, Boyd, *The Age of Atonement. The Influence of Evangelicalism on Social and Economic Thought, 1785–1865* (Oxford: Clarendon Press, 1988).

Hitchcock, Tim, *English Sexualities, 1700–1800* (Basingstoke: Macmillan, 1997).

Hitchcock, Tim, Peter King and Pamela Sharpe (eds.), *Chronicling Poverty. The Voices and Strategies of the English Poor, 1640–1840* (London: Macmillan, 1997).

Hobman, J. B. (ed.), *David Eder. Memoirs of a Modern Pioneer* (London: Victor Gollancz, 1945).

Hoggart, Richard, *The Uses of Literacy*, orig. pub. 1957 (Harmondsworth: Penguin, 1958).

Hole, Robert, *Pulpits, Politics and Public Order in England, 1760–1832* (Cambridge: Cambridge University Press, 1989).

Honeyman, Katrina, *Women, Gender and Industrialisation* (Basingstoke: Macmillan, 2000).

Hudson, Pat, *The Genesis of Industrial Capital. A Study of the West Riding Wool Textile Industry c.1750–1880* (Cambridge: Cambridge University Press, 1996).

   'Proto-industrialisation. The Case of the West Riding Wool Textile Industry in the 18th and early 19th Centuries', *History Workshop*, 12 (1981), pp. 34–60.

   'The Role of Banks in the Finance of the West Yorkshire Wool Textile Industry', *Business History Review*, 55:3 (1981), pp. 379–402.

Hudson, Pat and Steve King, 'Two Textile Townships, c.1660–1820. A Comparative Demographic Analysis', *Economic History Review*, 53:4 (2000), pp. 706–41.

Hunt, E. K., 'Marx's Theory of Property and Alienation', in A. Parel and T. Flanagan (eds.), *Theories of Property. Aristotle to the Present* (Waterloo, Ontario: Wilfred Laurier for the Calgary Institute for the Humanities, 1979), pp. 283–315.

Jackson, Mark, *New-Born Child Murder. Women, Illegitimacy and the Courts in Eighteenth-century England* (Manchester and New York: Manchester University Press, 1996).

Jago, Judith, *Aspects of the Georgian Church. Visitation of the Diocese of York, 1761–1776* (London: Associated University Press, 1997).

Jago, Judith and Edward Royle, *The Eighteenth-century Church in Yorkshire. Archbishop Drummond's Primary Visitation of 1764*, Borthwick Papers 95 (York: University of York, 1999).

Jenkins, D. T., *The West Riding Wool Textile Industry, 17770–1835. A Study of Fixed Capital Formation* (Edington, Wiltshire: Pasold Research Fund, 1975).

Jenkins, Keith and Alun Munslow, *The Nature of History Reader* (London and New York: Routledge, 2004).

Johnson, James William, 'Chronological Writing. Its Concept and Development', *History and Theory*, 2:2 (1962), pp. 124–35.

Jones, Vivien, 'Scandalous Femininity: Prostitution and Eighteenth-century Narrative', in Dario Castiglione and Lesley Sharpe (eds.), *Shifting the Boundaries. Transformations of the Language of Public and Private in the Eighteenth Century* (Exeter: Exeter University Press, 1995), pp. 41–70.

Joyce, Patrick, *Class* (Oxford: Oxford University Press, 1995).

   Democratic Subjects. The Self and the Social in the Nineteenth Century (Cambridge: Polity Press, 1994).

Karsten, Peter, *Between Law and Custom. High and Low Legal Cultures in the Lands of the British Diaspora, the United States, Canada, Australia, and New Zealand, 1600–1900* (Cambridge and New York: Cambridge University Press, 2002).

Keeling, Frederic, *Child Labour in the United Kingdom* (London: P. S. King, 1914).

Kent, D. A., 'Ubiquitous but Invisible. Female Domestic Servants in Mid-Eighteenth-century London', *History Workshop Journal*, 28 (1989), pp. 111–28.

Kotkin, Stephen, *Magnetic Mountain. Stalinism as a Civilization* (Berkeley, Los Angeles and London: University of California Press, 1995).

Kussmaul, Ann, *Servants in Husbandry in Early Modern England* (Cambridge: Cambridge University Press, 1981).

Landry, Donna, *The Muses of Resistance. Labouring-Class Women's Poetry in Britain, 1739–1796* (Cambridge: Cambridge University Press, 1990).

Landau, Norma, 'The Eighteenth-century Context of the Laws of Settlement', *Continuity and Change*, 6:3 (1991), pp. 417–39.

'Going Local. The Social History of Stuart and Hanoverian England', *Journal of British Studies*, 24:2 (1985), pp. 273–82.

'Laws of Settlement and the Surveillance of Immigration in Eighteenth-century Kent', *Continuity and Change*, 3 (1988), pp. 391–420.

Lane, Joan, *Apprenticeship in England, 1600–1914* (London: UCL Press, 1996).

Laslett, Peter, *The World We Have Lost* (London: Methuen, 1965).

Laslett, Peter and Richard Wall (eds.), *Household and Family in Past Time. Comparative Studies in the Significance and Structure of the Domestic Group over the Last Three Centuries* (Cambridge: Cambridge University Press, 1972).

Laurence-Anderson, Judith, 'Changing Affective Life in Eighteenth Century England and Samuel Richardson's *Pamela*,' *Studies in Eighteenth Century Culture*, 10 (1981), pp. 445–56.

Lees, Lynn Hollen, *The Solidarities of Strangers. The English Poor Laws and the People, 1700–1948* (Cambridge: Cambridge University Press, 1998).

Lefkowitz, Mary, *Greek Gods, Human Lives. What We Can Learn from Myths* (New Haven and London: Yale University Press, 2003).

Levere, Trevor Harvey and G. L' E. Turner (eds.), *Discussing Chemistry and Steam. The Minutes of a Coffee House Philosophical Society, 1780–1787* (Oxford: Oxford University Press, 2002).

Levi-Strauss, Claude, *Totemism* (Boston: Beacon Press, 1963).

Levine, David, 'Illiteracy and Family Life during the Industrial Revolution', *Journal of Social History*, 14:1 (1980), pp. 3–24.

Lucker, Richard, 'Bishop Challoner. The Devotionary Writer', in Duffy, *Challenor and his Church*, pp. 71–89.

Lüdtke, Alf (ed.), *The History of Everyday Life. Reconstructing Historical Experiences and Ways of Life*, trans. William Templar (Princeton, N.J.: Princeton University Press, 1995).

Luke, Carmen, *Pedagogy, Printing and Protestantism. The Discourse on Childhood* (Albany, N.Y.: State University of New York Press, 1989).

McBride, Theresa, *The Domestic Revolution. The Modernization of Household Service in England and France, 1820–1920* (London: Croom Helm, 1976).

Mack, Peter, *Elizabethan Rhetoric. Theory and Practice* (Cambridge: Cambridge University Press, 2002).

MacPherson, C. B., 'Servants and Labourers in Seventeenth-century England', in MacPherson (ed.), *Democratic Theory. Essays in Retrieval* (Oxford: Clarendon Press, 1973), pp. 207–33.

Manuel, Frank E., *The Eighteenth Century Confronts the Gods* (Cambridge, Mass.: Harvard University Press, 1959).

Márquez, Gabriel García, *Living to Tell the Tale*, orig. pub. 2002 (London: Jonathan Cape, 2003).

Marx, Karl and Frederick Engels, *Selected Works. In Two Volumes* (Moscow: Foreign Languages Publishing House, 1958).

Mascuch, Michael, *Origins of the Individual Self. Autobiography and Self-Identity in England, 1591–1791* (Cambridge: Cambridge University Press, 1997).

Mather, F. C., 'Georgian Churchmanship Reconsidered. Some Variations in Anglican Public Worship, 1714–1830', *Journal of Ecclesiastical History*, 36:2 (1985), pp. 255–83.

Mautner, Thomas (ed.), *Francis Hutcheson. On Human Nature. Reflections on our Common Systems of Morality. On the Social Nature of Man* (Cambridge: Cambridge University Press, 1993).

Maza, Sarah, *Servants and Masters in Eighteenth-century France. The Uses of Loyalty* (Princeton and Guildford: Princeton University Press, 1983).

Meldrum, Tim, *Domestic Service and Gender, 1660–1750. Life and Work in the London Household* (London: Longman, 2000).

Michael, Ian, *The Teaching of English from the Sixteenth Century to 1870* (Cambridge: Cambridge University Press, 1987).

Miller, Pavla, *Transformations of Patriarchy in the West, 1500–1900* (Bloomington: Indiana University Press, 1998).

Mink, Louis O., 'Everyman His or Her Own Annalist', *Critical Inquiry*, 7:4 (1981), pp. 777–83.

Mitchell, L. G. (ed.), *The Purefoy Letters, 1735–1753*, 2 vols (London: Sidgwick and Jackson, 1973).

Mitchell, W. Fraser, *English Pulpit Oratory from Andrewes to Tillotson. A Study of its Literary Aspects* (London: SPCK, 1932).

Mokyr, Joel, *The Gifts of Athena. Historical Origins of the Knowledge Economy* (Princeton, N.J.: Princeton University Press, 2002).

Moretti, Franco, *The Way of the World. The* Bildungsroman *in European Culture* (London: Verso, 1987).

Morris, R. J., *Class and Class Consciousness in the Industrial Revolution, 1789–1850* (London: Macmillan, 1979).

Mullan, John, 'Feelings and Novels', in Roy Porter (ed.), *Rewriting the Self. Histories from the Renaissance to the Present* (London: Routledge, 1997), pp. 119–31.

Myers, Mitzi, '"Servants as They are Now Educated". Women Writers and Georgian Pedagogy', *Essays in Literature*, 16:1 (1989), pp. 51–69.

Neale, R. S., *Class in English History, 1680–1850* (Oxford: Basil Blackwell, 1981).

Neeson, Jeanette, *Commoners. Common Right, Enclosure and Social Change in England, 1700–1820* (Cambridge: Cambridge University Press, 1993).

Niethammer, Lutz, 'Zeroing in on Change. In Search of Popular Experience in the Industrial Province in the German Democratic Republic', in Lüdtke, *History of Everyday Life*, pp. 252–311.

Nussbaum, Felicity, *The Autobiographical Subject* (Baltimore: The Johns Hopkins University Press, 1989).

Obelkevich, James, *Religion and Rural Society. South Lindsay 1825–1875* (Oxford: Oxford University Press, 1976).

O'Brien, Patrick K., 'The Political Economy of British Taxation, 1660–1815', *Economic History Review*, 41 (2nd Series) (1988), pp. 1–32.

'Public Finance and the Wars with France, 1793–1815', in H. T. Dickinson (ed.), *Britain and the French Revolution, 1789–1815* (Basingstoke: Macmillan, 1989), pp. 165–87.

Orr, Mary, *Intertextuality. Debates and Contexts* (Cambridge: Polity Press, 2003).

Ovid, *Ovid, Metamorphoses. A New Verse Translation*, trans. David Raeburn (London: Penguin, 2004).

Parry, Keith, *Trans-Pennine Heritage Hills. People and Transport* (Newton Abbot: David and Charles, 1981).

Pateman, Carole, *The Sexual Contract* (Cambridge: Polity Press, 1988).

Pickard, Lisa, *Dr Johnson's London. Life in London, 1740–1770* (London: Weidenfeld and Nicholson, 2000).

Pidock, Barbara, 'The Spinners and Weavers of Swarthmore Hall, Ulverston, in the late Seventeenth Century', *Transactions of the Cumberland and Westmorland Antiquarian and Archaeological Society*, 95 (1995), pp. 153–67.

Pocock, J. G. A., 'The Mobility of Property and the Rise of Eighteenth-century Sociology', in Anthony Parel and Thomas Flanagan (eds.), *Theories of Property. Aristotle to the Present* (Waterloo, Ontario: Wilfrid Laurier for the Calgary Institute for the Humanities, 1979), pp. 141–66.

Poovey, Mary, *A History of the Modern Fact. Problems of Knowledge in the Sciences of Wealth and Society* (Chicago: University of Chicago Press, 1998).

Porter, Roy, *Enlightenment. Britain and the Creation of the Modern World* (London: Penguin, 2001).

Poulantzas, Nicos, *Classes in Contemporary Capitalism* (London: Verso, 1975).

Jacques Rancière, *The Names of History. On the Poetics of Knowledge* (Minneapolis: University of Minnesota Press, 1994).

Reade, Aleyn Lyell, *Johnsonian Gleanings. Part II. Francis Barber, the Doctor's Negro Servant* (London: privately printed, 1952).

Reay, Barry, *The Last Rising of the Agricultural Labourers. Rural Life and Protest in Nineteenth-century England* (Oxford: Clarendon Press, 1990).

Robbins, Bruce, *The Servant's Hand. English Fiction from Below*, orig. pub. 1986 (Durham and London: Duke University Press, 1993).

Roberts, T. A., *The Concept of Benevolence. Aspects of Eighteenth-century Moral Philosophy* (London: Macmillan, 1973).

Rosaldo, Renato, 'Celebrating Thompson's Heroes. Social Analysis in History and Anthropology', in Harvey J. Kaye and Keith McClelland (eds.), *E. P. Thompson. Critical Perspectives* (Cambridge: Polity Press, 1990), pp. 103–24.

Roth, P. A., 'Narrative Explanation. The Case of History', *History and Theory*, 27 (1988), pp. 1–13.

Royle, Edward, 'The Church of England and Methodism in Yorkshire, *c.*1750–1850. From Monopoly to Free Market', *Northern History*, 33 (1997), pp. 137–61.

'Religion in Huddersfield since the mid-Eighteenth Century', in E. A. Hilary Haigh (ed.), *Huddersfield. A Handsome Town* (Huddersfield: Kirklees Cultural Services, 1992), pp. 101–44.

Rule, John, *The Experience of Labour in Eighteenth-century Industry* (London: Croom Helm, 1981).

Russell, Anthony, *The Clerical Profession* (London: SPCK, 1980).

Schwarz, Leonard, 'English Servants and their Employers during the Eighteenth and Nineteenth Centuries', *Economic History Review*, 52 (1999), pp. 236–56.

Scott, Joan Wallach, 'Women in *The Making of the English Working Class*', in Scott (ed.), *Gender and the Politics of History* (New York and London: Columbia University Press, 1988), pp. 68–90.

Sewell, William H., 'How Classes are Made. Critical Reflections on E. P. Thompson's Theory of Working-class Formation', in Harvey J. Kaye and Keith McClelland (eds.), *E. P. Thompson. Critical Perspectives* (Cambridge: Polity Press, 1990), pp. 50–77.

Seznec, Jean, *The Survival of the Pagan Gods. The Mythological Tradition and its Place in Renaissance Humanism and Art*, orig. pub. 1940 (New York: Harper, 1953).

Sharpe, Pamela, *Adapting to Capitalism. Working Women in the English Economy, 1700–1850* (London: Macmillan, 1996), pp. 87–108.

———, '"The Bowels of Compation". A Labouring Family and the Law, *c*.1790–1834', in Tim Hitchcock, Peter King and Pamela Sharpe (eds.), *Chronicling Poverty. The Voices and Strategies of the English Poor, 1640–1840* (London: Macmillan, 1997).

Singer, Irving, *The Nature of Love, 2. Courtly and Romantic* (Chicago and London: University of Chicago Press, 1984).

Slack, Paul, *The English Poor Law, 1531–1782* (Cambridge: Cambridge University Press, 1996).

Slattery, Wilhelm C. (ed.), *The Richardson–Sinistra Correspondence* (London and Amsterdam: Southern Illinois University Press, 1969).

Smail, John, *Merchants, Markets and Manufacturers. The English Wool Textile Industry in the Eighteenth Century* (Basingstoke: Macmillan, 1999).

Smail, John, 'The Sources of Innovation in the Woollen and Worsted Industry of Eighteenth-century Yorkshire', *Business History*, 41:1 (1999), pp. 1–15.

Smith, Alan, *The Established Church and Popular Religion, 1750–1850* (London: Longman, 1971).

Smith, Bonnie G., *The Gender of History. Men, Women and Historical Practice* (Cambridge, Mass.: Harvard University Press, 1998).

Smith, Mark, 'The Reception of Richard Podmore. Anglicanism in Saddleworth, 1708–1830', in Walsh *et al.*, *The Church of England, c.1689–1883*, pp. 110–23.

———, *Religion in an Industrial Society. Oldham and Saddleworth, 1740–1865* (Oxford: Clarendon Press, 1994).

Smith, Roger, *The Human Sciences* (New York: Norton, 1997).

Snape, Michael, *The Church in an Industrial Society. The Lancashire Parish of Whalley in the Eighteenth Century* (Woodbridge: Boydell Press, 2003).

Snape, Michael, 'The Church in a Lancashire Parish. Whalley, 1689–1800', in Geoffrey S. Chamberlain and Jeremy Gregory (eds.), *The National Church in Local Perspective. The Church of England and the Regions, 1660–1800* (Woodbridge: Boydell Press, 2003), pp. 243–63.

Snell, Keith, *Annals of the Labouring Poor. Social Change and Agrarian England, 1660–1900* (Cambridge: Cambridge University Press, 1985).

———, 'Pauper Settlements and the Right to Relief in England and Wales', *Continuity and Change*, 6:3 (1991), pp. 375–439.

Soloway, R. A., *Prelates and People. Ecclesiastical Social Thought in England, 1783–1852* (London: Routledge and Kegan Paul, 1969).

Spufford, Margaret, 'First Steps in Literacy. The Reading and Writing Experiences of the Humblest Seventeenth-century Spiritual Autobiographers', *Social History*, 4:3 (1979), pp. 125–50.

Staves, Susan, *Married Women's Separate Property in England, 1660–1833* (Cambridge, Mass.: Harvard University Press, 1990).

Steedman, Carolyn, *Dust* (Manchester: Manchester University Press, 2001).

'Enforced Narratives. Stories of Another Self', in Tess Cosslett, Celia Lury and Penny Summerfield (eds.), *Feminism and Autobiography. Texts, Theories, Methods* (London: Routledge, 2000), pp. 25–39.

'Inside, Outside, Other. Accounts of National Identity in the 19th Century', *History of the Human Sciences*, 8:4 (1995), pp. 59–76.

Landscape for a Good Woman (London: Virago, 1986).

'Lord Mansfield's Women', *Past and Present*, 176 (2002), pp. 105–43.

Past Tenses. Essays on Writing, Autobiography and History (London: Rivers Oram Press, 1992).

'Poetical Maids and Cooks Who Wrote', *Eighteenth-century Studies*, 39:1 (2005), pp. 1–27.

'The Servant's Labour. The Business of Life, England, 1760–1820', *Social History*, 29:1 (2004), pp. 1–29.

'Servants and their Relationship to the Unconscious', *Journal of British Studies*, 42 (2003), pp. 316–50.

'Englishness, Clothes and Little Things. Towards a Political Economy of the Corset', in Christopher Breward, Beckey Conekin and Cardine Cox (eds.), *The Englishness of English Dress* (Oxford: Berg, 2002), pp. 29–44.

Strange Dislocations. Childhood and the Idea of Human Interiority, 1780–1930 (Cambridge, Mass.: Harvard University Press, 1995).

'The Watercress Seller', in Tamsin Spargo (ed.), *Reading the Past* (Basingstoke: Palgrave, 2000), pp. 18–25.

'A Weekend with Elektra', *Literature and History*, 6:1 (1997), pp. 17–42.

'What a Rag Rug Means', *Journal of Material Culture*, 3:3 (1998), pp. 259–81.

'A Woman Writing a Letter', in Rebecca Earle (ed.), *Epistolary Selves. Letters and Letter-Writers, 1600–1945* (Aldershot: Ashgate, 1999).

'Writing the Self. The End of the Scholarship Girl', in Jim McGuigan (ed.), *Cultural Methodologies* (London: Sage, 1997), pp. 106–25.

Steinfeld, Robert J., *The Invention of Free Labour. The Employment Relation in English and American Law and Culture, 1350–1870* (Chapel Hill and London: University of North Carolina Press, 1991).

Stephens, W. B., *Education, Literacy and Society, 1830–1870. The Geography of Diversity in Provincial England* (Manchester: Manchester University Press, 1987).

'Literacy Studies. A Survey', in Stephens, *Studies in the History of Literacy. England and North America. Educational Administration and History*, Museum of the History of Education Monograph 13 (Leeds: University of Leeds, 1983), pp. 1–19.

Stokes, Francis Griffin (ed.), *The Blecheley Diary of the Reverend William Cole, MA, FSA, 1765–67* (London: Constable, 1931).

Stranks, C. J., *Anglican Devotion. Studies in the Spiritual Life of the Church of England between the Reformation and the Oxford Movement* (London: SCM Press, 1961).

Styles, John, 'Involuntary Consumers? Servants and their Clothes in Eighteenth-century England', *Textile History*, 33:1 (2002), pp. 9–21.

Tadmor, Naomi, 'The Concept of the Household Family in Eighteenth-century England', *Past and Present*, 151 (1996), pp. 111–40.

Family and Friends in Eighteenth-century England. Household, Kinship, and Patronage (Cambridge: Cambridge University Press, 2001).

Taylor, Barbara, *Mary Wollstonecraft and the Feminist Imagination* (Cambridge: Cambridge University Press, 2003).

Taylor, James Stephen, *Poverty, Migration and Settlement in the Industrial Revolution. Sojourners' Narratives* (Palo Alto, Calif.: Society for the Promotion of Science and Scholarship, 1989).

Thaddeus, Janet, 'Swift's Directions to Servants', *Studies in Eighteenth-century Culture*, 16 (1986), pp. 107–23.

Thompson, E. P., *The Making of the English Working Class*, orig. pub. 1963 (Harmondsworth: Penguin, 1968).

'The Patricians and the Plebs', in Thompson (ed.), *Customs in Common* (London: Penguin, 1993), pp. 16–96.

Thrale, Hester, *Thraliana. The Diary of Mrs Hester Lynch Thrale (Later Mrs Piozzi)*, ed. Katherine Balderson, 2 vols. (Oxford: Clarendon Press, 1951).

Tomalin, Claire, *Samuel Pepys. The Unequalled Self* (London: Penguin, 2003).

Tompson, Richard S., *Classics or Charity? The Dilemma of the 18th-century Grammar School* (Manchester: Manchester University Press, 1971).

Townsend, John Rowe (ed.), *Trade and Plumb-cake for Ever, Huzza! The Life and Work of John Newbery, 1713–1767. Author, Bookseller, Entrepreneur and Pioneer of Publishing for Children* (Cambridge: Colt Books, 1994).

Tully, James, *A Discourse on Property. John Locke and his Adversaries* (Cambridge: Cambridge University Press, 1980).

Valenze, Deborah, *The First Industrial Woman* (London and New York: Oxford University Press, 1995).

Verdon, Nicola, *Rural Women Workers in Nineteenth Century England. Gender, Work and Wages* (Woodbridge: Boydell Press, 2002).

Vicinus, Martha, 'Helpless and Unbefriended. Nineteenth-century Domestic Melodrama', *New Literary History*, 13:1 (1981), pp. 127–43.

Vickers, Noreen, *Parson's Pence. The Finances of Eighteenth-century North Yorkshire Clergymen* (Hull: University of Hull, 1994).

Vickery, Amanda, *The Gentleman's Daughter. Women's Lives in Georgian England* (New Haven and London: Yale University Press, 1998).

Vico, Giambattista, *The New Science of Giambattista Vico*, orig. pub. 1744, trans. Thomas Goddard Bergin and Max Harold Fisch (New York: Doubleday, 1961).

Virgin, Peter, *The Church in an Age of Negligence. Ecclesiastical Structure and Problems of Church Reform, 1700–1840* (Cambridge: James Clark, 1989).

Wadsworth, A. P. and J. de Lacey Mann, *The Cotton Trade and Industrial Lancashire, 1660–1770* (Manchester: Manchester University Press, 1931).

Walsh, John and Stephen Taylor, 'The Church and Anglicanism in the "Long" Eighteenth Century', in Walsh *et al.*, *The Church of England, c.1689–1883*, pp. 1–64.

Walsh, John, Colin Haydon and Stephen Taylor (eds.), *The Church of England, c.1689–1883. From Toleration to Tractarianism* (Cambridge: Cambridge University Press, 1993).

Ward, W. R., *The English Land Tax in the Eighteenth Century* (London: Oxford University Press, 1953).

Watkins, Owen, *The Puritan Experience. Studies in Spiritual Autobiography* (London: Routledge and Kegan Paul, 1972).

Weber, Max, *The Protestant Ethic and the Spirit of Capitalism*, orig. pub. 1904–5 (London: Allen and Unwin, 1930).

Wells, Roger A. E., *Dearth and Distress in Yorkshire, 1793–1802*, Borthwick Papers 52 (York: University of York, 1977).

'The Development of the English Rural Proletariat and Social Protest, 1700–1850', in Mick Reed and Roger Wells (eds.), *Class, Conflict and Protest in the English Countryside, 1700–1880* (London: Frank Cass, 1990), pp. 29–53.

Wretched Faces. Famine in Wartime England, 1798–1801 (Gloucester: Alan Sutton, 1988).

Whatman, Susanna, *The Housekeeping Book of Susanna Whatman, 1776–1800*, intro. by Christina Hardyment (London: National Trust, 2000).

White, Hayden, *Metahistory. The Historical Imagination in Nineteenth-century Europe* (Baltimore and London: The Johns Hopkins University Press, 1973).

Winnicott, D. W., *Playing and Reality* (Harmondsworth: Penguin, 1971).

Wokler, Robert, 'Anthropology and Conjectural History in the Enlightenment', in Christopher Fox, Roy Porter and Robert Wokler (eds.), *Inventing Human Science. Eighteenth-century Domains* (Berkeley: University of California Press, 1995), pp. 31–52.

Wood, Andy, *The Politics of Social Conflict. The Peak Country, 1520–1770* (Cambridge: Cambridge University Press, 1999).

Woodforde, James, *The Diary of a Country Parson. The Reverend James Woodforde 1758–1781*, ed. John Beresford (Oxford: Oxford University Press, 1924).

Wrightson, Keith, 'Politics of the Parish', in Paul Griffiths, Adam Fox and Steve Hindle (eds.), *The Experience of Authority in Early Modern England* (Basingstoke: Macmillan, 1996), pp. 10–46.

Wrigley, A. and R. S. Schofield, *The Population History of England, 1541–1871. A Reconstruction* (Cambridge: Cambridge University Press, 1989).

UNPUBLISHED THESES

Holmes, Jane, 'Domestic Servitude in Yorkshire, 1650–1780', PhD, University of York, 1989.

Meldrum, Tim, 'Domestic Service in London, 1660–1750. Gender, Life Cycle, Work and Household Relations', PhD, University of London, 1996.

Walsh, John Dixon, 'The Yorkshire Evangelicals in the Eighteenth Century, with Especial Reference to Methodism', PhD, University of Cambridge, 1956.

WEBSITES AND ELECTRONIC RESOURCES

'The House that Jack Built', http://homepage.eircom.net/~lawedd/HOUSEJACKBUILT.htm

'Why Bellastown?', http://www.bellastown.demon.co.uk/btown.htm.

Index